TUDOR BOOKS OF SAINTS AND MARTYRS

HELEN C. WHITE

tudor books
of saints and martyrs

THE UNIVERSITY OF WISCONSIN PRESS

MADISON
1963

Published by the University of Wisconsin Press
430 Sterling Court, Madison 6, Wisconsin

Copyright © 1963
by the Regents of the University of Wisconsin

Printed in the United States of America
by North Central Publishing Co., St. Paul, Minnesota

Library of Congress Catalog Card Number 63-13741

ACKNOWLEDGMENTS

h aving been in process for a good many years, this book is widely indebted to a variety of generous friends and institutions. The beginning of it goes back to the year I spent at the Henry E. Huntington Library and Art Gallery on a fellowship from that institution. Since then it has been pushed on, thanks to a summer grant and two semester research leaves from the University of Wisconsin, the Achievement Award of the American Association of University Women for 1947, and a summer grant from the Folger Shakespeare Library.

I wish to express, too, my warm appreciation of the courtesy and helpfulness of the authorities and staffs of the Huntington Library, the Widener and Houghton Libraries of Harvard University, the Boston Public Library, the Folger Shakespeare Library, the Library of Congress, the British Museum, the Bodleian Library, the Library of Cambridge University, the Newberry Library, and the Libraries of the University of Wisconsin and the State Historical Society of Wisconsin.

Finally, I wish to thank for aid in preparing the book for publication, my sister Harriet, who checked the citations for some of the earliest work; Mrs. Barbara Davis, who supplied items for the bibliography; Mrs. Peggy Barry, who helped with the footnotes; Mrs. Eugenia Loyster, who typed and helped proofread the manuscript; and Mrs. Elizabeth Steinberg of the University of Wisconsin Press, who has made invaluable suggestions for improving the form of the book.

In the references to sixteenth- and seventeenth-century texts, titles have been given in as brief a form as possible, with the spelling and, as far as practicable, the punctuation of the original, but with the type and the capitalization standardized. In citations the original spelling and punctuation have been kept, with these exceptions: all contractions have been extended, merely typographical peculiarities of the printing of the time, including ligatures in English words, have been disregarded, and the varieties of type reduced to two, roman and italic, with the italic reserved for special purposes.

HELEN C. WHITE

The University of Wisconsin
February, 1963

CONTENTS

I   The Saint's Legend as a Literary Type   3

II   *The Golden Legend*   31

III   The Attack on the Saint's Legend   67

IV   The Catholic Martyrs under Henry   96

V   Foxe's *Book of Martyrs*   132

VI   Foxe's Ecclesiastical History   169

VII   The English Mission   196

VIII   The Triumphs of Death   240

IX   Continuing Classics and Emergent Types   277

Notes, 325

Bibliography, 349

Index, 363

ILLUSTRATIONS

following page 166

The Golden Legend

The Lyfe of Saynt Radegunde

Certayne Sermons or Homilies

The Seconde Tome of Homelyes

The Life of Syr Thomas More

The Book of Martyrs

Saint Peters Complaynt

The Works of John Jewell

TUDOR BOOKS OF SAINTS AND MARTYRS

THE SAINT'S LEGEND
AS A LITERARY TYPE

Of all the incidental paradoxes of Christianity, none is more striking than that of the martyr, and it might be added, none more characteristic. No contrast could be sharper than that between the usually painful and often sordid and horrifying circumstances of the martyr's last earthly appearance, the charter of his claim to remembrance, and the magnificence of the form which its commemoration has assumed in the veneration of later times. In the gleaming shrines of the high Middle Ages, for instance, every grace of material and artifice of craftsmanship is devoted to the preservation of the crumbling tatters of agonized mortality. Often the long-past torture is recalled through direct presentation in painting or sculpture, or, more commonly, suggested through some symbol like the sword in the hands of Saint Paul. But the gold and gems of shrine or altar, and the light of the encircling candles, have an even more immediate significance, for they dimly foreshadow the splendor of that heavenly galaxy in which the martyr now shines and in which his devotees look one day to behold him in their own triumphant participation. For even the flame of the tapers, perhaps the least material aspect of this physical commemoration, is but a bodying-forth of something more imaginative and spiritual, and that is the legend of the martyr, in which both what he was and is, and still more what he means, is gathered up and defined in a pattern for both art and devotion. It is that legend that is of primary interest to the student of literature.

Like the martyr himself, the legend has a foot in two worlds, the world of historic fact and the world of spiritual significance. In addition, the legend has its own richly involved life as a literary form of major importance in the perspective of literary history and, in spite of many vicissitudes, by no means obsolete today. Some of the greatest literary as well as religious minds of Christendom have contributed to the development of the martyr's legend as a literary genre, but from the beginning the martyr's legend has been a form designed for popular consumption and for popular influence. As in all such writing, the relationship between author and audience has been, therefore, far from one-way. Indeed, as we shall see presently, the interaction is apparent in the very origins of the materials with which the martyrologist and the legend-maker work.[1] The result is, therefore, a literary form of a good deal of complexity and of exceedingly varied interest.

To understand that type, we might well begin, as the sixteenth-century preacher loved to do, with the word itself. To us today the word "martyr" in its commonest use suggests "sufferer." But in the beginning of Christian history it meant "witness," from the late Greek form μάρτυς.[2] Tertullian at the end of the second and the beginning of the third centuries used the term "martyr" not only for those who had already given their lives for the faith but for those who, having borne witness, were awaiting death, and even for those who, having confessed Christ, escaped the final penalty.[3]

It was the very nature of Christianity that made that witness so important. For it was not a philosophical system which the Jews and Gentiles were asked to accept in first-century Palestine and presently the whole Mediterranean world, but a story, and a very remarkable story at that.[4] Those who first carried the good tidings of that story of God become man, dying for man, and rising again with promise of eternal life for those who accepted that story with its implications for life here and hereafter, could themselves vouch for what they had seen and heard. Their conviction of its literal truth, evidenced by the pains they were prepared to take to bring their story to their fellows, was their most persuasive answer to the Jew or pagan who said to himself that this looked like what he had been groping for, but was it true? The fact that the first tellers of this story were prepared to stake their lives on its truth and, indeed, with one exception did give their lives for it, and all with a cheerful confidence in the future, vindicated their conviction as nothing else could.

The problem of truth was of the first importance at the beginning, then, and the evidence of the actual witnesses its best solution. When it came to what may be called the second stage, that of the testimony of those who had heard the wonderful tidings at second hand from those who had themselves seen and heard, the problem of truth became in some ways more acute and in some ways less important. By now there was the momentum of success, however modest, the reinforcement of the brotherhood, however humble, the mounting evidence of the continuing presence of the Saviour among his own, the transforming operation of grace apparent in the demeanor of those who had received and tried to live the faith. All of these things were important; but they were not all. The work of understanding, of accounting for, of defining, of explaining, was already under way, and here, as lively minds trained in one of the most acutely metaphysical ages of history began to lay hold upon the basic data of revelation and experience, there was bound to be difference of opinion. Furthermore, as numbers grew, there was sure to be difference of degree of fervor and staying power, and the spirit of self-criticism was startled into being. These were, of course, just a few of the things that happened in the first centuries of the new religious dispensation, but they are enough to show that the issue of truth had become not so much less important as less all-absorbing; it had been complicated by other issues.

And still more was this true when the great persecutions, particularly of the third and early fourth centuries, fell upon them. Although it was still true that every convert became, as Tertullian so well put it, a candidate for martyrdom,[5] yet something like confidence had been built up, if nothing more than the confidence of what was now a considerable period of continued existence. By this time there were not a few people in the Christian congregations who had never known anything else, and who consequently had come perilously close to taking themselves and their position in the world for granted.[6] Many of them were solid citizens in every sense of the very solid citizenship of the Roman Empire. They were not at all the kind of people who would go out looking for a new religion, or join any fanatical new movement or enthusiastic little conventicle. The outbreak of the great persecutions was the sharpest kind of shock to them, as it would be to any well-adjusted person.[7] It not only cut the ground from under them, but it raised prospects before them which they had the best of reasons for knowing they were not prepared for, for which, indeed, they might be said to be constitutionally unsuited.[8] They were not peasants of a defeated people living a hard and bare life close to a harsh soil, with little but Messianic dreams to leaven the laborious monotony of their days. Many of these Christians upon whom the terror of the great persecutions fell were men and women who had been gently and even luxuriously nurtured, with a great deal in the way of human satisfaction to sacrifice.[9] Martyrdom in the heroic sense was in all their traditions, pagan as well as Christian,[10] but they doubtless thought of it as something remote, appertaining to beings of less delicate nerve and lively imagination than theirs, and here it was upon them.

Sudden terror can be stimulating, but terror prolonged and exacerbated by the pendulum swing of impossible hope and imminent but still delayed disaster is, as too many men in our own day have learned, confusing and demoralizing. In such a human predicament the martyr appears as something little short of a miracle in his very being. His assurance, his confidence not in himself but in his faith, the very integrity of his resolution, are like a fresh revelation to his fellows. He is what they cannot be and yet by their very profession would like to be; indeed, feel they ought to be. But he is more than an example. A superman might be that and yet leave the ordinary man bemired in his all-too-excusable inferiority. But the brother who has just met the dreaded challenge and stood fast belongs to the brotherhood; they have a part in him, and they take courage from his vindication. For they see that their faith is not only something that exposes them to this unthinkable peril, but that it is also something that nerves a believer to face it. So the girl Felicitas at Carthage in 203 reassures her fellow prisoners that she, who was almost too frail for the stress of childbed, will yet be strong enough for martyrdom, for Christ will be in her.[11] The whole Christian body is quickened by the martyr's faith and his courage. That Christ is with his own, in his own, is demonstrated in their midst.[12] The martyr is more than an example; he is a revelation.

And here it is important to remember something about these early passions that it is easy to lose sight of. Later writers were, in the course of a process of embellishment, to endow the agents of the great persecutions with the most unsavory and even monstrous attributes, so that the examining magistrates emerge as fit functionaries for Dante's hell. Some doubtless were deserving of their later caricatures, but there must have been others who were more recognizably human, relatives, old and respected friends, with claims of both a personal and a civic character upon the consideration of the martyr that made defiance, if not perplexing, at least painful. Under such circumstances even the envied resolution of the martyr was harder to come by than the hagiographers could realize. And so with the passion itself. Later imagination was to refine the physical tortures to the point that any historical sense must protest. Even a twentieth-century man, for whom there can be few surprises in the darker regions of human nature, may well doubt if some of those brews of horror can have happened very often. But conversely there was much less blowing of trumpets and majesty of procession to those final scenes than memory suggests. Not the least of the sufferings of the martyrs was in the affronts to human dignity and the wasting-away of the basic physical resources. Many a man must have felt that he had lost whatever human grace he had ever possessed when he was finally dragged out to that last noisy, confused, often squalid, scene.

It is not surprising, then, that what followed came to seem to those who watched, a miracle, and still more wonderful to those who heard only the awed report. That the martyr could endure the worst which could be inflicted on him without losing his hold on his faith was a triumph of the most heartening and inspiring kind. But it was something more. From the beginning the Christian had been told by his Master that he should not fear him who could destroy the body, but only him who could destroy body and soul.[13] Now he must have wondered how a spirit so frightened and so confused as his own could withstand the corrupters. The martyr in his willing acceptance of suffering had shown him how it could be done.[14] Again, the Christian had heard often enough from the reading and the expounding of Scripture in church that suffering permitted by God was a good and not an evil, that suffering for the faith's sake was a participation in the sacrifice of Christ, and the fruit of it a share in Christ's victory.[15] All this was familiar enough, but we may be sure that it took on a quite new meaning when the imminence of persecution brought the prospect of martyrdom home to those who had never thought of it as a personal possibility.

It seems only logical, therefore, that one of the earliest and most influential of hagiographic genres to develop was the address of consolation and encouragement to the faithful in time of persecution. Particularly is this type moving when it emanates from one who is to be a martyr, from one who is already under the shadow of death, for then the voice of the teacher comes with the deepening authority of the witness. The first of this type (after the New Testament) is to be found in the series of letters which the second of Saint Peter's successors in the see of Antioch, Ignatius, wrote on his last journey from Antioch to Rome, somewhere about the year 110.[16] This journey Ignatius made under a guard of Roman soldiers, and of the end he had no doubt, death in the Colosseum. One thing only he feared on that journey, on which he had witnessed an outpouring of homage and solicitude from the Christians along the way, and that was that the Christians of Rome might use their influence to save him.[17] It was to dissuade that mistaken kindness that he wrote the most famous of the seven epistles now accepted as authentic, that to the Romans, the heart of which is in these sentences from the great fourth paragraph: "I beg you, do not show me unseasonable kindness. Suffer me to be the food of wild beasts, which are the means of my making my way to God. God's wheat I am, and by the teeth of wild beasts I am to be ground that I may prove Christ's pure bread." [18] Ignatius had his wish, and the anniversary of his victory is kept in the West on the first of February, and in the East on the twentieth of December.[19]

More common than this plea of the martyr to be left undisturbed in his course is the exhortation to the prospective martyr to stand fast. There must have been a good many of these letters and messages and addresses of encouragement to those who stood in danger of losing their lives for their faith, those whom Tertullian in a very eloquent epistle addressed as "Blessed Martyrs Designate." [20] The letters that came from notable pastors and preachers would, of course, be especially treasured. And if later the writer himself joined the ranks of the martyrs, then the message of encouragement would take on an especially persuasive and even sacred character. Perhaps the classic example of the genre is the *Exhortation to Martyrdom* which Origen composed about the year 235 to encourage his friend and patron, Ambrose, and a priest friend, Protoctetus, who had been imprisoned in the persecution of Maximin Thrax.[21] Origen holds up before his friends the "great reward prepared in heaven for those who are persecuted and mocked *for justice's sake* and the Son of Man," pointing out that denial cuts off and bearing witness joins the soul to God, and urging his friends not to weaken resolution for fear of the taunts of the enemy, or affection for loved ones, or concern for property.[22] He reminds them, too, of the great company of witnesses, visible and invisible, to whom in their combat they are become a spectacle, and he offers for their emulation what will become the classic medieval examples of martyrdom, Eleazar and the Seven Maccabees.[23] Martyrdom, he further reminds them, is the chalice of salvation, and the baptism of blood which effects the remission of sins.[24] Above all, martyrdom is the supreme way to glorify God.[25] Here in the middle of the third century the main lines of the classic exhortation to martyrdom are already laid down.

And only a little later what one may call the other side of the coin is apparent, too, this time in Saint Cyprian's famous address on *The Lapsed*, delivered at the close of the Decian persecution in 251.[26] The Bishop of Carthage opens with a paean of thanksgiving and a salutation of triumph to the surviving confessors that sets the standard for the judgment of those who failed: "Valiantly you repudiated the world; to God you offered a glorious spectacle, to your brethren an example to follow."[27] But there are those who failed to meet the test, who offered the idolatrous sacrifice. With tears Cyprian lashes at the too-prevailing laxity that made possible the fall of so many. Greed, clerical laxity, luxury, and devotion to the world's fashions sapped the strength of the Christian community, and made men rush to conform.[28] The tortures inflicted on those who resisted, Cyprian retails graphically enough, with compassion for those whom they broke, but not for those whom they frightened. And now he finds a fresh danger in those who seek and give a too easy reconciliation without the rigorous penance and almsgiving that alone can win the forgiveness of the God whom they have betrayed.[29] And he reinforces this warning with dramatic instances of retribution that have already overtaken the guilty, and he holds out to the truly penitent "not merely God's forgiveness, but His crown." [30] That crown, the crown of martyrdom, the author of this eloquent appeal was himself to win only a few years later, in 258.

The message of all these writers, that martyrdom is the greatest of all human privileges and the readiest way to the supreme good, the presence of God, was a noble thing for the man of that time, as of any time, to hear, but we may be sure, as Saint Cyprian's condemnations show only too clearly, that it did not commend itself any more readily to the natural man then than now. It would take something much more infectious than the preaching of even a Cyprian to stir the lethargy of the mediocre to the spiritual exertions that would make the acceptance of martyrdom possible. Only the example of the martyrs could do that.

We have practically no contemporary literary records of the earliest martyrdoms after that of Saint Stephen, so movingly described in the sixth and seventh chapters of the Acts of the Apostles. When the literary records do begin, in the middle of the second century,[31] they are sober enough, keeping close to the ascertainable facts.[32] Early in the year 156 the persecution at Smyrna had claimed a number of victims, among them the well-known bishop of that city, Polycarp. The Christian community at Philomelium in Phrygia heard of this and sent for information. The answer to this inquiry was the famous circular letter designed not only for the satisfaction of the brethren at Philomelium but for the Church at large, the *Passio Polycarpi*, giving a proudly full account of the magnificent way in which the Bishop and his flock had met the challenge,[33] and ending its account of Polycarp's death with the eminently fitting prayer: "May we be privileged to follow in his footsteps and arrive in the kingdom of Jesus Christ." [34]

There are a number of these early accounts that have a certain simplicity and even homeliness that have never failed to go to the heart of all the very different centuries that have passed since. Perhaps the most moving is the voice of the twenty-two-year-old Perpetua, who died in the amphitheater at Carthage in 203: "A few days after we were lodged in prison; and I was in great fear, because I had never known such darkness. What a day of horror! Terrible heat, thanks to the crowds! Rough handling by the soldiers! To crown all I was tormented there by anxiety for my baby."[35] Then there was her father, who tried to dissuade her: "And I grieved for my father's sake, because he alone of all my kindred would not have joy in my suffering."[36] There is the same feminine touch, too, to the story that her fellow Christians told of her encounter with the mad heifer in the arena: "Perpetua was tossed first, and fell on her loins. Sitting down she drew back her torn tunic from her side to cover her thighs, more mindful of her modesty than of her suffering. Then having asked for a pin she further fastened her disordered hair. For it was not seemly that a martyr should suffer with her hair dishevelled lest she should seem to mourn in the hour of her glory."[37]

But it would be a mistake to think that there were no wonders in the very human simplicity of these early accounts. There were dreams and visions, for one thing. Polycarp, praying, fell into a trance three days before his capture and saw his pillow afire and knew then the manner of death he should die.[38] Perpetua at her brother's request prayed for a vision that would reveal what was in store for her and was rewarded with a very elaborate vision of a narrow, peril-beset ladder up which she went to a garden where a shepherd gave her of the milk which he was taking from a sheep, and she awoke with sweetness on her lips and knew that she had no more hope of this world. There was her dream, too, of her brother Dinocrates, who had died miserably as a child, and of the miraculous font which lowered its inaccessible rim so that he might drink its healing waters.[39]

Then there was the voice from heaven that greeted Polycarp as he entered the stadium: "Be strong, Polycarp, and play the man." And when the fire was lighted, there was another marvel to gladden the memory of those who were to survive that scene: "For the fire forming a sort of arch, like a ship's sail bellying with the wind, made a wall about the body of the martyr, which was in the midst, not like burning flesh, but like bread in the baking, or like gold and silver burning in a furnace. For we caught a most sweet perfume, like the breath of frankincense or some other precious spice."[40] There were also, a century later, those wonderful white horses with their white-clad young riders that appeared in the sky above the Numidian martyrs Marianus and James and their fellow martyrs, and though with their bandaged eyes they could not see them, they knew their brethren's account of them was true, for they heard the neighing of the horses.[41]

The stories of the martyrs play a very large part in the work of the first great historian of the Church, Eusebius Pamphili, Bishop of Caesarea, who in the first quarter of the fourth century wrote the ten books of his *Ecclesiastical History*. The most learned and famous writer of his time, Eusebius had lost his master Pamphilus in the last days of the persecution of Diocletian, and shortly thereafter had been elected to the see of Caesarea, where he proceeded to take an active and prominent part in the controversies of the time.[42] Although Eusebius obviously took great pains to assemble the best authorities he could, often quoting from his sources at length, there was certainly nothing academic or disengaged about his work. What he saw in the events he recounted was "a vindication of the divine Word, in whom the faith of Christians centers."[43] In the first chapter of his work Eusebius tells us quite clearly what he purposes to do. Beginning with a full account of the dispensation of God in Christ, Eusebius plans to give an account of the successions of the holy apostles and of the times from Christ to his own, of the main events and the main leaders in the major dioceses, of the great teachers and preachers, of the leading promulgators of heresy, of the Jews, of the various assaults on the faith by the Gentiles, and of the martyrs and the martyrdoms that resulted therefrom, "and with them all the gracious and kindly succor of our Saviour."[44]

The story of the apostles is, of course, a story of martyrdoms, and so is the story of many of their successors. Interspersed in the accounts of the events of the years that followed are numerous brief accounts of obscure martyrdoms, and some very full accounts, often including the extended reproduction of the original documents, like the letter on the death of Polycarp which we have already encountered, in the fifteenth chapter of the fourth book,[45] and in the first and second chapters of the fifth book, the famous letter from the brethren at Vienne and Lyons, giving an account of the persecution in Gaul in which the slave girl Blandina so signally triumphed, because although "small and weak and greatly despised, she had put on the great and invincible athlete Christ."[46] Indeed, a favorite term of Eusebius for the martyrs is "the athletes of religion," and "glorious" is his favorite adjective for martyrdom, the greatest of all victories.[47]

The eighth book Eusebius devotes for the most part to the terrible persecution of Diocletian, which he had, as we have seen, known firsthand.[48] Now it is the "wonderful martyrs" that he celebrates with harrowing details of their sufferings, of which a good example is the tortures inflicted on Christians in the Pontus.[49] Happily, the history can end on a triumphant note with the gracious decrees of Constantine bringing peace to the Church.[50] Eusebius does have his marvels, like the apparition of Potamioena, three days after her martyrdom, to the soldier Basilides, who had shielded her from the crowd, with the crown which foretold his own approaching martyrdom for the faith,[51] or the terrible punishment of loathsome disease sent in retribution to Galerius, who had been chiefly responsible for the persecution of Diocletian.[52] But the greatest of his marvels is ever the constancy of the martyrs and the outpouring of divine grace that made it possible. The miraculous element is always, therefore, both relevant and functional.

Eusebius is not only a responsible church official, but a serious historian trying to work out a comprehensive view of man's experience on this earth in the light of Christian thinking about his nature and destiny. It is easy to imagine how in less responsible or less experienced hands the bare story of the wonder of one of these martyrdoms must have grown as it was whispered in the crowded darkness of the prisons in which still other prospective martyrs awaited their hour, among travelers leaving the city of the martyr's suffering to carry the story to the sympathetic or the curious in other towns, or in the hiding places of Christian refugees in country hut or cave. And it is still easier to imagine how the story grew as the proud brethren of the martyr's congregation told it to their children.

For here the martyr's story passed out of the cautious record of the church official into the exuberance of the popular imagination. Precise reporting of any exciting event is very difficult, as we all know, even when the facilities for accurate record are available and the critical spirit is present to compare memories and weigh probabilities. But here, where the only provision for precise reporting was in the cold-blooded if not hostile record of the official interrogatory and trial proceedings, so eagerly purchased at a stiff price by the Christian survivors,[53] and all beyond that was caught up in the wonder of those who had been so profoundly moved by their own reactions, it is not surprising if the story grew, as fact and feeling interacted in the supercharged imagination of the devout. A modern mystic, the late Baron von Hügel, in his study of Saint Catherine of Genoa and her friends, has shown how, even outside the peculiar tensions of the martyr situation, the elements not easily understood in a remarkable personality may find their description at the hands of what von Hügel has not unfairly denominated "her materializing biographers" in the popular version of a marvel.[54]

The stages of what might be called hagiographic evolution have been admirably defined by the Bollandist Hippolyte Delehaye, as follows: first, the official reports of the interrogatories of the martyrs, of which only a few survive in some of the earliest accounts, like that of the martyrdom of Cyprian; second, the accounts of eyewitnesses, direct or credibly reported; third, acts "*of which the principal source is a written document* belonging to one or other of the preceding categories"; fourth, historical romances; fifth, imaginative romances with even the hero himself an invention; and sixth, plain forgeries.[55]

But the memory of the martyr's passion, however transmuted in the rich amber of folk imagination, is but the imaginative vesture of what may be called the after-life of the martyr. That really begins with the gathering-up, where possible, of whatever remains of the martyr's body, broken or burned, blood or dust, and the careful burying of it. The craze for relics will later tear afresh and scatter those battered remnants, but in the beginning the Roman respect for the body of the dead [56] will insure the careful preservation of what remains in a spot to which the friends and followers of the martyr can return for those commemorative rites that, rooted in pagan antiquity, are the real foundation of the cult of the martyr.[57] Of these the most important is the anniversary observance of the day of the martyr's death and his entrance into glory, an observance involving not only the celebration of the Mass in what is now a sacred spot but also a night vigil before, and afterward a commemorative feast, supplemented and presently supplanted by the giving of alms to the poor, and as a part of the service something in the nature of a panegyric on the virtues and triumphs of the martyr.[58] Such an observance, when conditions permitted, would focus attention on the tomb of the martyr so that between anniversaries it would continue to be an object of pious resort; becoming in time, when imposing basilicas began to be erected over the tombs of notable martyrs, a rival to what we would call today the parish church.[59]

But by now something more than commemoration had come into the evolving situation. We have seen how the Christian had come to feel not only an admiration for the martyr but a deep gratitude to him. From that it was but a short step in that age, when the relation of patron and client was one of the basic social relations, for the Christian to take the martyr for his patron. And after that final scene of the martyr's triumph, in which the veil between this life and the next had been, if not torn asunder, at least worn very thin, it must have seemed in that world in which the address to the dead is a commonplace of funeral inscription, pagan and Christian alike,[60] only natural to seek the martyr's intercession for the perseverance of those whom his story had heartened and inspired to attempt to follow his example.[61]

So here now at the martyr's tomb those who especially felt the need of the spiritual graces so signally exemplified in his life would make their supplication, and here they would come to return thanks for help given, and to leave evidence of their gratitude, as the heathen were accustomed to do in their temples.[62] In the beginning, perhaps, the petitions offered to the martyr for his intercession would bear a special relevance to his character, but in time they would extend to the whole gamut of human need, spiritual and physical. Not the least of these petitions would concern health of body and mind, so that very often the tomb of the martyr would come to be regarded as a center of healing,[63] and the cures would swell dramatically the list of miracles wrought through the martyr's intercession.[64] And these miracles, the wonderful things brought to pass through the intercession of the martyr from his place in heaven, would be added to the record of his virtues and his sufferings.

Again, gratitude and admiration would warm piety with the glow of human feeling, and the imagination taking over in retrospect would heighten the colors of memory. The pride of the group to which the martyr had belonged would make precious each fresh evidence of his continuing concern for them, and of the potency of his intercession. The need for help in a time of persecution would not dispose devotion to the critical examination of the testimonials of gratitude, especially when they served to warm afresh the inspiration of the treasured memory.[65] And later, when peace gave both leisure for proud recollection and fresh motive for the rekindling of zeal, the vitality of the martyr's influence would seem more urgent than its restriction or definition. The essentials were clear enough, the recognition of the martyr as a man of faith and devotion and courage, the memory of his suffering on a certain day and at a certain place, the preservation of his remains and the observance of his anniversary in this place or one nearby, and the growing list of supernatural favors and beneficences wrought through his intercession.[66]

Sometimes, of course, the situation was not so clear, particularly in cases of bitter and widespread persecution, where burial was made hastily and in danger, and records were destroyed or lost, and the anniversary observances were prevented by the watchfulness of civic authorities or the scattering of the faithful. Then we have the martyr known only to God, whose burial place is completely lost until through vision or miracle the presence of the sacred remains is revealed.[67] Ambrose, to whose insight is attributed the discovery of the bodies of the ancient martyrs of Nero's time, Saints Gervasius and Protasius, at Milan, is hardly to be considered a credulous man; nor are Augustine and Paulinus, who report the event.[68] Pride in the martyrs and the enthusiasm for their cult made every fresh discovery a welcome addition to the corporate spiritual treasure of devotion, to say nothing of more mundane considerations of local pride and prosperity.

In the heat of persecution the making of detailed records must have seemed the least of the concerns of harassed church officials, and their preservation a hazard to the suspect and an encumbrance to the fugitive. Even when the crisis had passed, the disorders of the barbarian invasions and the confusions of the resultant breakdown of ancient ways of life made the business of preserving records still more difficult.[69] Yet the effort of at least minimal record-keeping was made in the interest of liturgical observance, that the anniversaries might be properly celebrated. The day of the martyr's triumph, his birth into glory, and its place were preserved, and, where possible, the location of his tomb and the site of his cult. These were the hagiographic indispensables, and they came to be included in the calendar of any church having any interest in the martyr, and presently in the universal calendar.[70]

Out of the needs of this cultus came the brief account of the martyr's passion and acts to be read in the office of the day of his commemoration, the *legenda*, or what was to be read.[71] When the Sanctorale was superimposed upon the Temporale for certain important feasts, in the eighth century, the number of lessons in the case of a major figure like Saint Martin might run as high as a dozen.[72] There was, of course, no want of material for Saint Martin, but the matter was not so simple for many saints. Writing chastens and restrains the exuberance of talk, but it has also its own necessities. With the lapse of time the details of even the most remarkable narrative blur, and any piece of formal writing, particularly one to be read aloud, must have a certain extension if nothing else. Moreover, it was not historic precision but edification that was the object of these lessons.[73] It was the moving of the hearer's will that was sought, and the stirring of feeling and imagination was more appropriate to this than the mere rehearsal of fact, of which there might not be too much to begin with.

Hence the development of the logical probabilities — such a man was sure to have had such and such qualities; indeed, one might be sure that one possessed of such grace as the martyr's would possess all virtues [74] — and since it is very unlikely that many of these lessons were composed by writers who had never heard any lessons read before, the common stock of martyrology was sure to be drawn upon, and the familiar formulae of hagiography supplied the deficiencies of both knowledge and style of the writer.[75] For the theme of all the martyr stories is the same, the wonder of the divine goodness and mercy, and the individual story, however unique in its local importance, becomes when seen in the larger context of the universal Church but another episode in the divine epic. Nowhere is the communion of the saints more a fact than in this, that the spiritual treasure is a common one into which all the particular contributions are poured, from which particular and deserving need may replenish itself.[76] That is, perhaps, the most important source of that cavalier indifference to plagiarism that has so much shocked or amused the modern source-hunter.

Moreover, familiarity is no handicap in community observance of any type, and least of all in worship, where the recurrence of the expected reinforces the essentially conservative nature of piety. In a world of such cataclysmic confusions and changes and uncertainties as that in which these early martyrologies took shape, the very repetition of established hagiographic detail would give welcome reassurance of the unchanging dependability of the heavenly realm of which the martyrs constituted so important an evidence.

The hazards of the primitive martyrology were increased by two developments which followed the triumph of Christianity. The first was the expansion of the local martyrology to include martyrs of other regions, as was appropriate to the conception of the universal Church.[77] Of this the supreme example is the development of the Roman martyrology. The details of that development can only be conjectured today by the combined resources of historical, iconographic, liturgical, archaeological, and philological research. But it is clear that all the difficulties of the local operation were many times compounded when the universal martyrology was attempted. To establish the bare liturgical essentials of name, day, place, and manner of death was in a reeling world a task almost beyond the resources of the time.[78]

The second development was in the long run to bring even more complication, and this was the expansion of the categories included in the martyrology. From an early date the local martyrology had included the names of the founders and the bishops of the various churches,[79] in a large number of cases, martyrs too. In the great persecutions another category became prominent, that of confessors.[80] Some of the potential martyrs were restored after supposed execution in a mass holocaust, others survived sufferings that killed many of their fellows, still others spent themselves in heroic endeavors for the menaced community. Conspicuous among these latter were, of course, the bishops and other leaders of the threatened churches. They were clearly of the same breed as the martyrs, and when they died, perhaps prematurely as a result of their sufferings and exertions, it would seem only fair that they should be remembered, too.[81] Indeed, such men would already be viewed by their surviving friends and followers in much the same light as the martyrs.

Those who followed the Master's injunction to the rich young man of the Gospel and sold all to give to the poor and followed Him had from the first excited gratitude and admiration in proportion to the magnitude of the position which they had sacrificed.[82] The development of the ascetic life in the fourth and fifth centuries, with its rebuke to the luxury of the world and its even stronger admonition to the too often low-flying, earth-keeping Christian of that more secure time, added still another category, that of the spiritual athlete who eschewed the temptations of the world and the natural life of man, to conform himself wholly to the example of his Master.[83] Again, the contrast between what the ascetic had been and what he became stirred the popular imagination, and the Roman lady of high rank turned ascetic, like Paula or Melania the Younger, and the beautiful harlot repentant, like Mary of Egypt and Thais, joined Paulinus and Augustine in popular wonder and awe. And among these athletes certain ones achieved still further distinction as the ascetic life in that age of the breaking and making of institutions became organized, and great personalities like Saint Antony drew their flocks of disciples and followers after them into the desert and the wilderness.[84]

That the ascetic was joined to the martyr in the witness to the faith is indicated by the subtitle, "The Book of the Triumphs of the Holy Fathers," which Palladius, Bishop of Helenopolis, affixed to the account which he wrote in 420 of the monks and ascetics of the Egyptian desert, the *Paradise*, better known from the dedication to Lausus, a chamberlain at the court of Theodosius II, as the *Lausiac History*. While Palladius does include some martyrs, such as the famous Alexandrian virgin Potamioena,[85] his theme is rather the feats of endurance of the ascetics. So remarkable are some of these stories, like that of Macarius the Alexandrian, for example,[86] that no other marvel would seem necessary to do justice to this example of the power of grace. But Palladius' *Paradise* flowers with an abundance of marvels of quite remarkable range. There is Kopris' story of the heathen who stole vegetables from the monks' garden only to find it was impossible to cook them, and so he became a Christian.[87] There is the story of the helpful lions who dug a grave for Antony to bury the body of the blessed Paul.[88] There is the story of the converted thief and tomb-robber, Petarpemôtîs, whose prayers procured a respite for a dying brother, that he might have a chance to repent of his laxity.[89] It is hardly possible to exaggerate the marvels of Palladius, but the morals which he draws from his narratives are always salutary in their warnings and their reassurances, and the rigor of penance is constantly sweetened by the spirit of charity.

The overrunning of the various provinces of the empire by the barbarians gave new importance to the role of the missionary, both the man who, like Saint Patrick or Saint Columba, brought the faith to new realms, or, like Saint Martin of Tours or Saint Cuthbert of Lindisfarne, addressed himself to the no less arduous task of converting the masses within the official Christian lines.[90] And after these came the great institutional figures, notably the founders of monasteries and orders, like Saint Benedict, and one may say the way is open for the leaders of an almost limitless variety of enterprises arising out of the Church's effort to meet the ever-changing circumstances of the Christian pursuit of the unchanging spiritual in an all-too-changing material world. Again, the mood is one of expansion.

Not that all martyrs were accepted without question. Just as the outbreak of the great heresies had led to not a little of the work of the Fathers in defining and developing Christian thought, so the problem of the heretical martyr had to be faced, to say nothing of the martyr for heresy. And the principle that it is the cause and not the death which defines the martyr was early established.[91]

But the Christian taste for saints was seemingly insatiable. And each new category added to the possible ranks created its own opportunities. A very good case is that of the founder or first great leader of a monastic establishment. Personal affection and corporate pride would warm admiration for the stellar exemplar of one's profession into a very full-hearted promotion of the institutional cult.[92] Men who had forsaken every earthly interest of their own would glory in the growing prosperity of the monastery which was the center of a popular cult, and would bask in the prestige which invested everything associated with their founder or their great man. And this is but one example of how motives human and divine would encourage the expansion of the heroic list.

Perhaps the thing that most exposed the martyr's legend to the hazards of historic change was its very responsiveness to the climate in which it found itself. That is not so apparent in the great collections, in which a lengthy process of adaptation and a sort of functional standardization has reached its culmination, though even here a careful comparison of details will show the surviving evidences of origin. But it is at once apparent when one takes up any early life of a new saint or martyr, or any fresh recension of an old one. For all its tales of demons, Saint Athanasius' life of Saint Antony in the mid-fourth century is still a classical encomium, carrying the traditional praise of the hero and the sage to the saint.[93] It is a study in the classical manner of a great personality and his ideas and his way of life, of his example and his teaching, a study that reflects the poise and the balance of the classical world out of which it came and which it was designed to influence. At the other end of the world, the Cynewulfian account of Saint Andrew's mission to Mermedonia, the *Andreas*, is an Anglo-Saxon heroic tale, in which a mighty champion of Christ strives for his faith as Beowulf strove for his people.[94] Yet this Anglo-Saxon epic mood is softened in the *Elene*, the story of Saint Helena's finding of the Cross on which Christ suffered, with mysticism and romance.[95] The story of Saint Brendan is an adventure story into unknown lands.[96] And the life of Saint Columba, the founder of Iona, by Adamnan, the ninth abbot, is a Celtic wonder tale.[97] Indeed, in the high Middle Ages, when the legend and the romance reach their fullest development, it is often very difficult to draw the line between them, as witness the more mystical portions of Malory's handling of the Arthurian legend in the thirteenth to seventeenth books.[98]

But the adaptability of the legend is not confined to literary fashion. From the beginning the saint's or martyr's legend was an instrument of propaganda for convert-making, designed to convey the wonder and excitement of conversion and the subsequent missionary zeal of the convert. This is especially true of Severus' famous life of Martin of Tours.[99] And still more remarkably the story of *Barlaam and Josaphat*, a Christianized adaptation of the legend of the Buddha found in the work of the eighth-century Saint John Damascene, garners up a treasure of picturesque tales far come from the little-known world of India, and turns them not only to the glorification of the ascetic life of monasticism but also to the defense of the veneration of relics, and other topics controverted in the eighth century.[100]

Later the martyr's legend is used as a weapon in the thirteenth-century battle to rescue the Christian community from the corruptions of the passion for wealth and material splendor, as in Saint Bonaventura's famous life of Saint Francis.[101] Likewise, the life of

Saint Catherine of Siena by her confessor, Fra Raimondo of Capua, for all it concentrates on the devotional life out of which her public activity sprang, is implicitly a plea for the unity and peace of the Church as well as for the contemplative life.[102] And the always vital issue of the relations of Church and State receives its contribution from the highly business-like life of Saint Thomas à Becket by his friend and supporter, John of Salisbury. Clearly, the fact that he could style his hero "assertor ecclesiasticae libertatis, et quasi turris erecta in Jerusalem contra faciem Damasci,"[103] added to John of Salisbury's enthusiasm in his famous life of his master. One might multiply the categories of the uses to which the saint's life was put in the defense of the teachings and the privileges of the Church and in the never-ending battle for the purification and the elevation of its life. And in so doing, one might build up a formidable roster of both its allies and its enemies in its unremitting battle for the souls of men.

But with the expansion of the martyrology came also an expansion of its complexities. As the new civilization shaped itself out of the shattering and the transmutation of the old, one may say that the resources for the creation of saints' legends increased, and the facilities for their control diminished. Communications were much slower and much more difficult than they had been in the sociable fourth century, say, but they existed. Images and ideas traveled far, and stories farthest of all. In the common frame of Christendom a wide variety of tribes and peoples brought together an even greater variety of influences and traditions and habits of thought and feeling. On the shores of a remote island like Britain washed tides of influence, intellectual and imaginative, from the heathen civilizations of the west and north, from the ancient Mediterranean world, and presently from the remoter Orient. And one of the main channels of these influences was the saint's legend, come from the ends of the earth, and gathering up as it moved all that devout enthusiasm could impart to it of wonder and miraculous splendor.[104] For it ministered not only to the pious credulity of the Middle Ages, but to another quality of the medieval mind, no less striking even if not so well publicized, its insatiable curiosity.[105] The literary enterprise to cope with all this treasure trove of pilgrimage and trade was not lacking, but it was sadly handicapped. The Europe of the seventh and eighth centuries was rich in imagination, but it was poor in material things, and in nothing poorer than in books and the tools of literary research. The great libraries of the ancient world had vanished, and nothing like them had arisen to take their place. Bede, at Jarrow, was probably the most learned man of his day in Western Europe, and he was living in a recognized center of Christian learning and culture, but it is estimated that he did not have access to more than about five hundred volumes at most.[106]

By the end of the sixth century some enterprising writer or writers had made a collection of the martyrs, in view of the later collections a mere outline, to give body to the commemorations of the calendar, and put that martyrology under the protection of the mighty name of Jerome.[107] As Bede himself tells us in the biographical note which he appended to his famous *Ecclesiastical History*, he compiled "The Martyrology of the Birth-days of the Holy Martyrs, in which I have carefully endeavoured to set down all that I could find, and not only on what day, but also by what sort of combat, or under what judge they overcame the world."[108] On this foundation Bede based what is really a new hagiographic type, the historical martyrology, the martyrology that enriched the bare calendar entries with a résumé of the saint's story.[109]

It is characteristic of Bede's scholarship that the narratives appended to the martyrological entry were brief and sober, and the blanks in the calendar numerous. And it is characteristic of the period that followed that the story of the historical martyrology is one of almost steady expansion. In the first half of the ninth century Florus, a canon of Lyons, filled in some of the blanks which the cautious Bede had left in his martyrology. In the middle of the same ninth century, Adon, Archbishop of Vienne, expanded freely and boldly the work of his predecessors, and by the third quarter of the ninth century the diversity of the materials and their arrangement seems to have aroused the concern of Charles the Bald, who asked Usuard, monk of Saint-Germain-des-Prés, to try to bring some order into the work. This Usuard did, pruning the luxuriances of Adon in the accounts of martyrs already recognized, but also notably expanding the number of saints commemorated. With Usuard one may say that the traditional martyrology has reached its maturity. The process of adaptation and expansion will, of course, continue, thanks to the efforts of a variety of writers, including some of such literary eminence as Notker of Saint Gall at the end of the ninth and the beginning of the tenth centuries, and Herman Contractus, monk of Reichenau, in the eleventh.[110] But the martyrology of Usuard will hold the field until Baronius,[111] and is still the basic text from which comes the contemporary Roman martyrology.[112]

But though dominant, the universal martyrology is far from alone. There were, of course, from an early date calendars and martyrologies of particular regions and dioceses.[113] And in the course of time the great religious orders came to have theirs, too. The first is the Benedictine, with the appropriate flowering of the type not only in the parent order but in the various branches that stemmed from the efforts of a succession of monastic reformers, such as Romuald of Camaldoli and Robert of Molesme. And later came the Dominicans and Franciscans with their burgeoning martyrologies.[114]

But important as it was, the martyrology was not the only type of hagiographic collection in the medieval period. The legendaries or passionaries constituted another very important one, for they gathered up accounts of varying length of the lives of the saints, following the classic patterns of life, martyrdom, translations of the relics, and miracles. The oldest surviving example, the Codex Velseri in the Royal Library of Munich, goes back only to the seventh century, but there is evidence of the existence of the type at an earlier period.[115] It was, of course, a literary genre of the greatest usefulness for lessons in the liturgical office, or for texts for public reading in the monastic community, because it made accessible in compact summaries the necessary details for meaningful commemoration.

In the thirteenth century this traditional type underwent a further development, both an expansion and in a sense a reorientation, so that it is possible to consider a series of works that appeared at this time a new type. For these collections of lives of the saints are not made for liturgical use or for monastic observance but for what might be called popular education, since they are designed for preachers to use as a source book for edifying examples to illustrate the points urged in their sermons, or for pious readers, particularly laymen and laywomen, to read for private devotion.[116] In view of the popular character of this undertaking it is not surprising that these great thirteenth-century collections are the work of Dominicans, of Jean de Mailly, the pioneer with his *Abbrevatio in Gestis et Miraculis Sanctorum* of the first third of the century (1230?), and of Vincent of

Beauvais, who in the vast collections of the *Speculum Historiale* (1244) finds room for a good deal of hagiography, and finally of the master of the genre, Jacobus de Voragine, Archbishop of Genoa, whose *Legenda Aurea* appeared sometime between 1258 and 1270.[117]

In this new hagiographic type the legend of the martyr and the saint has burst out of the margins of the calendar and the formal limits of the lessons of the daily office, and taken on a life of its own. In view of the contempt that later ages were to visit on his great work, it is worth remembering that Jacobus de Voragine was a man of learning and of practical experience in ecclesiastical government and in what would today be called public relations. An Italian of humble origin, he entered the Order of Preachers in 1244, when he was somewhere between sixteen and eighteen years old.[118] Like the Franciscan order, the Dominican had been founded early in the thirteenth century to meet the religious needs of a new social situation, the rapid growth of the population in the expanding cities of the time. Popular education was from the beginning the concern of Saint Dominic and the Order of Preachers which he founded. In a generation of able men, Jacobus from the little town of Varaggio on the Gulf of Genoa made his mark early. At the age of somewhere around thirty-five he became prior of his convent, and in 1267, when he was not much over forty, he became the provincial of his order for Lombardy, an office which he held for eighteen years.[119] He refused the nomination to the see of Genoa in 1288 but suffered himself to be persuaded to accept that office in 1292. He was archbishop of Genoa at a time when the contacts of that rich trading city with other parts of the world, particularly the Near East, were at their height, and he made such a reputation for himself as a peacemaker and a friend of the poor that when he died in 1298 his people regarded him as a saint.[120] In view of some later complaints about the way money that should have gone to the poor was squandered on doing honor to the bodies of saints, it is worth remembering that he forbade his mourners to deprive the poor of the cost of his burial.[121] It is pleasant, too, to remember that this lover of the saints was himself beatified in 1816, long after most of his contemporaries had been forgotten.[122]

His great work was composed, then, in the midst of a busy and active life; so it is not surprising that its writing, with perhaps some revision, extended over a considerable number of years between 1250 and 1280.[123] What Jacobus sought to do was to provide a *legenda*, or lectionary, containing lives and works to be read as the various feasts of the liturgical year came round, this time not by the clergy, who already had their liturgical *legenda*, but by the layfolk. That is why Jacobus includes with the feasts of Our Lord and Our Lady and the saints explanations of the four seasons of the year, as expression of the four periods of the religious history of mankind, and the main features of their observance.[124] Thus he would put the pious lay reader in possession of the history of God's dealings with his creature man. His motive was, in the most liberal sense of the word, educational.

Jacobus cites various sources, but often these are at second hand, as is so often true of medieval citations. Modern studies of his relations to his sources have disclosed that Jacobus took the legends that were in existence in his time, notably those of Usuard and of Caesarius of Heisterbach, and used them with a good deal of freedom.[125] Nearly all his saints are to be found in the *Speculum Historiale* of Vincent of Beauvais,[126] but where there is close agreement between the two versions, it is because both compilers used a common source.[127] Jacobus was by no means unaware of the problem of sources, and he seems to have made an effort to discriminate between them. But even when he pointed out that the source was doubtful, he still included the story if he thought it a good one.[128] It is clear, too, that he was not concerned with literary originality. Even where he had known the saints in question personally, he does not attempt to give a fresh view. His originality lies rather in the skill with which he adapts his materials to the psychology of the lay audience which he knew so well from his own experience as a popular preacher.[129]

The success of Jacobus' undertaking may be gauged by what happened to his work after his death. He himself had included only one hundred and eighty legends in his original work. By the fifteenth century various editions and translations had expanded the number to four hundred.[130] In other words, the *Legenda Aurea* had taken on a life of its own. When the invention of printing came to make books cheaper and so more easily available to the reading public, the *Legenda Aurea* led even the Bible in number of imprints, one hundred and fifty-six as against one hundred and twenty-eight for the fifteenth century.[131]

But not only was the *Legenda Aurea* paid the tribute of imitation and expansion; it was also paid the characteristic medieval tribute of abbreviation, and one of these abbreviations in English quite explicitly underscores the educational aspect stressed above. It was John Mirk's *Festial* or *Festyvall*, a collection of homilies largely, as Mirk put it, "drawen out" of the *Legenda Aurea*,[132] composed somewhere about the beginning of the fifteenth century by the prior of Lilleshall in Shropshire and printed in 1483 by William Caxton, shortly before the *Golden Legend* itself. It continued to be printed as late as the twenty-third day of October, 1532, by Caxton's successor, Wynkyn de Worde. The purpose of this work is very well summed up in Mirk's own explanation that he wished to give help to the parish priests, "holden to teche theyr parysshens of all the pryncypall feestes that come in the yere, shewynge unto them what the holy sayntes suffred and dyd for goddes sake and for his love, so that they sholde have the more devocyon in good sayntes and with the better wyll come to the chyrche to serve god and praye his holy sayntes of theyre helpe."[133]

In whatever form it finally found its way to the hearer or reader, such a collection as that of Jacobus de Voragine would meet the needs of the late Middle Ages as the more leisurely and ambitious biography could not. For it would meet the predicament of the poor monastic preacher, or still more the poor parish preacher, who would find in such a collection an anthology or a compendium to take the place of the library he did not possess. It would, as Mirk said, enable him to put his congregation in systematic possession of the riches of the ecclesiastical year, and thereby to present the basic elements of the faith and the moral teachings of the Church in a form which would be within reach of the illiterate and often half-barbarous village which it was his duty to civilize for this world as well as to save for the next. For the collection of martyr legends would present the striking episode, the unforgettable speech, the picturesque gesture that would carry home to the uncluttered imagination and the unsophisticated heart of the villager the warning and the inspiration of the heroic example. And if in the process the far-off story of the martyrology, half a world and now more than half a millennium away, were brought into the village itself, and the actors in the sacred story took on the familiar features of one's neighbors, to say nothing of oneself, so much the better.[134] And in that village world where the resources for instruction and for entertainment which we take for granted were unknown, and the laboriousness and monotony and bareness of life were such as the modern man would find hard to imagine, the bright figures of the legend must have brought an excitement and a delight to hungry minds that would be very difficult for members of our richly possessioned and constantly stimulated age to appreciate.[135] The medieval preacher did not scruple to terrify, and he apparently felt no qualms about laughing within the sacred walls. In many a medieval village the sermon must have been an entertainment as well as an inspiration to look forward to and back upon. And of no sermon was this more true than of the sermon based on the saint's or martyr's legend. As the late Donald Stauffer once said, "the saints' lives became a religious Arabian Nights Entertainment for every day of the year."[136]

And it should not be forgotten that this was a form of entertainment which a man could enjoy with a good conscience. Ecclesiastical authority was likely to take a dim view of many of the pleasures of the natural man, dancing, and singing of dubious songs, and dicing, and drinking. Here was a form of escape from the day's routine, and from the constant struggle to keep body and soul together, that the earthy but well-intentioned Christian could enjoy to the full. And here was an instrument which the preacher, anxious with more than the normal speaker's concern about holding his audience, would be tempted to exploit to the full. For the Christian pastor was no longer addressing himself to a select and devoted few gathered out of a hostile or indifferent world. After Christianity became the official religion, and still more after the mass conversions of the barbarians brought whole tribes and provinces into the churches, the preacher found himself dealing with the full range of normal humanity, from zeal to recalcitrance, with a wide spread of laziness and indifference between. The martyr's legend must, therefore, have seemed a heaven-sent answer to one of the most difficult and constant of the preacher's problems.[137]

Again, historic accuracy was the least of the village pastor's concerns. Effectiveness for edification was the thing which he sought in his collection of legends, and it was that which he found.[138] It is not surprising, then, that the collectors and the editors and the composers of such anthologies for the help of preachers, usually quite familiar from actual experience with the needs of the audiences to whom their work would presently be relayed, should have done their best to make the stories they told effective. Many of them were quite aware of competition in the secular romances current in more sophisticated centers at least, and they would be quite alive to the pity of leaving the best tunes to the Devil. Many of them, too, had their own very considerable literary gifts for the magic effect, to say nothing of the fantastic, and so on. Indeed, side by side with the elaboration of genuine legends went the fabrication of a certain number of what can only be called religious romances, in which, very much as a modern historical novelist builds his story of what might well have happened in a certain setting at a certain time, so the pious romancer of the Middle Ages made his story of what might have happened in the wonderful world of the hagiographer.[139]

For the villager the competition of secular romance would be limited except in so far as it filtered down to him through the popular vulgarizations which the wandering minstrel or storyteller would provide, but there were prospective audiences among the well-placed and the literate with the means to buy things as expensive as books were before the invention of printing, for whom the competition between the saint's life and the romance would be an actuality. Here again the imaginative satisfactions of the saint's life would make the pious choice the easier and the more stimulating.

It would, of course, be a mistake to think of the process as always as self-conscious and deliberate as this brief analysis suggests. Such happy adaptations as these are usually more instinctive, arising out of a sharing of tastes between writer and reader quite as much as a calculation of effects.[140] Certainly, there can be no doubt of their success, as is evidenced by the succession of great collections of saints' and martyrs' legends, often one pyramiding upon another. That success is, also, apparent in the part which the saints' legends played in the development of medieval drama.[141] It is apparent, too, in the use that was made of them not only in verse and prose but in the visual and the plastic arts as well. How much of the endless charm and eloquence of the medieval cathedral is due to the telling of these stories in painting and sculpture upon its walls![142] And every record of the time shows how intimately these stories were interwoven with the warp and woof of daily routine and the most casual of earthly intercourse. And their constant expansion with fresh examples, even drawn from the immediate neighborhood and the acquaintance of the storyteller, doubtless contributed to that medieval sense of the supernatural and the miraculous, not as something that stopped a long time ago when the age of revelation was closed, but as something continuing even to the present and likely to continue.[143] Under such circumstances that line so often drawn sharply today between the obsolete past and the modern present could have hardly existed, and the Christian brotherhood could be inclusive temporally as well as spatially. In a very effective way the ever-increasing roster of the saints not only bridged the gap between the past and the present for the quite unhistorically-minded medieval man, but between this world and the next.[144] In so doing, it made the Church's teaching on the communion of the saints a living reality to the least mystical of her children.

THE GOLDEN LEGEND

*t*he readiest way to understand the *Legenda Aurea* as sixteenth-century England saw it is to consider it in the form in which it was for the first time printed in England, by William Caxton in his own translation in 1483. Caxton's approach was as impersonal as Jacobus de Voragine's, but the very circumstances of the making of his translation give it a personal quality that makes it worthwhile to take a look at the man who was responsible for this, the best-known form in which the *Legenda Aurea* has ever appeared in English.

In spite of all the differences between the Archbishop of Genoa and the London printer, their basic undertakings had not a little in common. Born about 1424, Caxton came out of the middle class at a time when that class, long of growing importance, was accelerating its rate of progress to an epoch-making degree.[1] He made a notable success of foreign trade, so that by 1463, when he was only a little past forty, he was the Governor of the English Nation beyond the Sea. During the half-dozen years of his tenure of that position he traveled and served his government in various negotiations of importance.[2] About the time he concluded his service to his fellow merchants he entered into the service of Margaret, sister of King Edward IV, and Duchess of Burgundy. It is not always in such matters easy to say which is cause and which is effect. But certainly this successful businessman was to a remarkable degree free of the court world of his own country and free of the Court of Burgundy, the most brilliant in Europe from the cultural and intellectual point of view.[3]

He had already begun to occupy his leisure with literary work, particularly translation from the French, as early as 1469 beginning his translation of Raoul Lefèvre's *Recueil des Histoires de Troyes*.[4] It was apparently in order to satisfy his noble friends' desire for copies of his literary work that during a visit to Cologne in Germany in 1471–72 he investigated and learned the new art of printing, printing his translation of the Troy book, the first book to be printed in English, at Bruges in or about 1475.[5] The autumn of 1476 found him established in Westminster[6] under the patronage of King Edward IV,[7] in the first printing shop of England, from which in the next seventeen years emanated a series of works, the most famous of which were, after the *Golden Legend*, the *Canterbury Tales*, Gower's *Confessio*, and Malory's *Morte d'Arthur*.[8] But a third of Caxton's printing was religious, and, therefore, it is only fitting that he completed the translation of the *Vitas Patrum* the day he died in 1491.[9]

During these busy years of printing he translated twenty-four works from Latin, French, and Dutch, all but one of which were printed on his own press.[10] Of these, the greatest in volume and, from our point of view, in significance was the *Golden Legend*, completed, as he tells us in the colophon, on the twentieth day of November, 1483.[11]

According to Caxton's own preface to the *Golden Legend*, he used not only the Latin version but a French one and an English one. The French one is the well-known translation that the Hospitaler Jean de Vignay made sometime after the first third of the fourteenth century.[12] He also used an English version, of which eight manuscripts survive, all representing one translation made before 1438. It has been suggested that this version may be the work of an East Anglian Augustinian, Osbern Bokenham, and there are some who think that it is better than Caxton's own.[13] But it is Caxton's translation that was printed and so made widely available, and it is the relation of this to Jacobus' that is important for this study.

Caxton's is the most comprehensive of all known versions of Jacobus' work. It is about a third larger than the original Latin. Caxton omitted four of the original one hundred and eighty-two chapters, he added ten chapters on feasts represented in the post-

Voragine accretions, and he included fifty-nine legends not found in the Latin, but, most of them, in the English or French versions. With the freedom characteristic of the translators of his age he did not scruple to add several passages of his own composition.[14] But the most remarkable addition to the *Legenda Aurea* is the series of Biblical lives which Caxton inserted after the preliminary ecclesiastical-year material in the 1483 edition (concluding with "The dedicacion of the chirche") with the simple heading, "Here folowen the storyes of the byble": the lives of Adam, Noah, Abraham, Isaac, Joseph, Moses, Saul, David, Solomon, Rehoboam, Job, Tobit, Judith, thirteen in all.[15] In general, as we have seen, Caxton follows the basic pattern of the *Legenda Aurea*, but here he has made a distinct innovation, for, as Charles C. Butterworth has pointed out, nothing like this series of Old Testament lives is to be found in any of the three sources, the Latin, French, and English versions of the *Legenda Aurea* which Caxton acknowledged in his famous prologue to his book.[16] They are, so far as we can judge, his own translations from the Latin Bible. In general these stories follow the lines of the Bible, with some condensation or abridgment, with omission of irrelevant material, and with occasional supplementation from ecclesiastical historians and Church Fathers — in the case of Moses, for example, where Josephus' story of the test of the burning coals is added to the scriptural account of the youthful Moses.[17] But, on the whole, the scriptural originals are followed with such fidelity that Butterworth is certainly justified in including the name of Caxton in his account of the literary lineage of the King James Bible, where on the strength of this first edition of the *Golden Legend* he claims for Caxton the honor of being the first to print passages from the Bible in English.[18] What, of course, makes this achievement so noteworthy is that the prohibition of 1408 against circulating the Bible in English was still in force.[19]

It may well have been caution, therefore, that made Caxton refrain from calling attention to this feature of his work in the otherwise fairly inclusive description in the colophon, which he signed that twentieth day of November, 1483. One other possible measure of prudence he took, and that was to call attention to the liturgical position of these portions of Scripture, as, for example, that the story of Moses was read on mid-Lent Sunday.[20]

This impression of caution, a caution, it may be added, thoroughly justified by the circumstances of the times, is confirmed by the rather confused history of these lives in later editions of the book. As regards the next edition, that of 1487, it is very hard to be sure about what happened to the lives, because so many surviving volumes, like the British Museum copy, have been made up of leaves from both the first and second editions.[21] It is not too clear, either, what happened in the third edition, that of 1493, for in the copy of that edition in the Huntington Library used for this study, the stories of the Bible do not appear at all, and the book moves on from the dedication of the church to the first of the saints' stories, that of Saint Andrew, quite as if the lives had never been.[22] Or so it seems, but when one checks the signatures, it becomes apparent that there has been some interference with the orderly sequence.[23]

It looks as if in this copy, at least, the omission was made in the course of printing the book, and something like this seems to have occurred in the case of the British Museum copy of this edition. The suggestion in the British Museum Catalogue description of this book, that although the Bible stories are omitted, "there is a blank of a column and a half between the 'Feestes' and the 'Legende' as if to allow of their insertion at pleasure" is a possible explanation, in view of what is known of the fluidity of the English situation at this time.[24]

The whole problem of these lives becomes more puzzling when their history is followed in succeeding editions of Caxton's work, published in the next thirty-odd years. In the edition which Caxton's successor, Wynkyn de Worde, published at Westminster in 1498 they are boldly put at the very beginning of the work.[25] And they have the same preëminent position in the editions printed by Julian Notary in 1503, and by Wynkyn de Worde in 1512, and even so late as 1527.

But whatever the explanation of these changes, Caxton's *Golden Legend*, for all its obviously orthodox intention, came to make a modest contribution to the spread of the Bible in English.

In his omissions from the Latin, too, Caxton showed a tendency to carry Jacobus' adaptation of his source materials to the general lay public even further. This was, of course, necessary, because where Jacobus had used the Latin of scholars and so addressed his materials to the non-Latinate lay public through the medium of the clergy, Caxton had in using the vernacular ventured much lower in the educational scale. It is not surprising, therefore, that he omitted certain materials that would not be of much interest to laymen. For example, as Sister Mary Jeremy has pointed out, he omitted panegyrical passages, citations of authorities, groups of scriptural quotations, and controversial or doctrinal dialogues. He also omitted certain expressions of the critical spirit in his source, an omission understandable in view of the fact that the more popular audience would hardly be interested in the weighing of evidence as to authenticity. On the other hand, his omission of certain narrative passages, most of which offer variants of episodes narrated elsewhere, suggests a concern for not wearying the general reader, and perhaps an instinct for economy.[26]

When on that twentieth day of November, in the year of Our Lord 1483, and the first of the reign of King Richard III, William Caxton completed at Westminster his great edition of the *Golden Legend*, he unquestionably enjoyed the exhilaration of the accomplishment of a great undertaking. But however much he may have triumphed in the consciousness that he was a beginner of new things in the field of translation and publication, nothing can have been further from his thoughts than any innovation in the materials of his great book. There is in every line of his *Golden Legend* the secure and opulent poise of the recognized and consummated classic, the spacious ease of the acclaimed expression of a great and long-established and secure civilization. That does not mean that there is anything complacent or sentimental in the groundwork of the book itself. The moral and physical crises out of which martyrs are made, and the intellectual and spiritual tensions through which saints come to their glory, are far too essential to the drama of the book to be glozed over or minimized, but all of these things are viewed, not from the dusty battleground of this earth, but largely and triumphantly, as from the heights of that heaven in which the suffering and the struggling alike have become but precious memories, the pledge of everlasting beatitude.

There is, also, that sense of context, no less characteristic of the classic. For Caxton thoroughly understood and maintained the basic framework of Jacobus de Voragine's book, and the homiletic purpose that inspired it. Caxton followed the Archbishop of Genoa in his endeavor to give the layman a bird's-eye view of the ecclesiastical year, emphasizing, as in his colophon description, the feasts of Our

Lord and Our Lady.[27] He enriched this survey with detailed recollection of the scriptural history behind it, reinforced often with the
interpretations of the Fathers. In his account of the Feast of Corpus
Christi he carefully supplied a full summary of the theory of the
Blessed Sacrament, including some historical material with regard to
past usage, and in the section on "The Dedication of the Temple or
Chirche" he explained the Mass and the Hours, and the way in which
men should approach the services of the Church.[28] This is all done
very faithfully and systematically in order that, even as he becomes
absorbed in the wonders of the *Golden Legend*, the reader may be
reminded of the spiritual whole in which the saint plays his appointed part.

For there is nothing individual or private or removed about the
glory of the Church Triumphant. The saint belongs to all. And what
is true of the saint is even more sharply and dramatically true of that
most dramatic and heroic of the Christian heroes, the martyr; as
"saint austyn sayth," repeated Caxton, "the moost prouffytable forme
for tenforme the peple to god, is the fayre speche of martyrs."[29]
Indeed, it would be difficult to find a more inclusive summary of
the Christian program for any age than that which is suggested in
those three things which Caxton tells us Saint Laurence preached to
us by his famous example: the strong suffering of adversities, the
greatness of his faith, and the fervor of his love.[30]

But this was not merely the example of a past time. The fires that
warmed Saint Laurence's gridiron were centuries cold, but the love
that had strengthened his courage was of an immortal heat, which
might still warm the tepid spirit of the as yet peaceful years of the
close of the fifteenth century. Some of the saints and martyrs at the
time could take this long view, Saint Patrick, for example, praying
"that none yrisshe man shal abyde the comyng of antecryst," a large
undertaking even for the racial solicitude of the patron of the Irish;[31]
but not unnaturally most of the victims of fire and sword were more
narrowly tethered. Yet all of them in their degree finally took on the
burden of sanctity, both direct and indirect. With all humanity for
his clients, the saint was, of course, assailed with a variety of importunities, from the arrogant, like the indignant client of Saint Nicholas
who at the onset of misfortune directly challenged his patron as to
why he had allowed this thing to happen to one who had always been

his faithful servant,[32] to the humble, like the sick nun who, knowing herself not worthy to address herself to God, besought her founder, Saint Dominic, to heal her.[33] And once at least the patron admitted the need of still more help himself. Characteristically, it was Saint Peter who, when one of his monks, a sinner as Peter knew himself to have been, begged for help, turned to Mary to ask that the devil-beset monk might be permitted to return to his body to do penance.[34] In all the entanglements of human frivolity and weakness and materialism that were soon to have their consequences in the widespread criticism of the cult of the saints, this element still remained central, that the saint was not something past and gone, but a force immortally present in the life of the mystical body, and perennially operative in the affairs of his succeeding brethren.

Even when it comes to the individual histories which are the main business of the book, the *Golden Legend* operated on the basis of a carefully-thought-out and long-established pattern or ground plan which in effect, as we have seen in the preceding chapter, recapitulates the history of the Church and the development of the cult of the saints. That plan is explained at considerable length in the account of All Hallows. There are really four classes of saints that are remembered in the course of the ecclesiastical year. Of these the first and the most important are the apostles. Then come the martyrs, and then the confessors, and then the virgins. Needless to say, a good many saints come into more than one of these categories. But each class has its appropriate and, one might almost say, expected excellences. The apostles excel first of all in "soveraynte of dygnyte," as befits the "wyse prynces of the chyrche mylytaunt." Moreover they are also "the puyssaunt accessours of the Juge perdurable, they ben swete pastours of the shepe and the flock of our lord." Verily, "the lyf and conversacion of Jhesu cryste shone in theym as in a myrrour." Finally, they excel in "the effecte of prouffyte." From the humblest and simplest of men were they raised to eloquence and to wisdom,[35] two gifts that any writer, lay or ecclesiastical, will prize.

The second class is the martyrs, whose excellence lies in "that they suffred in many maners prouffytably: constauntly and mu[l]typlyengly." Here as so often the hagiographer remembers that most of his readers are not likely to find their opportunities of excellence in striving with Roman emperors and heathen provosts. So he goes on to translate martyrdom into terms more nearly applicable to the average Christian, whose combat must be with humbler and more weary-ing foes, patience in adversity, compassion of them that are in afflic-tion — "who that hath compasyon of ony that is in necessyte, he bereth the crosse in his thought," he quotes some unknown author-ity — and love of those that wrong one. So the great battle and the little are made one. And so, too, the profit: remission of sin and "joy perdurable," for them, and for us, "an example to fyght" and "patrons for to ayde and helpe us." For in their martyrdom God "examyned theym for to enseygne and teche us . . . He breketh theym for to gadre us." [36]

After the martyrs come the confessors, whose dignity and excel-lence lie in the fact that "they confessyd god in their manners, by herte, by mouth: and by werke." And again the example of the saints is brought down to the level of the generality of men: "as ofte as we done ony good, we confesse god." [37] Finally, but far from least, are the virgins; they are "the spouses of the eternall kyng." [38]

These are the basic patterns of sanctity, but, of course, each indi-vidual manifestation will have its own character, its own emphasis. To begin with the most obvious in the purely human picture, the saints in their social origins cover every class of society. Edward the Confessor was King of England,[39] and Saint Eloy was a goldsmith, a good workman and charitable to the poor, quite deserving of being made a bishop, as was possible in the more easygoing times of King Dagobert.[40] Mary of Egypt was a harlot [41] and Scholastica, sister of the founder of the Benedictine order, was a nun.[42] But the author of the *Golden Legend* did not exploit the social ranges of the martyrol-ogy as fully as he might have. He had a taste for the remarkable and the dramatic, and in view of the suffering ahead of the martyr and the bare, hard life in store for the saint, it is not surprising that, as a rule, he selected those who in choosing the straight and narrow path gave up most, and that he delighted in emphasizing the splendor of the sacrifice and the magnitude of the conversion. Saint Rock is one of his favorite types, noble, rich in dominions, "also vertuous in all humanytee," [43] the medieval counterpart of the more ancient senator's son of the failing Roman Empire, likewise rich and learned, who be-came Gregory the Pope.[44] Still more romantic is the feminine coun-terpart of this noble young man, the virgin, like Saint Agatha, "right fayr, noble of body and of herte, and . . . riche of goodes," whom the base-born and low-minded provost of her Sicilian city coveted,[45] or the British Winifred, whom the King's son loved and, thwarted in his suit, beheaded with results so dramatic for all concerned.[46]

But much as the author of the *Golden Legend* cherishes the rich and noble and brilliantly endowed young man or woman who gives up so much of worldly felicity for martyrdom, he delights even more in the great sinner who gives up his evil ways for true faith and devotion. The conversion of Saint Paul, he explains, is hallowed more than that of other saints because he that was such a sinner is now in great joy.[47] It is not surprising, therefore, that he shows no disposition to minimize the preconversion records of his reformed sinners. Saint Mary of Egypt lived seventeen years in sin before the day she found herself unable to enter the church to worship the True Cross in Jerusalem.[48] Saint Julian had slain his father and mother under the impression that he had found in his bed his unfaithful wife and her lover.[49] Indeed, most grievous of all from the point of view of the classic martyrologist, Marcellinus the Pope, in fear of torment, offered incense to the gods, bringing joy to the pagans and grief to all good Christian people, and yet having deposed himself and been reëlected, he met martyrdom valiantly, giving orders that his body should not be buried among Christian people, as not worthy of the honor.[50] Perhaps the most glowing account of the great sinner in the whole book is the description of the unconverted Pelagia, surely a rival to the Cleopatra of Plutarch:

Pelagyenne was the formest and noblest of the wymmen of anthyocke full of richesses in all thynges. She was ryght fayr of body, Noble of habyte, vayne and varyable of courage and not chaste of body. On a tyme as she wente thorugh the Cyte with grete pryde and ambycyon, that ther was no thynge sene on her, But gold and sylver and precious stones: and overall where as she wente: she fylled thayer wyth dyverse odours, and swete smellys, and to fore and after her wente a grete multytude of yonge men, and maydens: whiche were also cladde wyth ryght noble vesture and ryche.[51]

The young Bernard, who at the age of twenty-two is followed to Citeaux by thirty companions, is another example of the magnetism of the saint, all the more impressive because now the first enthusiasm of a new revelation is more than a thousand years spent.[52] Again, Childeric of France was still a pagan, but he held Saint Genevieve in such reverence that when he had some prisoners whom he intended to put to death, he left Paris so that Saint Genevieve might not get their lives from him. He had the gates of the city shut behind him, and doubtless felt safe. But he had reckoned without his saint. She soon heard of it, and went after him. The gates opened without key, and, needless to say, she obtained the prisoners from the doubtless still-unconvinced but helpless King.[53]

Indeed, on occasion this magnificence of the saint can take on dimensions that are larger than life to an almost flamboyant degree, as in the case of the man who before his baptism was named Reprobus and afterwards Christopher — "he was of a ryght grete stature: And had a terryble and ferfull chere and countenaunce. And he was xii cubytes of lengthe. And as it is redde in somme hystories, that whan he served and dwelled wyth the kyng of canonees It came in his mynde that he wolde seeke the grettest prynce that was in the world, and hym he wolde serve and obeye." [54] Here is one of the figures of high romance, indeed, a figure older than romance, one of the strong men of the world of folk tale and legend with the authentic idealism and extravagance of the folk hero. The story of such a man can hardly fail to be widely appealing, and, as we shall see presently, Jacobus did one of his best pieces of storytelling when he came to it.

Perhaps that is the most important thing to say about the saint and the martyr alike: they are on the whole remarkable people. True, there are the nameless men, here as in every crisis of history, and the writer today would be more likely to pick one of them. There is, for instance, that host of bystanders who were converted in Nicomedia when an angel came and shattered the bloody wheel on which Saint Juliana had been broken and healed her wounds — "And anone after for the fayth of Jhesu cryst, were byheded men and wymen to the nombre of C and xxx persones."[55] They are but an interlude in the prolonged tortures of the beautiful Christian woman who was given in marriage to the heathen provost of Nicomedia, but their names, though forgotten in history, which is so necessarily selective in its spotlight, are written in the book of life, and who shall say that their glory is any the less in that other world? But for this one the beautiful and valiant heroine who withstood so many tortures is the central figure, and here the instinct of the hagiographer is at one with that of the romancer and the teller of heroic tales.

In nothing, of course, is the remarkableness of the saint so apparent as in his attitude toward the martyrdom which so often puts the final seal upon his sanctity. There are some ages when the achievement of martyrdom is easier than in others. Saint Thomas Aquinas must have known that he was more likely to go on laboring long and painfully with the arguments of heathens and heretics and muddleheads than to fall to their swords. Yet the memory of the glory of martyrdom is one of the brightest ideals of the *Golden Legend*. And there is no question of the rich abundance of examples from the early days to be so remembered. Indeed, even in the quiet days of the composition of the *Golden Legend*, and the still-peaceful days of its printing, the martyrs are always regarded as the great source of the faith and the zeal of the Church, and every detail that can be gleaned not only of the actual martyrdom but of the attendant circumstances of these ancient sacrifices is treasured.

Not the least remarkable aspect of this cult is the grasp on the psychology of the martyr. Not so long after Caxton's own time, Thomas More was to look long and thoughtfully upon the possibility of martyrdom, not feeling himself so good a man that he might rush rashly upon it. But not so the martyrs of the *Golden Legend*. Theirs is the spirit of the superb taunt of Saint Vincent to his tormentors from the midst of his passion: "This is that I have always desired" — they could not invent any torment he could not suffer.[56] Saint Agatha at first refused the heavenly medicine which Saint Peter brought from another world for her wounds, for she was loath to mar the perfection of her trust in Christ by accepting even so divinely appointed a relief.[57] Saint Peter himself, who was usually so generous of his healing powers, in turn allowed his daughter Saint Petronilla to suffer from a painful illness because it was good for her soul, and she happily acquiesced.[58] But it is more than merit that is at stake. It is the fullness of the Christian life, the final triumph of the Christian enterprise.

That is why so many of the martyrs seem to rush headlong upon their felicity. Especially those candid, even brutally candid, souls like Saint Ignatius of Antioch, who undertook to tell the Emperor himself that the gods he worshiped were thieves, ribalds, and men of abominable life.[59] In this category the women martyrs seem rather to have the preëminence, perhaps because women so often are forced to fight with words for their only arms. Indeed, there are in the *Golden*

Legend a number of plain-speaking virgins who make one feel some sympathy for the masculine tyrants who had to cope with them. There is Saint Agatha, who told the provost Quintianus that his gods were devils dwelling in idols of stone and wood, and beings of quite as evil life as himself.[60] Saint Christina told her father that he was the son of Satan, and when she was haled before the judge and her tongue was cut out, she threw it into the judge's face, knocking out one of his eyes.[61] There is Saint Barbara, who cursed the shepherd who betrayed her miraculous flight and turned his sheep to locusts, and very tartly defied the judge, expressing her scorn for the devils that the heathen gods really were and for all their worshipers.[62] Perhaps the most ironic touch in a by no means naïve book is her prayer for the frailty of our common human kind, before her final execution by the sword.[63]

But man or woman, the martyrs do not confine their stoutness to words only. It is with tremendous pride that their historian records the sharpness and the ingenuity of their sufferings as they storm from martyrdom to martyrdom. One does not know which to marvel at more, the dogged persistence of the pagan tyrants who in the face of incredible frustrations still persisted in trying to kill these seemingly indestructible zealots or the toughness of the victims. Neither does one know whether to marvel at the ingenuity of the pagan torturers or to be nauseated by the fruits of their imaginations, for some of their contrivances are particularly horrid and nasty. And they lose nothing in the telling at the hands of a writer who is a master of the swift phrase and the detail that plays on the nerves, as in the martyrdom of Saint Julian, whose body on the wheel "was to broken in suche wyse that the mary cam out of the bones."[64] The executioners of Saints Primus and Felician tried fire, boiling lead, lions and bears, and still their incredible victims lived. At last they resorted to the means that doubtless they had rejected in the beginning because of its swiftness, the axe, and this did its work.[65]

Not the least curious thing in these accounts is this respect for a sharp edge. Again and again what fire or boiling lead or wild beasts or hanging or starvation cannot compass, the sword brings off.[66] There are, however, a few cases where the victim recovers miraculously, notably that of Saint Winifred. But it should be noted here that Saint Beuno was at hand at the critical moment to set the severed head to the body and to lead the people in prayer for her restoration. It cannot be denied, either, that her after-life, noble and useful as it was, did not quite match her martyrdom in dramatic interest. Indeed, the well that sprang where her head fell to the ground was her most lasting monument.[67]

It goes without saying that whatever the tortures, the victim bore them resolutely, and even on occasion joyously. The principle that the increase of torments increases glory was as well known to the martyrs as to their panegyrist.[68] There is some evidence, however, that the hagiographer was torn between dwelling on their sufferings, with the consequent enhancement of their heroism, and doing justice to the joy of suffering in so glorious a cause. Once at least, in the case of Saint Laurence, he points out very reasonably that the body could feel no pain on earth when the soul and courage were in heaven.[69] The solution of the difficulty is to be found in the thoroughly adequate compromise of the resolved and composed surrender of the whole heart and will to the great business in hand, as in the description of Saint Matthew lifting up his hands and commending his spirit to God.[70]

But sometimes, eager as he was for his release from this imperfect world, the martyr yet lingered. There are some very remarkable stories of the activity of practically dead and just dead men in the *Golden Legend*. Saint Basil, near death, this time in the course of nature, and feeling already the magnetism of heaven, yet lingered another day to convert his Jewish physician, who had said he could not be won.[71] Saint Cecilia with her head almost cut off lived three days.[72] Saint Denis, in one of the most famous post-mortem feats of all romance, carried his head in his hand from the place of his beheading to the place where his body was to rest.[73]

The part which women play in these stories of the ancient martyrs is a striking feature of the *Golden Legend*. It would seem that there was a remarkable number of these energetic and hardy young women to be found in the early days of the Church in the ancient world and later among some of the backward peoples. Noble girls of ancient Rome and Alexandria and princesses of Britain seem to have possessed an independence and a resourcefulness not so common among women of a later time. Consequently, they play a larger part in the roster of the saints and martyrs of the early day, as women seem to do in a pioneer world, while as the struggle of the spirit settles into the long war of the established and mediocre, they seem less likely to emerge from the ranks of the more easily settled sex.

The young female martyrs certainly bring the light of their beauty and the pathos of their youth and many a touch of answering chivalry into the story, and doubtless the hagiographer felt that the frailty of the sex of these conquerors was the greater tribute to the wonder of the power of God, but it is impossible to avoid the conclusion that his enthusiasm has betrayed him into admitting into his Paradise some very dubious precedents for the well-behaved miss. It may be rash to suggest the heroines of the *Golden Legend* for the ancestry of Shakespeare's Beatrice, but these young women have an amazing competence that goes far beyond the exigencies of the Sunday School lesson.

No less interesting is the contribution which women make to the stories of the virgins, another of the four categories from which their sex would not bar them. As we have seen above, virginity was the human estate closest to the angels in the eyes of the hagiographer, but physical abstention in itself was not enough. The author quotes the "Pastor Hermes" as to the virtues "wyth out whyche noo vyrgyn may be agreable to god." It is an impressive list, twelve, numbered with that precision dear to the heart of the author, and that recklessness of logical discrimination no less characteristic: faith, abstinence, patience, magnanimity, "symplesse," innocence, concord, charity, discipline, chastity, truth, and prudence — not a bad summary of the undertakings of the Christian life.[74]

But there are a number of episodes and passages in which some very curious arguments are advanced in support of the angelic state, arguments that sometimes have a faintly feministic tinge that can hardly have been intended as anything but a concession to human weakness. The most striking is the sermon which the eunuchs Nereus and Achilleus preached to Flavia, the niece of the Emperor Domitian. It was a striking picture that the lady made, sitting "curyousli" arrayed in her robes of purple and precious stones, as the two eunuchs preached to her of the faith of Christ and the virtue of virginity. The sermon began properly enough with eloquent praise of the virtue in general and in theory. Then the two preachers, perhaps not entirely unaware of the inner being of the gorgeous young woman before them, took up a line of argument that would do credit to the less cheerful moments of Innocent III, but can hardly in any age have been part of the orthodox religious instruction of a young woman who seems already to have been bestowed in marriage. For they went on to set against this glowing picture of the high estate of virginity, a picture of the married woman, "subget to man, and is beten wy staves and fystes in suche wyse that they be delyverde of their childerne or their tyme dysformed and lame: And where in her youth she myghte uneth suffre techynges and admonestynges of her moder whyche were but soft and amyable, She sholde now by the contrarye suffre of her husbonde grete shames repreves and vylanyes." But orthodox or not, their argument must have struck home, for we find the niece of the Emperor agreeing that her mother had had a hard time with her jealous father, and that she knew well that her husband would be the same sort of man. It is not surprising, therefore, that she decided to be a Christian and a virgin. But there must have been something more to her conversion than a fear of the woes of marriage, for she persisted in her resolution to the test of the headsman's sword.[75]

For its period, that may be taken as a fairly representative, even if unusually dramatic, story. But some of the stories concerning virginity are among the least conventional in the book. There is, for instance, the story of Saint Lupus or Leu, who when he was archbishop of Sens kept in his company a devout nun who was the daughter of his predecessor. Not surprisingly, there were plenty of people to see evil in his conduct. So when he heard of the gossip, he took the nun and before all the detractors and the doubters, he kissed her, saying that evil words could not hurt a man whose conscience was sound, an heroic measure, doubtless not often to be emulated.[76]

Another type of story about women saints that arouses in the mind familiar with latter-day arguments the same sort of suspicions aroused by some of Shakespeare's page-boy heroines is that of the enterprising young lady who for some always unimpeachable reason disguises herself as a monk or a hermit and so lives without any suspicion of scandal, other than that proper to her supposed sex. There is an interesting variety in the women who did this. Theodora, for all her nobility and wealth and beauty and apparent holiness, must have been a little simple-minded when she yielded to a seducer who as-

sured her that God did not see in the night, but there is no other indication of light-mindedness in her story, and she lived a model life
in the monastery to which she went for penance, and behaved hero-
ically when she was accused of being father to a child.[77] The Cleo-
patra-like Pelagia, whose motives might properly have been suspect
in view of her record before her conversion, very wisely did not go
to a monastery but to the desert. In such circumstances her masculine
disguise had some justification, though Saint Mary of Egypt, whose
record was even worse, had not needed it.[78]

But one's feminist suspicions receive more certain confirmation in
the case of Eugenia, the daughter of the Roman provost of Alexandria, who was a very learned lady. When she decided to become a
Christian, she dressed as a man and went to a monastery and became
a monk. The charge of trying to force a woman under cover of practice of medicine would doubtless have been received with the proper
indifference of the saints to the world's opinion, had not the charge
been made the pretext of an attack upon the still-pioneer profession of
Christianity; so it had to be refuted, as was done with spirit. There
are a number of elements of classical romance in the story of Eugenia,
including the conversion of her provost father and his resigning the
provostship to become a bishop, but the most important from our
point of view, as from the point of view of the hagiographer, is her
return to Rome and her conversion of many people there. In the
whole story one has the impression of a vigorous woman quite capable of operating confidently on the intellectual front of the new
religion.[79]

Nor is Eugenia the only woman to do so, or indeed the most conspicuous. Saint Mary Magdalene we find actually preaching to the
crowds, probably, like so many things that remarkable woman did,
not to be taken as typical, but certainly not viewed as unbecoming
or ineffectual.[80] Likewise, Catherine of Alexandria seems early to have
been as famous for her wisdom as for her beauty and to have received
an education that was quite as much a tribute to her taste and capacity
as to her prospective rank in society. Her progress in contemplation
and mystical illumination is another evidence of her mastery of the
things of the mind. So is the work of conversion she did among the
people around her. But the most famous manifestation of her competence is the dispute with the Emperor Maxentius. He had come to

Alexandria and summoned the people to do sacrifice. Those who would not, were, in the summary fashion of the time, put to death. Catherine heard the tumult, and when she found out what was going on, she went "hardely" to the Emperor and challenged him in a fashion startling enough from the lips of a beautiful woman of eighteen: "The dygnyte of thyn ordre, and the waye of reason have meoved me to salewe the, yf thou know the creatour and maker of heven, and woldest revoke thy corage fro the worshyppnge fro false goddes." What followed was such a flow of argument and exhortation that the Emperor seemed at first to have been completely overwhelmed. But presently he recovered, pointed out that the business immediately in hand was the sacrifices, and had Catherine taken to his palace. But even at leisure the Emperor found himself no match for her; so he sent abroad into all the neighboring provinces for experts in all worldly wisdom, and them, too, she not only abashed but convinced, so that they were ready for martyrdom. Only the Emperor seems to have been inaccessible to the force of her wit, for the rest of her story is one of the classic stories of torture heaped upon torture until the sword ends it all.[81] But one of the striking things about the handling of this story is the time and detail devoted to it. Clearly, it was one of the hagiographic favorites.

The relations of learning and sanctity are, of course, a classic subject of speculation and controversy in the history of religious feeling. Clearly, there are involved in the matter two of those extremes so dear to the heart of the spiritual enthusiast. There is the wonder of the way in which the suddenly manifest wisdom of the simple and the unlearned confounds the wisdom of the wise — naturally, one of the most popular manifestations of the power of God. The conquest of the pagan masters was obviously still a subject of deep pride centuries later to the teller of Catherine's wonderful story. At the other extreme, there is the satisfaction to be found in the reflection that one's own humble faith is shared by those who know all there is to know. Both extremes have their liabilities, as the medieval hagiographer very well knew. On the whole the *Golden Legend* preserves the balance, or perhaps, rather, does justice to both points of view at once, a harder but surer way to justice.

The simplicity of the apostles and the wisdom to which they came by the grace of God are, of course, a lasting source of pride to their descendants, not least to those of learned aspirations. At the opposite end, the triumphs of the brilliance of the faithful are recognized as a source of the corporate intellectual life of the Church. The marvelous books of Saint Thomas Aquinas, for instance, had replenished the whole Church with his learning, and after his death one of his brethren saw that other great source of wisdom humane and divine, Saint Augustine, appear with Saint Thomas in a jeweled cope to reveal the ratification of his glory.[82] But there is another facet to this complicated matter. And that is represented by the great mystic and ascetic writer, as well as ecclesiastical reformer and lawgiver, Bernard of Clairvaux — "He sayde that all that he had lerned of holy scrypture: he hadde lerned it in woodes, in feldes: moost by medytacyon and prayenge, and confessyd that he had none other maystres but Okes and Holme trees this confessyd he amonge his frendes." It would be tempting to see in this passage some foretaste of the theories of the romantic poets, but it must never be forgotten that the man who said this rode all day along the lake of Lausanne (Geneva) without seeing the lake or even knowing that it was there.[83] Rather, it is a matter of another way of acquiring wisdom, for at this point two aspects of the religious life, too often severed by a false dichotomy, become one — what may be called the discursive method of research and the concentrative method of meditation, the latter operating upon a rich store of both individual and group experience in the ascetic and mystical fields to which Bernard devoted his efforts.

Wisdom, however, is never taken as enough for any saint. Good works are indispensable as the expected fruit and authentication of grace. In general, they fall into two classes, works of devotion or piety, and works of charity. They are really two halves of the same whole, and to separate them even momentarily for discussion is to run the risk of violating the essential integrity of the saint's functioning. The first, the works of piety, will, of course, vary from age to age, partly because of the accident of personal genius, partly because of available resources and opportunities. In an age of persecution, the burial of the dead, especially of those who died for the faith, will assume an importance not likely in more settled times. It was thus that the piety of Abdon and Sennen first attracted attention as men became aware of their zeal in burying the bodies of the martyrs.[84] So the conversion of the unbeliever in a mission land will have a dramatic urgency and a potential importance that no conversion can have under normal circumstances. Especially is this true of the conversion of the ruler of a country. Saint Augustine's conversion of Ethelbert, King of Kent, is but one example of the way in which the faith advanced in mission lands.[85] In such a case it must be remembered that not only did the ruler's conversion facilitate the spread of new ideas, but the virtue of a good king might be a prime source of the felicity of his land, a notion very deeply imbedded, of course, in folklore. So, according to Caxton, when good King Edward sat on the throne of England, there was no pestilence in the land, the crops were good, there were no disastrous storms at sea.[86] In other words, the very elements made their contribution to the age of gold.

Analogous in importance to the conversion of the men of power in the pioneering period of a new faith is the defense of the faith, once it is established, against heresy or the threat of heresy. Pope Innocent III's vision of Dominic supporting the church of the Lateran is but a picturesque testimony and symbol of an intellectual reality widely appreciated at the time.[87]

But in all ages the basic work of piety is the life of devotion, with its instruments of prayer and meditation. The story of Saint Bernard is proof enough that the enterprise of direct access to the source of wisdom and insight is in no danger of undervaluation by the authors of the *Golden Legend*. Indeed, what may well be called professional experience of prayer is revealed in some of the passages on the subject. For instance, the handling of the story of Saint Antony clearly recognizes the problem of the weariness that befalls human nature too long strained in prayer, as in any intellectual activity. The famous parable of the bow that cannot be kept bent too long without loss of resiliency, so often attributed to Saint Benedict, is here given to Saint Antony; and to him is attributed the discovery, through the teaching of an angel when he complained of distraction from weariness, of the necessity of physical labor to relieve the exhaustion of too-prolonged prayer.[88] The whole handling of this episode indicates the practical sense of the man for whom these matters are no mere abstraction of religious idealism but the very stuff of day-to-day experience.

Not that the author of the *Golden Legend* is unaware or unappreciative of the loftier heights of contemplation. Mary Magdalene, when she had brought Christianity into France, preaching with her

disciples at Marseilles, sought a very grim desert for "soverayn" contemplation.[89] And enthusiastic as is the author's tribute to the wisdom
and the debating skill of Saint Catherine of Alexandria, the episode
that engages his deepest sympathies and his most prolonged literary
appreciation is the famous mystical marriage that was to prove the
prototype of some of the loftiest expressions of contemplative experience. But here it is again obvious that the account is for the
generality of men, not for the rare spirits to whom the delight of
the ineffable is possible without the mediation of the symbols of this
earth. The splendor of the scene at the monastery of Catherine's
vision, with the host coming out in white with crowns of lilies and
in purple vestments with red roses on their heads, is representative
of the resort to the properties of romance for the suggestion of the
supermundane.[90]

Still more is this true of the representation of the spiritual combats
through which so many of the saints have come to their glory. The
medieval mind was quite aware of the mixed nature of all human
experience and the struggle inseparable from any human achievement, spiritual or otherwise. But by and large, the writer for a popular
audience was not so likely to deal with introspective problems as the
writer for the practising specialist in the spiritual and contemplative
life. The result is that the dim marchings of the awakening consciousness and the struggles of the encumbered will are more likely
to be presented in dramatic episodes than in ecstatic description. And
this is the easier because the forms of devil and angel are clearer
and more familiar to the reader of the *Golden Legend* than to the
superstition-fearing rationalist of a later generation. One of the most
homely episodes in the book is the story of Saint Dunstan's catching
the Devil's nose between a pair of tongs.[91] Saint Germanus routed
a whole tableful of devils, a feat that, the author admits, would be
but for his merits a marvel.[92] Then there is the founder of the Abbey
of Bath, Saint Alphege, who was misled by a devil in the likeness of
an angel over mud and mire until finally rescued by a real angel
and brought safely back to his prison and to martyrdom, the safest
of all conclusions to a life in the time when the Danes were still
wasting England.[93]

As for the works of charity, they do not greatly vary from age to
age in spirit or impulse, though the forms may vary with the circum-

stances which charity tries to meet. Love of God is the mainspring, human compassion the concomitant. The pity of Francis of Assisi for the poor is notable because it is expressed in such direct and absolute terms. The famous story of the leper is told very briefly with no exploitation of its implications, and yet so told, it still keeps clear the classic pattern of Christian charity as regards both impulse and practical consequences: "On a tyme he mette a lepre: whom naturelly men abhorre, but he remembred him of the worde that was sayd of god, and ranne to him and kyssed him. And anone the lazare vanysshed away: wherfore he went to thabytacyon of the lazares and kyssed devoutly their hondes, and gaaf to theym money. And lete them have no nede of suche as he myght doo." [94]

The lady giving bread at the gate is of course one of the classic figures of medieval romance, but even her luminous figure pales beside the lady wanting to be poor with the poor, Elizabeth, the Landgravine of Thuringia.[95] Her legend is one of the longest and most enthusiastically told in the whole book. One element is especially interesting in view of the social preoccupations of Caxton's time, the fact that when traveling, the Landgravine refused any food not obtained by good and just labor.[96] This note of respect for labor recurs more than once in the course of these stories. Saint Edmund's mother, for instance, gave the spinners more wool to spin for the pound than they could make a living by. When they complained, Saint Edmund threw all the wool into the fire, and then after a while he took it out, and the just pound was not damaged, but all that was above the pound was burned.[97]

This instinct for justice, the necessary foundation of charity, receives its due emphasis in some rather surprising forms. One of Saint Nicholas' clients, a group that, if we can believe the stories told of them, must have been a rather mixed lot, evolved a very ingenious trick of a hollow staff to cheat a Jew of the gold which he had sworn upon the altar of Saint Nicholas to return to him. When summoned to court, he gave the Jew the staff to hold while he swore that he had repaid the money, and then he took back the staff and the gold from the unsuspecting creditor. The trick seemed to have worked, but soon afterward he was run over by a cart, and killed, and the staff broken, with the consequent revelation of the gold. The Jew very generously refused to take the gold again unless the dead rascal were restored to life by the merits of Saint Nicholas, and in that event he promised to be baptized. The story ended happily with the dead man restored to life and a very superior Christian added to the list of Nicholas' clients.[98]

Doubtless the saints had their work cut out for them in keeping the less worthy of their followers in order, and there must have been a good many stories of what happened to the rogues and rascals who tried to use the good name of their patrons as a cloak for their knavery. Saint Pancras was even more direct than Saint Nicholas, for when a young man had sworn falsely, and no sign was apparent at the altar of Saint Peter, the judge appealed at the tomb of Saint Pancras, and the young man putting forth his hand to swear falsely again was unable to draw it back and so died soon after, a horrible example to other false swearers.[99]

But it would be a mistake to assume that the saint had no sympathy with human weakness. One of the characteristic good works of Saint Eloy was to bury the bodies of those who had been hanged. When he found that one of the hanged still lived, he strenuously defended him against a second execution.[100] So Saint John the Almoner and Patriarch of Jerusalem would not allow some of his clergy to curse a young man who had ravished a nun and thereby, as the clergy very properly pointed out, put two souls in jeopardy. Saint John invoked the commandment "Judge ye not," and insisted that they could not tell whether the culprits had continued in sin and not repented.[101]

Nothing shows better the popular character of the *Golden Legend* than the proportionate time given to the good works of the saints and their works of piety. The active will always make better copy for a story than the contemplative. But there are very few of these saints who are so forthright as Saint Christopher, who flatly declared that fasting was not within the scope of his possibilities, and that waking and praying were beyond his comprehension. So the wise hermit who was counseling him set him beside a dangerous river to bear travelers over the flood. And Christopher embraced this task and

bare over all maner of peple wyth out cessyng and there he abode thus doyng many dayes: And in a tyme as he slepte in his lodge he herde the voys of a childe whiche called hym and sayd, Crystofre come out, and bere me over. Thenne he awoke and wente out. but he founde noman And whan he was agayn in his hous, he herde the same voys. and he ranne out and fond no body. The thyrde time he was called and came thyder and fond a chyld besyde the ryvage of the ryver: whiche prayed hym goodly to bere hym over the water. And thenne crystofre lyft up the child on his sholdres and toke his staffe and entryd in to the Ryver for to passe. And the water of the ryver aroos and swellyd more and more. And the child was hevy as leed, and always as he wente ferther, the water encresed and grewe more, and the chyld more and more wexed hevy in soo muche that crystofre had grete anguysse. And was aferd, to be drowned. And whan he was escaped wyth grete payne and passyd the water. And sette the chyld a grounde, he sayd to the chyld: Chyld thou hast me put in grete peryll, thou wayest al most as I had had all the world upon me I myght bere no gretter burdon, And the childe answered: Crystofre merveyle the noo thyng, For thou hast not onely born alle the world upon the, But thou hast born hym that created and made all the worlde, upon thy sholders, I am Jhesu cryst the kynge, to whom thou servest in this werke. And by cause that thou knowe that I saye to the trouthe, sette thy staf in the erthe by thy hous. And thou shalt see to morne that it shal bere floures and fruyte and anone he vanysshed from his eyen: And thenne crystofre sette his stafe in therthe, and whan he aroos on the morn he fonde his staf lyke a palmyer berying floures leves and dates.[102]

Nor does the beneficent activity of the saint stop with his death and burial. Sometimes there are marvelous happenings to reveal a body that has been hidden or lost or dishonorably buried. A notable example is that of the young Edward, king and martyr, who had been murdered at the instigation of a stepmother of folk-tale wickedness.[103] It was not that the saint or martyr was any tenderer of the dead body than of the living; rather, the dead body so revealed might be the occasion of fresh help to the martyr's fellow Christians. The cures at the tombs of Saint Alphege [104] and Edward the Confessor [105] are famous English examples, paralleled in every land. But sometimes something more than cures is involved in the tomb cult. One of the best of the stories in the *Golden Legend* concerns the tomb of Edward the Confessor, the story "Of the deposycion of saint wulfstan. And how he was restored agayne." It begins with admirable directness: "Whan wyllyam conquerour had goten all Englond: and hadde it under his power, thenne he began to medle wyth the chyrche and by the advys of lanfrank the holy bysshop saint wulfstone was chalenged that he was not able of lettrue ne of conning for to occupye the reame and offyce of a bysshop: And was callyd to fore Lanfranke: and wylled hym to resygne by the consente of the kynge, to the said

lanfranke archebysshop, that a man of gretter connynge myhgt occupye the dygnyte." Characteristically, Wulfstan agreed with those
who had challenged his capacity, but said that he would resign his
charge only to him who had pressed it upon him, the dead King
Edward. So he went to the saint's tomb and placed his staff on the
hard stone of the tomb, which took the staff and held it so fast that
none could move it. Both William and Lanfranc were abashed and
asked Wulfstan's forgiveness; Lanfranc bade him take his staff again,
and at Wulfstan's prayer the staff was released by the stone, and
Wulfstan happily restored to his office as bishop.[106] The elements of
this miracle, involving as it does both the manifestation of the sanctity
of the dead and the authentication of the living saint, are characteristic of many of these stories. Miracles such as this are a revelation of
the spiritual reality otherwise not apparent to mundane eyes.

This is especially true of those stories of prenatal wonders that
again and again signal the appearance of the saint. There is, for
example, that Candlemas Day when all the people were assembled
in church with tapers in their hands. Suddenly all the lights were
quenched save only that in the hand of Saint Dunstan's mother, and
the rest of the congregation, knowing that it was only by the power
of Our Lord that hers had burned again of itself, came and lighted
their tapers at hers.[107] Akin to this is the childhood prophecy, like
that of the young Ambrose, who, having seen his elders kiss the hand
of the priest when they offered, gave his hand to his sister to kiss (the
hagiographer has not forgotten to record that she in the usual way
of small sisters refused).[108] Of much the same order are those stories
of amazing precocity told of some of the saints. Probably the most
remarkable is that of Saint Quiricus, who, seeing his mother scourged
because she would not do sacrifice, scratched the face of the provost
who was trying to caress and win him, and so beat at his mother's
foe and struggled with him that the latter dashed him to the pave-
ment, and he perished, surely one of the youngest martyrs after the
Holy Innocents, and unlike them, though so young, yet a chooser of
his fate.[109] Indeed, Caxton presents an alternative version of this story
in which the young saint gives the provost a very remarkable rebuke
for his folly in not seeing that only the Holy Ghost could have taught
one not yet three years old such wisdom as he had just displayed in
his confession of the Christian faith.[110] The hagiographer has left the

two stories side by side, obviously giving precedence to the more reasonable story, yet clearly unable to resist the more marvelous exhibition of wisdom out of the mouths of babes. After such a tale the five-year-old Elizabeth of Hungary haunting the chapel in her father's castle seems but the normal pattern of pious precocity.[111]

This half-revelatory, half-authenticating character is typical of a good many of the marvels in which these accounts of the lives of the saints abound. They are a sort of supernatural materialization of spiritual value and significance. There is Earl Leofric's story of seeing Christ in the elevated Host blessing the kneeling King Edward;[112] there is the golden engraving of the name of Jesus found on the dead heart of the martyred Ignatius.[113] The earth shook when Saint Agatha, who had refused to escape from prison for characteristically feminine double reasons—the keepers might suffer and she would lose the crown of martyrdom—was rolled on burning brands.[114] There is the harp that sounded on Saint Dunstan's wall without the touch of human hand, and the songs of the angels that bore his soul to heaven,[115] and the singing of the monks in the distant church of Saint Francis that the sick Clare heard on Christmas Eve.[116] And there are the apparitions, like the appearance of Christ to Saint Edmund in his school at Paris as one of his schoolfellows.[117] There are the straight visions, like the one in which the young Prince Josaphat, the Christianized Buddha, saw Paradise as "a medowe arayed with fayre floures, there where the levys of the trees demened a swete sounde, whiche came by a wynde agreable, and therout yssued a mervayllous odour, and the fruyte was righte fayr taste, and there were to see ryght delectable of setes of golde and sylver and precyous stones . . ."[118] And there are also the dreams, like that of the sceptical bishop, who in the story of the conversion of Saint Pelagia dreamed of a black dove that was washed white,[119] and then there are those wonders of this world, half travelers' tales, half visions, like the magic islands which Saint Brendan came to in his marvelous travels, including the Earthly Paradise and that merciful place where even Judas may enjoy a brief respite from the most thoroughly earned tortures of hell.[120]

Perhaps most beautiful of all the marvels of the senses are the miraculous lights which shine upon the way of the martyrs and the saints for all these centuries. There is the light of innocence that shone about Saint Agnes in the Roman brothel and kept all profanation away,[121] there are the candles that lighted miraculously for Saint Genevieve,[122] and the shining tree of Saint Kenelm's dream, the cutting of which foretold his martyrdom.[123] There are those wonders of jewels, like the sleeves of gold set with precious stones that covered the naked arms of Saint Martin when he began to say Mass in the half a coat that was left after he had given the other half to the beggar.[124] All these things shed a radiance upon the blood- and tear-stained pages of the *Legend* that gives it a mortal and sensuous splendor worthy of its name, like some jeweled reliquary to hold a fragment of the charred and twisted bones of a martyr.

But the ethereal character of the book should not be overemphasized. For that would be to do less than justice to a number of other elements, like, for example, the animal wonders that add their own distinctive flavor to many a page. There is nothing ethereal about the two otters that came out of the sea and licked the freezing body of Saint Cuthbert when he had fainted from the midnight chill of the ocean in which he had been standing naked.[125] And quite as practical are the birds that brought food to Saint Blaise when he took refuge from the persecutors in a ditch.[126] So in a different way are those various creatures that help to bury the outworn bodies of the saints. Foremost among them is the lion that dug the desert sand for the grave of Saint Mary of Egypt;[127] and there are the wild bulls that meek as lambs drew the body of Saint James into the palace of the cruel Queen who would not receive him while living.[128] The poetry never far from the pages of the *Golden Legend* comes into these stories of the friendly and responsive creatures, and, of course, it dominates the more purely symbolic stories, like that of the three doves bearing in blood on their breasts the names of the new martyrs, Denis, Rusticus, and Eleutherius, to Bishop Regulus at Arles, who had just put their names into the canon of the Mass he was saying, and settling upon the cross of the altar at which he was celebrating.[129]

But, of course, the prime marvels concerned with any saint's or martyr's life are the miracles which he performs, or rather, it would be more accurate to say, for which he is the instrument or occasion. The heart of the matter is in an episode in the life of Saint Brendan at the time he was in the marvelous island abbey. He wondered that the tapers in the church, which an angel flying in the window had lighted, burned without being consumed, but the abbot reminded him that it is written that Moses saw a bush afire, and yet it burned not, and he bade him marvel not, for the might of God was as great now as ever it was.[130] Certainly, miracles are the expected manifestation of the presence of a saint. Some of them are concerned primarily with the preservation of the saint, like those various escapes which we shall study presently in later patterns of maryrdom. (The miracle by which Saint Benedict escaped drinking the venomous wine which some enemies had prepared for him is an example of what might be called a peacetime miracle of this type.)[131] But by and large, the great majority of a saint's miracles are concerned with the welfare of other people. Some of these are pretty extensive in their scope and significance, like the victory without shedding of blood which is attributed to the merits of Saint Martin,[132] or the appearance of the knight with the drawn sword behind Pope Leo, which awed Attila and saved Rome for that time.[133] But most of them are, like most things in life, relatively humble and obscure, and it is the habit of the writer, while stressing the wonder of the manifestation of grace, not to enhance the essential homeliness of the character of the miracle itself, an evidence of his sound respect for the unspectacular dignity of ordinary human life.

No student of the time and the years following but must have felt considerable envy of that fortunate man whom Saint Basil helped to speak Greek.[134] Even wider must have been the appeal of one of Saint Blaise's miracles. He persuaded a wolf to return a stolen pig to a poor widow. When he was in prison, the grateful widow killed the pig and brought the head and the feet with bread and a candle to the generous saint, who in turn bade her offer a candle in his church every year, with highly gratifying results for her temporal estate thereafter.[135] Still humbler is the miracle of Saint Swithin, who, when a poor woman's basket of eggs was dropped in a tussle with some workmen on a bridge, made the broken eggs whole.[136]

Of course the healing miracles are the commonest, not a surprising circumstance in view of the relatively low state of the healing art and the general state of public health in the Middle Ages. Here again the essential nature of the saint's miracle is to be emphasized. When Simon Magus and Saint Peter rivaled it out, Saint Peter was able to raise the dead because he operated in the name of Christ.[137] Saint Genevieve, for instance, was able by her prayer to restore the mad and the possessed to sanity.[138] Saints Cosmas and Damian performed one of the most dramatically attested cures on record, because when they wished to heal a man who had a cancerous thigh, apparently the only freshly dead thigh they could lay hands on was that of an Ethiopian; so the miracle was unusually conspicuous.[139] Then there was the blind bell-ringer of Westminster, who, waking from a sleep in which he had heard a voice bid him ring the bells, obeyed and saw Saint Edward going before him, crowned with a light about him, and he watched him till he came to the high altar, when he saw him no more, but ever after he had his sight.[140] But there is no need of multiplying examples, especially in view of the fact that many of the best stories concern the activity of the saints after their death.

One special variant of the cure story must, however, be noticed, because it involves larger issues even than those of life and death, and that is the restoration of the damned sinner to life for a period long enough for penance or absolution. The plight of the damned has always lain heavily on tender consciences, and the saints have been no exception. Of these tales the most famous concerns Saint Augustine of Canterbury. Once when at the beginning of Mass the saint liturgically bade all the accursed to withdraw, he was shocked to see a dead body arise, and with a white cloth on his head leave the church and wait in the churchyard until the Mass was finished. Augustine inquired the reason for this unhappy state, and discovered that it was a matter of unpaid tithes. So the charitable saint, doubtless not unaware of the salutary effect of this lesson upon his congregation, had the dead lord bring him to the place where the curate who had cursed him was buried. There Saint Augustine, reminding the priest of the mercy of God, bade him arise and absolve the accursed man. So he did, and when Augustine told the released sinner to go to his grave and stay there till the day of doom, the body went back into the grave and fell happily into dust.[141]

There is no need to say more of the miracles and wonders so dear to the heart of the teller of the *Golden Legend*. The ensuing age was to take a very severe view of the lies and superstitions that it claimed were thus palmed off on a credulous populace in the name of religion. But the student of literature may take a gentler view of the rich store of romantic treasure enshrined in the *Golden Legend*. Most of the imaginative resources of the popular literature of the Middle Ages are represented here. The four chests in the story of Saint Barlaam,[142] two full of filth but gilded, two covered with pitch but full of treasure, are as authentic properties of the folk tale as one could ask, quite as classic as the wicked stepmother of the young King Edward the Martyr,[143] or the ugly mother of ugly daughters into whose malevolent and envious hands the beautiful Saint Agatha is delivered by the lecherous provost.[144] The very villains of the martyr stories seem to come from the world of the folk tale and the romance; the pagan provost, the heathen emperor, the enchanter and the pagan priest, the marauding Danes, the northern barbarians in the fields of Germany and France. They are pictured darkly enough, and now and then the right epithets are joined to the appropriate nouns, but there is very little real feeling in the condemnation. There is no sign of any suspicion that these are perils that may be encountered again; so there is no reason for regarding them as a possible menace, and no point to getting really excited about them. Anyway the villains have long ago expiated their crimes or been safely buried in that hell from which there is no chance of their returning to harm the martyrs or their now secure clients and successors. At best their reality was hardly ever more than functional, and now their memory is dramatic rather than exciting.

As for the more sophisticated romances of the medieval world, their spirit is to be caught at every turn of the *Golden Legend*. The range is wide, too, within the genre. The tale of the adventures of Saint Eustace is an exceedingly rich and complicated and exciting story of romantic adventure.[145] The story of the Seven Sleepers of Ephesus is another sophisticated story, in which the mystery of time and its passing lifts the folk tale to new heights.[146] Of the same type, combining both speculative and romantic interest, is the charming story of the archer and the nightingale, which Barlaam told to King Anemyr to illustrate the folly of those who worship idols. The nightingale saved its life with a promise of teaching its captor the three wisdoms: "never to take that thynge that thou mayst not take, and of thyng loste, which mai not be recoveryd, sorowe never therefore: ne byleve never thynge that is incredyble." But the archer proceeded to demonstrate both his need of the wisdom and his inability to profit from it, whereupon the nightingale taunted him with his folly and went on to tell the story of the man who fled from a unicorn and fell into a great pit with a dragon at the bottom but managed to catch on with his hand to a branch of a tree which was nearly gnawed apart by a white mouse and a black, and so put his feet on a "slyding place" from which issued the heads of four serpents, and yet turned aside from these dangers to enjoy a little honey he saw in the boughs of the tree. And this story he explained as a figure of man's life in this world, and the behavior of the foolish amid its perils.[147]

Even the desperate lover finds his place, in the lovesick young man who promised himself to the Devil in return for help in winning his girl, and whom Saint Basil saved from the fiends.[148] But usually the romance is the romance of divine love, of which the prototype is the very young and very beautiful Saint Agnes setting against each other the two lovers, the son of the prefect of Rome and the Son of the King of Heaven, with never a moment's doubt as to which she shall choose, the earthly jewels or the vision of heavenly glory.[149] The light of that romance is on every page of the *Golden Legend*, and the certainty of that choice.

Even the handling of Scripture is touched with that spirit. The author of the *Legend* does not vouch for it, but he does embellish the story of Mary Magdalene, already rich fare for the romanticist, with the report that some say that she was wedded to Saint John the Evangelist and that it was from that wedding that Christ called John. Thereupon the forsaken wife fell into evil ways, and Christ took pity on her.[150] Something of the same sort is done again with the story of Judas. For here the storyteller draws on the Apocrypha for a most Oedipus-like past for the unhappy traitor. Judas' mother foresaw that he would be the destruction of his people. So he was exposed, taken up by the King's wife, and brought up as the heir, but he could not escape his destiny. He murdered his foster brother, killed his father, and unwittingly married his mother. It was his discovery of these things that sent him to Christ.[151]

These materials the hagiographer, with a sound instinct, knows for his own. But he is not, it is apparent, quite devoid of the critical spirit. He will not pass up the opportunities of a doubtful story, but even his strong appetite for romance has its own sense of responsibility, intermittent as it may be in its operation. He does have his moments of doubt, and though much of the time he is quite oblivious to the claims of chronology in a genial "once upon a time" contemporaneity, still he is now and then worried by discrepancies in the evidence. He is, for instance, disposed to doubt whether the Seven Sleepers slept the three hundred and sixty-two years his authorities claimed, but the more reasonable figure which he adopts, two hundred and eight years, is still generous enough not to spoil the story.[152] Sometimes he is too uncertain as to the relative claims of two stories to risk either, and presents both. Some say that the beautiful hart with the cross between its horns, the meeting with which changed the course of Saint Eustace's story, spoke to him and said he was Christ, but others say that it was the image of Christ on the cross between the horns that so spoke.[153] Either way it is a story to delight a lover of legends and to shock an iconoclast. Again, when he comes to the Julians he realizes that he has his hands full, and perhaps, too, that selection and organization are not his strong points. So he gathers up a whole sheaf of wonderful stories about an assortment of Julians, and even manages to include the name of Julian the Apostate, purely for the sake of completeness.[154]

Again, it should not be forgotten that like most medieval writers the author of the *Legenda Aurea* has a great reverence for authority and love of bolstering his own humble efforts with the opinions of learned doctors. Saint Augustine and Saint Ambrose are favorite authors of his, and again and again he appeals to their judgment, usually for an analysis or definition of some matter under discussion, for reinforcement of his own storyteller's verdict. He is certainly more than capable unaided of doing justice to the peculiar opportunities of Saint Laurence's martyrdom, but he prefaces his own judgment with the four standards which Saint Maximin and Saint Augustine had set up for martyrdom, "sourness of his passyon or bytterness, . . . prouffyte or effect, . . . constaunce or strengthe, . . . merveilous bataylle and manner of his victorie." It is an imposing analysis, hardly to be controverted, but not, I think, to be set beside the hagiographer's own summary of the martyrdom, "And after that he was all to broken and brente, he shedde in all the chyrches of the worlde the odour of noblesse." [155]

For the good Archbishop has his own narrative gifts, not by any means limited to those of a romantic storyteller, and they lose nothing in the transmission through Caxton's vigorous and even at times racy English. To begin with, Jacobus de Voragine has a very good sense of the comedy of human life, not the same thing as a sense of humor but no less indispensable to the humane spirit. His story of the two rascals, a lame and a blind man, who made the most of their infirmities for their sustenance in a hard world, is a case in point. The body of Saint Martin was to be translated, and they were afraid that if it were brought before their house, they might be healed, which was the thing furthest from their desires. So they ran away to a church in the neighborhood where they felt sure the disturbing body would not come, but on the way they met the body, and "by cause god gyveth many benyfayttes to men not desyred: and that wold not have theym, they were both heled: agaynst theyr wylle."[156] Altogether, it is a variant of the healing story that sheds a new light on one classic branch of the miracles tradition.

The author of the *Legenda Aurea* had no illusions about the nature of human life on this earth. When Saint Ambrose on his way to Rome met a rich man who boasted that his estate was "happy ynough and glorious . . . I have never thynge that may angre ne trouble me," the saint warned his companions, "Flee we hens for our lorde god is not here."[157] And he had a keen eye, too, for the foibles of the respectable as well as the rascally. He gives us many a glimpse of the gossip of bygone days in the interstices of noble stories. There is Saint Chrysostom, for instance, who seems to have set about reforming the clergy of his bishopric of Constantinople a little hastily, and encountered the inevitable reaction. One of the things the growing hostility fastened on was the fact that the new Bishop would not dine with his clergy or have them to dine with him. Some said it was because his food was so bad, others said that it was because his own table was so good, implying that he did not like to leave it or to share it, but the truth, said the historian, was that he had a weak stomach and suffered often from indigestion.[158]

And if he had a lively sense of the absurdity of human nature in its ill-doing, Jacobus had also a vivid sense of the frailty of human nature in its nobler aspirations. There is the pitiful tale of the martyrdom of Saint Adrian, the first of the Emperor Maximin's "knights" in Nicomedia, who seems to have been with his wife Natalie a secret Christian. The bold behavior of a company of Christians taken in a sudden persecution seems to have fired his timidity so that he leaped among them and declared himself one of them. Natalie was overjoyed when the news came to her, and she ran to the prison and kissed the chains that bound her husband. But when Adrian came to fetch her to witness his passion, she misjudged him, and thinking he had run away, she reviled him bitterly, because now she would not have the honor of being the widow of a martyr, but only the wife of a renegade. Only when he had convinced her that it was to his martyrdom that he had come to bring her did she admit him joyfully, and she valiantly served the martyrs in prison. But though she encouraged him stoutly in his preliminary sufferings and comforted him proudly, yet when it came to the final scene she was afraid that the sight of the sufferings of his companions might weaken his courage; so she begged the executioners to begin with him. This they did, and he gave a very good account of himself, to the lifelong pride of his wife, who ever after kept one of his severed hands at the head of her bed for a proud token of his victory.[159]

Much has been made recently in the discussion of seventeenth-century literature of the mingling of many contrary elements in the subtle complexity of baroque art. But, however great the gap between the sophistication of the faith of the seventeenth century and the naïveté of the faith of the fifteenth, there is no question that the mingling is already there in Caxton's *Golden Legend*. There can be no better example than the martyrdom of Saint Peter. That robust spirit, who seems to have had no illusions as to his own nature, begged to be crucified upside down, because he was not worthy to be crucified like his Master, who had come down from heaven to earth, whereas he, Peter, had been a creature of the earth whom it had pleased God to raise from his low ground. Yet as he hung there, "as leo witnesseth our lorde opened the eyen of them that were there and wepte, soo that they sawe the angelles wyth crownes of roses and of lilyes stondynge by Peter that was on the crosse wyth the angelles."[160]

It is this combination of the courage of the earth, vigorously realized and expressed with sensuous sharpness, and the answering splendor of the divine, moving through whatever the earth-bound imagination can conceive of beauty or joy, that makes the distinctive flavor of the *Golden Legend*. It is grounded in this earth, earthy, but there is a light of glory on the broken bodies and the straining hearts that is of another world, yet not alien; rather the fulfillment of the hopes of this valiant dust, the flowering of its hidden and unestranged nature.

It is at this point of style in the larger sense that the *Golden Legend* was well served by its English translator. Viewed from its relation to the Latin original, Caxton's style has not been free from criticism. Sister Mary Jeremy has called it "a blurring of the original Latin," but she adds, "If it sometimes mars or even cheapens the thought and imagery of its original, it also from time to time improves upon it."[161] Here again, Caxton's audience should be taken into account, and so should Caxton's relation to that audience. His frequent insistence upon his own simplicity and lack of learning is not, of course, to be taken too literally in view of the familiar auctorial disclaimers of the time.[162] But his own frequent complaints of the difficulties of finding the right expression at a time when the idiom of the language was still being hammered out, and his often-expressed interest in words for their own sake, should not be overlooked.[163] And perhaps most important of all, his obvious desire to put things clearly so that the common people might understand should receive perhaps more attention than it has.[164] Here Caxton clearly anticipates that movement in sixteenth-century prose writing that was to put so much stress upon clarity and simplicity, that was in turn to influence the seventeenth-century emphasis on the plain style of the Puritan preachers and the scientists. But in a certain dramatic quality of his homely immediacy even in the presence of the supernal, Caxton is very much of his age, of his age at its best.

There are a great many stories that illustrate this combination of homeliness and splendor, but none better than the story of the hallowing of Westminster. Ethelbert, King of Kent, had made a church in the west end of the city which was then called Thorney, and that church he asked Mellitus, the Bishop of London, to hallow in honor of Saint Peter:

And the nyghte before that he had purposed to halowe it, saynt peter apered to a fysshar in temse, and badde him sette him over from stangate to westmestre: And he prayed the fysshar to abyde him there tyll he came agayn: and he wold rewarde hym for his labour. And soone after the fysshar sawe saynt peter entre in to the chyrche wyth a grete lyghte: whiche lyghte endured contynuelli as long as he was in the chirche And a certen space after he retourned to the fysshar: axing him if he had take oni mete to ete: And the fysshar was so gretly abasshed of the lyght that yssued out of the chyrche wyth him, that he durst not speke to him. To whom saynt peter sayd Broder drede the not: I am a man as thou arte. Hast thou take ony fyshe, and he sayd naye, for I have awayted on you all this nyghte, while ye have be in the chirche. And thenne they entred in to the boot And saynt Peter commaunded hym to cast oute his nette. And whan he had soo doon. There came soo grete a multytude of grete fysshes in to his nette: that unneth they myghte drawe up the nette for brekyng:

And whan they were comen to the londe. Saynt Peter devyded the fysshes And badde the fysshar bere the gretteste unto Mellyte bisshop of London, and delyver it to him. And telle to hym that I have halowed the chryche of westmestre this nyghte. And saye to hym, that he saye masse therin tomorough. And if he wylle not byleve it, saye to hym whan he cometh, he shall fynde there tokens suffycyent. And I shall be patrone of that chirche, and vysite it oftymes, and bere in the sighte of almyghty god, the prayers and devocyons of tru crysten peple that prai in that place. And take thou the remenaunt of the fyssh for thy labour, and this sayd saynt peter vanisshid away. Thenne this sayd fyssher merveyllid gretly of the sight that he had seen: And erly by the morough he went to the bysshop myllyte of London: and delyver to him the fyssh that saynt peter had sente to him, and tolde to hym by order, lyke as saynt peter had given him charge. And as ye have herd tofore, but the bisshop wold not byleve him tyll he cam to westmestre and see the tokenes for to put him out of doubt. And whan he had opened the chirche door he fonde a crosse made of sonde, fro that one side of the chirche unto that other: wyth a/b/c/ lettres of grewe: And he fonde also xii crosses made on the walles in diverse places of the chirche, and thendes of xii candels almost brent oute: And also he sawe the places that were enoynted wyth holy oyle, whiche yet were moyst and apered newly doon. Thenne the bysshop bilevyd this thyng verely, and sayd masse that same daey in the chirche. And there preched to the peple a gloryous sermon And declared the grete myracle openly, wherfore the peple gaaf laude and praysinge to god, and to hys gloryous apostle saynt peter.[165]

The elements of direct edification in such a passage might be challenged, but there is no doubt that for the simple reader it would make him feel more at home in the great church at Westminster, and more hopeful, too, that with such help, at once so understand-

ing and so powerful, the great distance between the fisherman's boat
and the throne of Him who ruled wind and wave might be bridged
on Thames shore as it once had been on Gennesaret, and the divine
provision for human need, physical and spiritual alike, ever renewed
to the succeeding generations of the sons of man. After all, that was
the whole point of the *Golden Legend*.

THE ATTACK
ON THE SAINT'S LEGEND

*t*hat the second half of the third decade of the sixteenth century
saw both the last of the early printings of the *Golden Legend* in
English and the first printing of the Bible in English has already
been noted as a "curious bibliographical and historical coincidence."[1]
The chronological coincidence is, indeed, close. The last printing of
Caxton's *Golden Legend* by Wynkyn de Worde to be recorded in
the *Short-Title Catalogue* is dated August 27, 1527. Just a little before
this, the first printing of the entire New Testament in William Tyndale's version was completed at Worms in 1525 or 1526, and the volumes were undoubtedly being smuggled into England, where the
1408 ban against the unlicensed printing of the Bible in the vernacular still obtained, while Caxton's successor was contemplating this
final reprinting of his masterpiece.[2] And about two and a half years
after the completion of the *Golden Legend* printing, in January of
1530, Tyndale published his version of the Pentateuch, ostensibly at
Marburg, possibly at Antwerp.[3] This coincidence of dates is, of course,
a good deal more than a piece of historical irony, for the two events
are not only closely linked in symbolical value, but they are far from
lacking in causal relationship. For while it was not the printing of
the New Testament that ended the printing for that time of the
Golden Legend, it was the triumph of the revolution in religious orientation, signaled and served by that printing of Tyndale's book,
that ended the *Golden Legend*.

The religious elements are by no means the whole story in that revolution, as everyone recognizes today, and the cult of the saints is only one among them, but it is a central one. When Stephen Gardiner was commanded, as a test of his conformity, to preach before Edward VI in 1548 on the religious changes of the last twenty years, the third "great alteration" which he cited, after the renunciation of the Bishop of Rome's authority and the dissolution of the abbeys, was that "images were pulled down," that is, the images of the saints.[4] Gardiner's estimate was a sound one. The remembering and the honoring of the saints, the appeal to the saints for their intercession with God in the highest and the lowliest of human needs, the use of the saints' stories for the teaching and the exploring of spiritual truth, the taking of the saints for guides and models, all of these were an integral part of the very warp and woof of the religious life of the Middle Ages. In the very heart of the Church's worship, the canon of the Mass, in the offices of the day's public prayer, and in the primers of private devotion, the saints had their place, established and taken for granted. Nor was this recognition of the role of the saints limited to the word read or heard; it was expressed also in painting and statue, in mural and miniature, in music and drama and pageant.

Caxton himself in his thoroughly sober discussion of the fundamentals of Christian worship gives the classic statement of this multi-form approach to the problem of popular religious instruction, in the section of the *Golden Legend* on "The Dedication of the Temple or Chirche":

We have thre memories of the passion of our Lord, thone is the mynde of the passyon of him that we have in writyng, and the other ymagined in figure, and that is to the sight for the image of jhesu crist, and of thother Images that ben in the chirche, for the remembraunce of jhesu crist and of his saintes is for to move the devocyon of the people. Thyse ben also as the bokes of the laye people, and thise in memoires ben but one. The seconde memoire is in word. That is the passyon of our lord preched, and this mynde is as to the heryng. The third mynde is the passion of our lord transfigured in to this sacrament which is verely the soule: bodi and blode of Jhesu crist, and this minde is as to the tasting.[5]

That is, of course, a relatively simple and elementary approach to a very complicated matter, as one would expect from the very practical-minded author, at once both voice and shaper of the middle-class culture of his day. But it is a thoroughly central one, particularly in one respect, and that is in its emphasis on the value of the saint's legend for the pastoral work of instructing the people in the religious fundamentals.

But there were bound to be difficulties with anything so widespread, so spontaneous, so fortuitous, in short, so popular, as the devotion to the saints, and those difficulties were early apparent. Even in antiquity the African bishops had had to take measures to check a growing cult of what they knew to be false martyrs, whether men of bad character killed in a brawl with unbelievers, or misguided fanatics who had given needless provocation to the civil authorities.[6] In the disorders of the Merovingian period in France, as indeed in other times of confusion and violence, saints were made abundantly and sometimes too easily by panic-strained popular devotion.[7] Pope Gregory the Great, who not only told such good stories about the saints but who usually is credited today with the arrangement of the saints in the canon of the Mass, must have been quite aware of the problem.[8] As far back as the end of the tenth century, with the first recorded example of a formal approval by the Pope (in this case John XV) of a canonization, that of Ulric, Bishop of Augsburg, the work of bringing some ordered application of standards to the too often impulsive process of popular canonization was under way.[9] In the twelfth century Pope Alexander III ruled that for the future the decision for canonization should be reserved to the Holy See. From then on, the effort was to define procedure so as to avoid the scandal of a dubious saint. But it was a slow business, so that not until 1634 did Urban VIII arrive at what are substantially the main lines of procedure still in force.[10]

But there were other problems, too, notably that of relics. The problem of dubious relics goes back to antiquity, and it was not made any easier by the political disorders and the civic insecurity and difficulty of communication in the early Middle Ages. The passion of medieval piety for relics, the part which their possession consequently played in the competition for prestige not only of monasteries and churches but of towns, created a market for relics that was a sore temptation to the greedy and the unscrupulous. In 1215 the Fourth Lateran Council tried to regulate the use of genuine relics and to check the trade in the spurious, by requiring that any new relics should have the authentication of the Holy See before being exposed for veneration.[11] But the problem was as wide as Christendom, and greed and gullibility were hard to regulate or restrain.

A somewhat similar problem was involved in the use of the prayers of the saints that came to fill so large a proportion of the fully matured Primer or Book of Hours, like the very rich and complete *Hore Beatissime Virginis Marie ad Legitimum Sarisburiensis Ecclesie Ritum*, which François Regnault published at Paris in 1527, obviously for the English trade.[12] That the pious should be encouraged to use the prayers which the saints had made would seem a very natural way of realizing the whole purpose of the cult, the making available to the average Christian of the example and experience of the superior. To enter into a saint's prayer, to memorize it perhaps, to meditate on it, to make it one's own, would seem the readiest way of penetrating into the spirit of its author. So from the beginnings of the Christian community the prayers of the saints, from Saint Paul down, had been the very fabric of devotion, public and private. And as the roster of the saints had grown with the passing ages, so had grown the riches of the collections of their prayers in the books of private devotion.

It was natural, too, that just as the makers of the public liturgy had made their selections of Scripture and of saints' prayers with an eye to particular occasions and to special needs, so the makers of the books of private devotion should suggest that for a certain occasion or need a certain prayer by a particular saint would be helpful. Sometimes it was reported that the prayer had been composed by the author under such and such circumstances or for such an occasion as would make its use under similar circumstances or for a like occasion appropriate. From that it was but a short step in the hagiographic atmosphere to say that such a prayer would be peculiarly efficacious in such circumstances, particularly when there was something miraculous in the circumstances of its first use. And from that, in the context of such a book as this *Hore* of 1527, it would be all too tempting to take what at first might seem a slight step but in fact was an abysmal leap, to a promise that if this prayer were said, certain desired effects were assured. That this was done is clear in the *Hore* of 1527, as in the explanation of the origin of the famous *Versus Sancti Bernardi*, with its suggestion that he who said these verses daily would not only be saved but would have knowledge of the day of his death.[13] There is no question of the merit of the prayers themselves. For the most part, they were, as one would expect from their authors, impeccable in intention and elevating in effect. The danger lay in the promises with which they were pressed upon the reader, sometimes merely rash or extravagant, sometimes dangerous in their implications that heaven was to be had on such cheap terms.

There were similar difficulties, too, in the legends of the saints, particularly in the stories of their miracles. Here again the desire to find a certain and easy way to felicity was often father to the belief. As we have seen, careful writers took the precautions available to them of trying to get hold of the best authorities and support their work with references to them.[14] Even the author of the *Golden Legend*, Jacobus de Voragine, whose work was to become for the sixteenth-century Reformers the symbol of the worst extravagances of the genre, was, as we have seen, by no means unaware of the difference between good and bad authorities.[15]

But there was more at stake than the reputation of the authority available. There was a good deal that might be objected to in some, at least, of the saints' legends as they stood, as is all too clear in what we have seen of Caxton's *Golden Legend*. Plato had anticipated the sixteenth-century criticism in his complaints in the *Republic* on what the storytellers of his world had done with the gods. The picture they gave was frequently scandalous, he said.[16] The legends of the Middle Ages did not often depict the saints as taking the moral and religious standards of their day in quite so free and easy a style as the ancient poets had shown their gods doing. But they did too often present the saints as taking human iniquity much too casually, and sometimes they showed the saints as playing an undignified and even indecorous role. And they showed them as tolerating clients whose recklessness with law, human and divine, should, as Erasmus was to suggest, have put them beyond the pale of any socially responsible company.[17] Worse still, for anyone who felt that the rational acceptability of the universe demanded that the rascal should get the retribution coming to him, the saint's legend was often distressing and even shocking. And even for less exacting people whose general approach to the practical conduct of life might be summed up in the well-known Puritan sentiment usually attributed to Oliver Cromwell, "Trust God and keep your powder dry," there was something reprehensible about the

way in which a saint so often intervened in order to extricate a feck-
less client from a predicament from which he had no reasonable right
to expect to be rescued.

It is here that the growth of the middle-class reading public in
the fifteenth and sixteenth centuries might well be expected to pro-
duce a critical reaction. For the middle-class man then as now was
marked by habits of responsibility and forethought and efficient
matching of ends and means. He would be less disposed than either
his unenterprising inferiors or his more easygoing superiors to approve the very casual attitude of many of the saints and their admirers to poetic justice, and he would not have the same feeling,
humble or cynical, that he might one day himself be glad to "scape
whipping."

But the recognition of the absurdity of various aspects of the cult
of the saints did not have to wait for the sixteenth century. The intelligent medieval man was quite aware of the abuses. Here, as usual,
he saw no need of shutting his eyes to the known facts of human
weakness and infirmity, and it was not his way to defend the ideal
by denying the existence of the reality. Toward the end of the fourteenth century Chaucer handled the saint's legend exquisitely in the
Prioress' contribution to the *Canterbury Tales*, but he roundly mocked
the abuse of the cult of the saints in his account of the Pardoner in
the general Prologue and in the Pardoner's Prologue and the jesting
conclusion to the great moral tale of that rogue's telling.[18] That still
seemed in the next century the proper way to treat the absurdities of
the saints' cult to such a man as Reginald Pecock, Bishop of Chichester. Pecock was to suffer condemnation for heresy at the hands of
the Archbishop of Canterbury of his time, and to be included in
Foxe's calendar of martyrs as a confessor, a little over a century later,[19]
but on this point at least he was orthodox enough. For it was in reply
to the iconoclasts of his day that he wrote: "But so it is that these opin-
iouns, bi whiche symple men trowen at sumtyme that an ymage hath
withinne him vertu, such as God mai putte into a creature; or that
the ymage dooth miraclis, or spekith at sum tyme, or herith alwey,
or swetith at sum tyme . . . for hem discrete men mowe oonlie
lauȝe at suche folies of men, as thei doon at her othere folies, of whiche
no moral harme cometh."[20]

Pecock is still of the Middle Ages, even in his attitude toward absurdity. He was to be followed by men who, though they would not abolish the veneration of the saints, would laugh even harder at the absurdities of what had not too much worried Chaucer or Pecock. The advent of humanism certainly brought, if not a change in basic attitude, a change in emphasis from tolerance of absurdity to impatience with absurdity. Again, this is not a simple matter. Some of this impatience was the age-old revolt of an intellectually lively younger generation in an age of expanding horizons against its benighted grandfathers. Many of the humanists had had to battle against obscurantism and sheer resistance to any change. But they, also, had their own distinctive intellectual world, their own rationale, their "New Learning," and in many respects it was very different from the world of the Middle Ages.[21] Men like Vives and Erasmus saw the immediate past not only as superstitious and benighted but as totally lacking in that respect for learning and devotion to intellectual enlightenment that had driven them back to the leaders of classical antiquity.[22] There is, therefore, not a little of the familiar contempt of the enlightened modern contemplating the obscurantism and naïveté of the past in their view of the extravagances of the saint's legend, the very epitome of the Middle Ages. It was for their archaic absurdity that they laughed at them, even as they deplored the menace to religion in their capricious dealing with reality.[23] Indeed, Cardinal Nicholas of Cusa went so far at the diocesan synod of Brixen in 1453 as to forbid his priests to preach to the people about "superstitious matters" such as were to be found in the lives of certain saints in the *Golden Legend*.[24]

But perhaps the most characteristic expression of this humanist reaction against the saints' cult in all its aspects is one of Erasmus' colloquies, *The Pilgrimage of Pure Devotion*, that appeared in an English translation in 1536–37, without any indication of place, date, or printer, under the title: "*A Dialoge or Communication of Two Persons*, . . . by the noble and famous clarke Desiderius Erasmus intituled the Pylgremage of Pure Devotyon."

The work is a characteristic Erasmian performance, presenting dramatically the absurdities of the old order, doubtless with the selections and the exaggerations essential to caricature, and suggesting the author's serious criticism with ironic comment and innuendo rather than direct indictment. The range of Erasmus' attack on the pilgrimage cult is wide. Menedmus rallies his friend Ogygius on his cockle-shell-and-bead-bedecked costume, and his undertaking to discharge his mother-in-law's vow by his pilgrimage to Compostella.[25] When Ogygius reports that fewer pilgrims come to Saint James because of the influence of "this new learnynge," and those give little or nothing, on the excuse that it might be better given to the poor, Menedmus ironically deplores the new influence in terms that for the moment at least seem to deceive his more naïve friend.[26] The technique is now apparent; it is simple but nonetheless effective. Ogygius tells of a letter written by Our Lady by the hand of an angel, which he apparently accepts at face value, but Menedmus asks, "Do you know so well the hand of thangell whiche is secretary to our lady?" And when Ogygius reveals upon promise of secrecy the contents of the letter, it rather surprisingly reveals Our Lady as grateful to the Lutheran attack upon the effectiveness of the appeal to saints, on the plausible ground that she has been overwhelmed by the importunities of not too reasonable clients, some of whose petitions are too shocking to be recounted (although Our Lady gives a very adequate notion of their general character). But unfortunately the Lutheran attack has brought not only "more ease, but lesse honor and profett."[27]

When Ogygius comes to tell of his pilgrimage to Walsingham, the great Marian shrine of England, he is as usual enthusiastic, pronouncing the little chapel that is the center of the establishment, "a seate meete for sayntes, all thynges be so bright with gold, sylver, and precyous stones."[28]

But he has noticed that there are those who when they appear to make their own offering at the shrine contrive to steal what others have given, whereupon Menedmus confesses his uncertainty as to which is more marvelous, their wickedness or God's forbearance.[29] But he has no such uncertainty about the tale of a knight's miraculous escape, after prayer to the Virgin, through the perilously little wicket in the pale about the churchyard. Ogygius, however, is able to report that the sexton gave satisfactory evidence for his story in a copper plate in the wicket which showed the picture of the knight "with the same garmentes that the Englishmen were wontyd to wayre at that tyme, as you may see in that olde pictures, whiche wylnat lye."[30]

When it came to the showing of the relics, Ogygius was not so fortunate. For when he was told that a joint of a man's finger that he had devoutly kissed was Saint Peter's, he took another look, and observed that Saint Peter must have been a "great man of stature." At that, one of the bystanders could not keep from laughing, and that stopped the display of relics, to Ogygius' pious regret.[31]

Superstition and credulity are the themes of the visit to Walsingham. There is a more macabre flavor to Ogygius' no less enthusiastic account of the visit to Canterbury, where he saw the silver-mounted brainpan of Saint Thomas, with the upper part, which was "thraste quyte thorow," bare to be kissed, the hair shirt and other garments of penance belonging to the martyr, which Ogygius humbly takes as a rebuke of the pilgrims' "delycate gorgeousness" and, Menedmus adds, maybe of the slothfulness of the monks, too, and, finally, a display of relics that seems to have taxed even Ogygius' enthusiasm; for he exclaims, ". . . what a sort of bones be brought forthe, skulles, jawes, thethe, handes, fyngres, hole armes, whan we had worshipyd thaym all, we kyssyd thaym, that I thoght we shuld never have mayd an ende."[32] But the display ended because of the behavior of one of the company, an Englishman named Gratian Colte, whom Menedmus suspected of being one of Wycliffe's scholars. Apparently the last straw for the sexton was Gratian's obvious abhorrence when "an arme whiche had yet the redde fleshe apon it" was offered for his kiss.[33]

And when they came to the almshouse and one of the old men ran out to sprinkle the horsemen with holy water and offer for their veneration and reward a piece of Saint Thomas' shoe bound in an iron hoop, Gratian's disgust broke into anger.[34] But characteristically, Ogygius took a more sympathetic view, pointing out that "thys holy man, whyle he was yet alyve, by hys good example, hys doctryne, hys goodly exhortatyons provokyd us to vertuouse lyvynge, he dyd comfort the comforthlesse, he helped the poure, ye and now that he is deade, he is in a maner more profytable. He hathe buylded thys costly and gorgeouse churche, he hath caused great authoryte thorough out all Englande unto the ordre and presthode. At the last, thys pece of the show dothe susteyne a company of poure people."[35]

This work, also, makes its contribution to the old discussion over giving the wealth of the shrines to the poor. After the pilgrims had prayed at Canterbury in an inner chapel before the face of the saint, "overgylted and with many precyous stones goodly garnysshed,"

Gratian with seeming innocence asked the priest who sat by the head if the report he had heard was true, that Saint Thomas in his lifetime was merciful to the poor. When the priest responded by enlarging on Thomas' liberality to the poor, Gratian then pressed on to ask if Saint Thomas, who was so generous when he himself had need of money and who now had no need of anything, would not be content "if a poer woman havynge at home chylderne lakynge mete and drynke, or else doughters beynge in danger to lose ther virginite, for defaute of ther substaunce to mary them with, or havynge her husbande sore syke, and destitute of all helpe, in case she askyd licens, and pryvyly stole away a small porcyon of so greate riches, to sukkre her howshold, as and if she shold have it of one that wold other leane, or gyve it to herre?" Now there was no mistaking the priest's disapproval, but Menedmus is clearly sympathetic with Gratian's challenge.[36] But though Ogygius admits the abuse, he thinks it may better be suffered, in view of the behavior of those who rob the churches of whatever jewels may be found in them. He also reminds his companion that this church wealth is the gift of the great who might otherwise have made worse use of their riches, as for war. When it comes to taking it, there is the question of sacrilege, "then they hold their handes that were accustomed to gyfe, besyde that morover they be allured and movyde to robbynge and vaynynge," a touch of prophetic realism one would hardly have expected of the idealistic Ogygius.[37] The work ends with Menedmus still clearly of the mind that it is better for him to discharge his responsibilities at home than to go on pilgrimage — "That I shuld se unto these thynges holy scripture commaundethe, that I shuld commyt the charge to sayntes I dyd rede yt never commaunded."[38] This dialogue is, in other words, a typically Erasmian performance of the year of its original publication, 1526. It covers a wide range of intelligent men's complaints about the popular cult of shrines and pilgrimages. These are presented in terms which, the writer might plead, as he did when need arose, implied no rejection of the veneration of the saints but rather a rejection of palpable absurdities in the interest of the spiritual endeavor that was the excuse for being of the saints' cult. When the Sorbonne censured the letter to Glaucoplutus, Erasmus defended himself by saying that it was a satire on the Zwinglians.[39] Certainly, there is nothing of the passion of the iconoclast in this free-hearted mockery, nor anything of the single-minded determination of the fundamentalist to get back to the purity of a more primitive time. It is rather the contemptuous mockery of too-long-entrenched obscurantism by a sophisticated and urbane modern. In spite of all Erasmus' protests of his loyalty to the Church, the faculty of the Sorbonne censured the *Colloquies* including *The Pilgrimage* for paganism and mockery in 1526, and in 1564 the Council of Trent condemned them.[40] It was clearly too late for laughter when Erasmus jested with Thomas More and his other humanist friends.

Indeed, if men like Erasmus had only known, it had been too late for a long time. Particularly is this true of the major charge made against the cult of the saints, the charge of idolatry. As we have seen, the Middle Ages, like the Fathers, had been quite as aware of the dangers of the abuse of relics, for example, as were the humanist reformers like Erasmus. But for none of these were the abuses inevitable. To the Protestant Reformers they were. Their position is put succinctly in *A Very Profitable Treatise, made by Jhon Calvyne, Declarynge what great Profit might come to al Christendome, yf there were a Regester made of al Sainctes Bodies and other Reliques, which are as well in Italy, as in Fraunce, Dutchland, Spaine and other Kingdomes and Countreys*, which, "Set furth and authorised according to the Queenes Majesties Injunctions," was published in London in 1561. The target of the little book was, as the title implies, the duplication of relics: "And then men shoulde know that every Apostle shoulde have more then foure bodyes, and every sainct at the least two or thre and so many should be of all the rest."[41] Calvin begins quietly enough with a reminder of Saint Augustine's scepticism about some of the relics of supposed martyrs carried about in his day, but presently he is attacking the very desire to have relics as "almost never without suspition, and that worse is, it is the mother of ydolatry, which is ordinarely connexed and joyned therwith."[42] Indeed, the very existence of relics is proof of corruption: "This wycked pompe of canonisyng them was never broughte into the church, untyll such tyme as all was perverted, and as it were prophaned: partly by the beastlinesse of the priestes and pastors, partly by their couvetousnes, partly also because thei could not resist the custome, after that it was receyved: And partly in that the people did seeke to be abused in setting their mindes rather on childishe playes, then on the true worshippynge of God." It is not surprising, therefore, that he concludes that the only way to cure the abuse is to abolish the cause.[43]

Much, of course, to which these early reformers objected was not so much idolatry as magic,[44] but idolatry was a charge easier to get within range of the heavy artillery of the Ten Commandments. Magic, as the history of popular superstition in the sixteenth century and long after demonstrates, was a more elusive business. But regardless of such distinctions, idolatry was to be one of the most frequently recurrent of the official charges against the old religious order in this period, and probably nowhere did it prove more effective than in Henry VIII's campaign against the monasteries, one of the central strategies in his withdrawal of the Church in England from the jurisdiction of Rome and in the consolidation of his own establishment.[45] For the monasteries were involved not only in the cult of the saints but in the possession of the various types of shrines that were the object of pilgrimage. And the old argument that the wealth spent on pilgrimages and donations to shrines of saints might better be spent on God's living shrines in the persons of the poor was one of the arguments most frequently urged in this period, probably most eloquently by Simon Fish, whose *Supplication of the Beggars* in late 1527 or early 1528 is one of the most radical documents of the time from the point of view of the attack on the wealth of the Church. To get the spoils of the monasteries into the hands of the poor was not to prove so easy a matter as Fish had assumed, but the confiscated wealth helped to ease the transition for those who did not resist the disestablishment of the monasteries, it certainly contributed to the relief of the grave financial difficulties of the aggrandized Crown, and it helped to consolidate the financial foundation of many of the new gentry and new nobility, and even of the more ambitious members of the middle class.[46] Above all, it helped to disincline a very considerable portion of the nation to any thoroughgoing return to the past. Foxe, who esteemed Fish's work enough to reprint it in his own great book,[47] did not have much patience with those who complained that the poor did not get the monastic lands. For him the great thing was that the monasteries were destroyed, and he pointed out very sensibly that it was much harder to recover their lands for any possible restoration from the great than it would have been from the poor.[48]

There is no need of recapitulating the familiar stages of the series of events which culminated in the Act of Supremacy of 1534 and Henry's assumption of the title of Supreme Head in 1535. More important for the cult of the saints are the steps which Henry took to discharge his new responsibilities, the first of which was obviously to bag the whirlwind he had unloosed. That he was quite aware of the problem is manifest in the very title of the "Articles devised by the Kynges Highnes Majestie, to stablyshe Christen Quietnes and Unitie amonge us, and to avoyde contentious opinions," which were published in 1536. In the preface, Henry, speaking directly in his dual role as king and as head of the Church, expresses his concern about the diversity of opinions in the realm, not only for the "daungers of sowles, but also the outward unquietnesse." [49] On the issues that concern us Henry seems to have been anxious to preserve old values, even though he pays tribute to the current preoccupation with the dangers of idolatry. For on the much-controverted question of the use of images he directs bishops and preachers to teach the people

that they be representers of vertue and good example. And that they also be by occasion the kendelers and stirrers of mens myndes, and make men ofte to remembre and lamente thyr synnes and offences, especiallye the ymages of Christ and our lady. And that therfore it is mete, that they shuld stande in the churches, and none otherwise to be estemed. And to the intent the rude people shulde not from hensforthe take suche superstition, as in tyme past it is thoughte that the same hath used to do, we wyl, that our byshops and prechers, diligently shal teache them, and accordyng to this doctrine refourme theyr abuses. For els there might fortune idolatrie to ensewe, whiche god forbydde.[50]

Again, in "Of Honouringe of Sayntes," he bids bishops and preachers to instruct the people

that sayntis nowe eynoge with Christe in heven, be to be honoured of christen people in erthe . . . bycause they be knowen the electe persons of Christe, bycause they be passed in godly lyfe out of this transitory world, bicause they alredy do reygne in glory with Christe, and most specially to laude and prayse Christ in them for theyr excellent vertues, whiche he planted in them, for example of and by them to such as yet ar in this worlde, to lyve in vertue and goodness. And also not to feare to dye for Christe, and his cause as some of them dydde: and finally to take them in that they maye, to be the advauncers of our prayers and demandes unto Christ, By these wayes and suche lyke be sayntes to be honoured and had in reverence, and by none other.[51]

Much of this ground is covered in the next article, "Of Prayinge to Sayntes," with the addition that it be done "without any vayne superstition as to thinke, that any saynte is more mercyfull, or wyll here us sooner than Christ, or that any saynt doth serve for one thinge more than an other, or is patron of the same."[52]

In spite of Henry's obvious concern about popular feeling, such a passage as this last would disturb some of the most settled habits of popular devotion in the invocation of special saints for special needs; yet it would do nothing to satisfy the iconoclasts waiting in the wings. That the enforcement of this article would move in the direction which would encourage these hopeful watchers of Henry's progress is suggested by the terms of one of the *Injunctions gyven by Thauc-toritie of the Kynges Highnes to the Clergie of this his Realme*, which was issued in 1536 by Thomas Cromwell in a form with blanks to be filled in with date, name of particular deanery, and name of commissary. One of these injunctions runs as follows:

Besides this, to thintent that al superstition, and hipocrisy, crept into divers mens hartes, may vanyshe awaye, they shall not set forth, or extoll any ymages, relyques, or myracles, for any superstition or lucre, nor allure the people by any inticementes to the pilgremages of any sainct, otherwise than is permitted in the articles, lately put forth by thauctoritie of the kinges majestie, and condescended upon by the prelates and clergie of this his realme, in convocation, . . . But they shall exhorte as well theyr parishoners as other pilgrimes, that they do rather apply them selfe to the keping of goddes commaundementes, and fulfilling of his workes of charitie, perswadinge them, that they shal please god more by the true exercysinge of theyr bodyly labour, travayle, or occupation, and providing for their families, than if they went about to the sayd pilgrimages, and that it shal profyte more theyr soule helth, if they do bestowe that on the poore and nedy, whiche they wolde have bestowed upon the sayd ymages or relyques.[53]

This seems confident enough, but apparently Cromwell felt the need of reinforcement from greater and perhaps more widely acceptable authority than his own. For it was at this time, if the modern editor, Henry de Vocht, is right, that the translation of Erasmus' *Pilgrimage of Pure Devotion* that we have already looked at as an example of the humanist attack on the abuses of the saints' cult was published, a good illustration of how the humanist attack on absurdity could be used for destruction. For the time, the translation itself was faithful enough. It was in the presentation that the adaptation was effected.

It is for that reason that the unspecified date of this publication is of so much importance. Since this dialogue deals mainly with the great shrines of Our Lady at Walsingham and of Saint Thomas at Canterbury, it is hard to believe that the editor would have made no reference to the destruction of these shrines if the book had been printed after 1538, the date of their destruction, and the references to insurrection in the preface must be to the Pilgrimage of Grace, which started in October, 1536, and was finally ended in March of 1537. Less certain, but plausible in view of what is known about Cromwell's propaganda for further desired changes in these years, is De Vocht's suggestion that this book is one of Cromwell's instruments,[54] a suggestion that explains the anonymity of its publication. In spite of this caution we can learn a good deal about its motivation from the address "To the reder" prefixed to the translation. The opening sentence of this address is a very long one, of which the gist would seem to be "that ther is (as I suppose) no parte of the scripture, which is not so expowndyde, furnysshed, and setforthe, but that every Christen man, therby may lerne his dewty to god, hys prynce, and hys nebure." In spite of this abundance of help, there are still those who

shall not entre in to the kyngdome of god, bycause, of chaungynge the glory of gode immortall in to the ymage of a corruptyble man, and therfore so lycentiously he hathe suffrede them to wandre in theyr clowdes of ygnoraunce, preferrynge the lyes and corrupte judgmentes of man [to] the veryte and the truthe of god, rather servynge the creature then the creator, amongst all the parties of the whiche (as was spoken at the begynnyng) thys alwaye not alonely in the newe law, but also in the olde Testament was as a thynge moost abhomynable and displesant in the sight of gode prohybyte and forbyden: but our nature whiche hath in hym, the dampmnable repugnance of synne agaynst the omnypotent power of gode, lest evyn frome owre fyrst father Adam, is so enclyned to vyces, amongst the whiche it hath not gyven the least parte to thys desperate synne of ydolatrye, agaynst the immaculate, and fearefull commandemente of god, Thou shalt have no straunge Gods in my syght, that it is sore to be dreadde the same judgment to be gyvyn upon us that was gyven upon the cytye of Ninyve to be absorped of the yerthe in to the yre and vengeannce of gode, whiche hathe ben the cause that so many wryters bothe of late dayes, and many yeres passede, have evyn to deathe, resisted thes dampnable bolsterers of ydolatrye, gyven theyr selves to the crosse in example of reformacyon to theyr bretherne.[55]

The author of this address was careful to call the attention of any would-be iconoclast to the fact that Erasmus "notethe as it were of arrogancye the pryvate judgment of certayne that of theyr owne brayne wolde cast out ymages of the temple, with out a comen consent and authoryte."[56] But he reserved the full measure of his moral indignation for those devotees of relics and pilgrimages who, now that they found their business "decay," rebelled and made insurrection against their King, "provokynge and allurynge the symple comynaltye to theyre dampnable ypocrysye and conspiracy, myndyng and goynge about to prevente our most soveraigne lordes judgment, not yet gyven upon theyr Sodomiticall actes, and most horryble ypocrysy," and for the "develishe and detestable usurped aucthoryties" of the Bishop of Rome.[57] It was, therefore, to move the true subjects to do their duty "in ayding hys excellent hyghnes to the reformacyon of all pernicious abuses and chiefly of destestable ydolatrye" that he offered them the dialogue which Erasmus wrote to that "intent and purpose."[58]

After this forthright indictment the Erasmian irony might seem at first a little too frivolous for De Vocht's suggestion of Cromwell's sponsorship, but Foxe tells us that Cromwell "always retayned unto hym, and had about hym . . . sundry and dyverse freshe and quicke wyttes, pertainyng to his famyly, by whose industrie and ingenious labours, diverse excellente both ballades and bookes were contrived and set abroade, concernyng the suppression of the Pope and all Popyshe idolatrie."[59]

If these conjectures about Cromwell's undertakings in popular propaganda are correct, we can understand the need of caution and indirection in *The Institution of a Christen Man*, which was published in the next year, 1537, by the archbishops, bishops, and other prelates of the realm, with an address to Henry as the "supreme heed in erth immediately under Christ of the Churche of Englande." Generally known as "The Bishops' Book,"[60] this publication is a guide to the Christian life, on the traditional framework of an orderly exposition of the doctrinal essentials: a four-part exposition of the Creed, the Seven Sacraments, the Ten Commandments, and finally the Pater Noster and the Ave, with this time the Articles of Justification and Purgatory.[61] The second section of the exposition of the Second Commandment is decidedly traditional:

Seconde, that although all ymages, be they engraven, peynted, or waroughte in arrase, or in any other wise made, be so prohibited, that they may neither be bowed downe unto, ne worshipped (for asmoche as they be the workes of mans hande onely) yet they be not so prohibited, but that they may be had and sette up in churches, so it be for none other pourpose, but only to thintent, that we (in beholding and looking upon them, as in certayne bokes, and seinge represented in them the manifolde examples of vertues, which were in the sainctes, represented by the sayd images) may the rather be provoked, kendled, and stired, to yelde thankes to our lorde, and to praise him in his said sainctes, and to remembre and lamente our synnes and offences, and to praye god that we may have grace to followe their goodnes and holy lyvinge.[62]

Archbishop Peckham would have approved of this. But to this exposition is appended an "item" which makes the characteristic Reforming appeal on behalf of the poor against the images:

. . . And they also that be more redye with their substance to decke deed ymages gorgeously and gloriously: than with the same to helpe poor christen people, the quicke and lively images of god, whiche is the necessarye work of charitie, commanded by god. And they also, that so dote in this behalfe, that they make vowes, and go on pilgrimages even to the images, and there do calle upon the same ymages for ayde and helpe . . . In whiche thinges if any personne heretofore hath, or yet dothe offende: all good and well lerned men have great cause to lament suche errour and rudeness, and to put their studies and diligence for the reformation of the same . . .[63]

Now all this would be very well if what were at stake were only the reform of abuses. But such a statement must have seemed to many who had watched Henry's progress a retreat, and certainly it would never enable Henry to end the vexation of the homage paid at the shrine of that perfect pattern of the rebel masking himself with religion, and being canonized for it, to boot, Saint Thomas à Becket,[64] nor would it set the treasure carts rolling with their trove of superstition into the redeeming coffers of Henry. It must have seemed to many impatient watchers of the unfolding drama as if the time for exhortation were coming to an end, and the time for action at hand. They must therefore have welcomed the call to action in what was the culmination of this campaign, the single sheet of *Injunctions for the Clerge* which Cromwell by the authority of the King as head of the Church issued in 1538. The sixth of these injunctions commands

that ye shall make or cause to be made in the sayde churche and every other cure ye have, one sermon every quarter of a yere at the leaste, wherin ye shall purely, and syncerely declare the very gospel of christe, and in the same exhorte your herers to the workes of charite, mercy and faythe, specially prescribed, and commaunded in scripture, and not to repose there trust or affiaunce in any other workes devysed by mens phanthasyes besydes scripture, as in wanderyng to pilgrimage, offeryng of money, candelles or tapers to Images or reliques, or kyssing or lyckyng the same, saying over a number of beades, not understanded ne mynded on, or in such lyke supersticion, for the doynge wherof, ye not only have no promyse of rewarde in scripture, but contrary wyse greate threates and maledictions of god, as thynges tendyng to ydolatrye and superstition, which of all other offences god almyghtye dothe moste detest and abhorre, for that the same diminysheth most his honour and glorie.

But Henry and Cromwell were not content to leave it to sermons; they insisted on action, in the seventh of these injunctions:

Item that suche Images as ye knowe in any of your cures to be so abused with pilgrimages or offeringes of any thyng made therunto, ye shal for avoydyng of that moste detestable offence of Idolatrie, furthwyth take down and deley, and shall suffre frome hensforthe no candels, tapers, or Images of wax to be set afore any Image or picture, but only the lyghte that comenlye gothe acrosse the church, by the roode lofte, the lyght afore the sacrament of thaulter, and the lyght about the sepulchre, which for thadourning of the church and divine serv-yce ye shal suffre to remayn styll admonisshyng your parishioners, that Images serve for no other purpose, but as to be bokes of unlerned men that can no letters, wherby they m'ght be otherwyse admonysshed of the lyves and conversacion of them that the said Images do represent, which Images if they abuse for any other intent than for such remembraunces, they commytte Idolatrye in the same to the great daunger of theyr soules. And therfore the kinges highnes gratiously tendering the weale of his subjectis soules hathe in parte alredy and more wyll hereafter travayle for the abolisshynge of suche Images, as myghte be occasyon of so greate an offence to god, and so great daunger to the soules of his lovyng subjectes.[65]

There is no need to say anything about the destruction that followed. To some of its promoters it must have seemed the long-delayed triumph of Truth, as if Josiah had again purged Judah and Jerusalem of the altars of Baalim. To some of its agents and participants it must have had its own violent exhilaration, to say nothing of certain practical opportunities. But immemorial custom is a precious thing with the folk, and there must have been a good many who looked on the ecclesiastical scene of 1538 with misgivings if not resentment. There is still surviving *A Litel Treatise ageynste the Mutterynge of Some Papistis in Corners*, which Thomas Berthelet, the King's printer, had printed four years before, in 1534. Then the issue of the day was the rejection of the Pope's authority, and the burden of the whispering was the very human, "That if we do well nowe, thus to forsake the pope, then all our forefathers dyd amisse, and so dyd we also, tylle this present tyme."[66] The unidentified author of this tract reassured these doubtful souls: "For undoubtedly all men, that were before tyme, whiche were wise and well lerned . . . did abhorre the pompose and worldly state of the pope." And he went on to explain that this opposition was silenced by persecution "by reason that the noble princis them selfe were unlerned, and coude not juge in suche matters, but they gave alwey credence to the falce, subtyle, and slye persuasions of the pope and his bolsterers."[67]

So now the pulpits were set to work, particularly the pulpit at Paul's Cross, to reveal to the people how they had been misled. For the comparatively sophisticated London public some of the best preachers of the day took up the theme. In Lent of 1547 William Barlow, Bishop of St. David's, followed by Nicholas Ridley, preached at Paul's Cross against the veneration of images,[68] and in February of the next year Bishop John Hilsey, the successor of Fisher in the see of Rochester, preached in the same pulpit, exposing the Rood of Grace from Boxley, and in November of the same year he preached again, this time exposing the Blood of Hailes from the Cistercian monastery in Gloucestershire.[69] As for those out of range of the voices of the famous London preachers, Cromwell, according to Foxe, had, as we have seen, other resources.

But when it came time for Henry in 1543 to issue his own version of an *Institution of a Christian Man*, there is some evidence in what he has to say on the subject of images that he thinks things may have gone further than he had contemplated.[70] One ground of Henry's concern is to be seen in the exposition of the crucial Second Commandment. After printing the commandment in full, Henry adds the qualification: "By these wordes we be not forbidden, to make or to have similitudes, or ymages, but onely we be forbidden, to make or to have theym to the entente to doo godly honoure unto them, as it appereth in the xxvi chapter of Leviticus," and then he proceeds to give instructions for the proper use of images that repeat, often word for word, the directions of the Bishop's Book of 1537, ending with another caution to those who might wish to go too far: "for which causes, images may be set in the churche, and ought not to be despised, but to be used reverently, although we be forbydden to doo anye godly honour unto them. These lessons shuld be taught, by every curat to there parryshe."[71]

Henry manifested his own faith in the potency of images by an illustrated edition of this work which in the same year, if we can trust the date on the title page, John Mayler printed with the interesting note at the end: "Thys boke bounde in paper bourdes or in claspes, not to be solde above .xii.d."[72] These woodcuts look traditional enough, with, for example, the full-page one under the heading of "The Crede or xii. articles of the christen fayth" a depiction of the descent of the Holy Spirit in tongues of fire on the apostles, with the Virgin seated in the middle of the front row of the group,[73] and a full-page picture of Mary Magdalene kissing the feet of Christ for "The Sacrament of Penance."[74] But there are some innovations, as for the ninth article of the Creed, the holy Catholic Church, a half-page scene with a hatted king, presumably Henry, sitting with his sceptre on a canopied throne, with monks and priests and bishops on either hand, with one, apparently a bishop, at his left, expounding Scripture at a reading desk.[75] Some pages later the usurpation of the Bishop of Rome is illustrated by a triple-crowned woman sitting on the many-headed dragon of Revelation xvii.[76]

Clearly, Henry had worried about going too far. His death in 1547 gave Cranmer the opportunity to go ahead faster and further with the business of getting rid of what he and his followers considered still dangerous abuses.[77] For in the same year of 1547, the government of Henry's boy heir issued the *First Book of Homilies: Certayne Sermons, or Homilies, appoynted by the Kynges Majestie, to bee declared and redde, by all Persones, Vicars, or Curates, every Sondaye in their churches where thei have cure.* In this work the saints play their part, in the enumeration of "Papisticall supersticions and abuses, as of Beades, or Lady Psalters and Rosaries, of .XV. Oos,[78] of saincte Barnardes Verse, of sainct Agathes letters, of Purgatory, of Masses satisfactory, of Stacions and Jubilies, of feined Reliques, of halowed Beades, Belles, Breade, Water, Palmes, Candelle, Fire and suche other; of Supersticious fastynges, of Fraternities, of Pardons, with suche like merchaundise . . ."[79] In other words, it looks as if the author of this homily had come across some backsliders using an unreformed primer like the *Hore* of 1527, referred to above. It is hardly to be wondered at that the enemies of the cult of the saints should have asked what had become of their efforts.

But perhaps even more effective in the long run than direct attack upon the veneration of the saints was the strategy of omission and ignoring. This strategy was employed early in the handling of the Primer, the traditional book of aid to the layman in his private devotions. There are a number of sixteenth-century references that indicate that a primer in English, and, therefore, at that time to be suspected of Reforming tendencies, was known in England as early as 1530, when it was outlawed by the ecclesiastical commission of that year. One of these references specifies that it omitted the whole litany, because, it was assumed, the author opposed praying to the saints.[80] That work is lost, but there is a recently discovered English version of the *Hortulus Animae*, a book of private devotion very much like the Primer, which was popular on the Continent. This version, printed in Antwerp in 1530, has been identified as the work of George Joye, a well-known controversialist and translator of Scripture of the time. In this book the number of calendar entries has been reduced in the interest of Reforming commentary; most of the Marian prayers have been eliminated, and all the litany.[81] Enough examples of Reforming primers survive from the years 1534 to 1553 to make clear that the example of George Joye was not lost upon his fellow Reformers. The changes in the calendar, litany, and collections of occasional prayers in these books reflect not only the evolution of official thinking with regard to the honoring of the saints but a sustained effort to wean the public away from its accustomed reliance on their intercession.[82]

But pervasive as would be the influence of such a modification of the traditional aid to private devotion, even more decisive would be the effect of the changes in the books for the public services of the Church, since the use of the first Prayer Book of Edward VI, the Book of Common Prayer, published on March 7, 1549, was made compulsory by Parliament, and penalty for use of any other was provided by statute.[83] The preface to this work opens with a large observation characteristic of the time in its preoccupation with corruption, and perhaps more influential than has always been appreciated in creating that strain of pessimism about this world's ways that is to be discerned so often in Elizabethan reflection: "There was never any thing by the wit of man so well devised, or so surely established, which (in continuaunce of time) hath not been corrupted: as (among other thinges) it may plainly appere by the common prayers in the Churche, commonlye called divine service." It then goes on to explain that the original intention was that in these prayers the major part of the Bible should be read over in the course of the year: "But these many yeares passed this Godly and decent ordre of the auncient fathers, hath bee so altered, broken, and neglected, by planting in uncertain stories, Legendes, Responses, Verses, vaine repeticions, Commemoracions and Synodalles, that commonly when any boke of the Bible was begon: before three or foure Chapiters were read out, all the rest were unread."[84] For this situation the new book offers an order "muche agreable to the mynde and purpose of the olde fathers, and a greate deale more profitable . . . because here are left out many thynges, whereof some be untrue, some uncertein, some vain and supersticious: and is ordeyned nothyng to be read, but the very pure worde of God, the holy scriptures, or that which is evidently grounded upon the same."[85]

The result so far as the saints are concerned is much more radical than the quiet tone of this explanation would suggest. The traditional calendar has almost disappeared in "A table and Kalendar for Psalmes and Lessons, with necessary rules perteining to the same," as may be judged by the following samples: for January, there are three commemorations remaining: January 1, Circumcision, on the sixth, Epiphany, on the twenty-fifth, the Conversion of Paul; for February there are only two: on the second, "Pur. Ma.," and the twenty-fourth, Mathias; for March only the "Annuncia." for the twenty-fifth. Clearly the main interest of this calendar is in the distribution of the Psalms and the lessons from the Old Testament and the New for the offices of Matins and Evensong.[86]

The Marian elements have been eliminated from the Hours,[87] and the various commemorations and prayers to saints from "The Supper of the Lorde, and the holy Communion, commonly called the Masse," except for the passage in the prayer "for the whole state of Christes churche": "And here we do geve unto thee moste high praise, and hartie thankes for the wonderfull grace and vertue, declared in all thy sainctes, from the begynnyng of the worlde: And chiefly in the glorious and moste blessed virgin Mary, mother of thy sonne Jesu Christe our Lorde and God and in the Holy Patriarches, Prophetes, Apostles and Martyrs, whose examples (o Lorde) and stedfastnes in thy fayth, and kepyng thy holy commaundementes: graunt us to folowe." But even this section of the prayer, which also includes a petition for the saving of the dead and the living members of the mystical body at the general resurrection, concludes with an underscoring of the rejection of the intercession of the saints in the petition: "Graunt this, O father, for Jesus Christes sake, our onely mediatour and advocate."[88] And the saints have quite disappeared from the Litany and Suffrages.[89]

Of course, there would be some of Edward's subjects who would regret these omissions of familiar devotional material. Such backsliding was clearly anticipated and provided for in the general explanation of omissions: "Furthermore, the most weightye cause of the abolishement of certayne Ceremonies was, that they were so farre abused, partly by the supersticious blyndenes of the rude and unlearned, and partelye by the unsaciable avarice of such as soughte more theyr owne lucre then the glorye of God: that the abuses coulde not well bee taken awaye, the thyng remayning styll."[90] In that last clause the makers of this book stated the basic premise of the movement which finally triumphs in its pages.

The revision of 1552, among more important changes involving doctrine and rite, was in this area to carry the process of elimination a little further.[91] And this book was to be, with certain changes, notably the rubrical ones, which do not particularly affect the area of our interest, the basis of the Elizabethan Prayer Book of 1559.[92] Not only was the use by the clergy of the revised book of King Edward legislated by Parliament, but the attendance of the people upon the Reformed services was made compulsory, and penalties for failure to comply were provided in the Second Act of Uniformity, 1552,[93] and this policy of enforcement was followed with the Elizabethan Prayer Book.[94]

The little over five years of the reign of Queen Mary were to prove of the greatest importance for the making of martyrs, as we shall see when we come to Foxe, but they were but an interlude in the campaign against the cult of the saints. The Venetian Ambassador, who seems to have been sceptical of the spiritual aspects of the Marian restoration, reported to his government in 1557 that the images had been restored to the churches, with the ancient rites and ceremonies.[95] But in the same year Archdeacon Harpsfield in his visitation of the

diocese of Canterbury complained of the incompleteness and unsatis-
factoriness of the restoration in liturgical furnishings of every sort,
and there are other records of similar tenor.[96]

But whatever the over-all picture, certainly the restoration of the
outward manifestations of the cult of the saints had gone far enough
to give the new government of Queen Elizabeth concern. For, with a
marginal note of "False Miracles," the second of the Visitation articles
of the first year of Queen Elizabeth directed the visitor to inquire of
the parish clergy: "Item, whether in their Churches and Chapels, all
Images, shrines, tables, candlestickes, trindels, and rolles of wax, pictures, paintings, and all other monuments of fayned and false Miracles, Pilgrimages, Idolatrie, and superstition be removed, abolished
and destroyed."[97] Likewise the ninth article, with the marginal note
"Superstitions," asked: "Item, whether they use to declare to theyr
parishioners, any thing to the extolling or setting foorth of vaine and
supersticious religion, Pilgrimages, Reliques, or Images, lighting of
candles, kissing, kneeling, or decking of the same images."[98] And
the old appeal for the poor was repeated in the eighteenth article:
"Item, whether they have diligently called uppon, exhorted and
moved their Parishioners, and especially when they make their Testaments, to give to the said poore mens box, and to bestow that uppon
the poore, which they were wont to bestow upon Pilgrimages, Pardons, trentals, and upon other like blind devotions."[99]

All of these inquiries concerned the parish church and what went
on within its walls. But the forty-fifth article, with a marginal note
of "Images," carried the inquiry beyond the church: "Item, whether
you know any that keepe in their houses any undefaced Images,
Tables, Pictures, Paintings, or other Monuments of fayned and false
miracles, Pilgrimages, Idolatrie and Superstition, and doe adore
them, and speciallie such as have been set up in Churches, Chappels,
and Oratories."[100] These injunctions continued to be reprinted
throughout Elizabeth's reign.

All this must have encouraged some pretty thoroughgoing image-
breakers to think that the churches had again been opened for the
completion of their work, for there is a proclamation, dated September 19, 1560, "against breakinge or defacing of monumentes of antiquitie, beyng set up in Churches or other publique places for memory,
and not for supersticion," that complains that the spoiling of metal

and stone monuments had been extended to include those that had been erected in churches or other public places "only to shewe a memory to the posteritie of the persons there buryed, or that had ben benefactours to the buyldynges, or dotations of the same Churches or publique places, and not to noryshe any kind of superstition . . . to the sclaunder of such as eyther gave or had charge in tymes paste onely to deface monuments of Idolatry, and false fayned Images in Churches and Abbeyes."[101] Apparently the new regime acted in time, happily for the archival richness of the English parish church. There were others, more sober and responsible than these iconoclasts, who hoped that the new regime might go further than it had so far. Among them were the makers of the first Geneva Bible, who in 1560 presented the fruits of their more than two years of labor to the Queen and the English public.[102]

The first accent of this undertaking was, as the title page makes clear, on authenticity and availability to the unlearned: "The Bible and Holy Scriptures Conteyned in the Olde and Newe Testament, Translated According to the Ebrue and Greke, and conferred with the best translations in divers languages, With Moste Profitable Annotations upon all the hard places, and other things of great importance as may appear in the Epistle to the Reader." But the urgency of the issue of idolatry is emphasized in the address of the Queen's "humble subjects of the English Churche at Geneva." It begins with commendation to her attention of the importance of the task of building "the Lords Temple," and with assurance of the writers' support for the leadership of her "whome God hath made as our Zerubbabel for the erecting of this most excellente Temple." In view of the enemies to this undertaking, "whereof some are Papistes, who under pretence of favoring Gods worde, traiterously seke to erect idolatrie, and to destroy your majestie: some are worldlings, who as Demas have forsaken Christ for the love of this world: others are ambicious prelats, who as Amasiah and Diotrephes can abide none but themselves: and as Demetrius many practise sedition to maynteyne their errors," they offer their translation to the Queen, reminding her that the Word of God "is as a fyre and hammer to breake the stonie heartes of them that resist Gods mercies offered by the preaching of the same." And they go on to assure the Queen that it is necessary for her to destroy all that stands in the way of her building the

Temple, and to remind her that "when the noble Josias entreprised the like kinde of worke, among other notable and many things he destroyed, not only with utter confusion the idoles with their appertinances but also burnt (in signe of detestation) the idolatrous priests bones upon their altars, and put to death the false prophetes and sorcerers, to performe the wordes of the Lawe of God: and therefore the Lord gave him good successe and blessed him wonderfully, so long as he made Gods word his line and rule to followe, and enterprised nothing before he had inquired at the mouth of the Lord."[103]

The authors of this address rightly suspected that Queen Elizabeth might hesitate to face the consequences of so rigorous a course of action, for they proceeded at once to reassure her: "And if these zealous begynnings seme dangerous and to brede disquietnes in your dominions, yet by the storie of King Asa it is manifest, that the quietnes and peace of kingdomes standeth in the utter abolishing of idolatrie, and in advancing of true religion: for in his dayes Judah lyved in rest and quietnes for the space of fyve and thirtie yere, til at length he began to be colde in the zeale of the Lord, feared the power of man, imprisoned the prophet of God, and oppressed the people: then the Lord sent him warres, and at length toke him away by death."[104]

Queen Elizabeth was never to go as far as the makers of this book would have liked. Indeed, its Calvinistic bias, especially manifest in the marginal notes, prevented its adoption as the official Bible of the Church of England.[105] But the succession on Matthew Parker's death in 1575 of the more sympathetic Edmund Grindal in the see of Canterbury gave the promoters of the Geneva Bible their chance, and in that same year Christopher Barker received a special license to print it in England, and at once set about doing so.[106] The plainness of the style of the Geneva Bible assured its popular success, and it became "the household Bible of the English people" until it was supplanted by the Authorized Version of 1611.[107]

But even if Archbishop Parker was not prepared any more than Queen Elizabeth to go as far as these admirers of Geneva wished them to go, the campaign against idolatry was not by any means neglected. For the second homily of *The Seconde Tome of Homelyes*, published in 1563, is "Agaynste parell of Idolatry and superfluous decking of churches."[108] The first of the three parts presents the peril as a very present and actual one: "the corruption of these latter dayes, hath brought into the Church, infinite multitudes of ymages." Reminding the congregation that "the Scriptures use the sayde two wordes, Idols and Images indifferentlye for one thing alwaye," the homilist cites a number of places in the Old Testament which condemn both idolatry and the images themselves, and insists that these apply to Christians no less than to Jews: "For yf we be the people of God, howe can the woorde and lawe of God not appertayne to us?" [109] But in the interest of the peace of the commonwealth, private persons are given the familiar caution that the redress of "such publique enormities" belongs to the magistrates and the proper authorities. [110]

The second section of the homily undertakes to demonstrate that this scriptural teaching concerning images was held by the Fathers and the Primitive Church. [111] Gregory I was the first to let images into churches to instruct the minds of the ignorant. [112] Idolatry was responsible for the schism between the churches of the East and the West, leading to the overthrow of the Christian religion in Greece and the East, and the increase of the tyranny of the Saracens and Turks, a warning of what might befall the present-day Englishman. [113]

The third part is devoted to "the confutation of the principall argumentes . . . for the mayntenaunce of Images." [114] If the images are laymen's books, they teach nothing but lies and errors. The ban of Exodus xx on all image-making applies to images of Christ and his saints, for images placed publicly in churches cannot possibly avoid the risk of idolatry. [115] The homilist is careful to explain that none of this is written in reproach of the saints themselves, but against the "makynge of the true servauntes of God, false Goddes, by attrybutynge to them the power and honoure which is Gods, and due to hym onely. And for that we have such opinions of the power and readye helpe of Sainctes, all our Legendes, Hymnes, Sequences, and Masses dyd contayne stories, laudes, and prayses of them, and prayers to them: yea and Sermons also altogether of them, and to theyr prayses, Goddes worde beyng cleane layde asyde. And thys we do altogether agreable to the Saintes, as did the Gentiles Idolaters to theyr false goddes." [116] There is no possibility that people might be instructed in the proper attitude toward images by preachers, "as fewe are inclyned to credite sounde doctrine, as many, and almost al, be prone to superstition and Idolatry," for "the nature of man is none otherwyse bent to worshipping of images (if he may have them and see them) then it is bent to whordome and adultry in the company of harlots."[117]

Finally the homilist turns to the

foolyshnesse and lewdenesse in deckyng of our ymages, as great puppets for olde fooles . . . For after that our preachers, shal have instructed and exhorted the people to the folowyng of the vertues of the sainctes, as contempt of this worlde, povertie, sobernesse, chastitie, and such lyke vertues, which undoubtedly were in the sainctes: thinke you assone as they turne theyr faces from the preacher, and loke upon the graven bookes, and paynted scripture of the glorious gylte ymages and ydolles, all shynynge and glytteryng with metall and stone, and covered with precious vestures: or els with *Chœrea* in Terence, beholde a paynted table, wherein is set forth by the art of the paynter, an Image with a nyce and wanton apparell and countenaunce, more lyke to Venus or Flora, than Marye Magdalene: or yf lyke to Mary Magdalene, it is when she played the harlotte, rather then when she wepte for her synnes: whan I saye, they turne aboute from the preacher, to these bookes and scoolemasters, and paynted Scriptures: shall they not fynde them lying bookes? teachyng other maner of Lessons, of esteamyng of rychesse, of pride, and vanitie in apparell, of nycenesse and wantonnesse, and peradventure of whoredom, as *Chœrea* of lyke pictures was taught: and in Lucian, one learned of Venus Gnídea, a lesson to abominable here to be remembered. Be not these thinke you pretie bokes, and scriptures for simple people, and speciallye for wyves and yonge maydens to loke in, reade on, and learne such lessons of?[118]

And he ends with the old complaint that money is spent on this decoration while the poor are in need.[119] Taken as a whole, the homily is a fair recapitulation of the attack on the saints and their images and legends, as it has developed through this century. However complicated its origins, and obscure as its progress often was, this attack was to have important consequences for literature and for learning.

On those who, whatever their contempt for the immediate past, had no thought of destroying the existing religious order, it forced a more serious critical attitude. It was no longer possible to let the extravagances of the veneration of the saints pass with laughter. The decree of the Council of Trent on the abuse of images left no doubt on this point: "All superstition in the invocation of saints, in the veneration of relics, in the use of holy images, must be done away with; all shameful gain must be removed; all lasciviousness must be avoided; so that no images of a wanton beauty be painted or represented; and that in the celebration of saints' days, or in the visit of relics, people fall not into the abuse of orgy and drunkenness." [120] The issue of truth was important again, and truth both in the historian's and the poet's sense. By the beginning of the seventeenth century the Belgian Jesuits, asking themselves to what ends the higher studies to which they had dedicated themselves as a part of their program of saving the then modern world for the Church should be directed, had decided, at the suggestion of Heribert Rosweyde, that the critical study of the lives of the saints was the worthiest endeavor to which they could address themselves, and so the long labors of the Bollandists, still unfinished, were launched. [121]

For those who rejected the cult of the saints, and their legends, the results were no less consequential. The medieval legend-makers would seem to have proceeded on the tacit assumption that the more a man believed, the better. That careless confidence had been shattered, and believers were made more wary, and so the first steps were taken to that tender conscience of which we are going to hear so much in the seventeenth century, and perhaps toward that basic caution about all belief that we are going to meet in the eighteenth.

But, more immediately, the bright clutter of the saints and their ubiquitous traffic between heaven and earth was swept away. It was unquestionably a tidier world without them, like the village churches from which their often gaudy images had been obliterated. The well-ordered world of the state church was not distracted by their alien reminders, and the parish pieties could consolidate their indigenous securities. But in that clearer upper air it was perhaps a little easier for the more reflective to see emerging the impersonal, self-contained, mechanical universe of the scientists, and for the less reflective to find a freedom to devote themselves to the business of this earth without too many irrelevant reminders.

As for literature, the more serious-minded descendants of the readers of the old saints' lives turned to the well-publicized excitements of reading the Scriptures, and the less serious to the enjoyment of the fascinating new stories from Italy and France. Meanwhile, on all sides men for whom the religious issue was the only one that mattered went to their deaths, and whatever their theory of the cult of the saints, made their contribution to the martyr's legend of their tradition, and so brought the *Golden Legend* back to its beginnings in the martyr story.

THE CATHOLIC MARTYRS
UNDER HENRY

*t*he history of the attacks on the saints' cult very well illustrates the character of the religious changes under Henry VIII: on the surface, a rather unsteady seesawing between the appeals of tradition and reform; underneath, a fairly steady progression in the destruction of the old order and the setting up of a new. In an age of revolution like the first half of the sixteenth century it is not easy for anybody to know what is really happening, much less what it portends or heralds. It is not surprising that sincere reformers often became impatient, and tried to force the issue, or assumed that because certain things had been said or done, it was now the time to go further. We know from Foxe what happened to at least some of them.

What is surprising is that there was not more resistance to Henry on the part of those who were not sympathetic with the changes under way, even when those changes concerned something as obvious as the control of the Church. The great sixteenth-century historian, Edward Hall, summed up the situation very well in his account of how, when commissions were sent over England to take the oath of all men and women to the Act of Succession, "fewe repyned," except Fisher and More and Nicholas Wilson, parson of St. Thomas the Apostle in London. After various exhortations and imprisonment, the last "dissembled the matter and so escaped: But the other twayne stode against all the realme in their opinion."[1]

Various explanations have been advanced, ranging from J. D. Mackie's suggestion that when Wolsey succeeded in welding into one the powers of the *regnum* and the *sacerdotium*, he created a tremendous authority which on his fall he in fact bequeathed to his master, Henry VIII,[2] to Father Philip Hughes's survey of the confusion and corruption that resulted from a disastrous combination of monastic decay, of ill-trained and submissive clergy in the lower ranks, and of typical bureaucrats in the hierarchy,[3] to say nothing of a weak and vacillating Pope.[4] But the psychological problem of resistance to change on the part of those who had no desire for it, and probably not too much understanding of it anyway, should not be underestimated.

The martyr story was, as we have seen, part of the religious inheritance of all sixteenth-century Englishmen. The heroism of the martyrs had been commended often enough to them, as to Christians of all times, and the steadfastness of these heroes had been admired, probably as an almost supernatural virtue, more conceivable in the first times of the faith than now in these easier days when such virtues were not likely to be demanded by circumstances, and the grace for them not likely to be given. Such is almost inevitably the psychology of any settled and long-established group. Of course, England had seen men suffer for their faith, but that was for disturbing the peace of Church and State with dangerous innovations. Such was clearly the general reaction except where doctrinal or personal sympathy, or pity for an especially hard or moving case, overcame the prejudice of settled society against the innovator. But quiet men who kept to the established ways with no intention of disturbing the known laws of God and the King did not expect to be challenged by martyrdom.

Moreover, Henry, as we have seen in general, and shall see presently in more detail, knew how to discourage resistance with striking examples that would reinforce the caution of the natural man. Particularly is this true of the most famous Catholic martyrs of his reign, the Carthusians, Bishop John Fisher, and Sir Thomas More. Henry, with his customary political acumen, was, also, quite aware of the possibilities of propaganda in sympathetic accounts of martyrdoms, and could be counted on to react to them with the vigor with which he received any overt opposition to his will. One remembers the exuberant note of "Now it can be told," in Foxe. Except for the very brief and much preoccupied reign of Mary, the story of the Henrician Catholic martyrs could not be told in England. The fact that Sir Thomas More had not only held the highest position in the realm that a subject could hold but had long enjoyed a reputation among Continental humanists, makes the history of the accounts of his life and death particularly illuminating for the possibilities of Catholic martyrology under Henry. It was on the Continent, at Basel, that the first account of More's execution was printed, the "Paris Newsletter" of July 23, 1535, which Erasmus composed from material sent from England and had printed for the information of his friends by his host, Froben.[5] And it was also at Basel later that year that Froben printed the famous *Expositio Fidelis de Morte D. Thomae Mori et quorundam aliorum insigniorum virorum in Anglia.* In both cases Erasmus, mindful of his English interests, took pains to conceal his authorship, and his friend Froben published the later book without any indication of the printer, or even the date of printing.[6] Another good example is the fate of the account which More's nephew, William Rastell, wrote of his uncle's trial. A plausible case has recently been made by De Vocht for the theory that this contemporary English account survives in a rough but fairly accurate Latin version, the *Ordo Condemnationis Thomae Mori* (which was published for the first time in 1947 by De Vocht)[7] and that the same English account was used more elegantly and less accurately by Erasmus for his *Expositio Fidelis.*[8] Thomas Stapleton's Latin life of More was published as Part III of his *Tres Thomae* at Douai in 1588, but it had to wait until our day for publication, in 1928, in an English translation.[9]

The earliest surviving English account of More, with the possible exception of the Rastell fragments,[10] the famous life by his son-in-law, William Roper, comes from a period some twenty years after the events it records.[11] We have evidence from the works of those who used Roper's account that his recollections of his father-in-law circulated in manuscript, but they did not find their way into print until 1626 and then on the Continent, ostensibly at Paris, actually at Saint-Omer. The English lives written by the still-unidentified Ro. Ba. and by Nicholas Harpsfield in the reign of Queen Mary had to wait until our own day to find publication, although Harpsfield was described by Lord Acton as the most important intellectual figure of his group to remain in England.[12]

There was, therefore, nothing in print, at least, to challenge the official view of the Catholic resistance to Henry. For that a brief and sober summary may be had in the pages of Hall, in the famous chronicle first published in 1548. The three Carthusians, Exmew, Middlemore, and Newdigate, Hall said, deserved the traitor's death they died for denying the King to be Supreme Head of the Church:

> These men when they wer arreigned at Westminster, behaved them selfes very stifly and stubbornly, for hearyng their inditement red how trayterously they had spoken against the kynges Majestie his croune and dignitie, they neither blushed nor bashed at it, but very folishly and hipocritically knowleged their treason whiche maliciously thei avouched, havyng no lernyng for their defence, but rather beyng asked dyvers questions, they used a malicious silence, thinkyng as by their examinacions afterward in the Tower of London it did appeare, for so they sayd, that they thought those men which was the lorde Crumwel and other that there satte upon them in judgement to be heretiques and not of the Churche of God, and therfore not worthy to be either aunswered or spoken unto.[13]

Bishop Fisher was more puzzling to Hall: "This bishop was of very many menne lamented, for he was reported to be a man of great learnyng, and a man of very good life, but therin wonderfully deceived, for he maintained the Pope to be supreme head of the Church, and very maliciously refused the kynges tytle of supreme head . . . wonderful it is that a man beyng lerned should be so blind in the scriptures of God that proveth the supreme aucthoritie of princes so manyfestly." [14]

Nor was Hall entirely sure about Thomas More. Of the main facts he had no doubt. "This manne was also coumpted learned, and as you have heard before he was lorde Chauncelor of England, and in that tyme a great persecutor of suche as detested the supremacy of the bishop of Rome, whiche he himselfe so highly favored that he stoode to it till he was brought to the Skaffolde on the Tower hill where on a blocke his head was stricken from his shoulders and had no more harme." But there was a weakness in More that made it hard for Hall to strike the balance in his final judgment: "I cannot tell whether I should call him a foolishe wyseman, or a wise foolishman, for undoubtedly he beside his learnyng, had a great witte, but it was so myngled with tauntyng and mockyng, that it semed to them that best knew him, that he thought nothyng to be wel spoken except he had ministered some mocke in the communicacion . . ." This habit stayed with him to the block — "thus with a mocke he ended his life," concluded Hall.[15]

The function of the martyr story is not only to record but to edify and fortify, as we have seen. All three services were desired and needed by adherents of the old faith in the England of Henry and Elizabeth, we may be sure, but the need had to be satisfied surreptitiously under circumstances in which the possession of such works as those described above, to say nothing of the composition or printing of them, would constitute evidence of treasonable activity. The hazards to manuscripts circulated in a group suspected of harboring subversive literature are, of course, many times those of normal manuscript circulation, as is well illustrated by the story which the sixteenth-century biographer of Fisher tells of the fate of the large volume which Fisher had compiled telling the whole story of the divorce. He had entrusted the volume to Phillips, Dean of Rochester, for safe-keeping, but on the news of the approach of some commissioners of Edward VI to search his house for books, Phillips burned the volume.[16]

The result is that the story of the martyrs of Henry's reign on the Catholic side must be picked up outside the main stream of sixteenth-century literature, often in Latin accounts not translated into English until long afterward, or in English accounts that, circulating in manuscript underground, were not printed until many years later. It is, of course, stretching a point to include such a Latin account as the Carthusian Dom Maurice Chauncy's *Passio XVIII. Carthusianorum in regno Angliæ* in a study of an English literary type, but it is too important a link in the martyr story of the time to be omitted, and it is of its kind deserving of more general literary knowledge than it enjoys today.

Henry chose his first victims well, from the point of view of strategy, and from the point of view of literature. For the execution of the Carthusian martyrs in 1535 was the inspiration of one of the notable martyr stories of the time in the classic tradition, the *Passio XVIII. Carthusianorum in regno Angliæ: Qui pro eo quod schismati adhærere et ab unitate Ecclesiae Catholicae segregare nolebant semetipsos,*

crudeliter martyrizati sunt of Dom Maurice Chauncy, which constituted the major portion of the Carthusian *Historia Aliquot Nostri
Saeculi*, published at Mainz in 1550.[17] Characteristically, Chauncy's
account had to wait nearly three and a half centuries for the publication, in 1890,[18] of an English translation, the work of a member of the
restored London Charterhouse. While Chauncy's book was several
times reprinted in the next half-century or so after its writing, and
was widely known and used by the writers of the time in this field,[19]
it is not surprising that it waited so long for a translator. For like the
men whom it commemorates, it looks back to the past, to a past soon
to be quite irrecoverable. It is, also, an old type of saint's life, full of
premonitions, of prophecies, of wrestlings with evil spirits, of visions,
of miracles. But still more important, it is a specialized type of
martyr's life, the story of contemplatives, written by a contemplative.
It could have nothing like the general public appeal, say, of the life
of Thomas More, or even of Bishop Fisher, of whom brief accounts
were prefixed to the Carthusian story in this book. And Chauncy's
general approach, though, as we shall soon see, it is by no means
lacking in human appeal, is fairly specialized, even professional. His
symbolism, his very language, though familiar enough to anyone
conversant with medieval contemplative literature, must have seemed
to the general reader even of the sixteenth century fairly technical, and
the things Chauncy obviously most cared for, remote. On the other
hand, the audience which would read Chauncy with delight, his
fellow monastics, would not need an English translation.

Though Chauncy's account was to be read widely by the world of
learned piety, it was in its initial impulse a report to his fellow Carthusians, explicitly to the prior of the Grand Chartreuse, the Primate
of the Carthusian order, of what had happened to his brethren. It has,
therefore, the character of an official report, like some of the greatest
of the early martyr stories, with a certain further specialized quality
of a report within the family, in this case a spiritual family. It has the
matter-of-factness of such a report, and that matter-of-factness is enhanced by the highly traditional character of so much of Chauncy's
language, as suggested above, the conventional language of contemplative literature, perhaps a little more concentrated in its scriptural-
ism because as a Carthusian priest Chauncy was a thorough and
constant student of Scripture. And the phrases of Holy Writ, not only

the Psalms, but the Prophets, and the other writers of the Old Testament, as well as of the New, were the habitual idiom of his thinking.

But there is nothing remote or academic about Chauncy. Indeed, of all these writers of the Henrician period he is in a certain sense the one most intimately involved with his subject. It is not only that he has known these men of whom he writes. He was one of them, and their predicament was his, though not their glory. "Satan was present among the sons of God, but is never praised; I indeed, went forth from these; the thing is notorious: but I was not of them, for if I had been of them, I should have remained with them to drink of the chalice which they also drank," he says in his address to the prior of the Grand Chartreuse.[20] Through the formal scriptural language breaks the remorse that, one may believe, led Chauncy to wear through his long and laborious life the penitential chain which at his death was found worn into his body,[21] and that led him to present so highly idealized a portrait of his former brethren.

It is ironic that the first victims of the Henrician reform should be perhaps the finest representatives of contemporary English monasticism, the Carthusians. Indeed, it was probably the very excellence of the reputation they enjoyed that made it imperative that Henry should secure their acquiescence in his new order. And when that acquiescence, in spite of every form of pressure, was not forthcoming, the swiftness of Henry's retribution was the most convincing evidence possible of the fate which awaited anyone who should dare to refuse his submission. If the Carthusians, whose devotion to their primitive monastic ideals was the admiration of devout London, had met such retribution, then what could the ordinary run-of-the-mill monk or friar look for?[22] It is characteristic of this early group of martyrs that Prior Houghton himself, though he had no doubt of the significance of the oath on the King's marriages when it was first demanded of him, was in no haste to rush upon the martyrdom he clearly foresaw. He even allowed himself to be persuaded by "certain honest and learned men" that this was not a cause to die for, and took the required oath "so far as it was lawful."[23] When the next year the Oath of Supremacy was demanded, Houghton considered throwing himself on the mercy of God and consenting to the King's will, *si licite fieri possit*, if his consent would spare the rest of the house.[24] His first thought was of the brethren in his charge, particularly the younger ones, for it is one of the evidences of the health of his institution that, as Chauncy tells us, so considerable a proportion of the brotherhood were under forty.[25] When Houghton's efforts to obtain some mitigation of the oath to renounce the Pope's authority and accept the King's in spiritual as well as temporal matters failed, the whole brotherhood faced the problem.[26]

We shall see presently that it was not an easy problem for men like More, who by their public position were abreast of the current of affairs in the great world. But it had been of the very heart of the Carthusian undertaking not to know what was going on in the world, and the rumors which gossiping seculars, friends and relatives and clients of various types, brought into the cloister were deliberately rejected as temptations to frivolous distraction.[27] The shock of this intrusion of the outer world must, therefore, have been peculiarly shattering to the peace of the Charterhouse.

From the fact that he was one of four sent away to other houses at this time, one may guess that Chauncy, although one of the younger members, had taken a strong position on the side of resistance. It may be, too, that he had already manifested that talent for leadership that was to characterize his later career. Upon his return to the Charterhouse after the death of Houghton he seems to have been one of those who thought a nominal submission would save the house for the future. Indeed, although Chauncy permits himself no sign of excuse or mitigation for the grief that, in spite of his personal reticence and his concentration on his martyrs, every so often breaks through his matter-of-factness, it may well have been that his elders persuaded him to submit as the best hope for the survival of the house. Whether because of the breaking of definite promises or only a disappointment of hopes that had been encouraged by the authorities, that compromise with his conscience soon proved fruitless, and, a fugitive in a strange land, Chauncy was left with no prospect but to bear witness to men who now seemed to him to have been braver and wiser than he.[28]

Of these the most important, indeed, the key personality, was the prior, John Houghton. On Houghton's early years Chauncy is brief enough, partly because he was not the man to say much of what he did not know for himself, partly because the personality of even the prior was subordinate to the house. A man of honorable parentage,

Houghton had won the bachelor's degree in both laws at Cambridge, and had then left his family to study secretly with a devout priest until he could take holy orders. He was in his twenty-eighth year when he came to the Charterhouse. There he devoted himself completely to the hidden life of the Carthusian. The impression he made on his brethren is shown by his being entrusted successively with the offices of sacristan, procurator, and prior, first of Beauvale, and then of London. Obviously the good opinion of his brethren was shared by the order at large, for he was appointed by the Reverend Father of the Chartreuse principal Visitor of the English Province.[29] With such a career, one is not surprised to learn that Houghton was considered a model monk and an administrator of great devotion and prudence. "He was kind to all, but to himself very strict and hard,"[30] might be said of a good many of the right kind of monastic leaders before his time and since.

Other qualities emerge in Chauncy's account of his administration, and these are interesting not alone for Houghton but for the light they shed on the time. One of the most attractive of these personal glimpses is what Chauncy has to say of Houghton's relations to his brethren: "When in another's cell with any of the brethren, he behaved, not as a Prior, but as a humble Brother, saying he had left the priorate in his own cell."[31] And of a piece is his habit of sending some little present to a brother whom he had had to disappoint of some request, or to discipline.[32] But this personal graciousness, however important for the men with whom he lived, is in perspective less important than his approach to the main business of the Carthusian, his life of prayer and worship. It is this which Chauncy stresses with a circumstantiality that leaves no doubt of what he thought most important about the ideal prior. And however limited Chauncy's Carthusian-blinkered view of the crises of his time might be, anyone who has read such a modern analysis as Hughes's of the decay of English monastic life on the eve of its destruction[33] will be struck by the appositeness of Houghton's analysis of his problem, and Chauncy's awareness of it.

For Houghton realized that in his day many religious were "mightily wearied when not occupied with vain and external consolations"; so he insisted on full devotion to the Divine Office, pleading with the less zealous: "If we, who live on the patrimony of Christ and alms, and are very strictly bound to pray for all, hurry in God's service, or invent excuses for leaving the church, regarding as too long, the short and little time we are here, assuredly I know not how we shall excuse ourselves from injustice, in taking, retaining, and expending the alms of our benefactors and founders." So he urged his brethren to lengthen out rather than hurry the chant in the church, and yet he would not tolerate their singing languidly, or in a low voice, for he thought such lukewarmness of performance an indication of luke-warmness of heart. "He was also always displeased, if any sang out of tune or a wrong note."[34] Long afterward in exile Chauncy remembered: "It was commonly said, If you would hear the service of the Church devoutly celebrated, go to the Charterhouse."[35] In other words, the foundation of Houghton's administration was the proper performance of the Divine Office, the central purpose of the common life of the Charterhouse. And what might so easily have been administrative rigor was redeemed by the prior's love of God: "The most devout Father was himself as burning flame or glowing iron, in the love of God, and desired that all about him should in like manner be ardently inflamed."[36] The similes to which Chauncy resorts are stereotyped enough; there is nothing stereotyped about the reality they describe.

The same combination of sweetness and fortitude is apparent in the final scene, in which, having refused a last offer of pardon, Houghton declared "that not through any pertinacity, malice, or rebellious spirit, do I commit this disobedience and denial of the will of our lord the King, but solely through fear of God, lest I should offend His Supreme Majesty." Even in the disemboweling of the traitor's death, the voice was still "sweet" that cried: "Most sweet Jesu, have mercy on me at this hour."[37]

Beside Houghton the other seventeen Carthusian martyrs remain shadowy, and the details of their execution are hurried over. Indeed, for those who died in prison, we have more precise, even if brief, detail in the life of Mother Margaret Clement, the daughter of the adopted daughter of Thomas More, who came to their relief.[38] But Chauncy manages to create a sense of the brotherhood as a spiritual group, and looking back upon them from the ruin that was to come, he remembers, "It was sweet to witness their combat and fervour."[39] Even the lay brothers shared in this community enthusiasm. With characteristic insight into the phenomena of the daily life about him, even though full understanding was only to come later, Chauncy explained how "being very simple and illiterate, they became possessed of wonderful ideas from what was read, and from what they heard in the church and refectory; and emitted brilliant sparks of spiritual knowledge to those who questioned them."[40] Chauncy could not foresee the spiritual efflorescence of the simple and the illiterate to come in the seventeenth-century development of the sects, but he already had the key.

Chauncy himself is not far from these simple brethren in one respect, and that is in his handling of the miraculous. Here his story makes an effective transition from the *Golden Legend* to the latter-day martyr's life. Not only premonitions and prophecies such as the later sixteenth century would still admit, but miracles and visions in the traditional sense grace his pages. It is significant that Chauncy never tells these as of his own knowledge. Indeed, the most remarkable of them, the story of the miraculous transport of the Irish prior, William Tynbygh, from the prison in Jerusalem in which he was awaiting execution at the hands of the Hagarenes to the chapel in his father's house in Ireland, where hung the picture of Saint Catherine which had so fortunately come to mind in his extremity, was supposed to have happened long before Chauncy was born.[41]

But of all Chauncy's miraculous stories none is more moving in its witness to what Chauncy conceived the spirit of the Charterhouse to be than the story of Brother Richard Crofts, of the House of Saint Anne near Coventry, who "despairing of the mercy of God . . . purposed to drown himself in a pond in the garden of the Convent." When his departure was discovered, one of the searchers saw a great light around the pond and called his companions — "Having entered the garden, they saw the Brother walking on one side of the pond, trying repeatedly to drown himself, yet always prevented, and they (not all, but two only) saw the great light on the other side, and in it, as they affirmed, they saw all our Fathers who had suffered, interposing themselves between the Brother and the water, as often as he tried to drown himself."[42] As Chauncy with characteristic candor had admitted, there were reprobates and backsliders even in the Charterhouse of London.[43] It is touching to think of the martyrs leaving their newly- and hard-won glory to save one of these. Less charitably, but quite in the spirit of his time, Chauncy added an epilogue to explain that "none of those who brought about the dissolution, long outlived the work, or received any lasting pleasure from their evil deeds; since, not long afterwards, all perished by a violent and ignominious death, or came to great poverty, or fell into the worst calamities of human life."[44]

But all this is by way of appendix, the witness of subsequent judgment and miracle to the glory of the martyrs. The real ending of the story proper is in the quiet paragraph at the end of the thirteenth chapter, in which Chauncy goes back of the *Golden Legend* to the early classics of martyrology: "This, Reverend Father, is the end of my report, and that was the sleep which God gave to your sons, His beloved ones, because fruit is to the just. So God judged them in the earth, to bring forth more fruit in patience, and to acquire greater glory in the inheritance of the Lord, which, we cannot doubt, God gives to his Saints (for whom all things work together for good), who have never swerved from their faith in Him."[45] In the formal dignity of those sentences the *Golden Legend* returns to the immemorial reality out of which it came.

The record for the Carthusians is, for all its distinction, limited enough. It is not much ampler for John Fisher, Bishop of Rochester, the next of Henry's most notable victims. An interesting sixteenth-century English life, *A Treatis Contayninge the Lyfe and Maner of Death of that Most holy Prelat and Constant Martyr of Christ John Fysher Byshop of Rochester and Cardinale of the Holy Church of Rome*,[46] survives in a number of manuscripts, in both English and Latin, that prove that it was appreciated under trying circumstances.[47] But it was not printed until 1655, and then in London, with various additions, as the work of Dr. Thomas Baily.[48] Curiously enough, certain preliminary drafts and working papers survive in one of the Arundel manuscripts, suggesting that the composition of this life extended over a considerable period of time, perhaps from some time before 1568 to 1577.[49] But the problem of authorship still remains. The author to whom it has been traditionally ascribed, Richard Hall, can hardly, as the Bollandist editor Van Ortroy has shown, have written it, since he was exiled to the Continent not later than 1562, and this life was not finished until around 1577. Van Ortroy's candidate for the main responsibility for what he thinks a collaboration, Dr. John

Young, Master of Pembroke Hall, Cambridge, of which Richard Hall was fellow in 1556, is a reasonable conjecture, but cannot be proved.[50] Whoever wrote the life was a scholar and a writer of real literary talent, but the work remained in manuscript.

Superficially, one would say that Fisher was a less interesting person than More. But on one score, and that the most important when one is thinking of the martyr genre, he far outstripped More, and that was in his religious concentration. And if he seems less many-sided, narrower and less colorful than the great chancellor, we must never forget that the man who claimed the admiration of so varied a range of people as the Lady Margaret Beaufort and Margaret Roper, and Erasmus and Henry VII, to say nothing of More, must have possessed a good deal of what we today call personality.

It is probably in that word "personality" that we shall find the key to a certain distance that we feel in Fisher. We put a great deal of stress on individuality when we assess character. The Middle Ages were much less interested in what was individual, and much more interested in what was representative of the universal, much less impressed by the dramatically engaging and much more concerned about the functional in personality. In this sense there is something medieval about Fisher that there never was about More.

And yet there is nothing of the reactionary about Fisher. He was a reformer, and an effective one. He was himself a model priest and university doctor and administrator. When he attracted attention and won the opportunity to influence the great, he used his opportunities as the chaplain of the Lady Margaret Beaufort, the grandmother of Henry VIII, to promote the increase and the improvement of education, particularly for the training of preachers.[51] When he became a bishop, he did a bishop's work as it should be done, visiting the poor, and supervising his clergy, setting an example, in the age of Wolsey, of evangelical poverty and simplicity.[52]

One might say, remembering Foxe, that Fisher was the great representative of the reform that for England at least failed, or, remembering Wolsey, was never attempted. Thomas More, writing *A Dialoge of Comfort against Tribulacion* in the Tower in 1534, was obviously haunted by the thought that if he and his contemporaries had been better Christians, all this might never have happened.[53] And

Fisher himself, also in the Tower, writing for his half-sister, a nun, a shorter treatise of what seemed on the surface a much more classic, not to say conventional, type, stressed particularly his remissness, his not using the time he had had to the best advantage: "O yee that have tyme and space to make your provision against the houre of death, defarre not from day to day lyke as I have done . . . And therefore delay it not as I have done, but before all other buzinesse put this first in suertie, which oughte to bee chieefe and princypall businesse. Neyther buildyng of Colleges, nor makyng of Sermons, nor giving of almes, neyther yet anye other manner of buzynesse shall helpe you without this." [54]

Clearly whoever printed this little treatise, doubtless, from the absence of any indication of time or place, to say nothing of edition or printer, a sympathizer, could not believe that the martyred Bishop was anything but dramatic in the personal allusions above, as may be seen from the title: *A Spirituall Consolation, written by John Fyssher Bishoppe of Rochester, to hys sister Elizabeth, at suche tyme as hee was Prisoner in the Tower of London . . . Also to admonishe them, to be at all tymes prepared to dye, and seemeth to bee spoken in the person of one that was sodainly prevented by death.*

Of course, the Bishop's thoughts in the Tower were not all penitential, for he also made for the same Sister Elizabeth a little treatise which the same editor entitled "The wayes to perfect Religion made by John Fyssher, Bishop of Rochester, being Prysoner in the Tower of London" and printed with the foregoing treatise. This is a moving and, at times, charming guide to the spiritual life, on the general text, "For love maketh everie worke appeare easie and pleasaunt, though it bee ryghte displeasaunt of it selfe." [55]

Yet in the end Fisher must have had a great sense of failure. The reform he had striven for was to come elsewhere, when the work of the Catholic Reformation was under way, but the great post-Tridentine bishops do not look quite like Fisher. Rather, the later-age bishop whom Fisher makes one think of is a countryman of his, Richard Challoner, who published the great recension of the lives of the English martyrs in 1741–42, and who carried the Catholic Church in England across the desert of the eighteenth century into the "Second Spring" of the nineteenth. But when Fisher put his fur tippet about his neck to avoid any betraying shiver that twenty-second day of June of 1535 and set out for the scaffold, he could not know how durable his model was to be.[56]

However different they were as men, More and Fisher have two things in common when they are compared with both the Carthusians and the martyrs of the Elizabethan period. They were great figures of their world, with what may be called international reputations, and they were very diffident about their calling to martyrdom. Of the first fact their biographers were fully appreciative, as we shall see. Of the second, they were less so, and of the connection between the two facts they were aware only to a limited and conventional extent. They knew, all of them, that both men had a great deal to give up, and that both were habitually modest about their own capacities. But it is doubtful if they knew the depth or the complexity of their predicament. The fact of it Roper clearly perceived in his recording, for instance, of his father-in-law's remark as he seated himself in the boat that was to carry him away forever from his loved home in Chelsea, "Sonne Roper, I thancke our Lord [God], the feild is wonne."[57] And Rastell, if he is the source of the account of his uncle's trial in the *Acta Thomae Mori*,[58] understood the great lawyer's plight as he addressed himself to his defense in a cause that he knew was prejudged.[59] But the way in which all the biographers speak of the isolation of the martyrs and the failure of their fellows to rise to the occasion as they did,[60] clearly indicates a failure to understand their predicament. That was largely because their own situation was so different; the world of the Henrician martyrs had passed away so completely.

Both Fisher and More were familiar with the traditions enshrined in the liturgy and in the *Golden Legend*. Some of the magical short cuts of the contemporary saints' cult would be abhorrent to the moral fastidiousness of Fisher, and the absurdities of the *Golden Legend* contemptible to More, but martyrdom was something of which they had a high opinion, something which in their younger days they would doubtless think of as belonging to the heroic ancient days, quite out of their range and expectation. One cannot imagine either the young Fisher or the young More, like the young Teresa of Avila, going out to look for martyrdom in his neighborhood.[61] Of course, they both came officially in contact with men who did risk and sometimes incur death for their religious views, but to both, these latter would seem at best misguided fanatics, at worst obstinate enemies to law and order, rash in their risk of martyrdom as of everything else.

Certainly, they could find very little in common between these men of their own time and themselves. They were both very successful men. Fisher, as we have seen, was eminently suited to the career he chose; More was the type of man who could have been successful in half-a-dozen callings. Both were quite aware of the shortcomings of many of the members of their respective professions, but in both cases their answer was a model performance. Both were men of great natural gifts, but they were, also, borne up by the social currents of their time. Dr. Baily in the mid-seventeenth century dedicated his travesty on the sixteenth-century life of Fisher to a merchant cousin, commending the son of a merchant, Fisher, as an example of the height to which his class could come.[62] The remarkableness of More's promotion was publicly noted by the Duke of Norfolk on the occasion of his installation as Lord Chancellor, on the ground that he came but of a modest family.[63]

Both careers might be regarded, then, as evidences of the triumphant advance of the middle class, although that advance in the Church was no new story. Certainly, no two men could look less likely to find themselves in radical conflict with the status quo. Fisher was, as we have seen, very much the institutional type of person, and men who thrive in institutional life are generally men who have some capacity to live and let live, and, generally, they are not men with a taste for standing alone. More was a more independent type of person. "I never intend to pin my soul at another man's back," he said at the end of his life when he was pressed to take account of other men's yielding on the issue of the Royal Supremacy.[64] But, again, he was not the type one would expect to find upholding alone a lost cause. He had all his life been very much the forward-looking progressive, loyal to the best of tradition but optimistic about the possibility of the improvement of practice. Nor was he the man one would expect to carry an issue to the death. The man who saw so clearly how precarious was the glittering favor of Henry VIII at the height of its most flattering manifestations,[65] to say nothing of the man who wrote the *Utopia*, had a capacity for seeing beneath the surface

of things, for perceiving the far-from-inevitable character of the rules
of most of the games men play, that only a great faith could save from
cynicism. Even in those last days in the Tower when he, who had so
clear a sense of the imperceptible thrust of events, could have had no
doubt of what the end would be, he could imagine the ground on
which a prince had built his castle laughing at his pride of possession
and thinking to itself, "Ah thou sely poore soule, that weneste thou
were halfe a God, and arte amidde thy glory, but a man in a gaye
gowne."[66] Such a mind is a rare one in any context, perhaps rarest of
all in those who find themselves so committed to a principle as to
die for it. It would perhaps be easier for More to stand alone than
for Fisher, but it would be a more surprising position for him to find
himself in.

But the loneliness of their predicament, though perhaps the feature
in their story that most impressed their biographers, intensified the
effect of another element that their biographers could not so fully
appreciate. As we shall presently see, the charge of treason never
ceased to be a bitter one to the Elizabethan Recusants. But they were
so habituated to the suspicion involved in that charge that they could
hardly imagine what its impact was on men who had been accustomed
to have their loyalty taken for granted. They had some of them
known it, of course — Roper for instance, in spite of all his father-in-
law's warnings[67] — but that was now twenty years behind, and in
all the griefs that had intervened, that had been veiled. Besides it is
always hard for the young to realize that their elders, especially when
of so heroic a stature as this, could ever have known the queasy uncertainty of conscience that led to such caution as More, for example,
displayed.

The dilemma was a real one. Whatever the modern reader may
think of Henry VIII, whatever later on the Elizabethan Recusant
might think of him, he had moral claims on both Fisher and More
that we must not underestimate. And those claims were highly personal to a degree that it is not easy for the post-feudal world to understand. Fisher had received his bishopric from Henry's father.[68] More
owed to Henry's highly personal favor his brilliant public career, in
which the master-and-servant relationship was much more than a
formality. Roper gives a very attractive picture of the companion-
ableness of the younger Henry: "And other whiles wold he, in the

night, have him uppe into his Leades, there for to consider with him the diversities, courses, motions, and operacions of the starres and planetes."[69] And this personal relationship was reinforced by the tremendous impressiveness of gathering power consolidating itself. The sheer magnetism of such a consolidation of power would have attracted most men in any age.

And the determination of that power to brook no challenge was early manifest. Question was itself made a treasonable activity,[70] and the very facilities of the new form of promulgating opinion, the printing press, made the enforcement of this control easier. Indeed, Fisher's pastoral conscience, that obliged him, when asked for his opinion for the personal enlightenment of the King, to give that opinion, was used to entrap him, according to the sixteenth-century life.[71] And according to the report of his trial, More's failure to speak in support of his master's position was taken as evidence of a treasonable attitude.[72]

Fisher's sixteenth-century biographer blamed Wolsey, as did most of these writers, for the insinuation of the fatal scruple in the King's conscience, and he found the motive for that fatal strategy in Wolsey's pride and ambition.[73] He knew from friends and acquaintance, if not firsthand, the magnificence of Wolsey,[74] and he appreciated the enduring scandal which that magnificence had given. It was against that disastrous brilliance that he set his own sober portrait of Fisher. No contrast to the splendor of Wolsey could be sharper than the vivid picture of the Bishop sitting for several hours in the smoke of a cottage so poor as not to have any chimney, to comfort a sick person, even when his attendants were unable to stay with him in the smoke, or of the Bishop, frail as he seems early to have been, climbing the ladder to a loft to visit the sick poor.[75]

And to those who stressed the ignorance and superstition of the past his biographer held up Fisher's devotion to learning, the partner of his devotion to his priestly duties and his charity to the poor. The greatest library of any bishop in Europe,[76] he said, making that appeal to the common world of intellectual Christendom in which Fisher had played an honored part with his writing and the report of the learned men who visited him and enjoyed his encouragement.[77] And yet the collecting of books can be a form of self-indulgence, however noble. So he took pains to point out that Fisher had given his library to St. John's College and kept but the use of it for his lifetime.[78] And of course he recorded that upon Fisher's arrest for treason, his books were seized, too, and scattered among the King's commissioners, and that none of the bequest ever reached Cambridge.[79] But more than anything else he stressed the devotion of his hero to prayer and to penance, his austerity, his ascetical devotion.[80] Indeed, Fisher might well be considered a champion of the ascetic life, and so a martyr in the classic sense ere ever he came to the Tower.

The manuscripts which Van Ortroy has published include that most precious of all aids to the understanding of literary method, what may be called the author's working papers, in this case not only first drafts of fragments, but outlines, lists of points to be determined, and even a couple of the questionnaires which he had addressed to people who might be in a position to clear up doubtful points or fill gaps in his information.[81] In these working papers are clearly apparent the author's anxiety to establish the facts of the record, and the pains which he took to do so. Many of the homely details which he included suggest that he did not confine his inquiries to the learned but, perhaps mindful of the contribution of Wolsey's Cavendish, included surviving servants.[82] Such a detail as Fisher's care for regularity of meals would suggest fussiness in any but a man who had obviously to take care of his health, and its inclusion can hardly have been dictated by hagiographic motives.[83]

But he used the basic hagiographic pattern in his organization of his material: the merchant's family, in this case sympathetic; the remarried mother who devoted the legacy of her first husband to the education of the promising sons; the early manifestations of devotion to learning; the detailed if not always accurate account of his studies; what one may call his recognition and advancement in the world [84] (this more, perhaps, in the tradition of the fall-from-greatness lives); his fulfillment of the pattern of the good bishop; [85] his meeting of the fatal challenge; [86] his battle; [87] his condemnation; [88] and his death.[89] The hagiographic pattern is apparent, too, in the set speeches of the hero, the sacred orations and pleas,[90] one might call them, going back like so much in the hagiographic tradition to the literary conventions of antiquity; in the summary of his virtues; [91] and in the careful relation of his story, particularly in the cause and circumstances of his death, not only to his namesake, Saint John the

Baptist, but to other saints and martyrs.[92] The author is quite aware of the tradition in which he is writing, though in the soberness and the precision of his procedure, one is reminded more of the early *Acta* of the martyrs than of the *Golden Legend*.

There is no suggestion of omen or premonition of greatness; there are no miraculous cures or conversions. For the greater part of the story the atmosphere is as sober as history, soberer, indeed, than most of the history of the period. There are a couple of narrow escapes, from poison and from shooting, the former a classic of hagiography from the life of Saint Benedict down, the second an innovation of the age of gunpowder.[93] "Providential," one might call the escapes, rather than "miraculous"; actually, as we shall see, more in the spirit of Foxe than of the *Golden Legend*. And the same is true of the retribution which so promptly overtook those responsible for the martyrdom, notably Anne Boleyn, Henry VIII, Cranmer, Cromwell, and Rich.[94] Again, the sixteenth-century attack on the miraculous spared retribution, and many who scoffed at the happy chances of the *Golden Legend* would have a grim satisfaction in Providence's avenging of innocent blood and bringing the persecutors of the saints to poetic justice.

Only at the end, when it comes to the martyrdom itself, does the author relax his sober self-vigilance. There are a number of touches here that invoke the hagiographical atmosphere. The first is a tiny thing, Fisher's opening of the New Testament with a prayer that his eyes might fall on the right text for his need. That prayer is answered with perhaps the text of all others most appropriate to Fisher's own nature and to his immediate need: "Haec est autem vita aeterna ut cognoscant te solum verum Deum et quem misisti Iesum Christum. Ego te clarificavi super terram, opus consummavi quod dedisti mihi ut faciam et nunc clarifica me tu, pater, apud temetipsum claritate quam habui priusquam . . ."[95] The second is the extraordinary accession of energy that came to the old man at the scene of his execution. The author has stressed the physical frailty of the victim, partly to underscore the effects of his lifelong asceticism, partly to emphasize the brutality of killing an old man already so far along the road to death. Indeed, like most of his contemporaries, he has exaggerated the age of Fisher, making him out to be a very old man, when the evidence would seem to indicate that he was not over sixty-five.[96] Yet frail and aged as he seemed, when he started up the steps of the scaffold, he went up with the speed and the strength of a young man. One remembers then, as the author surely intended one should, how in the oldest of the martyrologies the great miracle was the cheerfulness and confidence with which the martyrs met their fate. And the sun suddenly shining on the face of the old man, a touch of the hagiographic marvel familiar in countless paintings, is told with grave matter-of-factness.[97]

Of much the same symbolic quality are the other two marvels, narrated with the same sober homeliness. The first, clearly reminiscent of the scriptural story of his patron, tells how Anne Boleyn wished to see the head of her enemy and when it was brought to her, struck the dead lips, receiving an infection that left a scar that she bore to her own dying day.[98] The other is the remarkable lifelikeness of the parboiled head on the pole above London Bridge that stopped the crowds crossing there.[99] The sum total of these marvelous details is the triumph of the martyr in the oldest hagiographic tradition. This is the *Acta* developed with the homely fullness of nascent Tudor biography. It is a long way from the *Golden Legend*.

For the greatest of these Henrician martyrs, the record is much more abundant. Indeed, it is possible by going a little way into the next century to recapitulate in the development of the More legend the development of the whole of the preceding martyrological tradition from what might be called the prehagiographic record to the edge of the *Legenda Aurea*. For, unlike Fisher, More would be remembered today, even if he had never been a martyr. The greatest genius of his country in that day, is the claim that his biographers make for him again and again.[100] And even today the lineaments of his personality are better known than those of any of his contemporaries, with the exception of his King. For the picture of More does not have to be reconstructed from his works, as it has to be with so many literary personalities of that time. One of the greatest of his contemporaries has left it to us, Erasmus, especially in his famous letter of July 23, 1519, to Ulrich von Hutten.

The religious aspect of More's life was not what most impressed Erasmus, who after all had been a monk himself. It was More the humanist, the scholar and the wit, the man of great practical ability who used his eminent position for the patronage of the New Learning and the relief and encouragement of his friends, it was More the head and guide and teacher of his family, that fascinated Erasmus. In More, Erasmus found the old dream of the philosopher-statesman of Plato and the new one of the humanists come true. And in him Erasmus, who had so often been pinched and galled by circumstance, found a gracious plenitude that warmed his admiration to love. It is that man whom he presented to the humanist world of the Continent.[101]

That man is still to be glimpsed in the more limited arena of the *Ordo Condemnationis Thomae Mori,* which De Vocht believes to be a rough translation of the first version of the life written by More's nephew, afterward the distinguished judge of Mary's reign. And, a little muted by grief and caution, he is still to be seen in the elegant *Expositio* which De Vocht believes is the work of Erasmus.[102] And that man is still to be seen through the hagiographic radiance that invests the intimate personal memoir which William Roper, the husband of More's favorite daughter, Margaret, wrote some twenty years after the death of More, but which was published only in 1626 in Paris, *The Mirrour of Vertue in Worldly Greatnes, Or the Life of Syr Thomas More Knight, sometime Lo. Chancellour of England.* But now he is seen not only across the transforming tragedy but across the destruction of the whole world to which he belonged. Reading Roper, one thinks, on the lower level, of Castiglione's account of the vanished court of Urbino in *The Courtier,* where the brightness of the past shimmers through the memory of all the disaster that has intervened into a splendor that never was on this earth, nor could be. And, on the higher, one thinks of Plato's account of the death of Socrates. Not only Socrates but the whole world in which Socrates had lived had vanished, and the result was that Plato could present its triumph and its failure alike with that serene and ideal perfection possible only to the heroic scene that will not have to meet the disillusioning test of the morning after the crisis. Only of the dead may the hero-worshiper write with the certainty that is beyond complacency, and the pride which time divests of its arrogance.

There is possible, moreover, a certain impersonality that relieves the hero-worshiper of the onus of his too palpable weakness. There is no suggestion in Plato's *Phaedo* that here is a cause to be vindicated, or an example to be emulated. Nor is there in Roper's *More.* There was an aftermath to that story, grim and pathetic enough, but there is no suggestion of it in Roper's serene pages. It is with the man whose quality is beyond reach of attenuation that Roper is concerned. He does not in any way attempt to exploit it for sympathy for More's relatives, who were to pay their share for the vindication of his principles.[103] He does not even attempt to use the appeal of More's personality for the cause for which he died. Indeed, there is no suggestion in Roper's pages that there was a continuing cause. One might think that the specific issue for which More died had vanished from the world, and only the general remained, latent, like all the basic issues of experience. This is harder to understand than the author's absorption in his subject that made him dismiss the ensuing histories of More's family as irrelevant to the main effect of his theme, as they were, but it is, I think, explicable on one central count, and that is that the world of More had completely vanished, not only the physical but the moral and intellectual and emotional world. That peculiar blend of high Roman simplicity and dignity and English homeliness and humor that characterized this, the main figure of the early English Renaissance, might and probably did recur, but it was not to be found among the martyrs. Whether his son-in-law knew this, with that insight which his humility if not his intelligence gave him, is not easy to prove by anything he said, but one of the great fascinations of Roper's book is that he writes of these things which he had himself known as if they were quite as vanished for him as they are for us.

That is one of the secrets, too, of that Olympian simplicity and serenity that distinguish his account from those of the following period. In spite of the fact that his subject had shown from time to time an extraordinary prescience of the future, not, it should be added, of its triumphs, as in the case of most of the prophecies which men like to remember, but of its failures and its disasters,[104] Roper makes no effort to link up More's time with his own. His basic motive was simply to preserve a noble memory and bear his witness to what he had known and loved. For it cannot be stressed too much that this is a personal memoir, and at that a very special type of personal memoir, a memoir from out of the family which meant so much to More.[105] There is nothing of the professional writer, or even of the professional intellectual, about Roper, a fact that stands out most impressively when his account is compared with the accounts of his successors. This is most apparent in the capsule summaries of such relevant transactions in the great world as the disappointment of Wolsey over the papacy and the inception of "the king's business" as a scheme of revenge for the Emperor's responsibility for that disappointment.[106] It is not just that Roper took that whole business more simply than any modern historian would think of doing (more pretentious historians than he ever dreamed of being did, too, at that time), but his account shows that he saw the great world with the same directness and homely simplicity as the domestic world. His eye is for look and word and gesture, not for the diagrams which more intellectual men discern behind the shapes and colors of the sequence of events.

That is one of the reasons why he has been called naïve. Another reason is the role in which he has cast himself in the presentation of his relations with his father-in-law. That is almost always of a rather literal-minded, short-sighted young man whose chief function seems to be to give the wise and far-seeing More a chance to illumine him and us, a sort of hagiographic Dr. Watson, as it were. We must remember, too, that the man who writes this life of More is old Mr. Roper, the old Mr. Roper whom the author of Fisher's life was advised to consult,[107] who is looking back upon the folly and incomprehension of "sonne Roper" from the mature and experienced wisdom of a man now older even than the revered father-in-law of whom he is writing. But it is still true that only a man of a good deal of judgment or of uncommon taste would have been so sparing of his earlier folly, so reticent of his present superior vision. It is customary to say that Roper found help in the pattern of the classic saint's life for the very difficult business of organizing these personal reminiscences,[108] and that is true. From the first sentence of Roper's preface, which finds its kernel in "a man of singular vertue and of a clere unspotted consciens,"[109] to that wonderfully bare conclusion, "So passed Sir Thomas Moore out of this world to god, uppon the very same daye in which himself had most desired,"[110] the basic preoccupation is that of the martyr's life, albeit of a very special martyr, the man who mounted the unsteady scaffold smiling, with a jest: "I pray you, master Lieuetenaunte, see me salf uppe, and for my cominge downe let me shifte for my self."[111] Yet for all the jest, More knew that he was adding his mite to a great tradition. This Roper did not forget, as can be seen in his account of how More dressed himself in his best apparel and the lieutenant protested, "sayenge that he that should have it was but a Javill.

"'What, master Leiuetenaunt,' quoth he, 'shall I accompte him a Javill that shall doe me his day so singuler a benefitt? Nay, I assure you, were it clothe of gold, I wolde accompt it well bestowed on him, as St Ciprian did, who gave his executioner thirtie peeces of gould.' And albeit at length, throughe master Lieuetenauntes importunate persuasion, he altered his apparell, yeat after thexample of that holy martir St Ciprian, did he, of that litle money that was lefte him, send one Angell of gold to his executioner." [112]

One wonders how much Roper, like More, had had that ancient story of Saint Cyprian, one of the purest and the noblest of all time, in his mind throughout.

This general hagiographic approach governs Roper's selection of his material, leading him to say nothing of More's friendship with Erasmus, though he does cite in his preface the praise of Erasmus, more eloquent perhaps, but beside Roper's homespun a little ornate.[113] Nor does he speak of all the throng of visitors from home and abroad, except those who, like King Henry [114] and the Duke of Norfolk, play a part in the tragedy.[115] Nor does he say very much of all that colorful and delightful life of the house and the garden along the river with its view of the city below. But he is quite unpretentiously explicit about More's austerities and his care to conceal them,[116] about his fidelity to religious observance,[117] and his contribution to the intellectual defense of the Church,[118] about his early and late attraction to the contemplative life.[119]

But when it comes to the miraculous, Roper is as sober as the author of the life of Fisher. One miraculous cure, that of Margaret, is reported, with careful accounting for the means thereof in the remembrance of the healing "glister" in prayer.[120] And the appropriateness of the day of his death, Saint Thomas of Canterbury's "Even" and the Utas or Octave of Saint Peter, is noted, as More had noted it.[121]

But though Roper is even more sparing of the miraculous than his colleague, the author of the life of Fisher, he does admit one element of the *Golden Legend*, and that is the gift of prophecy. Clearly, as Roper looked back upon his conversations with More, one of the things that most impressed him was the way in which More had foreseen how things were likely to go when Roper himself had not had the slightest idea, and most even of those older and wiser than he were not much more alert. There is More's early anxiety about the consequences of the "king's matter."[122] Even more impressive is his great care in the midst of professional prosperity and domestic felicity to awaken his family to the possibility of a less comfortable future.[123] But of all these prophetic insights, the most remarkable is that implied in More's prayer that the day might not come when those who now sat on top, "treading heretikes under our feete like antes," would be glad to "let them have their churches quietly to themselfes, so that they wold be contente to let us have ours quietly to our selves." On this occasion Roper permits himself one of his rare rebuttals, "By my troth, sir, it is very desperately spoken!"[124] Perhaps in the light of what had happened since, that protest of his, which almost everyone at that time, heretic and orthodox alike, would have echoed, seemed ironic. But to Roper, who, it may be remembered, tells no stories of divine retribution, that too, now twenty years later, must have seemed prophetic.

It is not easy to tell how far Roper thought this prescience of More's the gift of prophecy of the saints, and how far he deemed it the evidence of his great wisdom. Certainly when More told the young man who had so proudly watched the King put his arm about his neck and walk familiarly with him, that the King would not hesitate to take his head if it would win him one castle in the current war with France,[125] he was merely expressing an estimate of his master's character which was to prove only too correct. And when he warned his friends, the Bishops of Durham, Bath, and Winchester, surely much more experienced men than young Roper, of the hazards of the seemingly nominal compliance of marching in the coronation procession of Queen Anne,[126] he may only have seen that very rapidly moving and complicated situation more steadily and whole than the wisest of his friends. Whatever Roper thought of it all, there is no question of the impressiveness of the cumulative effect. It has been commonly suggested that Roper had a remarkable memory; how remarkable has not been always appreciated. To remember across twenty years not only what his father-in-law said, but how he said it, the very inflection of his voice as revealed in his syntax, is a very remarkable feat. True, he had More's own writing to help him, and no writer was ever more constantly himself than More. Even at the end, in *A Dialoge of Com-*

fort, when he was most deliberately trying to rise above himself, he cannot, if he would, keep out the homely and breathtakingly apposite story, the flash of dramatic dialogue, the wryly humorous comparison, the ironic turn. All this Roper had to refresh his memory, and up to around some ten years before he presumably wrote his story, he had the help of his wife. With her he must often have talked over these things, doubtless finding in the later consequences much help for understanding what had once seemed so puzzling.

And yet some of Roper's speeches are pretty much the most characteristic utterances of More that we have, and some of them for dramatic incisiveness and grace are so fine that even Shakespeare would not be shamed by them. As A. W. Reed long ago pointed out, More himself not only had a flair for the dramatic, but his house at Chelsea must have been "an academy of dramatic writing and thinking." [127] Roper had remarkable opportunities, but he must also have had remarkable aptitude to profit from them. Only a very unusual sense of the dramatic could keep him from blurring another man's lines, to take it at the lowest.

Roper, also, has a sense of the scene. Take, for instance, the prophecy of the hero's future greatness from the lips of Cardinal Morton, close to the beginning of the life. It is introduced by that unforgettable picture of the brilliant boy stepping into the Christmas play, and without any rehearsal creating a part, on the spur of the moment, more entertaining to the audience than all the carefully prepared witticisms of the players. [128] And, even more important, Roper has a sense of dramatic pattern, of the thrust of action and the revelation of its meaning. When it comes to the final act, how dramatically Roper builds up his climax! How he rises above even the high rafters of Westminster Hall in that speech of More's when he had been condemned and could at last speak out fully. To the Lord Chief Justice, who had marveled that he should stand out against the bishops and the universities and the best learned of the land on the acts of Parliament making the King the Supreme Head of the Church of England, he answered:

> . . . I nothinge doubte but that, thoughe not in this realme, yeat in Christendome aboute, of thes well lerned Bishoppes and vertuous men that are yeat alive, they be not the fewer parte that be of my mind therein. But if I should speake of those whiche already be dead, of whom many be nowe holy sainctes

in heaven, I am very sure it is the farre greater parte of them that, all the while [they] lived, thoughte in this case that waye that I thinck nowe. And therefore am I not bounde, my lord, to conforme my consciens to the Councell of one Realme against the generall Councell of Christendome.[129]

Higher than that it would not seem that even More could go, but after the judgment had been given, which, horrible as it was, Roper did not stop to describe, More went even above the whole of Christendom with his reminder of Paul, who had consented to the stoning of Stephen, the most exquisitely tactful allusion he could have drawn from all the *Golden Legend*:

More have I not to say, my Lordes, but that like as the blessed Apostle St Pawle, as we read in thactes of the Apostles, was present, and consented to the death of St Stephen, and kepte their clothes that stoned him to deathe, and yeat be they [nowe] both twayne holy Sainctes in heaven, and shall continue there frendes for ever, So I verily [truste], and shall therefore right hartelye pray, that thoughe your lordshippes have now [here] in earthe bine Judges to my condemnacion, we may yeat hereafter in heaven meerily all meete together, to our everlasting salvacion.[130]

After that there is no surprise in that last scene, which Roper sums up so briefly, knowing as he did from all his years with More that even at his last minute on earth, he was thinking of another man's nervousness and how it might be relieved: "Then desired he all the people thereaboute to pray for him, and to beare witness with him that he should [nowe there] suffer death in and for the faith of the holy chatholik churche. Whiche done, he kneled downe, and after his prayers said, turned to thexecutioner, and with a cheerefull countenaunce spake [thus] to him: 'Plucke upp thy spirites, man, and be not afrayde to do thine office; my necke is very shorte; take heede therefore thow strike not awrye, for savinge of thine honestye.'"[131]

Needless to say, all the later lives of More are based on Roper, even though they will fill in the historic background with detail and understanding beyond Roper's resources, and will round out his memories with the results of a more systematic and ample research. The unique character of Roper's achievement is at once apparent when we turn to his immediate successor, the first formal biographer of More, Nicholas Harpsfield, the author of *The Life and Death of Sr Thomas Moore, knight*, that like Roper's volume circulated in manuscript through these years. Harpsfield was a very different sort of man from

Roper. According to Acton, he was the most eminent adherent of the old faith who in 1559 neither obeyed the Acts of Uniformity nor fled.[132] To Harpsfield, Chambers accorded the distinction of having been the first modern to compile in the English tongue a complete biography, and so present an all-round picture of his hero.[133] It was, of course, a much more ambitious undertaking than Roper's, an undertaking possible only to a man of Harpsfield's training and experience.

Yet his primary purpose was not, any more than Roper's, to write history but to compose a devotional work for the edification of his readers. Harpsfield admired More greatly, but from his own larger view of the issues of the time, he saw that the argument which More's adversaries had used against him — why should he alone of all men refuse to accept the judgment of the wisest and greatest of the realm? — was an argument still used against those who had refused to accept the Henrician changes. And to meet that still-vital argument he went beyond the position of Roper, that here was the purest conscience of his time, to the position of the Paris News Letter, of its author, Erasmus (if we accept De Vocht's argument),[134] that More was the brightest genius of his country, and that his taking up the position he did and holding it to the death was the act of not only the finest spirit of his time, but of the most penetrating genius of the realm.[135] He, therefore, went beyond the professional career and the passion of More to include the literary work which, after the admiration of Erasmus, had given him his international reputation.

Harpsfield himself was a humanist, as is shown perhaps a little incongruously in the praise which he gives to More's daughter Margaret, whom he styles not only appropriately as our Fabiola, Marcella, Paula, and Eustochium, but also, somewhat surprisingly, as our Sappho, Hypatia, Damo, and Cornelia.[136] So he tried to bring before his reader the brilliant wit and the humanist to whom Roper had hardly done justice. One of the finest things in Harpsfield's book is his description of the stimulating effect which More had on his friends through his conversation: "But he was therein so sweete and pleasaunt that there was no man of so dull and heavie disposition that he did not with his companie quicken, refreshe and exhilerate."[137] Harpsfield had a wider view than Roper of the catastrophe which overtook More, comparing the Henrician revolt with what had long before happened to the Greek Church, and what was then happening in Germany, and pointing out that in neither case had supremacy in religion been claimed by any lay prince.[138] Desperate heretics he found the greatest enemy to the peace of a commonwealth,[139] and the intercession of More and his fellow martyrs, the reasonable explanation of the speed of the restoration of religion under Queen Mary and Pole, an evidence that God had cast a pitiful eye upon the realm of England[140] — an ironic touch in view of what was so soon to happen to that restoration, and to Harpsfield himself, who was to spend many years in prison before his death in 1575.[141]

Artistically, Harpsfield had a much more sophisticated sense of form than Roper, a sense of form which led him to rearrange his materials and to organize them so as to make a readable and comprehensible whole.[142] And where Roper is often content to let the speech of More speak for itself, as in that last speech on the scaffold, Harpsfield underscores the point, as in this case explaining that More was the first layman in England to die a martyr for the defense and preservation of the unity of the Catholic Church, and the blessed proto-martyr of all the laity for the preservation of the unity of the Church.[143] Again, where Roper lets More's prescience about the future, as we have seen, illustrate itself in a number of anecdotes that suggest that he was quite aware of More's extraordinary foresight, if nothing more, Harpsfield does not hesitate to call attention to and emphasize More's ability to see the troubles that were coming upon them.[144]

But Harpsfield also carries the prophetic element in More's career further than Roper would seem to be willing to go. For example, he says that what More said as to the future of Anne Boleyn might well hang upon some private and secret revelation and divine information, rather than worldly foresight.[145] And he does not hesitate to say that the purpose of *A Dialoge of Comfort*, written in prison, was to prepare the minds of the English for the persecution to come and to help them withstand it.[146]

Harpsfield's lack of Roper's apparent diffidence about the miraculous is further evidenced in his suggestion that in the recovery of Margaret from sickness God seemed to show More a miraculous token of his special favor.[147] Here we are moving into the traditional psychology of the *Golden Legend*, even though Harpsfield's general demeanor is that of the careful and painstaking historian, and his style on the whole, though wanting in Roper's very individual charm, moves with a clarity and a homely directness that we do not usually expect in the self-conscious literary writing of these middle decades of the sixteenth century.

Both the scholarly and the hagiographical tendencies of Harpsfield are carried further in the third important life of More of the sixteenth century, that of Stapleton. In this life we come closer to the Catholic martyr lives of the seventeenth century in several respects. In the first place, it is the work of an exile, long settled on the Continent, written not only for the English but for the Continental public. It was published at Douai, the famous center of activity for the Catholic exiles, in 1588. It was written in Latin, and it found no translator until Hallett in 1928. Hallett deliberately made use of the language of More's own English works and of well-known phrases from Roper, but wisely refrained from any sacrifice of sense to antiquarianism.[148] The result does justice to the power and scope of Stapleton's work, but there is the inevitable loss of the personal flavor one feels in the English lives.

Stapleton's approach to his subject is apparent from the very title of his work, *The Life and Illustrious Martyrdom of Sir Thomas More, Formerly Lord Chancellor of England*, and from the additional fact that this life is one of a series of three, *Tres Thomae*, the other two Thomases being Thomas the Apostle and Thomas à Becket. This frankly hagiographic approach is maintained in Stapleton's careful prefatory exposition of the motives which led him to write this life: "first, the glory of God, and my love for the Catholic Church, for his loyalty to which More laid down his life; next, pity for my country in its present deep affliction and distress (More, in his lifetime, was its chief glory and proudest boast); then also the consolation my work will give to right-minded men and the just confusion it will cause to the wicked."[149] The latter is of course a far cry from Roper, but we must not forget that Stapleton is a leader in the Church Militant at one of the centers of the English Catholic resistance on the Continent.

Stapleton is, also, a very systematic writer, as is apparent in his explanation that he has thought it wise to divide up his material into chapters in order to aid the reader's memory and to "ensure order and method in the development of the narrative."[150] He makes use of Roper and Harpsfield, as he explains in his preface, but also draws upon both the Latin and the English works of More, and the reminiscences of his fellow exiles who knew More, notably John and Margaret Clement, John and Dorothy Harris, John Heywood, and William Rastell. And he has taken pains to search the works of contemporary writers, particularly Erasmus, for references to More.[151]

Early in his biography Stapleton struck the keynote which Harpsfield had struck, by quoting what Colet had said as to England's having but one genius, More.[152] And he proceeded to fit More into the literary as well as the political framework of his time, with an eye, it should be added, to the foreign audience as well as his countrymen.[153] Stapleton then went to considerable pains to reconstruct the context of More's time, now of course quite beyond the reach of the memories of even the old Mr. Ropers of the day. An example is his explanation of More's giving up the idea of entering religion, in spite of his attraction to the contemplative ideal: "for our religious communities had become lax, as the utter destruction and desolation of the monastic state, which followed so soon afterwards, showed with sufficient clearness."[154]

It is obvious that Stapleton sympathizes with More's estimate of the superiority of the contemplative life to the active, praising Archbishop Warham's resignation of the chancellorship because he wished for leisure.[155] But Stapleton is clearly aware of the activist temper of his own time, and does full justice to the brilliance of More's career of public service. He admits that More "took some little pleasure" in the life of the court "in so far as it was a school of goodness and piety, as it certainly was during the first twenty years of Henry's reign."[156] And in his report of More's views on the education of women, including quotations from his letters, he shows a sympathetic grasp of an aspect of More's humanism which Roper himself seems to have forgotten,[157] and he pays Margaret Roper the tribute of a chapter to herself.[158]

But all this is in the interest of something other than the great Renaissance figure, as he explains when he addresses himself to the crucial subject, " The Origin of the King's Anger": "For I have written his Life not to draw his portrait as a man of rank, learning, wit, or high position, not as a good father, a wise ruler of a household, a just judge, or a man of letters, but above all as a saint and a glorious martyr for truth and right." [159] And he goes on to explain how all this worldly success enhanced the merit of More's sacrifice, for the more temptations the martyr overcomes, the more powerful his example and the greater the praise of the Church, and that, he observes in passing, is why in the public litanies of the Church chiefly those of noble rank are commemorated. [160] And later, with a certain hard-headed realism which is characteristic of Stapleton in anything that touches on the area of contemporary controversy, he adds that there is a special advantage in the martyrdom of More as compared, say, with that of the Carthusians, for the evil might think the clergy died for the privilege of their class, but that no such suspicion can fall on More. [161]

Yet Stapleton hardly needs to remind us of this basic hagiographic purpose of his, for the very organization of his life from the beginning recalls the traditional hagiographic pattern. He begins with the parentage of More and follows this account with the classic portents that foretell the future glory of his hero. The first of these is the dream of the bride who on her marriage night saw upon her wedding ring the faces of her children, one shining with splendor beyond all the rest. [162] Another is the story of the child's escape from drowning when his nurse was carrying him across a ford, and here, as so often, Stapleton recalls a parallel to the episode in his hero's life or the trait in his character in a story from the calendar, in this case a story told of Saint Morontos. [163] Likewise in the classic hagiographic spirit he recounts the youthful More's struggles after perfection, including the wearing of a hair shirt, and watching, and fasting. [164] And at the height of More's public career, he relates how, though he cleverly concealed it, "as regards the service of God, he lived almost the life of a monk." [165] And from that love of God, he derives the efficacy of More's prayers as revealed in the story of Roper's conversion from Lutheranism, Margaret's recovery from the sweating sickness, Elizabeth Dauncy's deathbed vision of her escape from eternal pain through More's intercession, and especially the recovery of the melancholy citizen of Winchester whose despair More had relieved by his prayers. [166] And, like his predecessors, Stapleton stressed More's remarkable foresight, instancing his apparent prophecy of the change in the King's character, the persecution of religion, and above all the fate of Anne Boleyn. [167]

Stapleton is mindful of the classic pattern of the drama of the martyr when he describes More's first examination as "The first act of the tragedy that brought such shame to the King, but such glory to More," and then goes on to show his reader "how carefully and religiously the brave soldier of Christ prepared himself for the combat," in such matters as greater devotion to the defense of the Church against rising heresies, and redoubling of his austerities.[168] So again of the end of the trial, "After the judge had sentenced him, More knew that he was called to the grace of martyrdom, for hitherto he had been in doubt whether Almighty God would bestow upon him the favor of so high a vocation." [169]

And the execution brings its dramatic aftermath. Henry was playing at dice when the news was brought to him, and with a sharp word of blame to Anne, he retired "and shed bitter tears." [170] And there was the miraculous, too, in Dorothy Colley's finding in what she had thought an empty purse the exact money needed for More's shroud.[171] Stapleton, also, cited proudly the praise of the great and the learned who mourned More and praised him, notably, Cardinal Pole, Erasmus, John Cochlaeus, Paul Jovius, William Paradinus, the Lutheran John Rivius, and the Emperor Charles.[172] But the finest tribute of all was the encouragement of his example to his troubled countrymen: "I can remember quite well, and many others will bear me out, that when we were boys, More's fame and his illustrious martyrdom were constantly the subject of our talk, and fired our zeal for the Catholic faith." [173]

Compared with Stapleton's achievement, that of the last life of the century is a modest one. Indeed, Ro. Ba., otherwise unidentified, is most explicit as to his obligations to his predecessors and most modest about his own claims to attention.[174] But in spite of his modesty, Ro. Ba. has his own contributions to make to the story of More, and his own distinctive style and flavor. And it should not be forgotten that he writes in English, making available to the reader who was not at home with Latin the fruit of Stapleton's researches, for instance. That his contribution was appreciated is apparent from the number of manuscripts that survive of his work.[175] Ro. Ba. quite explicitly and self-consciously approached his subject as a saint's life, as a model for our self-criticism and our encouragement, as he explained, "for fitlie it runneth with the Currant of our noble nature not to rest in any inferiour brooke, but onely in the ocean from whence it first sprang." [176] He is thoroughly conversant with the literature of his subject, citing a considerable list of writers on the saints, Eusebius, Jerome, Palladius, Sulpicius, Simeon Metaphrastes, Beda, Usardus, Ado, Lippomanus, Surius, Mombritius — needless to say, a mixed lot of quite uneven merit.[177]

And he is quite aware, too, of the current criticism of the legends in English by "both grave and learned men who wish they were suppressed, and in theire places either the tomes of Surius translated, or some speciall and choice lines, fittest for our Countrie and tyme, out of the holy ancient fathers or other faithfull authors selected and compiled into one corps."[178] But in spite of all this there is still a good deal of the enthusiasm of the popular hagiographer in the terms in which he presents his offering to help fill that want, "the historie of a Confessour, Doctour and Martyr, so famous, so learned, so glorious, that what in the vast Ocean of Anceant recordes may be found to pleasure or profitt, here in this one life shalbe comprehended."[179]

On the other hand, Ro. Ba. has something of his own to add on the more human side of his saint. There is the pleasant little Judgment-of-Solomon story of the beggar woman's dog, which had been stolen and presented to his wife, and which, when the beggar woman claimed it, he took to the middle of the hall, bidding his wife at the upper end, and the beggar woman at the lower, call it by name. When the dog ran to the beggar woman, he adjudged it hers, and giving her the dog and a French crown, asked her to give it to his wife, which she did.[180] And at the end, where Ro. Ba. should be giving an account of his hero's virtues, he inserts between his hero's diet and his epitaph a paragraph on his "great pleasure to behold the forme and fashion of beastes and foules."[181] Nor does he hesitate to interject now and then his own comment on the matter he is relating, as when he says of Henry's making More his Lord Chancellor: "It may seem strange that Maister More should be thus advanced, for he alwaies shewed him selfe to have more respecte to [the] weale publique then to the kings gaine or pleasure. But it followeth that either the kinge was at this tyme a mervelous good prince, or that he had not that experience of his upright and plaine delinge, and this can I hardly beleeve."[182]

Although Ro. Ba. is so modest about his contribution to the legend, he has his own direct and homely power of storytelling that can on occasion rise to something dramatic and moving. There is Henry's reaction to the news that More was indeed dead: "He turned hym to Queene Ann, who then stood by, wistlie looking upon her, said, 'Thou, thou, art the cause of this mans death.' So presently went to his Chamber, and there wept full bitterlie." [183] And the story of the melancholy Winchester man whom More had saved from temptations of despair, and who had relapsed while More was in prison, fine as it is in Hallett's translation of Stapleton,[184] Ro. Ba. betters in the more dramatic form in which he tells it:

But when he hard that Sir Thomas was condemned, he poasted from winchester, hoping at least to see hym as he should goe to execution; and so determined to speake with hym, come what would of it. And for that cause, [he] placed hym selfe in the way, and at his comming by, he thrust through the throng, and with a loud voice said, "Maister More, doe you knowe me? I pray you, for our Lordes sake, help me. I am as ill troubled as ever I was." Sir Thomas aunswered, "I remember thee full well. Goe thy waies in peace, and pray for me, and I will not faile to pray for thee." And from that tyme after, so long as he lived, he was never troubled with that manner of tentation.[185]

The man who wrote that is not unworthy to close the line of those who, still faithful to the faith of their fathers, tried to bring the example of their own greatest martyrs to the inspiration and the comfort of their suffering countrymen.

FOXE'S
BOOK OF MARTYRS

But in the Henrician period there were, of course, Protestant martyrs as well as Catholic, for Henry was determined to maintain the traditional position on such much-controverted issues of the time as the English Books and the nature of the Sacrament of the Altar. Indeed, on certain occasions Protestants and Catholics suffered together in the Henrician executions. For instance, on July 30, 1540, two days after the death of Cromwell, six were put to death at Smithfield, the three Lutherans being burned for heresy, and the three Catholics hanged, drawn, and quartered for treason.[1] The Protestants found their record, too, in the beginning under circumstances not so dissimilar to those of the Catholics, though in the end the result was to be very different. Somewhere about the year 1552 a book about these martyrs was begun in England by John Foxe.[2]

Born in 1517 at Boston in Lincolnshire, John Foxe was in many ways a representative figure of his generation. Like Caxton he was of middle-class origin, but his early promise of mind and piety secured him a better intellectual opportunity in an Oxford education, culminating presently in a fellowship at his college, Magdalen.[3] In these early years Foxe shared not a little in the enthusiasms of the contemporary humanists, but it was theology, particularly that involved in the main controversies of the time, that engaged his deepest interest, and he emerged from this period of study a convinced Protestant, presently to be faced with a good deal of suspicion that resulted finally in his leaving Oxford and the academic life.[4] After much anxiety and privation (he had married in 1547), he found refuge as a tutor to the executed Earl of Surrey's children in the household of the Lutheran Duchess of Richmond, and began to publish translations and tracts of his own in the Reforming cause.[5] As an active and already well-known Protestant leader, he found it necessary to seek refuge on the Continent in 1554.[6]

When after some wandering and uncertainty, and considerable financial difficulty, Foxe finally established himself at Basel, he resumed his work on the book already under way. As originally planned, it was to include not only the more recent sufferers but, also, the Lollard martyrs, in whom Foxe saw the precursors of the movement that had burst forth in Luther's actions in 1517. The materials for the first part of that book had been gathered, and a rough draft made, when Foxe judged it wise to join the exiles overseas. Safe in Germany, with that sense of timing which was characteristic of him, Foxe decided to print at once, and the result was the Latin book published at Strasbourg on August 31, 1554, *Commentarii Rerum in Ec-clesia Gestarum, maximarumque per totam Europam persecutionem a Wiclevi temporibus ad hanc usque aetatem descriptio*, in which Foxe made the history of the Lollards known to the Continent as well as England.[7] His plans to proceed to the history of the Henrician martyrs were delayed by other writing, and by the news of the breaking-out of the Marian persecution in the burning of the first Marian martyr, John Rogers, on February 4, 1555. So at Basel he began to collect the materials on the growing persecution. It was, of course, a difficult and hazardous business, but already at Strasbourg, where Foxe's first book had been published, Edmund Grindal and a company of English exiles were gathering materials for an English book which they were projecting; and from them Foxe was able to obtain copies of examinations, disputations, information about lives and deaths, in other words, the classic raw materials of the martyr story.[8] The exiles at Strasbourg had planned an English book on the Marian martyrs, but the increase in their numbers and the difficulty of establishing the facts on the humble and obscure delayed that project, so that Foxe, who had intended to wait for the completion of their work, went ahead with the first part of his Latin account of the recent persecution, and published it at Basel in August of 1559: *Rerum in*

Ecclesia Gestarum, quae postremis et periculosis his temporibus even-erunt . . . Pars Prima, in qua primum de rebus per Angliam et Scotiam gestis, atque in primis de horrenda sub Maria nuper regina persecutione narratio continetur.[9] This he intended to follow up with a second part upon the recent Continental martyrs, but he never did. Even the account of the Marian persecution was left a fragment, ending with the execution of Cranmer on March 21, 1556, and merely listing the names of the later victims as Foxe had been able to learn of them.[10]

In a certain sense one may say that the rhyming martyrs' calendar which Thomas Brice published in 1559, so promptly after Elizabeth's accession, was a harbinger of Foxe's great work: *A Compendious Register in Metre, conteining the names, and pacient suffryngs of the membres of Jesus Christ; and the tormented; and cruelly burned within Englande, since the death of our famous kyng, of immortall memory Edwarde the sixte: to the entrance and beginnyng of the raign, of our sovereigne and derest Lady Elizabeth, . . .*[11] In the dedicatory epistle to Lord Par, Brice modestly expressed his confidence that one more learned than he would do justice to the theme,[12] and in the address to the gentle reader he repeated his confidence, this time describing the theme more specifically: "the martyrdome, and paciente sufferynges of Christes electe membres, and also of the tyrannical Tragedies, of the unmercifull ministers of Sathan."[13] Apparently "a good gentleman" had gathered together the information which Brice used for his rude rhymes.[14] These were arranged in the order of a calendar, according to the dates of martyrdom when known.[15] While Brice deplored the killing of the humble and the helpless, women and, in particular, virgins, in his address to the reader he stressed what was for the Reforming movement much more important, the killing of the preachers, "suche innocent lyvers, perfect preachers, and worthye counselours, learned ministers, diligent divines, perfecte personages, and faythfull shepherdes." These victims he likened to the martyrs of old, and their persecutors to the Roman emperors.[16]

The literary quality of the work may be judged from the opening stanza for the tenth and eleventh of June, 1555:

> When worthy Wattes, with constant crie
> Continued in, the flamyng fier

When Simson, Hawkes, and John Ardlie
Did tast the tyrantes, raging yre
When Chamberlaine, was put to death
We wisht for our, Elizabeth.[17]

The last line becomes a refrain, to be repeated at the end of each of the sixty-five stanzas until the triumphant conclusion of the third stanza under November, 1558: "God sent us our, Elizabeth." [18] Doubtless Brice achieved what he set out to win for the lives of the martyrs, "that by pleasantnes of reading, and easines of prices they myghte be the moore largely blowen and knowen." [19] His rhymes would certainly help, too, to create an audience for Foxe.

The death of Mary in November of 1558 had made it possible for the exiles to return, but Foxe did not arrive in England until October of 1559. There he became absorbed in collecting the details of the recent horror. But it was not until mid-1561 that he made his agreement with the printer John Day and embarked on the eighteen months of concentrated work under pressure that was to yield the nearly eighteen-hundred-page tome which was published on March 20, 1563, at about the time the Council of Trent was winding up its work.[20]

Nothing could be in sharper contrast to the large, easy serenity of the *Golden Legend* than the passionately controversial excitement of Foxe's great book. The very title itself is the swift thrust of indictment, comprehending pretty nearly all the main heads of his attack: *Actes and Monuments of These Latter and Perillous Dayes, touching matters of the Church, wherein ar comprehended and described the great persecutions and horrible troubles, that have bene wrought and practised by the Romishe Prelates, speciallye in this Realme of England and Scotlande, from the yeare of our Lorde a thousande, unto the tyme nowe present. Gathered and collected according to the true copies and wrytinges certificatorie as wel of the parties them selves that suffered, as also out of the Bishops Registers, which wer the doers therof.*[21]

The title page of the first edition defines the approach and sets the tone of the enterprise. It is an eloquent page with its woodcut embellishment, beginning at the top with a vivid Last Judgment. To the right of the Judges are the bearded Protestants in long robes, with crowns and palms, blowing their trumpets triumphantly aloft; to the left the generally smooth-faced, shaven-polled monks of Catholics, still puffing at their trumpets but falling downward, dragged by the devils clutching at them. And lest there should be any doubt of the significance of this iconography, there are below little pictures presenting the type of religious activities that led to these dramatic conclusions of heaven or hell, on the one side the Protestants at the stake, and, on the other, the Catholics at Mass. And below these in turn is another pair of pictures, representing, this time, both men and women listening to preaching, the one group with Bibles, the other with rosaries in their hands, the one group flanked by kneeling figures before the Tetragrammaton in a glory, the other by a procession which a very smug little devil is watching with his tongue hanging out. It is not especially delicate or finished art, but there is no mistaking some fine touches of the contemporary iconography, like the expression on the Protestant preacher's face, grave and venerable, and the smile on the face of the preaching friar, who looks as if he were telling one of those amusing stories that so engaged the attention of the friars' less-learned followers and so shocked their more sober-minded adversaries. But these details are only of incidental importance. It is the total effect that counts, and that is unmistakable.

It is eminently fitting, too, that the first of the series of addresses which Foxe put before his great work in 1563 should be a Latin *Eucharisticon* or Thanksgiving to Jesus Christ, the Saviour, giving thanks for the vindication of the martyrs and their cause, praying for grace for their sons to follow their example, and dedicating both the book and its author to Christ.[22]

As we shall see presently, Foxe was to reject vigorously the suggestion that there was anything in common between his book and the despised *Golden Legend*. But that Foxe was not entirely unaware of the possibility of making an effective substitution for the rejected *Golden Legend* is apparent in "The Kalender," followed by "An almanacke for 31.yeares," very much in the Primer fashion, which he prefixed to his book.[23] Of the ancient calendar, the foundation and the framework of the *Golden Legend*, the survivals are few, substantially those of the latest of the Reformed primers and the Book of Common Prayer,[24] for example, for January, the Circumcision on the first, the Epiphany on the sixth, and the Conversion of Paul on the twenty-fifth; for June, the Nativity of Saint John the Baptist on the twenty-first, and Peter and Paul Apostles on the twenty-ninth; for

December, Thomas the Apostle on the twentieth, the Nativity of Our Lord on the twenty-fifth, Stephen Martyr on the twenty-sixth, John Evangelist on the twenty-seventh, and Childer Mass (Holy Innocents) on the twenty-eighth. Of what might be called the non-apostolic saints, Saint George Martyr survives for April 23 and Mary Magdalene for July 22.[25]

But the empty spaces have been filled with a whole new set of confessors and martyrs, so distributed that no date is left blank. Sometimes the day of death coincided with the calendar commemoration; more often not. The day of the year is in general given in the last column of the calendar. For example, John Wycliffe, preacher martyr, is put opposite the second of January, with no day of death and the year 1387. John Aston, confessor, on the third is likewise given simply the year 1382, and so are the half-dozen fifteenth-century martyrs assigned to the opening days of the month, with the exception of one Swinderby, a priest martyr, who is given neither day of death nor year, and Richard Silbecke, martyr, who is given both, January 14, 1413. The sixteenth-century martyrs for January all have death dates (except for John Philpot and Thomas Stevens on the thirty-first, under the year 1557), but these death dates are different from the commemorations for the obvious reason that they are crowded into certain dates, often of group executions. Most of the entries are English, but there are exceptions, conspicuous among them: Zizka, a confessor, for February 5; and D. Martin Luther, confessor, for the eighteenth of the same month of February (the day of his death); John Hus, martyr, for May 2; and Hieronimus Savonarola for the third of May.[26] Perhaps the most interesting group of these foreign commemorations is that bracketed together with the label "confes" for December 30: Pico della Mirandola, Erasmus of Rotterdam, Martin Bucer, Paul Fagius, Philipp Melanchthon, Peter Martyr.[27] Some of the English martyrs are, as it were, starred by being entered in a different type, like that used for the survivals of the old calendar, as, for example, the series for October: the eighteenth, Luke Evangelist; the nineteenth, Nicholas Ridley, bishop martyr; and the twentieth, Hugh Latimer, bishop martyr; or for December: in the same type as the other major commemorations of that month, the final one of the month on the thirty-first, and the final of the calendar, King Edward VI, confessor.[28] From the Reforming point of view of

1563 these choices are understandable, even if not all of them were to be ratified by history. More puzzling are Reginald Pecock, bishop confessor, for February 11, and Eleanor Cobham, gentlewoman confessor, for February 13.[29] But the great majority of the martyrs are those of the tragic years 1555 to 1558. Of these the greatest concentration is for June, some sixty-odd martyrs for these years alone, to say nothing of a number of confessors. Some of these entries for martyrs are moving in their near anonymity: "A merchants servant . . . Elizabeth a blynde mayde . . . Alexander Hofmans man . . . Thomasina Woods mayde."[30]

But whatever the limitations of Foxe's information and the contemporary judgment of religious alignment, Foxe succeeded in filling up the calendar beyond the dreams of his most ambitious predecessors, and this not with the often dubious figures of the *Golden Legend* but with what, he was sure, were solid Protestant martyrs. The calendar had been shrinking in recent years almost to the vanishing point in the English primers and prayer books;[31] Foxe reversed the process with éclat.

It is significant that Foxe makes no mention of the *Golden Legend* in any of the English prefaces to his work. It is rather the name of Eusebius that he invokes in his address to the Queen, a happy choice which made it possible for him to remind her of Constantine's patronage of the selfless bishop of Caesarea, who asked only that he might have the imperial authority and sponsorship to collect the records of the martyrs of the persecutions then happily ended; and to pay graceful and grateful tribute to her ending of the late persecutions; and to plead for proper remembrance of the more recent martyrs who "geve their bloud in the same cause and like quarell."[32] The preface "To the Persecutors of Gods truth, commonly called *Papistes*," calls upon them to contemplate the cruelty now revealed and to repent of the inherent wickedness made manifest in that cruelty.[33] The more general prefatory notice, obviously designed for the general reader, reveals its orientation in the title: "A declaration concerning the utilitie and profite *of this history*."[34] The apologies for publication of Elizabethan writers are often ingenious, but the general approach of the address is for its day a surprising one. In the light of the "infinite multitude of bookes, dayly put foorth everywehre," Foxe is afraid his undertaking may seem "superfluous and needeles." He assures us that he too deplores "this insatiable gredines of wryting and printing" as much as any man. But when he weighed against this consideration "so great an history of so famous doinges, as this our age dayly hath ministred unto us, by the patient sufferinges of the worthy martyres: I thought it not to be neglected, that the precious monumentes of so many matters, and men moste meete to be recorded and registryred in bookes, should lye buried by my fault in the pit of oblivion." [35] He then goes on to remind his readers of the value of the martyrs' lives in terms that recall not only the traditional grounds for honoring the martyrs but, also, the Renaissance love of praising famous men and the Aristotelian faith in the moral value of contemplating the fates of tragic heroes. As against the godless and the Epicures, there is a witness to the rule of God in them "in whose lyfe appeared a certaine force of divine nature," and in their deaths even greater value, including "the manyfold sense and feling of the holy ghost, which they learned in many of their comfortes, and we by them." Like Aristotle he asks: "For if God gave adversity unto good men, what may either the better sorte promyse themselves, or the evyll not feare?" So salutary is the contemplation of the lives of these martyrs that Foxe wishes that "the heroicall wittes of kings and princes, which for the most part are delited with heroicall stories, woulde carye aboute with them such monumentes of Martyrs as this is, and lay them alwaies in sight, not alonely to reade, but to follow, and would paint them upon their walles, cuppes, ringes, and gates . . ." And he recalls wistfully "the zeale of aunctient Christians which flocked together with fervent desire unto the ashes of the Martyrs, and kissed even the verye chaynes wherewith they were tyed. Yea the swearde wherewith they were beheaded, was layde up as a precious juell, or relique." Perhaps it was the word "relique" that warned Foxe that he had let his enthusiasm run away with him, for he hastens to add immediately: "Howbeit I allow not the superstition that dyd after degenerate from sincere religion." But he cannot forfeit the example, perhaps more safely expressed in the hymns of Prudentius and Nazianzen, and the orations of Cyprian, Chrysostom, Ambrose, and Jerome.[36] For the main point of this looking back to past history is to be found in Foxe's conviction that "if Martyrs are to be compared with Martyrs, I see no cause why the Martyrs of our time deserve not as great commendation as the other in the primitive church, which assuredly are inferiour unto them in no point of praise, whether we looke upon the nomber of them that suffered, or the greatnes of their tormentes, or their constancy in dieng, or also consider the fruite that they brought to the amendement of mens lives, and the encrease of the gospel, for those did but water the truth with their bloud, that was nowe springinge uppe. And these by their deathes did restore it againe, when it was sore decayed and fallen downe." [37]

That Foxe was aware that his enemies would mock his effort with the title of "Golden Legend," we know from the Latin preface "Ad doctum lectorem," which follows the English address to the Queen. Indeed, without waiting to see his book, they had apparently sought so to discredit it in advance. That taunt he resented, for he shared the contempt of his party for the "leaden legend," and he claimed for his book, as we have seen, the status of sober ecclesiastical history. Likewise for the criticism that he was substituting a new calendar for the old, Foxe retorted that he did not have the official position to do so, nor the desire. What he had printed was only an "index" ("*pro Indice*") for the private use of the reader. As for the charge of substituting new martyrs for old, with its implications of novelty, to which Foxe like so many men of his party was especially sensitive, he invoked the classic position, *non poena, sed causa*, not the death but the cause, and to illustrate the principle asked if one Cranmer were not worth more than six hundred Beckets, an example in which Foxe with characteristic precision came to the heart of the issues of the time.[38]

Indeed, from start to finish this is a book directed to those issues with the greatest urgency and the greatest immediacy, and at that point Foxe certainly is correct in his insistence that his book is different from the *Golden Legend*. The author of the *Golden Legend* wrote for a world that was in no danger of sympathizing with the ancient pagan world that had warred upon the martyrs and been overcome. That had so completely vanished that its villains had become but instruments in the triumphant passion of the heroes of the *Legend*, no more menacing than the villains of a fairy tale, or a folk story, or a romance. The victory was so complete, so assured, so long established, that there was nothing to argue about.

It was very different with Foxe. The victory he celebrated was not so complete that the enemy was to be disregarded, or so secure that the defense of his cause could be dropped. Even when he celebrated the victory of his side, he was concerned with the maintenance of it. He was concerned lest the very relief of that victory should make its beneficiaries relax. That is why there is throughout a certain note of indignation. Like most men of his day, Foxe had seen changes in the incidence of power that made the possibility of future change, incredible as it might seem, something not to be left out of the long-time basic reckoning. He knew that there were a great many of his countrymen who for one reason or another were not satisfied with the recent changes in religion. He wanted to make sure that whatever direction they moved in, they would not move in one direction, and that was back to the situation which had existed before the religious settlement which had just been effected.

Yet for all its stress on the sufferings of the martyrs and the brutality of their persecutors, the book is the rationalization of a victory. True, it has its terror, but that terror is the terror of things remembered; it in no way impairs the confidence of the victory. Indeed, Foxe clearly uses that terror not to mitigate confidence in the justice or completeness of the victory but to whet the determination to defend it at all costs. Subtly memory becomes a reinforcement for the confidence of the present. Moreover, so far as Foxe is concerned, the period of which he writes is closed. What he conceives to be the right order is established. For him the front of Protestantism is firm and unbroken, and its security a fast vindication of its essential righteousness. Moreover, the very character of this victory is an integration of his world. What he has to say of Queen Elizabeth is more than a patriotic idealization; it is the glorification of a unity of religious faith and of national feeling that gives a remarkable sense of moral security and simplicity. True, the old enemy of mankind is still at large, and the flesh is known for what it is in its primal weakness. But the world has been won. That is what gives its glow to his panegyric of Queen Elizabeth. That is why the Church that was so soon to depart in so many ways from what Foxe considered the one and only way of looking at things gave his book the widest possible circulation.

In two respects, of course, Foxe is in his position typical of the transitional state of mind of the years of which he wrote. He hoped that the supporters of the old order, kept in check by the measures of the new settlement, would either acquiesce or, in the course of time, die out. That is the great hope of a triumphant party always, and there is a good deal of evidence that the hope was widespread in the first years of the Elizabethan Settlement. One of the points Foxe most emphasizes in his approach to the reign of Queen Elizabeth is her clemency, especially as contrasted with the rigor of the preceding reign — "then was no ende of butcherly killinge and bloudy murdering, so nowe is no beginning yet found of spilling anye drop of bloud"; [39] and "her raigne hetherto (raigning now fower yeares and more, hath ben so quiet, that yet (the Lord have al the glory) to this present daye, her sword is a Virgine, spotted and polluted with no drop of bloude." [40] Those who have most intimately studied Foxe's life and personality, like J. F. Mozley, believe that Foxe abhorred the death penalty for religious opinion, and the present writer would not be disposed to dispute that judgment, in view of Foxe's record of intercession for Anabaptists, and, according to his son Simeon, for Campion and other Catholic victims of the harsh penalties of the time. [41]

There is another aspect to the situation that should not be forgotten, and that is the problem of social disorder. Social disorder can be treated lightly by two classes of people: the beneficiaries of an established order enjoying the maximum of security and not aware of any threat likely to make itself good against its continued confidence, and revolutionaries who have never as yet had to face the problems of taking over the control of society. The nineteenth-century liberal in England and America and the nineteenth-century anarchist in parts farther east could both view the problem with equanimity. So could the sixteenth-century Anabaptist. But neither an old order on the defensive nor a new order entrenching itself could. In that respect the Marian and the Elizabethan situations have more in common than Foxe seems to have been aware of, as became apparent when the hope of a deliquescence of the old order vanished, and the fear of effective challenge materialized.

The problem of tolerance is not a simple one even in theory, and it is not to be wondered at that Foxe's most extended discussion leaves much to be desired in clarity and completeness. One thing is clear, that Foxe and men of his opinion would rather persecute men as disturbers of the peace and traitors than as heretics. It must not be assumed, however, that in practice or theory Foxe ruled out the possibility of persecuting men as heretics, or that he took heresy lightly. What he did object to, above all, was bishops persecuting as heretics men who, he was sure, were not heretics at all. Foxe explained his basic attitude at some length fairly early in the book, addressing himself directly to the gentle reader:

Firste of all that you do not interpreat any thinge whych shall be here spoken, in such manner, as thoughe I woulde maintaine anye improved doctrine: for as I doo not favoure heritickes, which are heretickes in dede, even so muche lesse do I not favoure false Byshoppes. And againe as I do not geve license unto neither of these, neither to the one to use his tiranny, or to the other to proceade in his errroures, so likewise doo I not goo aboute here to take away the power of the civil sword, because it is not borne by the Magistrate in vaine. For they have their lawes, their judges, and their punishmentes, necessary in a common welth wythout the which there should be no society, neyther any discipline amongst menne. But this my complaint doth only touch them, the whiche professinge a perfectnesse of spirituall life above all the reast of the common sorte of the people, and oughte to be the maysters of all pitie and godlinesse, yet shall you scarslye find any men more venemus in hatred, anger, malice, revenginge, and all kinde of tirannye . . . Neither doth everye errroure by and by make a man an hereticke excepte it have joyned therewyth an obstinate and frowarde will, neither do I knowe whether in thys poynte also the extremities are to be marked, and the rule of the Gospell is to be attempted or no: But the qualiti of the heresy is to be considered, what it dothe require, and what is convenient for every mannes profession, the profession of a seculer judge is one, the condition of an Evangelical minister is an other.[42]

That the device of turning the ecclesiastical victim over to the secular arm was profoundly unpopular seems apparent, an unpopularity that was to extend in turn to the Anglican bishops' later activities against the Puritans. Apparently in the sixteenth century and the early seventeenth century there was a widespread repugnance in England to the Church's using the State as an instrument of its purposes, but apparently less repugnance to the State's using the Church. It is, however, difficult to be sure on this point, for the issue was obviously of greater moment to those who for one reason or another were at war with the ecclesiastical establishment of the time than for those who acquiesced, and the State was in a far stronger position to repress criticism of its policies than the Church. There is a good deal to suggest, too, that the State was a more imposing and awe-inspiring material fact in an age when material facts exerted probably more moral effect upon men's minds than usual. Certainly, there was in *Actes and Monuments* abundant and constant reinforcement of whatever underlying psychology was here involved.

It is probably because they were so widely regarded as a menace to all social order that Foxe in his book does not worry about the known Anabaptists. He mentions some of the Anabaptist executions, but it is clear that he does not regard them as martyrdoms, and that he instances them merely to round out the religious picture. Even in the index they appear as "Anabaptistes justly condemned."[43] Usually, he does not bother to ascertain either names or circumstances of these anonymous victims, and he certainly wastes no sympathy on them, and what is still more significant, he does not arraign their persecutors for what he seems to have regarded as necessary keeping of order. For instance, between the merry story about a false alarm of fire at Oxford and a royal letter on religious measures in 1542, he just mentions the fact that twelve German Anabaptists were condemned about this time and that they were burned in different places.[44] For Joan of Kent and Dutchman George he is more explicit, but what he says implies that it must be clear to everybody that people who took such a position as theirs are not to be included in a list of martyrs.[45] And Foxe was quite willing to admit that if heresy disturbs the peace of the commonwealth, the severity of the magistrates is justified.[46]

In other words, Foxe is aware of the problem, and something like the later Anglican caution now and then looks out of his enthusiastic chronicling of the march of the Protestant cause. One of the most significant passages from this point of view is to be found in what he says about one of the sacramental martyrs of the Henrician regime. Peter, a German, and his companion defiled their quarrel over the Lord's Supper with false doctrine about Christ and his mother.[47] In other words, a common charge against some of the Anabaptists seems to have been made against this otherwise acceptable Protestant martyr, and Foxe qualifies his reception. Once at least, he laments the tendency of Protestantism to split up into sects, and the propensity of certain extremists to drive beyond the positions on which all reasonable men ought to agree.[48] He is not unaware of the presence of ideas which he considers false and dangerous in the ranks of contemporary Protestantism, but he is so little concerned about the prospect of their ever really disturbing the existing order that most of the time he pays very little attention to them. Some of the martyrs whom he celebrates clearly held ideas very different from Foxe's own. The result is that there is in his book no anxiety about the Protestant future, no premonition of the disputes and differences which were going to make of the English Church something rather different from what he thought it was.

As we have seen, the charges of heresy and innovation were probably the Catholic charges that went most sharply home in Reformation England. One way of rebutting these charges was to make clear a hatred of heresy. Another was to turn the charge back upon those who made it, to assert that the innovations were on the other side; to set up a new definition of heresy. "It is heresie to defend any doctrine against the holye scripture," said Foxe in defense of the marriage of priests.[49] In view of the disputes of the time as to what was the meaning of Holy Scripture, there was, of course, room for a good deal of argument here, and in view of the fact that the Catholic Church did not accept some of the leading interpretations of the Reforming movement, it was not difficult for a good many Protestants to become convinced that the old Church was in general the enemy of Scripture and of truth.

Certainly, Foxe was so convinced. Therefore, the battle between the persecuting bishops and the Reformers whom they martyred was basically a conflict between light and darkness, the most ancient, the most universal, the most profound, of all appeals to the militant heart of man. Foxe's final verdict on Gardiner, whose changes of position puzzled and disappointed men on both sides, "neyther a true frend to the Pope, nor yet a full enemy to Christ,"[50] defines the parties with admirable simplicity. Hooper comforts the Protestants who had been taken during a hidden prayer meeting by reminding them that they had been thrown into prison, not for wicked and superstitious prayers like the Papists', but for Christ's own.[51] Of a humorous story of the discomfiture of some divines of Oxford, Foxe says: "I have not thought good to passe it over with sylence, for God hathe oftentymes by dyverse manifest meanes deluded the crafte and subtiltie of the byshoppes and their vaine hypocrisie."[52] And when he is describing the effect of Henry VIII's proclamation against the dissemination of Coverdale's and Tyndale's translations of the Bible, and some of the early Protestant books on the Sacrament of the Altar, he sums it up finally by saying that the prelates' and Pope's side had made great headway against the Gospel.[53] It is no wonder that the changes which Mary made after the reign of the Protestant Edward brought grief to the good and joy only to wicked men.[54] Foxe, on the whole, does not make the mistake of arguing these black-and-white alignments; he takes them for granted as self-evident to all good and sincere Christians.

For always it is the battle between light and darkness that is the main standard of values, the focus of all issues for Foxe. Whatever furthers it is good, whatever hinders it is evil. His is the classic psychology of the crusade. This is well illustrated by what he has to say of the famous divorce case. The discussions of the issues involved in this transaction do not much interest him. He is much too serious a man to be engaged with the romantic or sentimental aspects of the matter; probably most of his graver-minded contemporaries were not much interested in them, either. And the psychological elements that have fascinated later minds held, so far as we can tell, no appeal for him. But the divorce was itself of prime importance for him, because through the providence of God it was the means by which greater things came to pass.[55] Through it the Pope lost his supremacy in England.[56] As for Anne herself, she is "the most vertuous and noble lady, Anne Bullen," a great favorer of the Protestants. She kept her ladies and gentlewomen busy sewing for the poor, so that in her court there was none of the idleness and pastimes such as now hold sway in princes' courts.[57] As for the end of Anne, Foxe simply states that she was cast into prison, with no suggestion of the cause, and that she made a good end. For her obituary he repeats that religion went forward with her, and growing more philosophic, he reminds his readers of the mystery of life by which the best things are soonest taken out of the world.[58] That was in that age a very safe observation and a very pertinent one. Later he permits himself to say that King Henry, playing the part of an unkind husband, had beheaded Queen Anne, surely an incontrovertible position for its very mildness, if nothing more.[59] Altogether, in view of the diplomatic complications of this discussion of the parents of the reigning sovereign, he acquits himself very well. Clearly he preferred Anne to Henry, as we shall see presently, but there were some very real difficulties in his position, not to be fully appreciated until we come to consider his view of the King.

Anne was a difficult case. There was no trouble whatever with King Edward or Queen Elizabeth. Across the troubled days of Queen Mary he looked back to the "meke and gentle times" of King Edward. No one suffered for the truth of religion except Joan of Kent and Dutchman George, and their positions were so different from what anybody could consider reasonable that he can hardly be blamed for discounting them.[60] And it is with the grimmest of regrets that he turns from the death of that "Impe of so great hope" to the troubled times that followed.[61] As for Queen Elizabeth, "the Quenes moste excellent majestye, and our redoubted lady," [62] his admiration for her was fervent. He admired her natural gifts, he admired the way she transcended "the naturall infirmitie of that sexe . . . her moderate and maydenlye behaviour . . . sobrietye in apparel . . . learnynge and knowledge . . . pacience and clemency." [63] He was proud, too, of the "advisemente" with which the changes of her reign were being made, in contrast to the last, in which "all was done in post hast." [64]

These are the great Protestant heroes who have advanced the cause of religion in England, who have protected its liberty, and secured its victory. After the princes come the ministers who pioneered in the teaching of the Reformation. One sees the basic pattern fairly clearly in what Foxe tells us of the saintly Master Thomas Bilney: "First this godly man beinge a batcheler of law was but of a little stature and very slender of body and of a strate and temperate diet, and geven to good letters and very fervent and studious in the scriptures, as apered by his sermons his converting of sinners. His preaching at the lazar cots wrappinge them in shetes helping them of that they wanted if they wuld convert to Christ: laborious and painful to the desperats, a precher to the prisoners and comfortles, a great doer in Cambridg, and a great preacher in Suffolcke, and Norfolke, and at the laste in London preached many notable sermons." Then Foxe reinforced the note of asceticism: "Concerning his diet which we spake of, it was so straight, that for the space of a yere and halfe commenly he toke but one meale a day. So that if he were disposed to sup, he would kepe his commons: And likewise his supper, if he were disposed to dine, and would beare it to some prison: Where he used commenly to frequent and to exhorte such as were infamed or prisoned for evil life . . . His scholler which had daily conversation with him, told us that to his thinking, no night he slept above .iiii. hours, and yet we speake of more then he reported to us." Still more strikingly for that great age of English music: "He could abide no swearinge, nor singing.

"Comming from the church where singinge was, he wold lament to his schollers, the curiositie of their deinty singing, which he called rather a mockery with god, then otherwise. And when Doct. Thurlby Bishop after, then scholler lieng in the chamber underneth him, wold play upon his recorder (as he wold often do) he would resort straight to hys prayer." [65]

Much the same pattern emerges out of Foxe's account of the life of Master John Bradford, another of the great leaders of the Reform:

His painful diligente reading and prayer, I might almost accompt it his whole life. He did not eate above one meale a day: which was but very lytle when he toke it and his continual study was upon his knees. In the myddest of dynner he used often to muse with hym selfe, having his hatte over his eyes, from whence came commenly plenty of teares, dropping on his trencher: very gentle he was to man and child, and in so good credit with his keper, that at his desire, in an evening (being prisoner in the kinges bench in Southwarke) he had licence (upon his promise to returne agayne that nighte) to go into London without any keper, to visit one that was syck, lying by the Stilliard. And (he that swete Bradford) going thither with hys frend, and the tyme of hys returne drawing nygh, he having respect to fidelity therin, more then life it selfe, went to prison agayne that night according to hys promise: so trusty was he in woord and dede. He was of person a tal man, slender, spare of body, some what a faynt sanguine coulour with an awburne beard. He slept not commenly above .iiii. howers a nighte: and in his bed till slepe came, his booke went not out of his hand. His cheife recreation was in no gamming, or other pastime, but onely in honest company, and comly talke, wherin he would spend a little leasure after diner at the bourd, and so to praier and his booke againe: he counted that houre not well spent, wherin he did not some good, either with his pen, studie or exhortacion to others etc. He was no niggard of his purse, but would lyberally participate that he had to hys felow prisoners. And commonly ones a weake he visited the Thefes, picke-purses, and such others, that were with in the prison where he laye, on the other side: unto whom he would geve godly exhortation to learn the amende-met of theire lives by theire troubles, and after that so done, distribute emong them some porcion of money to theyr comfort. [66]

In other words, the pattern is of piety, study, great industry, great sobriety, and austerity of life, sweetened by charity. Dr. Rowland Taylor, a successor to the evangelical work of Master Bilney in the town of Hadley, seems not only to have been himself charitable to the poor, but to have made some very successful efforts to stir up his parishioners to emulate his good example: "For this was his custome, once in a fourthnight at the least, to call upon syr Henry Doyll, and others the ryche clothmakers, to goe with him to the almoyse houses, and there to see howe the poore lyved: what they lacked in meat, drynke, clothing, bedding, or any other necessaries: The lyke dyd he also to other poore men, that hadde many chyldren, or that were with sickenesse oppressed. Then would he exhorte, and comfort them, and where he founde cause, rebuke the unruly: and what they lacked, that gave he after his power: and what he was not able, he caused the riche and welthy men to minister it unto them." [67] In general, however, this getting other people to join in the works of mercy is not stressed so much as the individual charity of the saintly hero.

As for the general types of the martyrs, the variety is considerable, and the emphasis of the martyrologist varies accordingly. It is the rank and the brilliant prospects of the Scotch martyr Patrick Hamilton that he stresses,[68] and the extraordinary personal promise of John Frith; [69] Dirick Carver, beerbrewer of Brighthamsted, he notes, had been blessed with temporal as well as spiritual riches.[70] But with a very few notable exceptions like Patrick Hamilton and Lady Jane Grey,[71] the beautiful lady of noble birth and the rich young man of ancient descent of the *Golden Legend* are missing. Another classic type does once or twice peep out, the woman martyr of high spirits and sharp tongue, most notably Anne Askew, who, according to her own account, when Christopher Dare examined her at Sadler's Hall, refused to explain how she took certain texts to which she had appealed, because "I woulde not throwe pearles amonge swine, for accornes were good inough." [72] There were some gentlemen, too. For example, a gentleman was burned with Anne Askew,[73] and a gentleman is noted among the unnamed seven who were burned at Smithfield in January of 1556.[74] But just as the center of the stage is taken more often by the learned doctors than by the men and women of rank, so the proportion of people from the humbler walks of life is higher in Foxe's book than in the *Golden Legend*. This popular character of sixteenth-century religious activity should be remembered in the light of the striking developments of the next century on the sectarian front. A study of the psychology revealed in some of the examinations of these humbler martyrs makes it quite clear why the Elizabethan Settlement did not succeed in holding the allegiance of some of the most powerful energies that had been released in the first half of the sixteenth century.

But in spite of this popular character of so much of Reforming religious activity in Marian times, the question of how the leaders of this cause were won to it is still of great interest, not only because it justified the cause for their followers but because it illustrates the way in which ideas are spread. Foxe, of course, is quite ready to attribute all to the wonderful working of the Spirit. In a classic case like that of John Bradford this was easy. For his life has many of the features of the traditional conversion story. He was in a very fair way to make his fortune in the service of a prominent public figure of the reign of Henry and of Edward, when he felt the call to give up worldly affairs and devote himself to the Kingdom of God. At Cambridge he studied Scripture and also enjoyed the conversation of men like Bucer, who urged him to become a preacher. Ridley ordained him deacon, apparently changing the rite to conform to the scruples which the young man already felt against the established order.[75] In such a case the young man's contacts seem to have reinforced an original bent.

A clearer case of a university conversion is to be seen in the story of Bartlet Green, gentleman and lawyer, who was converted to the Gospel cause by the divinity lectures of Peter Martyr. He was burned in 1555.[76] John Rogers was older when he came in touch effectively with the leaders of the new movement. He had completed his studies at Cambridge, and had been chosen chaplain to the Merchant Adventurers at Antwerp in Brabant. There he fell in with the exiled Tyndale and Coverdale, and seems to have been soon won to their cause.[77]

But the most instructive story is that of the conversion activities of Master Thomas Bilney, with whose austerities and charity we are already familiar. He had been at Cambridge from childhood. Moved by "the holy spirite of Christ . . . enduing his hart by privye inspiration, with the knowledge of better and more wholesome thinges," he devoted himself to the Gospel and converted many of his fellows, among them Thomas Arthur and Hugh Latimer.[78] With Master Arthur he also converted Master John Lambert, one of the most notable of the Henrician martyrs, who left Cambridge to cross the seas to Tyndale and Frith.[79] And he seems to have been responsible for the spread of his cause in Hadley, where another of the most distinguished of the martyrs, Dr. Rowland Taylor, conducted a very successful ministry until the accession of Mary.[80] Bilney's convert and pupil, Master Barnes, converted Master Bayfield, a notable Henrician martyr.[81]

Preaching and personal contact were not the only instruments, however, for this spread of ideas. Master John Tewksbury, leather-seller of London, who was put to death in 1531, was converted by the reading of Tyndale's Testament.[82] And clearly he had many fellows. Those Reforming books which Richard Bayfield confessed to having brought into the realm and landed at Colchester in the mid-summer of 1531 undoubtedly played their part in the maintenance of the Protestant tradition in that ancient center of unorthodox views.[83] Another important factor in the recruiting of martyrs was the magnetism which martyrdom itself exerted upon the imaginations and wills of earnest and sensitive men and women. The horrible punishment for heresy, like the punishments for treason and other major crimes of the time, was designed to strike terror into the hearts of prospective offenders. But sometimes it had quite the opposite effect. A good example is to be seen in the story of Mistress Joyce Lewis. The beginning of Foxe's story is dramatic and comprehensive. "Maistres Joice Lewis a gentle woman born, was delicatly brought up in the pleasurs of the world, having delight in gay apparel, and such like folishnes with the whych follies the most part of the gentle folkes of England were then and are yet infect." She went to Mass in the beginning of Mary's reign, but when she heard of the burning of Master Laurence Saunders, the minister of All Hallows in Breadstreet, London, in 1555, she seems to have begun "to take more hede to the matter, and inquired earnestly of such as she knewe feared god, the cause of his death." That was the beginning of a change of mind and heart that first brought her to be weary of the world and of her sins, and then to manifest her hatred of the Mass in such terms as eventually brought her to the same end.[84] While Foxe's reports of the effects of the martyrdoms on the people in general are perhaps not always to be taken at full value, still the accounts which he gives of the public reaction to the courage and fervor of the martyrs are too like some of the reports of the public reaction to some of the later Recusant martyrdoms and to the martyrdoms of the early Church to be disregarded.

An indirect witness to this effect of martyrdom on the public is to be seen in the pains that Foxe took to discount the deaths of those who would not accept the supremacy of the Crown in religious affairs. Of the execution of Friar Forrest, Foxe pointed out that he was hanged for papistry and therefore unworthy of a place in this catalogue. Besides, he took his death unpatiently.[85] Hanging, drawing, and quartering inflicted on a Protestant on a charge of treason trumped up to cover persecution for heresy, rightly seemed to Foxe a cruel death.[86] But in the case of the Carthusians of London, he was not troubled, for the charge was treason, and that was the appointed punishment. So with More and Fisher; they were not executed for religion but for treason.[87] What grieved Foxe was the blindness of an English novice in Antwerp who thought More and Fisher were martyrs.[88]

For Foxe, his martyrs are people whose characters and behavior may be taken as arguments for the truth of the position they have taken up. The character of their adversaries is clearly the opposite. Indeed, one may say that Foxe spends almost as much enthusiasm limning the portraits of his villains as of his heroes. These are no shadowy provosts or legendary emperors. They are people well known to the public for whom Foxe wrote, people about whom a good many of Foxe's readers would have strong feelings, and one may be sure that Foxe did nothing to impair the strength of those feelings. Wolsey is a case in point. Foxe rehearses effectively the familiar charges about Wolsey's pride and love of magnificence. But he goes further. He makes a good deal of Wolsey's treasons and abuses at the French Court when he went over to Amiens to help Pope Clement against the Emperor,[89] and he takes for granted in a passing allusion the story that at the end Cardinal Wolsey took poison.[90] Cardinal Pole he disposes of with a minimum of difficulty in a parenthesis, "a man of noble birth, but yet an Arch enemy unto God, and to Christes true religion yea altogether geven to papistry, ambicion and hipocrisy."[91] But his favorite villain is unquestionably Stephen Gardiner. It is Gardiner who, when the Commons were displeased with King Henry for the innovations he had made, told the King he might put himself right by demonstrating his aversion to heresy and making an example of John Lambert, who had denied the Sacrament of the Altar to be the body of Christ.[92] It was Gardiner who set even that friend of the Gospelers, Cromwell, against Lambert.[93] Indeed, on the occasion of the death of Gardiner, Foxe presents a full-dress portrait of "Stephen Gardiner, Byshop and Chauncelor, a man hated to God and al good men," that is a masterpiece of its kind. Foxe begins by admitting

his witte, capacitye, memorye, and other indumentes of nature not to bee complayned of, if he had wel used and applied the same, wherein there was no wante of nature in him, but he rather wanted to the goodnes of his nature . . . To these gyfts of nature were joyned againe as great vices and greater, which not so much folowed him, as overtoke him, not so much burdened him, as made him burdensom to the whole Realme. In stomacke high minded, in his own opinion and conceite flatteryng hymselfe to muche. In wit craftye and subtile, toward his superiour politike and pleasing, to his inferiours fierce, against his equal stout, and envious, namely if in judgement and sentence they anything withstode him, as appeared betwene the good lord Cromwel and him in the reign of king Henry, having the hart that the Poets attribute to Pelides Cedere nescius. And though he gave no place to men, yet I wish he would have given place to truth, as well as he seemed not to bee ignoraunt of the truth, that is, I wysh hys conscience had bene as good as hys knowledge was . . . Upon his estimation and fame he stoode to to much, more then was mete for a man of hys function, that shoulde be crucified unto the worlde, whyche thynge made him to stiffe in maintaining that he had once begon to take upon him. I wyl not here speake of, what hath bene constantly reported to me, of the monstrous makinge and fashion of his feat and toes, the nailes wherof are said not to be like other men, but to croke doune ward and sharp like the clawes of a beast. What [h]is learning was in the Civil and Canon law, I have not to say: What it was in other liberal sciences and artes, thys I suppose, that neyther hys continuance in study, nor diligence, nor reading was such (by reason of hys intermedlyng in Princes matters) as could truely geve hym tytle of a depe learned man . . . In tong and utterance somwhat perchaunce prayseworthy. In stile of writing far from all commendation . . . This we have al to thinke, his death to happen so oportunely, that England hath a mighty cause to geve thankes to the lord therfore: not so much for the great hurt he had done in time past, in perverting his Princes, in bringing in the .vi articles, in murtherng Gods sayntes, in defacing Christes sincere religion, etc. as also especiallye for that he hadde thought to have brought to passe, in murdering also our noble Quene that now is.[94]

After such an indictment it is hard to see how any good man could fail to rejoice at Gardiner's death, and easy to see how a large number of Foxe's readers would draw the conclusion that any man who failed to rejoice could not be a good man.

But more potent than any indictment of individuals is his indictment of the class of men that he held to be the main enemies of his cause, the bishops. It can hardly be wondered at that the attack upon the English episcopacy continued, even after the Elizabethan Settlement, to gather momentum. In this, as in so many other things, Foxe helped to lay the foundations of English Puritanism, for it may be said roughly that the only bishop that seemed good to Foxe was a bishop burned for Reforming principles. As we have just seen, even so staunch a Protestant as Cranmer could be misled by Gardiner into persecuting the light in the person of Lambert. The bishops are the generic villains of Foxe's story. True, the Pope is the archvillain, but though always a cloud on the Reforming horizon, he is often remote, and again of so elemental and cosmic a character as almost to take on a mythological significance, to be an evil force rather than a person. Not so the bishops. They are the actual authors of destruction, close and immediate. Anybody who read their record in Foxe and heard nothing more of bishops than he presents might well conclude that the institution of episcopacy was the root of the evil and must be swept away at all costs. And in view of some of the developments of the next century, it is perhaps significant that Foxe closes his discussion of the "florishing age" of the Church by citing the distinction made in a gloss to the Nicene decrees by some unspecified authority, that the primitive time of the Church may be divided into two parts, "the first primitive . . . when there was yet no difference betwixt a priest and a bishop: the second, when schismes came in, by reason wherof the office and autoritie of priest and bishop was distincted a sonder." [95]

True, Foxe sometimes is careful in his discussion of church government to invoke the temporal distinctions between the evil old times and the present, but usually he is more interested in arraigning the past than in taking any precautions for the saving of present authority. No region, he pointed out in showing how the profession of Christ's true religion had earlier "sparkled" in this world, had been more fruitful of martyrs than England, either by grace, "or els thorow the barbarous and folish cruelty of such as at that time ruled and governed the church." [96] Indeed, at one point in his account of the somewhat ambidextrous persecutions of Henry's reign, he made the bishops the defining element on the opposite side when he said that "it happened in this great slaughter of gospellers that the contrary secte of bishops, did not also clearly escape," and he went on to speak of the condemnation of Germain Gardiner and Lark for the Pope's primacy.[97] It was "the droncken rage of the byshoppes" which hurried on the death of Lambert,[98] just as when Stokesley took part in the defense of the traditional conception of the Sacrament, Foxe described him as "intending to fight for his belly," a charge perhaps sharpened by Lambert's attack on the over-rich prelacy.[99] But tyranny is the commonest charge, so often repeated that the two words "proud prelate" may be taken as one. And the tools these villains found to their hands were worthy of their masters, like those who set faggots to the burning of Dr. Rowland Taylor, one a man fit to be hanged, another a drunkard, another one who in King Edward's days had lost one of his ears for his seditious talk, and one who in former times had been a player of interludes.[100]

Against the bishops stand the martyrs, the martyrs of the present, worthy, as Foxe is careful to point out in his account of the martyrdom of William Gardiner, of being put with the great martyrs of the early days of the Church, the "Ignatians," "Laurentianes," "Ciriatianes," "Crescentianes," and "Gordianes." Foxe cites the ancient benefits of the good done to the Church by the martyrs, "with whose bloude it is watred, and fatted with theyr husbandry, strewed with their ashes, confirmed with theyr constancye, and witnesse, and finally through whose agonyes and victories the glory of the truthe and gospell dothe tryumphe."[101] It is the classic summary of the classic theme, and Foxe reverts to it again and again — Anne Askew is a singular example of Christian constancy for all men to follow;[102] the death of the martyr, as John Bradford pointed out in a letter written shortly before his own death, serves to confirm the believers in their faith;[103] indeed, as another martyr, George Marsh, wrote, the very work of the Gospel shall be saved by the constancy of the martyr.[104]

There are two values to be emphasized in this situation. The first is the cruelty of the tormentors; the second is the triumph of the martyrs. The suffering of the martyr is therefore doubly precious, but there is a basic difficulty in the handling of this, for the suffering of the martyr must be sharp enough to do justice to the cruelty of his tormentors; yet for the sake of his cause he must not be overcome. Tragically enough, there was plenty of material to Foxe's hand in the burning of these victims of the sixteenth-century religious struggle, and he gives us some masterly vignettes of the terror of the time as experienced on various levels. One of these is noteworthy not only because it shows that Foxe's gift of vivid, dramatic narrative was not a unique one in that intensely alive period, but because it shows certain qualities not usually found in Foxe's writing. First of all, it is more introspective than his work usually is. And then, though it is swift and confident, there is something nostalgic in it, quite foreign to Foxe's exultant mood. It was not in his nature to gaze back wistfully at a vanished comity and tenderness of habit. Probably that was a state of mind more common to the men who actually lived through the age of revolutionary transition. Anthony Dalaber gives an account of the search for a disseminator of heretical books at Oxford about the year 1526, which Foxe reproduces with an apparent fullness that gives a very lively idea of the terror of such a visitation. Dalaber had just arrived in an anxious frame of mind at St. Frideswide's:

And Evensong was begon, and the Deane, and the other canons were there in their Gray Amices, they were almost at Magnificat before I came thether, I stode at the quier dore and hard master Taverner play and others of the chappel there sing, with and among whome I my selfe was wont to singe also, but now my singing and musicke was turned into sighing and musing. As I thus and ther stode, in commeth Doctor Cotisford the commissary, as fast as ever he could go bare headed, as pale as ashes, I knew his grefe wel inough, and to the Deane he goeth into the Quier, where he was sitting in his stalle, and talked with him very sorowfully, what I know not, but wherof I might and did wel and truely gesse, I went aside from the quier dore, to se and heare more, the Commissarye and Deane came oute of the Quire, wonderfullye troubled as it seemed, about the middle of the church met them D. London, puffing, blusteringe, and blowinge lyke a hungry and gredy Lion seking his pray.[105]

This passage of Dalaber's is a good passage to set beside Foxe, because as prose, while it is as vivid as Foxe's prose, as incisive, as dramatic, it is beside Foxe's prose a little diffuse, a little meditative, a little too aware of too many elements in the situation. There is none of this in Foxe. Whether he is delivering his effect at a stroke, or detail by detail building up a harrowing indictment, Foxe is always swift, vigorous, resonant. There is nothing delicate, nothing elusive, nothing cloudy, about his style. He marches firmly in a world of black and white, and the result has the mark of his own simplicity and convictions. Yet he can suggest the agony of soul of the simple caught in the swirl of changing political-religious controls. John Tewksbury, who was, as we have seen, converted by the reading of Tyndale's New Testament, is a good example of the amateur theologian and tradesman disputant on the religious issues of the time. He was a leatherseller, expert in disputation on the Bible, and, according to Foxe, strong on justification. He retracted his views under extreme pressure of torture, and then he could not rest until "he had uttered to all his acquaintaunce, and asked God and al the world forgevenes, before the congregation in those daies, in a ware house in bowe lane." He also felt compelled to appear in the parish church of St. Austens with Tyndale's New Testament in his hand and *The Obedience of a Christian Man* in his bosom, and there he stood up in his pew before everybody, and declared "with weping teares that he had denied God, and prayed all the people to forgeve him, and to beware of hys weakenesse, and not to doo as he did. For he said, if I should not tourne again unto this truthe, having the new Testament in his hand, that this Gods word wold dampne him body and soule at the daye of judgement." The sequel is what might be expected. He was apprehended, imprisoned, and finally burned, acquitting himself quite to the satisfaction of Foxe.[106] The experience of Elizabeth Cooper, the wife of a pewterer of Norwich, was much the same. Having once given in, she could not rest until she had gone into the church where she had recanted, and there in the middle of the service revoked her recantation, and exhorted the congregation not to follow her example.[107] The end of the story was the same.

Like the martyrologists of old, Foxe prized the record of examinations of prospective martyrs, and even more the record of disputation when the Protestant champion was able to confront his adversary. For these records gave opportunities that Foxe made the most of for the presentation of congenial ideas. The history of Master John Lambert is a good example. Foxe first gave his history very briefly from the time he "did forsake his filthy priesthode of Antichrist" until the time he began to engage with Dr. Taylor in a private discussion on the nature of the Sacrament of the Altar. Foxe then indicated briefly how this private business became public and attracted attention until it came to the notice of Gardiner and the King. The dispute before the

King, of course, gave Foxe a good opportunity to air Lambert's views in detail and to expose the impudence and caviling of the Bishop of Winchester. Then he went on to give a summary of Lambert's book on the controverted subject, and then the articles objected against Lambert, and his answers thereto, to the extent of thirty-three double-column folio pages.[108]

In general, the sufferings of the prisoners in prison receive less attention than their examinations. A conspicuous exception is John Bolton, who was starved and chained in prison until he went mad.[109] Although there are stories of brutality on the part of sheriffs and pursuivants, there are not many charges of torture in the Marian executions. The racking of Cuthbert Symson, for instance, seems to have been unusual.[110] But the conditions of sixteenth-century imprisonment were grim enough in themselves, and the way in which these prisoners for principle rose above them is heroic, as may be seen in some of the letters of the time, from prison, in which news of the death or condemnation of friends is given with matter-of-fact steadiness and calm.[111] In the case of a leader like Hooper, who had been Bishop of Gloucester and Worcester, many visitors came to comfort, or take comfort from, him. One of these visits is admirably summed up in the crisp and highly concentrated dialogue characteristic of Foxe: "After that another came to hym, whom he knew to be a very Papist, and a wicked man, which appeared to be sorye for maister Hoper's trouble, saying: Syr I am sory to see you thus. To se me? why (sayd he) art thou sory? To se you (sayth the other) in thys case. For I heare saye ye are come hither to dye, for the which I am sorye. Be sory for they selfe man (sayd maister Hoper) and lamente thine owne wickednes: for I am wel I thanke god, and death to me for Christes sake is welcom."[112] Bishop Hooper had been one of the great leaders of the cause, and the steadfastness of his resolution corresponded to his eminence.

But even among the obscurer whom only the light of martyrdom rescues from the shadows of the past there is abundant evidence in this book, as in the *Golden Legend*, of the way in which devotion to a cause, and faith in a victory beyond the pain of this world, may overcome all the weakness of the flesh and even the natural affections of ordinary humanity. Agnes Bongeor had sent her child to nurse and had got her smock ready for her burning with the ten martyrs at Colchester in August of 1557, and she was grievously disappointed when she was for the time being reprieved, but she had her wish later, and seems to have felt, like her chronicler, that she at last had the chance of her glory.[113] There are stories, too, of wives exhorting their husbands to suffer, and of friends friends, and children their parents, but probably the most moving are the stories of parents giving up their children to the cause with gladness. For instance, the parents of William Hunter, overcoming nature, exhorted him to suffer patiently, as Foxe puts it, "rejoysing with wonderful gladnes." [114]

As in the *Golden Legend*, men found the courage they needed when they came to the test. Laurence Saunders was fearful of his own constancy, but in the event he had plenty of strength, an instance of God's grace which Foxe gratefully noted.[115] Latimer had seemed withered and feeble before to anxious friends, but in his shroud he stood up fresh and handsome, as if armed to the ordeal before him.[116] Especially did God give the weaker sex (and in the world of Foxe there was nothing conventional in that phrase) supernatural strength for their trial.[117] Mistress Joyce Lewis consulted her friends for advice as to "how she might behave herself, that her death might be most glorious to the name of god, comfortable to his people, and also moste discomfortable to the enemies of god." [118] It was reported that Cicelie Ormes stood in the flame at Norwich and died as if she felt no pain.[119] God, Foxe says in the grand tradition, "gave to his wytnesses faithe, and patience, with stoute and manlie hartes to despise all tormentes." [120]

It is in the final scene at the stake that the martyrs are at their best, and that their martyrologist is at his best. For he is a master of horror. Sometimes it is the number of victims involved in the execution that is stressed, as the number of thirteen burned at once at Stratford-the-Bowe on June 27, 1556.[121] But that terrible number is unusual, though its occurrence even once is appalling enough. Sometimes it is the horror of some unusual circumstance that augmented the agony of the victim. Laurence Saunders was burned with green wood.[122] For lack of faggots Bishop Ferrar was burned with turfs and sods in Wales.[123] The situation might be very different, for one accidental reason or another, for two victims in the same place. Latimer died with very little pain or none, but Ridley suffered much, and Foxe gives a careful account of it.[124] In general Foxe did this, partly to glorify his subject, partly to bring out the cruelty of the persecutors.

In some special cases, he puts unusual emphasis on the mercilessness of the persecutors, as in his account of "Maistres Smith widdowe of Coventry with sixe other men burned." [125] The fact that four of the others were shoemakers, one a glover, one a hosier, suggests that there may have been social reasons for the priority given to the woman, but there is no question that the fixing of the spotlight on her intensified the impression of mercilessness. The most atrocious single circumstance, the throwing back into the fire of a babe born in the fire, seems to have horrified authority, for Foxe himself says that the Queen's commissioners put the official held responsible into prison.[126] His noting that circumstance is worth remembering, for in general Foxe was quite ready to believe any cruelty of what he habitually calls the "murderous Papists."

But though he is by no means sparing of adjectives, Foxe is still more effective through the skill with which he selects striking and dramatic detail. He has the authentic Elizabethan genius for the unforgettable detail, especially of the homely, dramatic order. Richard Bayfield burning three-quarters of an hour, fixed, unmoving in prayer, is an impressive enough spectacle without the terrible detail of the burned left arm rubbed off unconcernedly by the right.[127] No one thing more constantly contributes to the dramatic quality of his narrative than this; indeed, in this as in so many elements of his vast book Foxe proves himself a storyteller of quite remarkable power, one of the greatest of a great age. And no dramatist of the time has a sharper eye for the dramatic gesture than Foxe. It is hard to choose among the abundance of examples he offers us, but two of very different atmosphere and final effect will illustrate this element in his literary power. The first is from a scene that is but one of many with no special historic importance as regards the persons or the occasion. It is simply a flash of light on a rather obscure transaction, the coming to the stake of one of the humble women martyrs at Colchester, of whom not much is known beyond this gesture: "When they had made their prayers, they rose and made them ready to the fier. And Elizabeth Folkes, when she had pluckte of her peticoke, would have geven it to her mother (which came and kist her at the stake, and exhorted her to be strong in the Lorde:) but the wicked there attending, would not suffer her to geve it. Therfore taking the said peticoke in her hande, threw it away from her, saying: fare wel al the world (quod she): farewel fayth, fare wel hope, and so taking the stake in her armes said: welcome love etc."[128]

In contrast to this more humble, though no less heroic, occasion, the burning of Cranmer, who had been Archbishop of Canterbury, was an event of great historic interest and importance. His behavior in recanting had from Foxe's point of view been a scandal. His recovery of himself at the end was regarded by Foxe as not only a personal triumph for his integrity but a vindication of his cause. The simplicity with which Foxe rises to the height of this occasion is an artistic triumph of a very high order (Cranmer, it will be remembered, wished to make clear to all men that he repented of his weakness by giving to the fire the right hand which had signed the recantation): "And when the wodde was kindled, and the fyre began to burn nere him, stretching out his arme, he put his right hand in the flame, which he held so stedfast and immovable (saving that once with the same hande he wyped his face) that all men might see his hand burned before his body was touched."[129]

The ending is not on the same high level because Foxe's interest does not remain concentrated at so high a pitch, but the same dramatic incisiveness is felt, especially in the use of the final revealing gesture. A Spanish friar, misunderstanding Cranmer's fortitude for desperation, ran to one of the attending noblemen saying that Cranmer died in desperation, "But he whiche was not ignorant of his countrimens constancie, being unknowen to the Spaniardes, smyled only, as it wer by silence rebuked the fryers folie."[130]

And always, however horrible the transaction he is handling, Foxe has a genius for the full sensuous presentment of a situation that will bring it to life in the reader's imagination with a vitality that will make it an ineradicable part of his consciousness. For much as Foxe protests at the horribleness of his material, he is singularly uninhibited in his exploitation of its sensuous possibilities. Literally nothing is too terrible to tell; indeed, it is precisely in the handling of the horrible that his extraordinary gifts are most powerfully revealed. The slow burning of Bishop Hooper, perhaps the most terrible episode in a terrible book, the full effectiveness of which is in

no degree blunted by the comparison of the passion of the modern
bishop with that of the ancient martyr, Polycarp,[131] presents the extremities of physical torment with every last ghastly sensuous detail:
"but when he was blacke in the mouth, and his tonge swollen, that
he could not speak: yet his lippes went, till they wer shrounke to the
gommes: and he did knocke his brest with his hands untill one of
his armes fel of, and then knocked still with the other, what time
the fat, water, and bloud dropped out at his fingers endes, until by
renewing of the fire, his strength was gonne, and his hand did cleave
fast in knocking, to the yron upon his brest. So immediatly bowing
forwardes, he yelded up his spirite."[132] It is hard for sheer horror to
surpass that.

In this exploitation of the physical details of the martyr's suffering
Foxe easily challenges comparison with the masters of the martyr
cult in the seventeenth century. It is customary to see in the detail
with which the later writers contemplate the sufferings of the martyrs
one of the most characteristic manifestations of the baroque influence
in literature. But Foxe is no less appreciative of the sensuous and dramatic possibilities of the extremes of physical torment. In general,
too, he illustrates the baroque tendency to develop its material in the
round, with sensuous fullness and material substance. There is a certain solidity, a certain literal and immediate and fully presented realism in Foxe's handling of detail, that leaves very little indeed to be
imagined. But it should be added that the emphasis is primarily upon
the physical appearance rather than upon the psychological or emotional or even nervous elements involved. In other words, the baroque
movement has advanced as far as the complete exploitation of physical
pathology in Foxe. By and large, the exploitation of the nervous and
the emotional remains for the next century.

This does not mean at all that Foxe is indifferent to the psychological elements, but the range of his subjective analysis is restrained
deliberately, in keeping with the sixteenth-century emphasis on sobriety for its godliness. Nowhere is this more apparent than in that
element that from the time of the first of the ancient martyr stories
might be considered the counterpoint to the horror on which we
have of necessity dwelt so much, and that is the triumph of the
martyr. "Patient" and "constant" are the words Foxe uses again and
again, as in the case of Saunders' "most constant pacience,"[133] or in

the account of how John Bradford at his execution "quietly and paciently suffred the violence therof." [134] But the word "mery," albeit not with the more playful connotations of today, does now and then come into the story of the triumph. John Rogers in prison was merry and earnest in all his undertakings.[135] Ridley was merry at supper the night before he suffered.[136] Among some simple folk burned at Ipswich, their neighbors were apparently surprised to discover that Michael Trunchfield's wife, who had not been so zealous as Potten's wife, when she came to the stake exceeded the latter in joy.[137] These are quiet descriptions, far from the ecstasies and the visions of the *Golden Legend*. After all, they are being written close to the event, with a practical rather than a contemplative interest, and in an area where the wind of the imagination, in the religious realm at least, is blowing cold.

But there are two episodes that have something of the old *Golden Legend* splendor of joy in the victory of the stake and the cross. The six martyrs of August 2, 1557, at Colchester, one of the great centers of religious enthusiasm at this period, clapped their hands for joy when the flames leaped up around them.[138] But the most dramatic is, as usual, the story of the particular man to whom Foxe knows how to give a particular name and personality. There is in the beginning an experimental, pragmatic note, foreign to the *Golden Legend*, but the final gesture has the authentic note of the ancient martyrologies. Thomas Hawkes, who had been a courtier, agreed with his friends that if the pain were too great, he would simply stand still, surely a valiant enough resolution in any event. But if it proved tolerable, such as a man might suffer, then he was to lift up his hands to heaven before he died. But the ending had a splendor that doubtless neither he nor they had contemplated. For just before he died, he lifted up his half-burned hands to heaven and with great rejoicing struck them together three times.[139] Foxe hardly needs to tell us that there was a cry of joy from the people around. Perhaps the witnesses of the *Golden Legend* would have been puzzled by the demonstration; they would have taken for granted what may have a little astonished as well as delighted the people of Coxehall in Essex. But then they had not been going through such a period of searching of hearts, of shaking of old confidences, as had these people of sixteenth-century England.

As for that other feature of the *Golden Legend* martyrdoms, the abundance of signs and miracles that, as we have seen, surrounded the martyrdom itself not only as an aura of the marvelous, but as a manifestation of the spiritual significance of the event, one would expect Foxe, in that age of revolt against supernaturalism, to reveal a very different attitude. And so he does. The book is full of the contempt of the sixteenth-century Reformer for the miracle and the miracle-monger. Clearly, they are regarded as belonging to the past of darkness and ignorance and superstition out of which the present, under the leadership of such men as are here seen in their martyrdom, has happily escaped. But old habits die hard. The friends to whom Dr. Ridley gave various little tokens, like a new groat, some napkins, some nutmegs, some "rasins" of ginger, his dial, and such other personal belongings, were clearly treasuring personal mementos. But there is more than a suggestion of the ancient relic-hunting in a sentence that follows Foxe's description of this touching scene: "Some plucked the poyntes of hys hose: happye was he that mighte gette anye ragge of hym." [140] Of course, it need not be said that there is no sign of the ancient use of relics as instruments for cure.

But Foxe seems a little reluctant to surrender the miracle, sometimes possibly because his competitive spirit is much too strong for him to resist any chance of vindicating his beliefs in any area. For instance, in his account of Tyndale's life he tells the story of the famous juggler at Antwerp who found himself unable to exercise any of his "develish magick artes" at a supper where Tyndale was, and gave as his excuse the presence of some man who restrained all his powers. To this Foxe adds: "So that a man even in the martyrs of these our dayes cannot lack the miracles of true faith, if miracles are to be desired." [141] So, too, James Bainam called out of the flames at Smithfield that the Papists who looked for a miracle might see one, for he felt no pain in the flames.[142] The taunt gives a topical twist to the old triumph of the martyr.

But that is, in fact, the original and basic miracle of the martyr. Once at least Foxe goes a little further than this, and in a passage hard to surpass for its combination of the triumphant and the macabre, adds a note of revelation to the marvel of endurance. It is in the account of the end of Robert Smith, who was burned in 1555. Smith had comforted the people about the stake by telling them that his body would rise again: "And sayde he, I doubte not, but that God wyll shewe you some token thereof. At length he being wel nigh halfe burnt, and al black with fyre, clustered together as in a lump lyke a blacke cole, all men thynkyng hym for dead, sodenly he rose up ryght before the people, lyfting the stompes of his armes, and clappyng the same together, declaryng a rejoycing hart unto them, and so bendyng downe agayne, and hanging over the fire, slept in the Lorde, and ended this mortall lyfe." [143]

But there is evidence of the survival of other types of marvels, evidently viewed by Foxe without any sign of apprehension. The dream is one of these. The story of Cuthbert Symson is full of dreams, though he at first refused to give credit to those of the minister of the congregation of which he was deacon, on the ground that dreams were only fantasies, unworthy of credit. The most striking of these dreams is that in which the wife of the minister saw a woman who was in the end to be burned at the same stake with him, "going downe the strete with a bloudy banner in her hand, and a fyre pan on her head." [144] Certain other types of portents are also admitted by Foxe, clearly as evidences of Heaven's concern. One of the most dramatic is also one of the most ancient, "the great miracle of Gods devine admonition or warning," the earthquake over all England at the time of the ecclesiastical assembly at the Greyfriars in London to inquire into the books of Wycliffe. [145]

But most of the marvels admitted by Foxe fall into two classes, miracles of Providence, usually of deliverance wrought on behalf of good Protestants to help them escape from their enemies, and miracles of retribution, wrought usually on the Papist persecutors of such good Protestants. What may be called the miracles of Providence are numerous. None enjoys greater social and public significance than that of the preservation of Queen Elizabeth through her perils. Everyone may see, says Foxe, confident that he will not be contradicted by any good subject, "that it was not without a singular miracle of God, that she coulde or did escape." [146] But though this was the most distinguished of the miraculous preservations, it was in no sense unique. After he had completed his story of the various minor victims of the persecutions of the Marian regime, Foxe added "An Other Chapter of Such, as by the providence of God miraculously have bene preserved from danger in the time of persecution." [147] A good example of these escapes is what happened when Thomas Christmas and William Wattes arrived as strangers in Rochester, Kent, looking for a place to stay with safety. They asked a little girl they met if there were any heretics in the town. She told them that they could find them at a certain inn. But before they went there, "God moving their hartes," they asked her how she knew, and she told them that they were active in rounding up Protestants. So they avoided that house, taking the warning "to be Gods marvelouse providence towards them."[148]

Quite appropriately to the psychology of the time, this chapter of happy deliverances is followed by "An Other Chapter or Treatyse of Tyrants and Persecutors, and concerning gods scourge and punishment exercised upon the same."[149] These are impressive enough. The bishop who condemned Bishop Farrar was stricken with a most unpleasant malady, that his meat would not stay down, and so suffered till he died. The sheriff, too, who seems to have tried to appropriate the martyr's cattle, felt the hand of retribution, for a number of the cattle refused to eat "but lay bellowing and roaring, and so died."[150]

But Foxe's catalogue of retributions is by no means confined to these final horrible examples. All through the book there are abundant evidences of the judgment of God. There is the classic case of the persecutor receiving his deserts in a mysterious and loathesome disease, one example of which, the death of De Roma at Avignon, receives very full treatment.[151] Closer to home, and doubtless more effective in its familiar detail, is the account of George Revet, who, though "a great reader of the scripture, or as a man may terme it, a talkative gospeller, woulde not be premonyshed by the workes of God." He let his son help the parish priest say Mass and become clerk of the town for the sake of money, and this in spite of the clear warning of the fate of his predecessor, who had apparently exercised the same office against his conscience until he went insane, so that his wife had to keep him chained up in the house to keep him from doing any harm. When some honest women of the town asked him, ". . . are ye not afrayd to let your sonne helpe the naughty priest say masse, and to serve that abominable idoll?" he said no. But their pressure upset him enough so that he prayed God for a token or sign if this behavior of his were displeasing. Soon after, his neighbor's

Hus endeth the legēde named in latyn legenda aurea/ that is to say in englisſhe the goldē legēde ꝼor lyke as paſſeth golde in valewe al other metallis/ ſoo thys Legende excedeth all other bokes/ wherin ben conteyned alle the hyghe and grete feſtys of our lorde ◖The feſtys of our bleſſyd lady/ ◖The lyues paſſiōs ⁊ myracles of mani other ſaintes hyſtoryes ⁊ actes/as all alonge here afore is made mency on/ Whiche werke J dyde accompliſſhed at the commaundemēte and requeſte of the noble and puyſ ſaunte erle ⁊ my ſpecyal good lord Wyllyam erle of Arondel/ And now haue renewed ⁊ fynyſſhed it at weſtmeſtre the xx day of May/ ◖The yere of our lord M CCCC lxxxxiii/ And in the viii yere of the reygne off kynge Henry the vii/ ◖By me Wyllyam Caxton/

INRI

Colophon (sig. gg4ᵛ) of the 1493 edition of Caxton's *Golden Legend*. Reproduced by permission of The Huntington Library, San Marino, California.

ℭℌere begynneth the lyfe of ſaynt Radegunde.

Title page of Henry Bradshaw's *Lyfe of Saynt Radegunde*, published in London, probably in 1521. Reproduced by permission of The Huntington Library, San Marino, California.

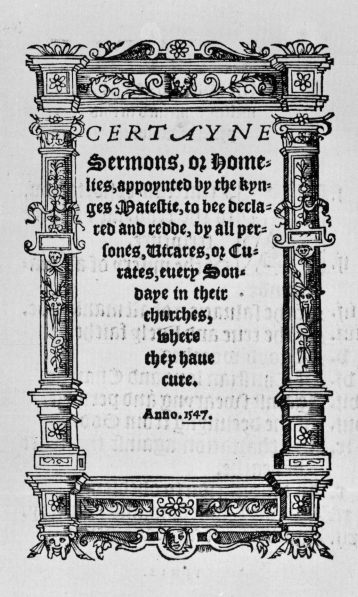

CERTAYNE

Sermons, or Home=
lies, appoynted by the kyn=
ges Maiestie, to bee decla=
red and redde, by all per=
sones, Uicares, or Cu=
rates, euery Son=
daye in their
churches,
where
they haue
cure.

Anno. 1547.

Title page of *Certayne Sermons or Homilies,* published in London in 1547. Reproduced by permission of The Huntington Library, San Marino, California.

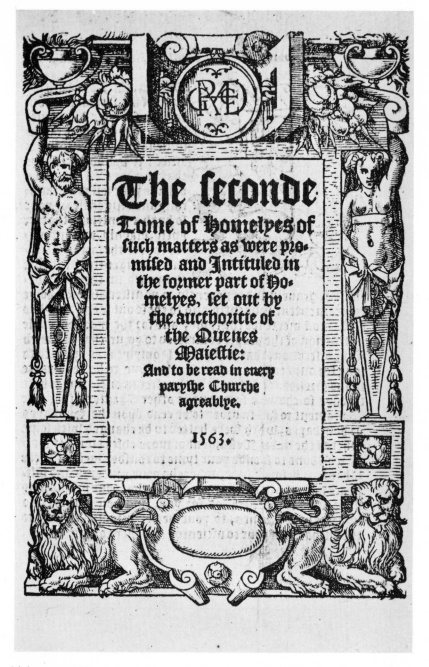

The seconde Tome of Homelyes of such matters as were promised and Intituled in the former part of Homelyes, set out by the aucthoritie of the Quenes Maiestie: And to be read in every paryshe Churche agreablye.

1563.

Title page of *The Seconde Tome of Homelyes*, published in London in 1563 by Richard Jugge and John Cawood. Reproduced by permission of The Folger Shakespeare Library, Washington, D.C.

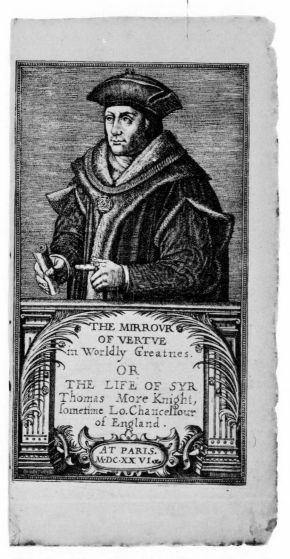

Title page of Roper's *Life of Syr Thomas More*, published in Paris in 1626. Reproduced by permission
of The Huntington Library, San Marino, California.

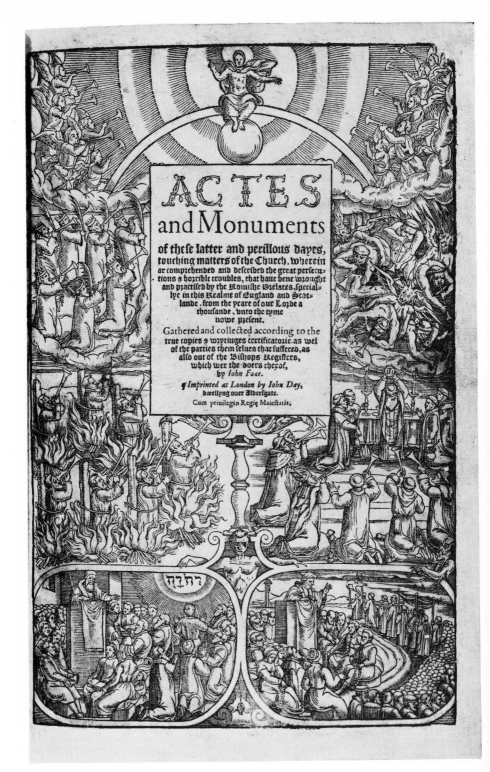

Title page of the 1563 edition of Foxe's *Book of Martyrs*. Reproduced by permission of The Huntington Library, San Marino, California.

SAINT
Peters com-
playnt.

With other Poems.

AT LONDON,
Printed by I. R. for G. C.
1595.

Title page of Southwell's *Saint Peters Complaynt*, published in London by Gabriel Cawood in 1595. Reproduced by permission of The Huntington Library, San Marino, California.

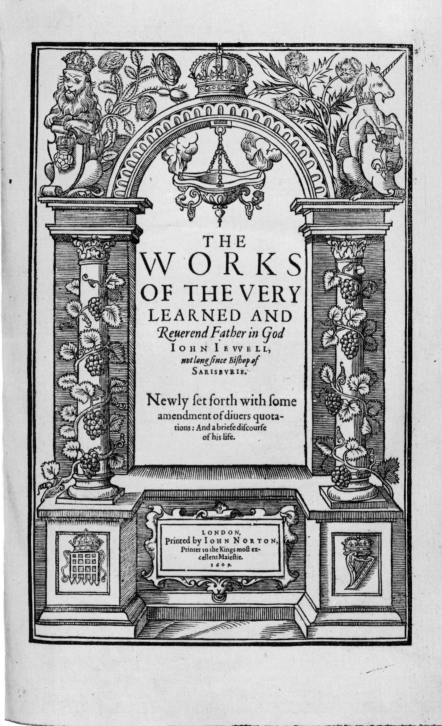

THE
WORKS
OF THE VERY
LEARNED AND
Reuerend Father in God
IOHN IEWELL,
nut long since Bishop of
SARISBVRIE.

Newly set forth with some
amendment of diuers quotations: And a briefe discourse
of his life.

LONDON,
Printed by IOHN NORTON,
Printer to the Kings most excellent Maiestie.
1609.

Title page of *The Works of John Jewell*, published in London in 1609. Reproduced by permission of The Huntington Library, San Marino, California.

bull came into his pasture and gored his gelding, which was the pride of his heart. But though he granted the judgment, yet he obstinately refused to do anything about his son. The result was a strange sickness, of which he "died most miserably in so impatient maner, that it terrified al good hartes to here therof." [152] That is the classic story of the sixteenth-century retribution, in which a man's behavior at his demise was scanned very closely by both friends and enemies for the evidence it afforded of his spiritual state and, more important still, though of course in indirect fashion, for the presumed effect of his religious professions, and the evidence his example gave for their truth or falsity.

That is why the example of the martyrs is so precious, for, as Foxe puts it, "in these men we have an assured and plaine witnes of God, in whose lyfe appeared a certaine force of divine nature, and in their death a farre greater signification . . . To be shorte, they declare to the worlde what true fortitude is, and a waye to conquer, which standeth not in the power of man, but in hope of the resurrection, to come, and is now I trust at hand." [153]

That he did offer a substitute for the rejected *Golden Legend* still remains true to a degree which Foxe could hardly foresee when he made his indignant protest. The popular title, *The Book of Martyrs*, under which it is best known, suggests that. And so does the success of the book as reflected in the record of publication. A second edition, much expanded, was published in 1570, a third in 1576, a fourth in 1583. After Foxe's death in 1587, an abridgment was made by Timothy Bright and published in 1589, and the fifth edition of the whole work appeared in 1596. The sixth edition in 1610 began the story of the seventeenth-century editions. In the new England which Foxe had so enthusiastically celebrated, his *Actes and Monuments* played a role in many respects not unlike that which the *Golden Legend* had played in the old. The familiar legend that the *Book of Martyrs* was by authority required to be kept in the parish churches together with the Bible, preferably for the legend, "chained," has been challenged in our day, mainly on the grounds that no legislation requiring it has been discovered, and that, from what we know of the publishing conditions of the time, the number of copies of the book available for such distribution is grossly inadequate. [154] But the upper house of convocation of Canterbury did in 1571 order that a copy of the Bishops' Bible of 1568 and a copy of Foxe's book should be installed in every cathedral church, and every member of the hierarchy from archbishop down to resident canon should have a copy of the latter in the hall or dining room of his house for the use of all who came there.[155] There is plenty of evidence, too, that it was chained beside the great Bible in many parish churches, and it was, with the Bible and chronicles and histories, one of the books to be found in the offices of the Court of Elizabeth, and the Companies of London had to keep a copy in their halls.[156] Even Leslie M. Oliver, who has challenged so effectively the legend of official prescription, places it second only to the Bible and *Pilgrim's Progress* for its influence upon Protestant England.[157]

FOXE'S
ECCLESIASTICAL HISTORY

But although *Actes and Monuments* has now for almost four hundred years held a quite unique position as the English book of martyrs par excellence, it is in fact a good deal more than that. Foxe clearly meant it to be. For, as we have seen from his address to Queen Elizabeth, he never intended to be considered a successor to the author of the despised *Golden Legend*, but rather to the first great historian of the Church, Eusebius Pamphili, the early fourth-century Bishop of Caesarea.[1]

The real model of Foxe is Eusebius' outline of his great project, with which he opened his *Historia Ecclesiastica*, and which Meredith Hanmer in his 1577 English version set apart in a "proeme." In that inclusive but admirably compact introduction to his ten books of history, Eusebius, beginning with the "dispensation" of Christ and "the successions of the holy Apostles," declared his intention of setting forth the main events in the history of the Church from Christ's time to his own. This included such matters as "who decently have governed the Churche, specially in the most famous provinces," who "have set forth the heavenly doctrine, eyther by preaching, or by writing," who also "through desire of noveltye, and error, falling into extremityes" have preached false doctrine and "cruelly rent a sunder as ravening wolves, the flocke of Christe," the evils that befell the Jews "because of their conspiracye against our Saviour," how the

Gentiles had striven against the "Word," the sufferings of the martyrs of the past, and finally of his own time, "together with the mercifull and comfortable ayde of our Saviour, towardes every one lovingly exhibited." [2] In short, Eusebius set out to write the story of the founding of the Church, of its spread and consolidation, of the perils from within and without, which with the help of Christ it had survived, all viewed triumphantly from the happy ground of the peace which had come with Constantine.

Although he organized his material systematically around certain leaders, events, issues, or problems, what might in short be called "themes," Eusebius did not in general go so far as to formalize the periods in which these themes successively take the lead, probably because there was a good deal of chronological overlapping. Nevertheless, because of the persecutions that took place in them, the reigns of certain emperors, like, for example, Marcus Aurelius in the fourth and fifth books, do give a certain temporal structure to the flow of the narrative. [3]

The notion of the division of all time into certain significant periods was, of course, a very ancient one, and so was its reflection in the ecclesiastical year. Jacobus de Voragine, for example, explained the division of all time into four periods: "deviationis," for the period from the fall of Adam to Moses; "renovationis" or "revocationis," for the period from Moses to the nativity of Our Lord; "reconciliationis," for the time in which reconciliation was effected by Christ; and "peregrinationis," for the time of the present life; and then went on to explain how that division was reflected in the familiar seasons of the ecclesiastical year. [4]

Something like this may have been in the back of Foxe's mind when fairly early in his book, after a brief summary of the growing corruptions of the Church from the year 600 to 1000, he stopped for "A Certaine Brief Description of the 4. Ages of the Churche." [5] And, as William Haller suggests, Foxe may also have been influenced, particularly in the later expansion of this history, by the mystical numerology of Revelation xi:12. [6] Foxe takes a very different approach, of course, from Eusebius or Jacobus, for clearly his main interest is the growth of corruption. His basic principle of historical criticism he gives almost at the beginning of his vast book: "In summe, to geve thee one generall rule for all, this thou shalt observe, the higher thou goest upwarde to the Apostles time, the purer thou shalt finde the churche: the lower thou doest descend, ever the more drosse and dregges thou shalt perceyve in the bottome, and especiallye within these laste 500 yeares, accordinge to the trew sayinge of Tertullian: quod primum, id rectum est, that which is the first, is right etc." Then, as so often, Foxe returns to his own time, which is never long out of his mind: "Therfore as that was the firste, and golden age: so I may well call this the olde, or brasen age of the churche." [7] Foxe relies on Eusebius for his account of the apostolic age, but he underscores his own points. There is no claiming of superiority by the apostles, including Peter, he insists; humbleness of mind was the characteristic of this first age. [8] And then after it came the second age, when the "word of God" was preached everywhere, not just in Jewry. This was, indeed, the "florishing age of the churche," when every church had its appointed honor. As for the duration of this primitive period, it may be said to end with the beginning of the middle age of the Church, which was when Polychronius, the Bishop of Jerusalem, about 440 began to claim the supremacy of his see of Jerusalem. [9] Then came "The midle age of the Churche," in which the Church wrestled with sects and schisms, especially such as contended for supremacy. Somewhere about eight or nine hundred years after Christ, the Church began to decay. This deterioration Foxe attributed to the fact that "through the great sufferance of princes" she had subdued not only all cathedral churches but all dispossessing princes. Popes and prelates, thus exalted by princes and emperors, began to forget themselves. The result is that the third age of the Church saw its strength begin to fail, "opprest with cold humors of worldly pompe, avarice, and tirrany." But the degeneration became most apparent when the thousand years were complete, and Sylvester II held the see of Rome. [10] Foxe carried this account of the third age down to 1374, about the time Master John Wycliffe became reader of divinity at Oxford. [11] The end of the first part of Foxe's history would seem to finish this discussion of the decay of the Middle Ages.

But when he began the second part of his history, with the marginal date of 1371, he nevertheless went back to pick up some of those who before Wycliffe had wrestled in the same cause. Then Foxe began what is really his fourth age, with John Wycliffe: "This is out of al doubt, that at what time al the world was in most desperate and vile estate, and that the lamentable ignorance and darknes of god his truth had overshadowed the hole earth: This man stepped forth like a valiant champion."[12] This was for Foxe really the beginning of the Reformation. He did, of course, pay tribute to other controversies of the period, including the work of a couple of Councils, and to the martyrs of the Bohemian and other foreign churches.[13] Then he returned to England, with a note to the reader, assuring him of the faithfulness of the present settlement to the real Christian tradition. The very plan of the book shows that Foxe belonged to that group of Protestant apologists who were most sensitive to the charges of heresy and innovation that their Catholic adversaries cast at them. In his preface to "the gentle Reader" before this third part of his ecclesiastical history, Foxe quite explicitly attacked the notion which he found widespread among the common people, "that this religion nowe generally used, hathe sprong up and risen but of late and few yeres, even by the space, (as many do think) of xx. or xxx. yeres," and assured his reader "that not only the actes and monumentes heretofore passed, but also the histories here after following, shal manifest and declare that thys professyon of Christes religion hath bene spread abrode in Englande, by the space almost of CC. yeres, yea and before that time, and hath oftentimes sparkled although the flames therof have never so perfectly burst out, as it hath done within these C. yeres and more."[14] And he proceeded to document that claim, beginning with William Taylor, "a favourer of Wickleffe," burned at Smithfield in 1422,[15] and going on to the end of the reign of Henry VIII.[16] The fourth part of the book treats of "the milde and Alcion days of king Edward the sixte,"[17] the fifth of "the horrible and bloudye tyme of Queene Marye,"[18] and the sixth of "the most florishing reigne of Queen Elizabeth."[19] So Foxe's history ends with the personal victory of Queen Elizabeth and the triumph of her religious settlement. As he said in the beginning of his great undertaking, Foxe wrote his book in order that his countrymen, instructed as to what they had escaped from and come into, might "therfore power oute more aboundant thanks to the Lord for this his so swete and mercifull reformacion."[20] It is really the victory of the Lord that Foxe is celebrating.

Actes and Monuments tells an exciting story of a great struggle and a great victory in the triumphs of the martyrs, but it does a good deal more than that. It gives the religious history of England from the beginning to the present in ever-increasing detail. It sets that history of the breaking of the light, and the struggle of the light with darkness, in its larger world context in the history of Christianity, presenting the ancient pedigree of the martyrs, as we have seen, and accompanying the story of the breaking English Reformation with that of the Continent. The result is that the local struggle is given dignity by its relation to the world struggle, and, on the other hand, the larger struggle is brought home to the English reader in homely local terms.

It is quite clear, too, from even the bare outline of Foxe's history, what he conceived to be most central to the whole history of Christianity, and that was the question of what should be the central organizing institution of Christian society. By and large, the question of whether the Church was international or national did not bother Foxe because the issue he was interested in was the supremacy of the king. Consequently, though the basis of the discussion of the relations of the national and the international Church that was so much to interest later controversialists is to be seen in his challenge to the primacy of the Roman see as an usurpation and an aggression with regard to other sees, he is much more interested in building up the case against the Papacy as a threat to royal authority, and documenting that menace from past history. No ultramontane ever took the importance of the Papacy to the continuing order of the Catholic Church more seriously than Foxe. Of the followers of the thirteenth-century Waldo, he says, for example: "Their chefe and principall poynt that they fixed their eies upon, the which toke away al the gloming darkness of ignoraunce, whych was spred over thearth was this, that they taking Christ for the only savior and hed of the church, did consequently judge and esteme the pope for very Antichrist, and his doctrine as a most mortal and deadly poyson." [21]

On this issue Foxe developed his attack along historic lines. The Church never knew any such papal supremacy in the religious sense until Boniface I called himself universal bishop six hundred years after Christ.[22] Indeed, the claims to papal supremacy were not known in the Primitive Church, which followed the injunction of Paul in the Thirteenth Epistle to the Romans that every soul should be subject to the superior power, the power which bears the sword, not the spiritual but the temporal.[23] That was to be the great foundation of the prince's power for the sixteenth-century Protestant, and that was, Foxe believed, the mind of the apostles for the Primitive Church, to which he looked back for his model. Indeed, Foxe quotes Niccolò Machiavelli, "the secretary of the cytie of Florence," in what must be one of his most respectable Elizabethan appearances, to the effect that "before Theodoricke kyng of Lombardes, that is, before the yeare of our Lorde 500. in all pollitike affayres the Byshoppe of Rome ever obeyed the Emperours and kynges." [24] It was only in the third age of the Church, about the year 1000, that "the supremacy of Rome raged in his ruffe, which being once established in consciences of men, the power of all other princes christian did quake and decay, for dread of the popes interdict, suspense, and excommunication, which they feared no lesse, then Christe his owne sentence from heaven." [25]

Foxe went on to document that thesis abundantly. Hildebrand was, of course, a notable villain in that story, and the episode of Canossa was presented in full detail with colorful comments in the margin. The famous waiting of the Emperor at the gates of the castle of Canossa is described marginally as "A wonderous submissyon of a valiant Emperour to a vyle pope." Against his account of the terms of the promise by which Henry bound himself not to exercise his imperial functions until a council should have passed on his conduct, Foxe wrote: "Here the beast of the Apocalipse appeareth in hys couloures." When Hildebrand refused to excommunicate Rudolf for his rebellious invasion of the empire until he should have a hearing, Foxe not only accused the Pope of using the law for a pretext, but labeled the whole transaction marginally, "The pope traitor to themperor." [26] And rifling the gossip of an age which might give even his own models in the art of denigration, Foxe drew a character of Hildebrand commensurate with what he judged his historic role. Hildebrand was, so almost all writers testify, "a sorcerer most notable, and a Necromansier." [27] The Countess Matilda was the Pope's paramour; [28] the Pope set in motion a device for murdering the King. While Henry was presented as a model of kingly virtue that would have doubtless astounded Henry himself, Hildebrand was depicted as "the first author, and patrone of all misrule that followed in Popes," a verdict which Foxe justified by explaining that "here came firste

the subjection of the temporall regiment, under the spirituall jurisdiction. And Emperours which before were theyr masters, now are
made their underlings." [29]

With such a reading of history it is not surprising that for Foxe
Thomas à Becket was "that olde Romish traytor." [30] True, the version
which he gave of the death of Thomas [31] is more like the traditional
one than like that which was reprinted among "Certain Injunctions"
published by royal authority in 1539, in which the false martyrdom
was explained as having "happened uppon a reskue by him made," [32]
but Foxe's opinion was no higher than Henry's of the character of the
traitor. On the other hand, the character of King John engaged the
attention of Foxe, who not unnaturally showed a good deal of sympathy for that worthy Prince, "so trayterously handled of his byshops
and Barons," and found in their constant treason the cause of John's
oppressions. Moreover, a story told of a jest by the King on the
obligation to hear Mass suggested to Foxe that John did not take
the Mass with the superstitious seriousness of most of the kings of
his time. And, of course, Foxe gave a full account of what he said is
the story of most writers, that the King was poisoned by a monk.[33]

But the climax of all his history of the troubles between popes and
kings came when Foxe began

> to intreate of the marvelous and moost gracious worke, of the holy providence
> of God, beginnyng nowe here to worke about this time in Englande, that
> whych nether durste be attempted before of anye Prince wythin this realme, nor
> yet could ever be hoped for of anye subject, concerninge the abolishinge and
> over throwe of the popes supremacy here in the English church . . . Thoc-
> casyon wherof began thus (through the seacrete providence of God) by a
> certaine unlawful marriage betwene Kinge Henrye the eight, and the lady
> Katherin his brothers wife Which marriage being found unlawfull, and so
> concluded by all universities, not to be dispensed withal by any man, at length
> brought forth a veritie long hid before, that is, that nether the Pope was that,
> he was recounted to be: And that again presumptuouslye he tooke more upon
> him than he was able to dyspence wythall. These little beginninges being once
> called into question, gave great lyght to men and ministred withall, great
> occasyon to seke further: In so much at lengthe the Pope was espied, both
> to usurpe that which he could not claime, and to claime that which he ought
> not to usurpe.[34]

Shortly after, Foxe is able to report that the Pope's "whole power
and authority began utterlye to be abolished, by the reason and oc-

casyon of the most vertuous and noble lady, Anne Bullen, who was not as yet married to the king. Howbeit in great favor, by whose godly meanes and most vertuous councell, the kynges minde was dailye inclined better and better." [35]

The last sentence is the key to Foxe's final verdict on King Henry, "Who of his owne nature and disposition, was so inclinable and forward in all thinges vertuous and commendable, that the like enterprise of redresse of Religion, hathe not lightlye bene sene in anye other prince christened." But there was the problem of the King's counselors: "So long as Quene Anne, L. Cromewel, B. Cranmer, M. Denney, D. Buts with such like were about him, and could prevail with him, what organe of Christes glory did more good in the church than he? . . . So againe when sinestre and wicked counsaile under subtile and craftye pretences had gotten once the fote in, thrusting truth and veritye out of the princes eares, how much as religion and all good thinges went prosperously forward before, so much on the contrary side al revolted bakward againe." [36]

Foxe was in a difficult position when he faced the record of Henry VIII. For as we have seen, Henry had to a preëminent degree the virtue of having resisted the Pope. Indeed, in that category of excellence he had no peer. It was hard to believe that such a man could have been so misguided on the subject of the Sacrament of the Altar as he clearly was. For it was one of the basic premises of Foxe's position that the king as an institution could be trusted to maintain religion — that is, a Scripture-devoted king. According to the theory of the Supremacy, the king was the final court of appeal for the maintenance of the establishment of religion. He undeniably had the sword and the right to use the sword. He used it to good effect against traitors who refused his supremacy, and Foxe approved. [37] But he used it also against Sacramentarians who refused to acknowledge the Real Presence and who preached and who agitated for the abolition of what they and Foxe himself regarded as idolatry. At that point Foxe was in trouble.

The case that seems most to have bothered him was that of John Lambert, who had found it wise to go abroad earlier in the reign to study, but who had thought that when Henry came under the influence of Cromwell and Anne, England might be safe for his views. The case was further complicated for Foxe by the fact that

Lambert got into trouble originally because the Gospelers with whom he first began to take up his views were not prepared at that time to go as far as he was. Foxe suggested that Dr. Barnes at least might have been afraid that a position like Lambert's would jeopardize the spread of the Protestant cause among the people, who clearly seem for the most part to have been conservative on the subject of the Sacrament of the Altar.[38] At any rate, the discussion went on until it came to Cromwell's attention. The result was that Lambert was condemned at the hands of men who had just accomplished the supremely Protestant work of the separation from Rome. Of course, Foxe looked for the villain who had so misled good men, and he did not have far to look. The later record of Cromwell made it clear that he must have been misled, just as the later record of the Bishop of Winchester, Stephen Gardiner, made clear who was responsible for the mischief. It was never easy for Foxe to grasp the notion of development of religious positions, any more than it was easy for most of his contemporaries. Indeed, much of his power lay in the very fact that he habitually dealt in black-and-white wholes, not in complex or intertwining strands of various shades between.

It was Gardiner, then, who was ultimately responsible, but even Foxe saw that Gardiner could never have compassed Lambert's ruin if Henry had not acquiesced. Foxe's explanation of that unhappy fact is ingenious. It was simply that "the commons had conceived a verye evell opinyon" of Henry, partly because of the suppression of the monasteries, but more because of the "abolishing" of the Pope; so Gardiner took advantage of the situation to convince Henry that he could pacify some of this resentment by showing how stoutly he resisted heresy, and that could be demonstrated by his dealing with Lambert.[39] But that explanation did not really satisfy Foxe himself. When he thought of all the appalling aspects of the condemnation of Lambert, it seemed to him that nothing could be worse than the "undecent and the uncomelye behaviour of the kinge's majestye at that daye, whiche assysted so manye proud and furious bishoppes to execute their cruelty in the death of one poore and miserable manne." So moved was Foxe at the memory that he directly apostrophized the dead King in an address that in its uncertainty as to his present whereabouts sounds more like a seventeenth-century

Puritan viewing royal authority than a sixteenth-century champion of the Supremacy:

But howe muche more commendable had it beene for thee, O kynge Henry (if that I maye a little talcke with thee where so ever thou arte) if thou haddest ayded and holpen the poore little sheape, beinge in so greate pearils and daungers, requiringe thy aide and healpe againste so manye Vultures and Libardes, and haddest graunted hym rather thy autoritye to use the same for his save garde, rather then unto the other to abuse it unto slaughter . . . But O kynge Henrye, I knowe you did not follow your owne nature there in, but the pernitious councels of the bishoppe of Wynchester, notwithstandinge your wisdome shoulde not have bene ignoraunt of this, whiche all other kinges also ought to consider, whyche at this present through the wicked instinctions of the Bishops and Cardynals doo so rage against the simple servaunts of Christ: that the time shall once come, when as ye shall geve accompt of all the offences whiche ye have eyther committed by your owne fault, or by the Councell or advise of others, what shall then happen (if these miserable heretickes whyche you here in this world doo so afflicte and tormente, shall come with Christe and hys Apostles and martirs to judge the xii. tribes of Israel, sitting upon their seates, if they with like severity shall execute their power uppon you) what then I saye, shall become of you? Wyth what face wil ye behold their majesty whyche here in this world have shewed no countenans of pity upon them?[40]

Such a speech is prophetic of the gathering of the hosts of the Lord in the seventeenth century. But in general, Foxe's respect for the royal authority makes him cling to the villainous counselor as the explanation of all the failings of kings, even in the case of Queen Mary. Her holding to her religion in the reign of her brother was, of course, to Foxe, "great stubbernes"; he stressed her bad faith in dealing with the Sussex "gospellers" who supported her when she needed help, on condition that she would not attempt the alteration of religion,[41] and her implacable hate against Cranmer because of her mother's divorcement. Indeed, his reflections on that theme inspired one of his few adverse reflections on the nature of princes: "And againe what can not princes doe in fyndyng cause whensoever they lyste to doe a man hurt, whensoever they beare one ill wyll, which maketh manye tymes muche hurte in common weales."[42] But in general he stressed the responsibility of the bishops and other ecclesiastical authorities rather than of the Queen, as in his brief record of her death, "God beholding us wyth mercy, called Queene Mary, (the which princes the Cardinal [Pole] and the rest of the

Byshops of England, miserably abused to the utter destruction of Christes churche) out of thys life." The consequent rejoicing in Providence may be pardoned, in view of the panegyric on the Princess Elizabeth which followed, and the old fiction of the wicked counsel conserved the regal proprieties.[43]

If the possession of a central theme be one of the prerequisites for a great view of human history, then it cannot be denied that Foxe has it. He goes through past history, garnering up every rebel against Rome that he can find whose position can be reasonably interpreted as involving a return to the position of the Primitive Church, and out of these figures and movements of the past he establishes what he regards as a continuing tradition of striving for the restoration of the Church to the purity of its first days.[44]

But even if one grant Foxe his ambition to be considered a sober historian, his history is a good deal more than a history. It is, also, an encyclopedia of the Reformation in England. All the main issues of the English Reformation are fought out before one's eyes, in résumés of books and pamphlets, sometimes in the reprinting of a substantial portion of a pamphlet, like Simon Fish's *The Supplication of Beggars*,[45] in full reports of councils and conferences, in oftentimes verbatim accounts of debates and disputes and inquiries, in official memoranda and definitions and articles and ordinances, in letters, personal and public. Certain issues are debated again and again, with the result that the most casual reader cannot help becoming familiar with the points in dispute. And if at any point his memory fails him, he has only to turn to the index which Foxe has very thoughtfully provided at the end of the volume: "A diligent index or table, of the most notable thinges, matters, and wordes contained in this whole worke." This is, in fact, an extensive analytical index of argument as well as topic and name and place, covering thirty-eight and a half three-columned folio pages.[46] For example, the crucial word "Image" (or "Images") is repeated thirty-two times, sometimes with subheadings and multiple page references,[47] and the entries beginning with "Pope" or "Popes" cover more than two columns.[48] The result is that the layman eager to keep abreast of the controversies of the time is here provided with easy and convenient access to a whole encyclopedia not only of historic information but of apologetics.

And the great thing about this apologetics is that it substantially represents the position which a large section of the English Church had reached at that period, as was realized plainly by those who used the book in the churches of the time. It is always hazardous to attempt to sum up anything so complex in its nature, and so diverse in its components and its possibilities, as the English Church of the year 1563. But it will be illuminating to take one example, particularly since it is at once central to the over-all situation and central to our inquiry, as we have seen, and that is the revolt against supernaturalism, to use a very rough term for a phenomenon that ranges from the crusade against superstition in which, say, a Thomas More or an Erasmus could take an active and convinced part, to the attack on sacramentalism that was to disturb the English Church for a good many years to come.

When Foxe says that Britain, of all nations, was the most superstitious in the old days, one wonders what has happened to his staunch patriotism. But it turns out that this is just another way of saying that in the old days Britain was exceptionally generous in its support of the monasteries.[49] For Foxe the monasteries were the great centers of the superstition of the time, but they were not the only offenders. There were the pilgrimages, which had long been the target of criticism on various social grounds, but which Foxe attacked for being sources of support for idolatry.[50] There were the shrines, which invited superstitious devotion, the offering of candles and, doubtless, of treasure for which the opponents of superstition could easily envisage a better use.[51] But, above all, there were the idols and the images. For this is, as we have seen above, one of the great ages of iconoclasm. Foxe was clearly one of those many men of the sixteenth century who seem to have been sincerely incapable of envisaging any use of the visual arts for religion that would not be idolatrous. The result is a genuine iconoclastic passion, not a negative reaction of rejection or neglect, but a positive, crusading fervor that was by no means satisfied by its own refusal to participate in idolatry but could not suffer anybody else to indulge in it. Here one may see already in Foxe's pages the first stirrings of the tender conscience that is to play so conspicuous a part in the Puritan assault upon the Established Church. For the iconoclast cannot understand how anyone can deny him relief from the horror he feels at the sight of an idol, the sheer compulsion of destruction. That there should be any sentiment of outraged reverence on the part of the idolater is only fresh fuel to his righteous indignation. Foxe's account of the hanging of three men for the burning of the "Idoll" or Rood of Dovercourt [52] is a case in point. That the punishment was excessive, that the image of God in the least of his creatures is more precious than any image in wood, was not the burden of his argument. Rather it was that these men had been punished for a deed for which any but blind and ignorant men would have applauded them.

This attitude is apparent, also, in Foxe's handling of the sacramental disturbances which played so conspicuous a part in the iconoclastic activities of the time. The nature of the Sacrament of the Altar was, of course, one of the most hotly debated issues of the time, the cause, more than any other one thing, of the Marian martyrdoms. From Wycliffe's time it had been the subject of many university disputes, some of the most notable of which took place at the accession of Queen Mary, like those of April, 1554, in which Cranmer, already under arrest, met the attack of a number of opponents.[53] The issue was debated on a great many levels. Frith's rejection of transubstantiation as false, vain, not grounded in the Scriptures, creedally unnecessary, and resulting in the exclusion of the German and other Protestant nations, represented the level of the eminent Protestant controversialist of the time.[54] But the debate was popular among the unlearned and the untheological, especially, so far as one can tell from the frequency with which the question of the Sacrament comes up in the case of women under investigation, among women. That is, of course, easy to understand, since it was at this point that the disputes touched most constantly and most intimately the daily lives of the people. There are a good many stories of the time that illustrate the crude level of much of this popular theologizing. Elizabeth Sampson, "convented" in 1508 before the consistory of London, said "she could make as good bread, as that which the priest occupied." [55] From some of the records of village gossip that have come down to us, it was obviously the happy hunting ground of the village sceptic. In Calais, Foxe says, even the old wives could distinguish between a superstitious Papist preacher and a true preacher of the Gospel on the Sacrament.[56]

Foxe entered into all these sacramental disputations with great sympathy and at great length. Once at least he suggested that it would be well if men agreed on the presence of Christ in the Sacrament, leaving the question of the how of the mystery alone.[57] But it is hard to reconcile with that position, so suggestive of the "comprehensive" position of a later day, the sympathy with which Foxe recounted in great detail a series of sacramental episodes, difficult to understand in terms of any belief in the sacred character of the Sacrament.

The most dramatic, and the most interesting in its implications, of all of these stories is that of William Gardiner, an Englishman who was burned in Portugal in 1552. In view of the international involvements, it is not surprising that Foxe laid a good deal of emphasis on this story as an example of the service of the martyrs to the Church and the advancement of truth. William Gardiner returned to a church where he had seen a royal wedding celebrated, and there the following Sunday, when Mass was being said by a cardinal in the presence of the King and a notable company, he seized the Host from the priest's hands and trod it under foot, and before the onlookers could interfere, overturned the chalice. One thing only bothered Gardiner, and that was the tumult he had caused in the presence of the King. He courteously told the latter that he was sorry to have vexed him with such seeming disrespect, but he reminded the King and his examiners that they were themselves to blame for having suffered such idolatry to go on in their presence.[58]

But though the rejection of transubstantiation was the essential spearhead in the attack on the old order in this region, the popular counterpart was the attack on the Mass, the central and sustained focus of the attack on the old supernaturalism in this period. That Foxe perceived this is clear from the fact that he opened his fifth section, on the "horrible and bloudye tyme of Queene Marye," with a substantial discussion of the "perilous idolatry of the Popish Mass."[59] The heart of his objection to the sacrificial conception of the Mass is to be found in a marginal note which he set against that section of the canon of the Mass, translated out of the Salisbury missal, in which the priest asks that his offering (of the Body and Blood of Christ) may be accepted: "What the masse? in the devils name, for what intent then dyed Christ?"[60]

For Foxe, of course, any notion of development of religious rite or practice was a confession of corruption or of artificiality. His final comment, after he had reprinted, with appropriate marginal comments and interlinear explanations, Coverdale's English translation of the canon from the Mass book of Salisbury Use, was on the way it had grown with time: "And thus have ye in some the gatherynges of the masse, with the canon and all the appurtenances of the same, which, not much unlike the crow of Esope being patched with the feathers of so many birdes, was so longe a getheryng, that the temple of Salomon was not so long in building, as the popes masse was in making." [61]

The seriousness with which Foxe took this charge of the idolatry of the Mass is shown in his discussion of the case of Master Hales, whose drowning of himself raised the old awkward problem of suicide for religious reasons. Foxe discussed with great sympathy the possibility that Master Hales killed himself to escape the defilement of hearing Mass, like those early Christian virgins who killed themselves to save their virginity from pagan spoilers. He did not feel justified in including him among the martyrs, but neither did he give him up for damned.[62] Again, the popular version of the issue was cruder and more dramatic. Young Rose Allen, who carried on the ancient tradition of the sharp-tongued virgin, declared that the Mass stank in the face of God.[63] There is no question that these Sacramentarians would agree with the later Recusants as to the central importance of the Mass, cosmically as they would disagree as to the character of that importance.

Such iconoclastic episodes must have caused a good deal of shock and even some social disturbance. Earlier Foxe had made it clear that if heresy disturbed the peace of the commonwealth, the severity of magistrates was justified,[64] and he had found himself unable to believe that a man with such sound evangelical ideas as John Ball could be mixed up in so un-Gospel-like a proceeding as the rising in Kent of 1382.[65] But in the case of the sacramental episodes Foxe clearly agreed with William Gardiner that the true cause of the social disturbance was not the curative violence but the initial idolatry that had challenged such drastic action. And this conclusion is confirmed by the exception which he made to what he defined as the chief of the good works which declare the faith of a Christian man, and that was to be obedient to the magistrates, unless they command idolatry.[66] That seemed so self-evident to Foxe that he did not bother to argue it, but in the event it was as grave a potential threat to the state Church as the ancient tenet of refusal of obedience to an heretical prince, which was to make the Catholics so feared, and in the hands of the Puritans it was to prove an even graver actuality as the conflict with the Established Church drew to the Civil War. But here again Foxe seems to have felt confident that his own stoutly Protestant position would hold the field, and, of course, in this he reflects the confidence of his point of view in this still pre-Hooker period in the development of the Established Church.

But it would be a mistake to take Foxe simply as the voice of certain elements in the life of his time, or even of certain movements gathering force for the life of succeeding generations. And it would be an injustice. For Foxe is very much more than the voice of his time. He is a propagandist of deep conviction and of deliberate and sustained purpose. There is nothing of the speculative philosopher or of the academically objective and impersonal reporter about him. He is always an advocate, even a champion, reporting every round of the struggle with the energy and delight of the devoted partisan. The result is to be seen not only in the judicious selection of material, but in the careful underscoring of the main lines of the evidence, in the frankly debating summary of the results, in the careful repetition and reinforcement of the lessons to be drawn, in the ardently interested and often highly emotional commentary on the whole transaction. There is in Foxe nothing of the modern, or even of the Shakespearean, sense of tragedy, nothing of the mystery of human fortune in which the greatest are brought low, and the best of human nature is spent seemingly for nothing. Any suggestion of that sort of tragic view of the world would have seemed desperate to Foxe, something not to be pitied but despised. For victory, and that in the fairly short run (at least as regards the Henrician and Marian martyrs), was to him not simply the reward of effort, but the vindication of the cause itself. For Foxe, to alter a little the definition of Milton's archangel, to be weak was to be miserable indeed, but to be beaten was to be proved wrong.

It is this conviction not only of the rightness of his cause but of its vindication in human history that gives such power to Foxe's passionate and unremitting partisanship, that enables him to sweep through the vicissitudes of the history he chronicles and deliver his verdicts as to their significance with so much confidence. For it is of something larger than anything man could do that he is speaking, and as he reports it, insensibly he assumes the large surety of omniscience. Very little, indeed, is said of the human agencies involved in the proud summary of the changes that were brought about by Edward's accession:

Masses extinct and abolished furthermore after softer beginnings, by little and little greater thinges followed after in reformation of churches. Then such as before were in banishment for the daunger of the truth, were againe receaved to there countre. To be short a new face of thinges began now to appere, as it were a stage, new players comming in, thold being thrust out. For the most part of churches the bishops therof were changed. Such as had bene domme prelates before were compelled to give place to other then that would preach and take paynes. Besides also other out of forren countries, men of lerning and notable knowledg wer sent for and received, emong whome was Petrus Martir, Martine Bucer, and Paulus Phagius.[67]

And this sureness of judgment still steadies the grief and indignation with which he sums up the disaster that followed on the death of the young King:

Nowe were come into the Churches blynde and ignoraunt massemongers, with their Latin bablinges and apyshe ceremonyes, who like cruell Wolves spared not to murther all suche, as any thyng at all, but once whispered against their Poperye. As for all the Godlye preachers whiche were in kinge Edwards tyme, they were eyther fledde the Realme, or elles, as the Prophetes dyd in kynge Achabs dayes, they were privilye kepte in corners. As for as manye as the Papistes could laye holde on, they were sette into prison, ther as lambes waiting, when the butchers would call them to the slaughter.[68]

It is significant, too, that though Foxe mentions the fact of the division of opinion at the accession of Elizabeth, he does not enter into the details of the struggle. He is content to record the victory without giving any information as to instruments or methods. The effect is, of course, immensely impressive. This is the victory of the Lord. The work of men may be criticized, may be impugned. It is vitiated by the passions of struggle and the moral imperfection of means. But the work of the Lord has an ease and a purity not possible to human effort. Nowhere has Foxe shown a sounder instinct than here in the simple summary of the parliamentary aspect of the Elizabethan triumph:

Although in this parliament some diversity there was of judgment and opinion betwene parties, yet notwithstandinge through the mercifull goodnes of the Lord, the true cause of the gospell had the upper hand, the papistes hope was frustrate, and their rage abated, the order and proceading of king Edwards tyme concerning religion was revived agayne, the supremacy of the Pope abolished, the articles and blouddye statutes of Queene Marye repealed, brefelye the furious fierbrandes of cruel persecution, which had consumed so manye pore mens bodyes, were now extincte and quenched.[69]

Not the least of Foxe's sources of strength is his complete incapacity to understand how anyone can fail to see the significance of this verdict of history. That is the source of the constant insinuation, which, operating on the known incapacity of most men to grasp how different the familiar world might look to another point of view from their own, impugns the basic integrity of his opponents, and makes them, as it were, witnesses against themselves in his cause. Perhaps the best example of this is to be found in the preface "To the Persecutors of Gods truth, commonlye called Papistes" at the beginning of the book, where having assured his adversaries that they are beaten and should give up so hopeless a cause, he goes on to suggest that those who still hold out in such circumstances must in their consciences know they are wrong:

Seing therefore the Lord doth and must prevaile, be counselled and exhorted in the Lord, leave of your resisting, and yeld to the truth, which your own boiling consciences (I am sure) doth inwardly witnes and testify, if for your own wilful standing up on your credit and reputation (as ye thinke) ye would come to the confession of the same. And what reputation is this of credite, to be found constant in errour against the truth, in Antichrist againste Christ, in your owne destruction, against saving of your soules? Briefelie and to be short, if my counsail may be heard, better it were for you in time to geve over while it is thanke woorthye, then at length to be drawen by compulsion of time, wil ye nil ye, to geve over your cause losing both thank and your cause also. For see you not daylie more and more the contrary part (the Lordes arme going with them) to grow so strong against you, that not onely ther is no hope, but no possibility, for your obstinate errour to stand against so manifest truth?[70]

Seldom has the argument from success been used with more force or assurance.

It would be a mistake, however, to impute any undue naïveté about the rationale of propaganda to Foxe. It is at the end of this same appeal to the erstwhile persecutors, that he shows that he very well appreciates the foundations of an effective revolution, especially the importance of the proper education of youth. For he goes on: "More-over, Universities and schooles in al quarters be set up againste you, and youthe so trayned in the same, that you shal never be able to matche them. To conclude, in Countries, kingdomes, Cities, Townes, and Churches reformed, your errours and superstitious vanities bee so blotted out within the space of these forty yeares in the harts of men, that their children and youth being so long nouseled in the sound doctrine of Christ, like as they never heard of your ridiculous trump-ery, so they wyl never be brought to the same." [71]

Foxe was quite aware, too, as we have seen, of the advantage of printing as an instrument of propaganda, for he pointed out that Gutenberg's invention made books so common and cheap that they could be spread abroad as never before to abolish ignorance and idolatry.[72] Of course, he could have no suspicion in his vigorous attack upon the idolatry of the image and the picture and the rite that a new idolatry had come into the world, the idolatry of the printed word. Rather, he followed with unflagging enthusiasm and excite-ment the progress of the English translations of the Bible. For ex-ample, the final English event he noted for the year 1526 was: "This yeare also the newe Testamente began firste to be translated into Englyshe by William Tindall, and was brought into the realme of England." [73] The circulation of this book was one of the prime in-struments of the new propaganda. For instance, one of the last things Master Bilney did before he was apprehended at Norwich was to give a copy of Tyndale's translation with *The Obedience of a Christian Man* to the Anchoress at Norwich.[74]

When in the thirty-eighth year of his reign King Henry issued a proclamation against English books, including Tyndale's and Cover-dale's translations of the New Testament, on the score that they had been used to sow abroad "sondry pernicious and detestable errours and heresies not only contrary to the lawes of this realme, but also repugnant to the true sence of goddes lawe and his worde," and that they had been used to "trouble the sober, quiet and godlye religion united and established, under the kinges majesty in this his realme," Foxe labeled the proclamation "A streight and cruell proclamation set forth and devised for the abolishing of english bookes," and went on to observe, "Here now the Prelates and the popes side thought, they had made a greate hand against the gospell." [75] Likewise when later, under Mary, the scriptural texts written on the walls of churches, which Bonner charged had been used to inculcate Protestant doctrine, were ordered to be taken down, Foxe at once pronounced the move a device to keep the people in ignorance of scriptural truth.[76]

But Foxe was not merely a master of the techniques of propaganda. He was also a master of those arts of emotional appeal that can alone give the mechanics of technique the vitality of inspired creation. Indeed, it is the sureness of his appeal to the basic human emotions that is the great strength of both Foxe's storytelling method and his incidental or implied apologetics. A good example of both is the story of the preacher Laurence Saunders and his infant son. His wife had come to his prison with her babe, and though the keeper did not dare to admit her, he did take the child and bring him to his father — "L. Sanders seing him, rejoyced greatly, saying that he rejoyced more to have suche a boy, than he shold if .ii. thousand pound wer given him. And unto the standers by, which praised the goodlynes of the child, he said: What man fearing god would not lose this life present, rather than by prolonging it here, he shold juge this boy to be a bastard his wife a whore, and himself a whoremonger? yea yf there were no other cause for which a man of my estate shold lose his life: yet who wold not geve it, to advow this child to be legitimate, and his marriage to be lauful and holy?" To this Foxe added: "I do (good reder) recite this saying, not only to let the se what he thought of priests mariage: but chiefly to let all maried couples and parents learn to beare in their bosom true affections, natural, but seasoned with the true salt of the spirite, . . ." [77]

Conversely, Foxe is no less expert in the techniques of denigration. He is a master of the emotional adjective, the label that can be counted upon to call forth the proper response. "Horrible" is a favorite adjective of his, as we have seen from the very title of the book. Where his Protestants are "symple" and "seely," his Papists are likely to be "craftie." [78] The epithet "franticke Francis" helps to dispose of the claims to serious attention of the founder of one body of the hated friars,[79] in a fashion that anticipates the seventeenth-century attack on "enthusiasm." What he can do in this important genre is brilliantly illustrated in that passage in his account of the education of the young

Cranmer in which he describes the condition of the universities at the turn of the century:

It was in that tyme when all good authors and fine writers being neglected filthy barbarousnes was embraced in all scholes and universities. The names and numbers of liberall artes did only remaine: the artes themselves were cleane lost. Logike was gone out of kind into sophistical trifles. Philosophy, both morall and naturall was miserablye defaced with infinite questions and subtleties. The use of tongs and eloquent learning was either smal, or none at al. Ye and divinity it selfe was fallen into the state, that being laden with articles, and distinctions, it served rather for the gayne of a few, then for the edification of many. Unluckelye therefore so good a witte falling into these unhappy tymes, is constreyned to spend a great part of his youthe (worthye of better instruction) in the pevish questions of Duns, and other maisters of the same sort, untill he was .20. yere olde. At the length after so long darknes of barbarisme, the tonges and other good learning began by litle and litle to spring up again, and the bokes of Faber and Erasmus beganne to be muche occupyed, and hadde in good estimation, wyth a number of good authours beside. In whome the same Cranmer takying no small pleasure, dyd dailye rubbe awaye his olde rustinesse on them, as uppon a whetstone, untyll at the length when Martin Luther was rysen uppe, the more bryght and happy day of gods knowlege did waken mennes myndes, to the cleare light of the truth.[80]

So Cranmer, now that he was about thirty years old, began to give his whole mind to the study of religious issues, first laying his foundation by devoting himself for three years to the study of Scripture.[81] This is a good deal more than an account of the intellectual awakening of one man. It is the familiar humanist view of the awakening of Western civilization after the slumber of the Middle Ages, presented as the preparation for the breaking of the light of the Reformation on the darkness of medieval Christianity.

This is certainly direct enough. But Foxe is, also, a master of the indirect attack that laughs the object of his contempt out of court with the life and energy it gives to its caricature or burlesque. His description of the Mass is a striking example:

What Democritus or Calphurnius could abstaine from laughter, beholding only the fashion of their masse, from the beginninge to the latter end, wyth suche turning, returning, halfe turning and hole turning, such kissinge, blissing, crowching, becking, crossing, knocking, ducking, wasshing, rinsing, lyfting, touching, fingring Whispering, stoping, dipping, bowinge, licking, wiping, sleping, shifting, with an hundreth thinges mo. What wise man, I saye, seing such toysh gaudes can keepe from laughter? And what bee all the Popes doynges, with the whole circumstance of his religion, and maner of his popelinges, but matters almoste to bee laughed at etc.[82]

The attack on the Mass was, as we have seen, one of the central strategies of the movement to which Foxe devoted his very great talents. There was nothing frivolous in the purpose of this exuberant mockery, and nothing careless in the spray of its needling contempt. Foxe had, as we have seen, thoroughly appreciated the enormous advantage that his side had enjoyed in the popular appeal of the cheaper printed books in the vernacular which had brought religious controversy with all its heady excitements to the unlearned and the unprofessional.[83] It was for that public that he wrote, and to that public that he shrewdly addressed all his remarkable powers of popular appeal. He understood that public, too, as few men of his time did, except for the great dramatists, with whom he has so much in common. He appreciated the passion of the time for history, particularly its own history, and he set out to satisfy it with what seemed to him, and to most of his contemporaries of a serious mind, the most important aspect of the recent national history, the religious settlement. He saw, too, the importance of having that history viewed in what he conceived to be its true light by the great mass of his countrymen. And he saw that to have that view of history accepted was the strongest guarantee possible of the defense of that settlement against the only adversaries he or most Anglicans of his time feared, the Catholics.

Foxe was quite aware of the national preoccupations of his age, especially of the passion for affairs of state which so many observers of the time, both harassed representatives of the government and disinterested visitors, noted as characteristic of the English of that period.[84] He knew, too, how much that public enjoyed being taken behind the scenes, and he took them there. And this was true not only of the actions on the main stage but also of the major decisions and definitions behind them. Foxe admitted the humblest subject who could read, or be read to, to the disputes of convocations and the debates of kings and lords.

To a lesser degree the *Golden Legend* had already done that, and presently Shakespeare was to do something like it in his histories, but there is something quite different from either in *Actes and Monu-*

ments. There are kings and popes and cardinals and great ones aplenty in the book, but the popes and cardinals are almost always seen at a disadvantage, and sometimes even the kings. And the infirmities of the great are in the last analysis overcome by the virtues of the humble. Foxe gives a gallery it would be hard to rival for the time, of men, and even women, of humble life who took the spotlight in at least one scene of their lives and acquitted themselves with the best for courage and resolution and often, from Foxe's point of view, intelligence and wisdom. Many of the familiar figures of the next century, the theological weaver, the Scripture-expounding and exhorting housewife, the disputing artisan and tradesman, appear in the roster of the martyrs. Of these manifestations of the lay preaching impulse the most impressive is that of George Egles, for his wandering called "Trudgeoner." He had, as Foxe says, "litle learning or none," following the occupation of a tailor, but after a while "being eloquent and of good utterance gave and applied himselfe to the profite of Christes church." Apparently he preached without interference in King Edward's days, and then when troubled times came, he continued for a year or two preaching the Gospel, especially about Colchester. This course of his Foxe expressly defended, reminding his readers that "often times Christes wil and pleasure is to beautify and adorn his kingdom with the weak and simple instrumentes of this world," and citing Amos and others from the Old Testament who "wer called from the heards and foldes to the honor of prophets," and the fishermen apostles of the New.[85] There was a power which the humble of this world, especially that section which was now feeling its strength and its ambition most strongly, could take on, and that was a power which overshadowed the power of the great of this world, the power of the Lord.

So viewed, this material must have been extraordinarily exciting to the braced wills of a class that was growing conscious of its strength and coming out of the shadows of an obscure past into a growing influence. This moral excitement is not to be overemphasized; it was more often beneath the surface than expressed, but it was there, and none the less operative because its triumph was still in the future. In this respect, Foxe must have contributed to the growing power of popular Puritanism at least as much as any man of his time. The reprinting of his book in the crucial year of 1641 is, as the great historian of the Puritan movement, William Haller, has pointed out, evidence that the seventeenth-century leaders of that movement were aware of the fact.[86]

But that is in the future. What Foxe did for the men of his own time, for whom *Actes and Monuments* was first written, was quite enough. He knew that most of his readers would not have the background to understand many of the things he discussed, and he gave it to them, both historically and theologically. And in giving what he considered the true history of the Christian Church, he built up the intellectual world he wanted his public to possess.

This great tome is not only a martyrology and a history and an encyclopedia all in one, but it is even more a whole library in a single volume, presenting the vast panorama of a centuries-old crusade and an epoch-making revolution. The whole history of a great and historic change is here unfolded in almost every species of literary record. There are accounts of personal experience from at home and abroad, histories of nations, trifling anecdotes and passions of valiant leaders, articles of arraignment and processes of examination, interrogatories and investigations, private debates and echoes of village arguments, and public disputations between protagonists of learning and power; there are manifestoes and petitions, supplications and protests, appeals and complaints of grievances, articles of religion, injunctions, decrees, proclamations, acts and processes of counsels and parliaments, judicial sentences, measures for the organization of church life, lists of books prohibited and commended, apologias, declarations of faith, testimonials, wills and testaments, letters, obituaries, accounts of ceremonies from the degrading of a bishop to the baptism of a princess, translations of liturgies (with careful annotations of a highly controversial character), orations, sermons, summaries and précis of books, and even at times whole pamphlets. There can have been few books in the world like it, few that would give an innocent reader such a sense of being in the know, past, present, and future, that would give a simple man so complete a picture of the world in which he found himself and how it came to be so; few books that would so completely furnish forth an untutored mind with a whole intellectual world, so perfectly suited to its tastes and adapted to its powers, so completely to arm it against the challenges and pressures of an age of unprecedented moral and mental aggression. The ordinary reader who worked conscientiously through the disputations and the reports of hearings and investigations must have been often at a loss to understand some of the issues that have challenged some of the finest metaphysical minds of the race. Here Foxe explained, and defined, and interpolated, and summarized. The result, on the whole, was lacking in subtlety of discrimination or breadth of imagination, but it was clear with the kind of simplicity and surety that will stand by a man in a fight.

But Foxe did something more; he dramatized all this in individual episodes, in stories. Whether his matter be horrible or merry, Foxe is a first-rate storyteller. He certainly needed all his gifts to keep his reader going through the enormous masses of controversial discussion, much of it of a very specialized and even technical character, with which he stuffed his book. But he has the born storyteller's sensitiveness to the limits of his reader's endurance, the dramatist's instinct for comic relief even to tragedy, and he does not scorn to yield to the necessities of the popular entertainer. Nor need he, for he knows how to turn even the comic interlude to the driving purpose of the main plot: "Hetherto gentle Reader we have remembred a great nomber of lamentable and bloudy tragedies of suche as have been slayne through extreme crueltie. Now I wilt here set before thee againe a mery and comycall spectacle, whereat thou mayst now lawgh and refreshe thy selfe, whiche for somuche as it dyd necessarely accorde with our present enterpryse, I have not thought good to passe it over with sylence, for God hathe oftentymes by dyverse manifest meanes deluded the crafte and subtiltie of the byshoppes and their vaine hypocrisie." He then reminds the reader of how this was manifest in the case of Pope Joan, whose sex was discovered by her being delivered of a child in the midst of a procession, a lasting disgrace to that see, and in a "pompous and rydiculous" embassy of Cardinal Wolsey.[87] Then, having, as it were, turned his reader's mind to jollity by these reminders, he proceeds to tell a very good story of how a cry of fire during a sermon at a recantation in Our Lady's church at Oxford created a panic in which many declared they felt the dropping of the melting lead from the roof, though there was no fire. One of the incidental absurdities is the episode of the boy who got out of the church in the press by jumping from the top of the door into a monk's cowl, and the resulting comedy when the monk became aware of the weight at his back and, hearing a voice, decided that the evil spirit which had caused the fire had flown into his cowl.[88] Doubtless the story had the effect which Foxe intended on the mind of the godly reader. But even the ungodly reader might be refreshed by it, for it is a good story told with all Foxe's power of conjuring up a scene, so that it comes to life for the reader as if he had been there.

This power of style in Foxe's work is important for two reasons. First of all, it is illuminating for the period. The pungent dialogue of the Elizabethan dramatists seems less of a miracle after one has read page after page of dialogue and dramatic narrative as brilliant as anything written for the stage. If this was pretty close to the most popular reading of the serious-minded public of those days, one is not so surprised at the color and verve of the literature of the less serious-minded. But it is even more important for the aid it gave to Foxe in the accomplishment of his propagandist purpose. The material he offered was as emotionally exciting as any romantic material of the time. It presented heroes of authentic proportions and villains of proper dye. It called forth all those emotions, of partisanship, of competition, of admiration, of hate, of horror, of pride, that not even the sober-minded have ever been able long to live without. And it offered them to edification and to salvation. The gravest of men could have a very good time with a very good conscience.

The age loved stories, even though that sober-minded public, the newly literate as distinguished from the cultivated and the learned, had been given grounds enough for having qualms about the works of the imagination, and suspicions of the adornments of art. What Foxe offered he offered as sober, even sacred, fact, and he offered it with a devotion to the matter in hand, a simplicity and directness, that suggest that he had caught the first undertow of that insistence on plain writing and talking that was to play so large a part in the history of Puritan preaching in the next century. But this material has another element of popular appeal. These stories abound in homely detail of everyday life, developed with often amazing precision. The result must have been an immeasurable heightening of confidence in the author who got so many of the things that could be checked so right. And this confidence made it possible for Foxe to do for his fellow countrymen what he had set out to do, perhaps more than he could ever have dreamed of doing, for there is usually in works of genius like his something that transcends intention.

In a time of great confusion, when most of his fellow countrymen had seen so many of the familiar landmarks of their lives swept away, Foxe gave them not only an explanation of what had happened but a rationalization and a justification. He gave them answers not only for the questions they were asking but for those they had probably never thought of asking. But more than that, for the view of the world by which they had lived for the most part tacitly and tra-ditionally, and which they were now assured they had been mistaken to accept so long, he offered them a substitute view of the world and of human history, past and present, that not only made it easy for them to accept the new order but persuaded them that it was their plain duty to do so. And, as we have seen, he did it with such power that he made acceptance of the new order seem an entrance into an heroic heritage that was in a very real sense the distinctive possession of the loyal and the up-to-date Englishman. In so doing, he gave to his countrymen a view of the world to live by, as Haller has again said, "a conception of universal history and of England's place in history, a conception which continued to prevail in the English mind long after the book had gone out of fashion though not out of use and memory." [89] Of course, the element of propaganda was in the martyr story from the beginning, but Foxe's ecclesiastical history must be pretty nearly in a class by itself, not only one of the greatest but one of the most effective examples of the literature of propaganda on record.

THE ENGLISH MISSION

 *W*hether viewed as martyrology or as history, Foxe's book is the story of a great victory. Nothing like this victory was going to be possible for the English Catholics who remained faithful to the old religious order, and consequently nothing like Foxe's book was going to be possible for them, either. The Catholic story in the years that followed the accession of Elizabeth is the story of the resistance of the defeated and the irreconcilable, a resistance that in the circumstances of the times had more and more to assume an underground character. The martyrological record will, therefore, remain a fragmentary and indirect one, dependent often on hostile accounts put forth by authority in justification or warning, and the often hasty rebuttal by the defenders of the martyrs. On both sides, the martyrological record is a part of a continuing struggle, and the controversial involvement heavy. It is necessary, therefore, to understand the situation that had developed in the twenty-odd years between the accession of Queen Elizabeth and the coming of Campion and Parsons on the mission of 1580.

The Elizabethan Settlement in its origins had been as complicated as most human arrangements are, but whatever the balance of forces that lay behind it, one thing is quite clear, and that is that it was designed to keep as many of the English people in the pews of one national church as possible. In the confusion of the ending of one world, however protracted that ending might be, and in the bewilderment of the rise of a quite new world, however slow in its self-definition the process might be, security received a new value, and integration as a guarantee of security, a fresh urgency. The uniting of the two kinds of piety, the love of God and the love of king (or queen), reinforced both. That integration of the nation's pieties was something which the government valued highly, so highly that it was prepared to do a good deal to preserve it once it was achieved. On the other hand, it had a real magnetism for the individual Englishman; it gave him the full plenitude of what might be called his Englishness. For it made possible a concentration and a deepening of his hold on his basic values that would make him very suspicious of anything that threatened that integration, so essential to his inner security.

Once the dominance of the royal power was established, that power, under Elizabeth at least, was ready to be conciliatory on those aspects of the religious situation which seemed less important. For those who looked below the surface, for those who took seriously their religious allegiance as distinct from their civic, there might be grounds for uneasiness. There would be those who, remembering Geneva wistfully, felt that the Elizabethan Settlement had stopped dangerously short of the ideal. Some of these men, of course, refused to have anything to do with the new order, but more of them continued working within the framework of the Elizabethan Settlement, hoping that with their persistent efforts at propaganda and education (weapons the effectiveness of which they had plenty of reason to trust), it might be possible to bring the national establishment closer to their desire. The hopes of such men were to die hard, and when they did, their resistance was to take a dramatic form. But the story of the Puritan martyrs belongs, on the whole, to a later period than this which we are studying.

There were others, to the left of the Puritans, if one may use a term of very dubious appropriateness, to whom the Elizabethan Settlement was deeply repugnant because it ran counter to their very radical disagreements with the whole social, as well as religious, thinking that lay behind it. The resistance of the Anabaptists deserves attention, but from the very circumstances of the case, that would be harder to study and harder to document than any of the resistances which we are studying. For the Anabaptists were banished from

England by the proclamation of November 22, 1538.[1] Still there are a few surviving accounts of executions of men who look and sound like Anabaptists, and even like Arians and Socinians. A ballad by Thomas Gilbart to be sung "To the Tune of, John Carelesse," commemorated the burning at Norwich on September 18, 1583, of John Lewes, "a Most Detestable and Obstinate Hereticke," for denying Christ. The ballad noted that he did "thou" everybody, without reverence for any rank. He smilingly turned his face from the preachers before burning, and when the flames surrounded him, and the crowd shouted to him to call on Christ to save his soul, he died without speaking.[2] But most Englishmen of this period, Protestants and Catholics alike, viewed such victims with horror, and their record is an obscure and fragmentary one. From the martyrological point of view, the dramatic resistance of the Elizabethan period is that of the Recusants, the Catholics who refused to conform to the Established Church.

Whatever the claims or the beliefs of the architects of the Elizabethan Settlement about the rational moderation of their position, they left nothing to chance when it came to making that moderate and reasonable position prevail in a not-too-reasonable world. The lurid glare of the Marian bonfires, particularly in the pages of Foxe, has so filled the sixteenth-century scene that it is often forgotten that there are much more intelligent and effective methods of pressure in the field of religion, as of everything else. It may well be that the fact that, after the Queen herself, certainly not to be suspected of anything like religious enthusiasm, the prime mover in the religious settlement was a practical man of affairs like William Cecil, led to the greater efficiency of the Elizabethan provisions for the enforcement of conformity.[3] The recognition of the Queen's spiritual as well as temporal sovereignty was exacted of all ecclesiastical personnel in the oath incorporated in the Act of Supremacy passed by Parliament in 1559.[4] The Act of Uniformity in religious observance, passed shortly afterward by the same Parliament, made a revised edition of the second Edwardian Prayer Book the standard of religious observance, and forbade any other form of service in England, imposing the obligations of attendance at that service under penalty, at first relatively modest, of a shilling a Sunday.[5]

This legislative provision was reinforced by propaganda from the pulpit in the sermons which all must hear, and in official proclamations and publications; and the line of this propaganda was constant and clear, and that was simply that the loyal Englishman accepted the religious order established by law as a matter of good citizenship and Christian duty.[6] For him to look abroad and remember his fathers' ancient allegiance to the Pope was to turn away from his duty to the Queen, to desert her for her enemies. On the other hand, the Englishman was assured that the religious order of the time was the familiar traditional order of his fathers, purged of corruption according to the greater light of the present day.

But there was a subtler element in the situation, one may say a matter of atmosphere. There was a basic folk piety, and nowhere was this stronger than in the English countryside where the village church, in which one's forefathers had worshiped, with the churchyard in which the bodies of the same forefathers lay awaiting the Resurrection, was the center of social life to a degree that is very hard for us to imagine today. It was for the villagers and the countrymen *the* church. It was the same church, very often with the same priest who had been there earlier, sometimes, it seemed, from time immemorial. The decorations had vanished, but whenever the villager was tempted to remember these, he was assured of his escape from idolatry, and any nostalgia would be labeled as a hankering after the fleshpots of Egypt. As for the changes in the service, there was enough that was familiar to give persuasiveness to the claim that this was the same service, and he was assured that any changes he noted had been made in the interest of removing corruptions and adulterations. So every effort was made to make the English public feel that all reasonable, balanced, sound men attended the parish church as good citizens should. The whole weight of Christian life for hundreds of years had been on the side of the production of a civilized human being, not only a pious individual, but even more a social human being. It was not a good preparation for individual nonconformity, as we saw in the Henrician debacle.

Moreover, with the passage of time during the first quarter-century of the Queen's reign, the Elizabethan Settlement came to gather to itself that further sanctity of the customary and the established that meant so much to the sixteenth-century Englishman. And by 1580 the very fact that more than two decades had gone by since he had known anything else made the now-established order seem the normal and inevitable one.

It is not surprising, either, that even among those who were aware of the extent of the changes that had taken place and found themselves unable to accept them there was a good deal of nominal conformity. When the nature of the Elizabethan Settlement was clear, many of the priests and scholars and leaders of the Marian regime who were still out of prison, and who found themselves with no possibility of functioning if they remained at home, had gone to the Continent, and so had a good many people of position with means to travel and live abroad. But this was a peculiarly drastic step for a sixteenth-century Englishman to take. And, of course, it was quite impossible for the great mass even of the concerned Catholic population. Many of them, therefore, thought it wise to make the minimal appearance at church and wait for a better day. There was always the hope of a change in the kingship, the possibility of the succession of the Scottish Queen, or of another Catholic heir. Even Queen Elizabeth's marriage with a Catholic prince might bring relief. And there was some hope, too, that the demonstration of Catholic quietness and loyalty might disarm government suspicion. A nominal conformity under such circumstances might seem justifiable to men who had a good deal to lose, and care to avoid attracting attention, a minimum exercise of prudence.

Such a situation had its obvious dangers from the point of view of anyone interested in the survival of the Catholic Church who had any idea of how institutions are affected by changing circumstances, and any notion of what those circumstances might be in the future.

Here one remembers the way in which the "English books" kept the Lollard movement alive in the fourteenth and fifteenth centuries. There were many works of controversy written on the Catholic side in this period, but the governmental censorship of books made the printing of such works in England impossible, except, as we shall see presently, at great risk on concealed presses.[7] The Elizabethan government was, also, quite aware of the danger of importation of books printed on the Continent. Indeed, the battle of the books from 1568 on was obviously one of the most constant worries of the Elizabethan government, as may be seen in the dozen or so proclamations on the subject in the Dyson collection of 1618. The proclamation of March 1,

1568, may be taken as the prototype, with its complaint of books made or translated without license, mostly by Her Majesty's subjects staying abroad (perhaps an indication that authority was aware of unlicensed printing at home), "contayning sundry matters repugnaunt to trueth, derogatorie to the soveraigne estate of her Majestie, and stirring and nourishing sedition in this Realme," and being circulated secretly by "malicious persons." Typical, too, is its warning of the loyal against them, and its command that all such books be turned in to the bishop of the diocese, and its forbidding of unlicensed keeping or reading of such books, with threat of severe punishment.[8] More detailed is the Royal Proclamation of July 1, 1570, "agaynst seditious and trayterous Bookes, Billes, and Writinges," directing anybody who finds any such forbidden materials to put them in the hands of proper authority, with promise of generous reward for so doing and punishment for failing to do so "as concealers and mayteyners of sedition and tumultes."[9]

But even if there had been easy access to the books written at home and abroad in behalf of ancient allegiances, the books alone would not have sufficed in this case. For it is the essence of the Catholic religious system that it is institutional and that it functions through the sacraments, and that most of the sacraments, though not all, require the priest, above all the sacraments of Penance and the Eucharist, and so does the central rite of the Mass. The sustained attack on the Mass as an idolatrous thing was an effective one, for the Mass was the cornerstone of the old religious order, and the Mass priest an indispensable need for the Catholic.

It was at this point that the Elizabethan Settlement worked with an almost automatic efficiency. It was simply not possible for any priest to continue functioning publicly, and any effort to function privately was at the risk not only of the priest but of his patrons and supporters. But still more important from the long-term point of view was the impossibility of recruiting any new priests. Here, then, the Elizabethan government could afford to be patient, and there is evidence that as time went on, authority was fairly negligent of the few remaining Marian clergy in England who had refused to conform to the new order. They were getting on in years now, and their numbers were dwindling from natural causes, if nothing else.

Nor was the danger unappreciated among the exiles on the Continent, particularly those who could turn their gaze from the defeats of the present to the possibilities of the future. Foremost among them was William Allen, perhaps the shrewdest and most statesman-like Englishman of his day on the Catholic side. Born in 1532, Allen represented the older generation of the Recusants, men who, though now exiles, had once been at the center of English academic life. He had early made his mark at Oxford, becoming Principal of St. Mary Hall in 1556,[10] but in 1559 he resigned, and in 1561 he went to Louvain in Flanders, where he found a good many other men from Oxford and Cambridge. He was ordained at Malines in 1567.[11] It was eminently characteristic of Allen that once having seen the need, he could not rest until he had found the answer to it, the seminaries on the Continent, where young men might be educated and trained, not to hold on to a vanishing order, but to meet the challenges of a new age with the resources of a new age. The first of these, the college which he opened at Douai on Michaelmas Day, 1568, was perhaps the first seminary to be established under the new rules of Trent made for the improvement of the training of the clergy, one of the greatest needs of the Church of the time.[12] The first of the Douai priests began to arrive in England in 1574 to work as auxiliaries to the Marian priests still active at that time.[13] Three years later, in 1577, they opened their martyr roster with the execution of Cuthbert Mayne at Launceston for treason.[14]

So intertwined were political and religious purposes and interests in the struggles of the sixteenth century that any delicate discrimination of motives and intentions is at best difficult. It is one of the ironies of the situation that the Pope of the period probably most dedicated to the spiritual interests of religion, the reforming Pius V, issued the Bull of Excommunication of Queen Elizabeth in 1570 to "quieten the consciences of the English Catholics, who scrupled to free themselves by arms from the tyranny that oppressed them, so long as they had not some official declaration that Elizabeth was a heretic, and that their oaths of allegiance no longer bound them." [15] Anyone who knew the English situation, as the Pope clearly did not,[16] could hardly be surprised by the reply of Parliament to this disastrous action, the Penal Statutes of 1571, the second of which, "An act against the bringing in and putting in execution of Bulls and other instruments from the see of Rome," declared anyone a traitor who after July 1,

1571, "makes use of any bull, writing, or instrument of absolution or reconciliation with the Roman see, who absolves or reconciles another, who receives such absolution or reconciliation," and made aiders and abettors of such traitors liable to penalties of praemunire (in reference to the medieval statute to prevent appeals from the royal to the papal court), and failure to denounce anyone who offered such absolution or reconciliation, a misprision or concealment of treason.[17]

It was never easy at any time to draw the line between the political and the religious elements in the sixteenth-century English situation, and the nature of Catholic political intrigue on the Continent, including that of Allen himself after 1582, did not make it any easier. Moreover, England might be the center of the universe for the loyal Catholic Englishmen preparing in the seminaries to labor for the salvation of their countrymen; it was not for Rome, or for the various Catholic princes jockeying for position at this time.[18] The men who embarked on the English Mission were men who deliberately embraced a very perilous calling. But by 1580, six years after their first coming, there were a hundred priests from Douai at work in England.[19]

It would seem invidious to single out one group rather than another among such men, but for the literary record the primacy for the Elizabethan age goes to the new order, the Society of Jesus. It was not a matter of numbers, for this period at least, for in the reign of Elizabeth there were rarely as many as a dozen Jesuits at work in England at one time.[20] It was rather a matter of impact and attention. Certainly the most dramatic episode in the English Mission, one may say the high and visible peak of that great iceberg of human effort, is the mission of the Jesuits Parsons and Campion, in 1580.

In spite of the suspicions of some of their detractors, the Jesuits had not rushed upon or seized the job. It was Allen who saw the potential usefulness of the new order.[21] Formally recognized at Rome in 1540, the Society of Jesus was the product of the new age, the device of a Spanish soldier and mystic, Ignatius of Loyola, to join the battle of the time head-on. The new society had certain advantages over the older orders. The first was their deliberate and calculated worldliness. The Carthusian story, as we have seen, is the classic example of the hazards of trying to keep oneself pure and unspotted from the world in a time of historical change. The Jesuits were not likely to be so surprised. And the second was their understanding of the resources of the new age, particularly of the consequences of the invention of printing for the art of propaganda. And closely associated with this was their alertness to the new psychological awareness of the time. In the *Spiritual Exercises* of Saint Ignatius they had not only an instrument that strengthened them for their independent and often solitary effort, but something which they could give to their pupils to enable them to carry on when they had to leave them. It would be a mistake to say that the *Spiritual Exercises* were a new method of organizing and disciplining the inner life of the devout Christian. They were not. But they were an answer to a search that had been going on for a long time, and that was for a way of making the techniques of meditation available, particularly to the layman, who did not have either the training or the framework of monastic life for the development and the cultivation of the art of meditation as a step on the way to contemplation.

It was characteristic of the Jesuits that when they were finally persuaded of the importance of their undertaking this enterprise, they so promptly took the center of the stage. This was due primarily to the character of the personnel they were able to put into the English Mission of 1580. Hughes does not exaggerate when he says of the selection of Parsons and Campion for this enterprise: "The miscalculations of the one were to be the foundation of the English anti-Jesuit legend — his virtues ignored, while the radiance of the other's spiritual genius, the richness which in him grace perfected, was such that later generations of Catholics have hardly seen any other figure in the Elizabethan Church." [22]

Parsons was made the head of the mission. The full story of Robert Parsons is still to be written. Born as he was in 1546, he was a member of the younger Recusant generation. Of humble origin, he gave up a successful university career at Oxford in 1575, went abroad, and later that year joined the Society of Jesus and presently plunged into both the political intrigues of his time and the work of the English Mission.[23] He was a tireless writer, an enthusiastic controversialist, a brilliant stylist. He defended the King of Spain against the suspicions of his countrymen,[24] and he mocked at Foxe's *Book of Martyrs*.[25] It is hard to believe that the same man also wrote what was incomparably the most popular book of spiritual guidance in six-teenth-century England, a book so much admired that an adapted version was made for the use of the Anglican, the famous *First Booke of the Christian Exercise Appertaining to Resolution* (1582), better known as *The Book of Resolution*.[26] As head of the English Mission, he was to prove a very able and active leader. In a letter from London to the Rector of the English College in Rome on November 17, 1580, he wrote of never remaining in one place more than two days,[27] and in August of 1581 he reported having a press and printers to publish books secretly, "using caves and holes in the ground and changing the place and their [printers'] names very frequently to avoid detection."[28] Indeed, modern scholarship has established that a number of books which it used to be thought were printed on the Continent were actually printed on Parsons' secret press in England.[29]

Among the first, if not the first, of these was a book which Parsons wrote to sound the keynote of the mission, and had printed with a Douai imprint at his secret press at Greenstreet, near London, some time before November 6, 1580.[30] It was characteristic of Parsons that he took up the crucial issue of church attendance in the very title of his book: *A Brief Discours contayning certayne Reasons why Catho-liques refuse to goe to Church*. Parsons used for this the device of a letter to a friend of his in England, and under the name of I. Howlet he dedicated it to Queen Elizabeth.[31] He obviously wished to give a notion of the impact on England of the persecution for refusal of church attendance, stressing, as he did, the imprisonment of gentle-men of position,[32] but, as he said, he wrote it mainly for those Catho-lics who for worldly considerations conformed to the requirements of church-going, assuring them that there was no Catholic in Europe but thought swearing the necessary oath and receiving the Sacra-ment as required damnable.[33] As for the hope of relief from the Recusants' hard position, the only suggestion he could offer was "in-stant and fervent prayer to almightye God, and humble recourse unto the good nature, mercye, and wisdome, of the Queenes most excellent majestye," and he reminded them that a hard ruler was the punish-ment of ill-living subjects.[34] This was, of course, the classic Tudor doctrine on the subject, and if this appeal to it may seem odd for a man with Parsons' later record, its political reassurance is in keeping with what is known of the intention at this time to keep the English

Mission clear of political entanglements. Indeed, the planners of the mission of 1580 had taken the precaution of obtaining a statement from Gregory XIII that no Catholic was expected to act upon the Bull of Excommunication of the Queen under present conditions.[35]

But even if Parsons thus sounded the alarm bell of the mission and remained throughout its nominal head, the stellar role was from the start taken by Edmund Campion. It was not because he was superior in energy or capacity to his leader. But he was superior in just those qualities that are so important for the martyr, for the warrior who in his end, which is both defeat and victory, opens the gates for his earth-bound fellows, and that is in purity, grace, and light. Here Campion is poetry beside Parsons' prose. Above all, it was he who died, and the legend is his. Perhaps the secret of the magnetism which Campion exercised on such a variety of people was that at first sight he looked so little like a martyr, and so much like something which most of the young men he encountered would very much like to be, the courtier of the high Renaissance, of Gloriana's Court as it still might appear to any young man of the position and talents that would admit him to its magnificent heights. One might add, that he looked so not only to young men, but to so seasoned a courtier and connoisseur of courtiers as the Earl of Leicester himself.[36]

Campion was, like so many of the men who play a part in this history, born into the lower middle class, in 1540, the son of a London bookseller who kept the old faith.[37] He escaped his proper lot of apprenticeship and received an excellent education because of the quickness of wit and intellectual promise he had shown from an early age.[38] Campion's gifts of mind and speech were impressive, not perhaps so much profound or original as quick, ranging, apt. He had the Elizabethan sense of the world in which he was moving, and the courtier's address in touching the mood of the moment. A junior fellow of St. John's College, Oxford, at seventeen, Campion had a brilliant university career as student and teacher, and finally as administrator in the capacity of proctor.[39]

There was, however, a cloud on that future. Though, like so many of his countrymen of the time, Campion had first reached religious awareness as a Catholic, conformity was the order of the day, and he conformed.[40] But authority was anxious about the universities

in those days, and with reason. The ranging quality of Campion's
mind, the breadth of his imagination, and the quickness of his wit
would betray him into indiscretion in the give-and-take of college
argument. He had gone as far as the diaconate, essential to a university career, in 1568, when suspicion fell on him, and he resigned his
scholarship and retreated to Ireland.[41] When suspicion closed in on
him there, he made his final decision and fled to the Continent, to
Allen's new college at Douai in 1571, and then late in 1572 he went
to Rome, to join the Society of Jesus in April of 1573.[42] Such a background fitted Campion for the mission which was to claim his life.
The temptations of conformity he knew, and he knew, too, the reality
of the ambitions that moved the young noblemen and gentlemen
who flocked to hear him. The exile, too, had its part, giving a warmth
to that love of country which he so often expressed even in the abbre-
viated record that remains to us, and that cosmopolitanism of out-
look implicit in the brief account of how, at the command of the
general of his order, he had gone from Prague to Rome and to England, "as I might and would have gone joyously into any part of
Christendome or Heathens, had I bene therunto assigned."[43]

   Both Parsons and Campion took the precaution of writing out
statements to explain their purpose in coming, in case they should
be captured before they could begin their mission.[44] Whether it was
that Campion was less cautious than Parsons,[45] or simply that chance
in which the hagiographer sees always the finger of God, it was
Campion's open letter which became public. The alarm which that
document produced is clear in the very title of what seems to be the
first of the spate of works that ensued, William Charke's *An Answere
to a Seditious Pamphlet lately cast abroade by a Jesuite, with a Discoverie of that Blasphemous Sect*, published as early as December 17, 1580. Apparently, a number of copies of Campion's letter
were in circulation, preparing "inconstant mindes to the mislike of
religion, and desire of Poperie."[46] As for Campion's claim that he was
not concerned with politics, Charke suggested a parallel between
Nicholas Sanders' expedition to Ireland to help Irish rebels against
England, the news of which had distressed Parsons and Campion
when they received it on their way to England,[47] and Campion's own
mission.[48] Finally, he pronounced impossible Campion's professed

undertaking to "avow the faith of the Catholike Church, by naturall and morall reason, which are two great enemies of true religion, and two great nurses of Atheisme and heresie." [49]

That would have seemed warning enough, but the fact that Charke, a former fellow of Peterhouse, was known to be of an extreme Puritan tendency [50] may have influenced the Queen's Council to seek a more central rebuttal. At any rate, Meredith Hanmer explained that it was at the request of the Council that on January 2, 1581, he published Campion's letter, with an answer many times as long, under the title of *The Great Bragge and Challenge of M. Champion a Jesuite.* [51] Hanmer, whom we have already encountered as a translator of Eusebius and other ancient Church historians, published the letter in full, and with a fair degree of accuracy except for one or two passages where the possibility of accident cannot be entirely ruled out. The tone of the letter is far too direct and serious for Hanmer's description. But it was undeniably a challenge, and a grave one, and that the Council saw at once.

For the very setting-out of so forthright a confession of purpose was embarrassing to those who, like Charke, regarded all such coming of priests from abroad as treasonable infiltration in the guise of religion. Sincerity was no easier to judge from rhetoric in the sixteenth century than now, but the candor with which the author of this document admitted quite enough to hang him, and worse, must have carried an alarming amount of conviction. And this was reinforced by the explicitness and circumstantiality of Campion's demand for an opportunity of disputation with "three sorts of indifferent audience. The first before your honors, wherin I woulde discourse of Religion so farre as is the common welth of your Nobilities. The second, whereof I make more accompt, before the Doctors, Masters, and chosen men of both Universities, wherein I undertake to vowe the fayth of our Catholike church, by proofes invincible, scriptures, councells, fathers, hystories, naturall and moral reasons. The thirde by the force of the lawe spirituall, and temperall. Wherein I will justifie the same faith by the common wisedome of the lawes standing in force, and practised." [52]

The most remarkable thing about this letter is its high-spirited assurance, and that in spite of the fact that the writer had no real doubt of what the end would be, as the last sentence of the letter makes clear. And here Hanmer, whether through carelessness or design, blurs a key idea, which is correctly translated in a modern version, as follows: "If these my offers be refused, and my endeavours can take no place, and I, having run thousands of miles to do you good, shall be rewarded with rigour, I have no more to say but to recommend your case and mine to Almightie God, the Searcher of Hearts, who send us His Grace, and set us at accord before the day of payment, to the end we may at last be friends in heaven, when all injuries shall be forgotten."[53] Hanmer changed the more dramatic "run" to "come," but more seriously, he blurred "your case and mine" into "your cause," with sad loss of effect.[54]

Here again, as so often, the very attacks on Campion testify to the impression he made. One of the official preachers to the Recusant prisoners in the Tower in May of 1581, John Keltridge, a well-known London preacher, in his dedicatory address of two of his sermons to Walsingham, complained of the way in which Campion and Howlet had put forth rebellious pamphlets and challenged all the learned in the realm to disputation.[55] And he went even more directly to the point in the address to his readers, where he reported the people of the land greatly troubled "because that the Papistes and Jesuites, with other the riffe raffe and scumme of this Realme, are nowe seene to appeare, who before this tyme have beene hidden in the dytches, and channelles of England."[56]

That same spirit of confidence that had made the challenge so alarming to his adversaries breathes through the little book with which Campion seized the opportunity which the circulation of the open letter had given him: *Rationes Decem: quibus certamen adversariis obtulit in causa fidei, Edmundus Campianus . . . allegatae ad clarissimos viros, nostrates academicos*, which appeared without indication of place or printer in 1581. Actually, it was printed on Parsons' secret press (which he had just transferred from Greenstreet near Barking to Stonor Park in Oxfordshire) and carried to Oxford, where the scholars assembled for a formal academic occasion found it on the benches of St. Mary's.[57]

The official line with regard to Campion's *Rationes Decem* was that it was contemptible theologically, but it is significant that authority took it seriously enough to ask the Regius professor of theology at Cambridge, Dr. William Whitaker, to answer it, and William Whitaker thought it worthwhile to answer it in a Latin *Responsio* in 1581, which aroused enough interest for a second edition that same year.[58] That same year, too, Whitaker published a *Defensio* of his *Responsio*.[59] And the next year both Campion's *Rationes Decem* and Whitaker's *Responsio* were printed together at Antwerp for the interested Continental public,[60] and the *Responsio* was answered on the Continent by at least one of Campion's fellow Jesuits, John Dury, a Scot, in a Paris publication of 1582.[61] Dury's objections were in turn rebutted by Whitaker in a reprinting of his *Defensio* in 1583.[62]

All this was in Latin, of course, for Whitaker had addressed himself to the same university audience for which Campion had written. But by 1606, when it was quite clear that the problem posed by Campion's challenge was by no means solved, and perhaps, when it was clear, too, that public opinion against the Jesuits was more consolidated and reliable than it had been in 1581, an English version of the controversy was published in London by Richard Stock, a London preacher. Stock printed in full his English translation of the Whitaker volume, thus making available for the first time in English Campion's work as well as Whitaker's.[63]

Like the other critics of Campion, Whitaker professed but a low opinion of the Jesuit's substance, yet took pains to answer him article by article and at such length as to enable his 1606 translator to claim on the title page that "In this treatise, most of the controversies betwixt us and the Church of Rome are briefly and plainely handled," and in the dedicatory epistle to William Lord Knowles to offer it as an "Enchiridion" of the controversy with "the Synagogue of Rome."[64] The charge of cruelty Whitaker rebutted with vigor, recalling at length the sufferings of the Marian persecution, and challenging Campion to name anyone who was put to death in the happy reign of Elizabeth, "whom every good man that heard of him judged not worthie of death threefold more than life?"[65] And yet at the end of his answer to the tenth reason Whitaker was still plainly worried, for he adjured the university scholars for whom this work was originally designed: "View it well, search it, and know it altogether, *Campian* is an adversary, and deceiptfull, trust him not, he is deceived himselfe, and laboureth to deceive you. By him none can be deceived, but such as willingly will be intangled with error."[66]

Whitaker was quite right in his warning, for there was a spirit of confidence in the *Rationes Decem* which the reports of Campion's death would in no way dim. Characteristically, he took the very taunts and jeers of his adversaries as the springboard for his own work. Perhaps it was a sentence of Hanmer's rebuttal of his first challenge that gave him his cue: "And me thinks by your words you are at a desperate poynct, yee wey neyther Crosse, nor racke, nor torment, nor prison, nor pikes, nor tyburne, nor Stories tippet"[67] — the last a reference to the execution of John Story, hanged, drawn, and quartered at Tyburn in 1553. His adversaries, Campion complained, would never give him the disputation he craved; instead, they called him a traitor — "as I perceive, our Bishops provide scourges, and not Schooles."[68] And the reason they behaved in so extraordinary a fashion for men supposedly interested in the free battle of ideas was that they were in despair. Then he proceeded to marshal the reasons for their despair to the number of ten: "1. Holy Scriptures. 2. True meaning of the holie Scriptures. 3. Nature of the Church. 4. Generall Councels. 5. Fathers. 6. Sure ground of the Fathers. 7. Historie. 8. Paradoxes of the Adversaries. 9. Sophismes of the Adversaries. 10. All manner of witnesses" — as Stock translated them in 1606.[69]

Whitaker was quite right when he pointed out that there was nothing really new in the lines of argument summed up under Campion's not always strictly parallel categories.[70] But that same assurance that informed Campion's first challenge breathes through the *Rationes Decem*, from the address to the scholars of Oxford and Cambridge to the end.[71] It is hardly to be wondered at that the scholars who found the little books in the benches of St. Mary's in 1581 should have read further, nor that the talk that resulted should have drawn the attention of an alert government.

The attacks upon Campion were not, of course, left unanswered. Campion's partner, Robert Parsons, was to miss the honor of martyrdom, but he was to carry on many years of fighting with his pen. Here if ever was a cause to engage his immediate interest, and he hastened at once to the defense of his colleague. His first effort was *A Brief Censure uppon Two Bookes written in Answere to M. Edmonde Campions Offer of Disputation*, published ostensibly at Douai but actually printed in England on Parsons' press at Stonor Park.[72] In this work Parsons took up the books of both Hanmer and Charke, and he met their refutation of Campion with hard-hitting directness.

On the treason charge, he asked, "Doe you hould, M. Charke, that noe man in Englande, can be of an other religion, then yours, but that of necessitie he must also be a traytor? This is hote doctrine?"[73] And he followed it up with a characteristic thrust: "Moreover in Queen Maryes time wil you saye that al Fox his martirs, were traytors to the state?"[74]

Needless to say, this defense of Campion at once drew forth a reply from Charke, which in substance retorted that the unknown defender had only confirmed Charke's original thesis "that Papists can not teache or mainteine the pretended Catholike religion, but they must be traytours to GOD and enemies of the State."[75]

Parsons returned to the attack the very next year, 1582, with a reiteration of his charges in the teeth of Charke's reply, set now, as the title page indicates, in the context of Campion's death: *A Defence of the Censure, gyven upon Two Bookes of William Charke and Meredith Hanmer Mynysters, whiche they wrote against M. Edmond Campian preest, of the Societie of Jesus, and against his offer of disputation, taken in hand since the deathe of the sayd M. Campian*, . . . The next year, 1583, Parsons' efforts were to receive their due reply in *An Answeare for the Time, unto that Foule and Wicked Defence of the Censure, that was given upon M. Charkes Booke, and Meredith Hanmers*, by an unidentified writer who seemed to be writing to hold the fort until Charke's more adequate answer could be published.[76]

Meanwhile, on July 17, 1581, Campion's brief career of missionary work in England had been brought to an end, appropriately enough, by a betrayal. And it is typical of the public interest which he had aroused that even the betrayer, in the spate of books that followed, should have hastened to tell his story: *A Very True Report of the Apprehension and Taking of that Arche Papist Edmond Campion the Pope his Right Hand, with Three Other Lewd Jesuite Priests, and Divers other Laie People, Most Seditious Persons of Like sort*. George Eliot, the author, "one of the ordinary yeomen of her Majesties Chamber," had been for a quarter of a year a Recusant, "deeply bewitched and drawn into their darknesse, as the blindest Bayarde of them all," as he told the story.[77] He came to see through their "doings" but apparently continued for some time thereafter to frequent their company. Then having made his submission and been reconciled to the Established Church, he obtained a commission from the Council with one David Jenkins "for the apprehension of certain lewde Jesuite Priestes, and other seditious persons of like sort, wheresoever wee shoulde happen to finde them within England."[78] In trying to think where he might find Campion, Eliot remembered Thomas Cowper, a cook who had formerly been a servant with him in the house of Thomas Roper of Kent. He had heard that the cook had also left Roper and gone to Master Yates, a Papist who entertained any of the sect that came his way. So he went to Yates's house at Lyford in Berkshire about eight on a Sunday morning, sure that if there were a Mass there, he would hear of it.[79]

Eliot's account of what followed is interesting not only for what it has to say of the taking of Campion, but for the light it throws on Recusant life in a large country house in those days. Eliot, calling on the cook, was invited to stay for dinner, and as a supposed Papist, for his friend had not heard of his reconciliation, invited to the secret Mass. He found Satwell (Ford) saying Mass, and Campion and Peters (Collington) kneeling by, with three nuns and thirty-seven other people. When Satwell had finished, Campion said Mass, and then sat down in a chair beneath the altar and delivered a sermon nearly an hour long.[80]

Eliot went to his friend Jenkins waiting in the buttery and told him of what he had discovered, and together they went off to get help from a nearby Justice of the Peace. In fifteen minutes the Justice with forty or fifty armed men arrived at the house. Here Eliot gives a brief glimpse of the house, surrounded with a moat in which, in the long years of peace, fruit and other trees had sprung up. The hedgerows around had had a chance to grow thick, too; so the result was what must have seemed the ideal retired and sequestered refuge. Mistress Yates denied the charges of the invaders, but they searched the house, without finding the priests. So they appealed to the other justices and secured a force sufficient to guard the house for that night. Next morning they obtained still more reinforcements for another effort, and then Jenkins, who apparently had not given up the search, discovered a hollow place, and breaking a hole, found the priests lying close together on a bed with bread, meat, and drink sufficient for three or four days. They did "courteously yeelde themselves," and Eliot triumphantly sent word to the Privy Council of his success. The bag of captives was increased when Filby, another priest, coming to the house to see Peters, was also taken. Apparently still more reinforcements were obtained; so it was with a large armed company that they set off for London.[81]

Campion, with a paper stuck in his hat, "Campion the seditious Jesuit," was brought to the Tower, under the escort of a considerable company, it would seem, both of the armed men who had secured him and of Catholic admirers.[82] There, according to an anonymous diary kept by an unknown prisoner in the Tower at that time, which we shall look at in more detail presently, he was put to the torture to gain information about the Catholics who had sheltered him and who had come to hear him.[83] Of course, there was consternation among the friends of Campion when reports began to drift out of the Tower that he had broken under torture.[84] For no witness against the Recusants could be found more devastating than the priest who surrendered, and no witness more disheartening to the Catholics who had trusted him. That is why Campion's appearance again from the depths of the Tower was so eagerly awaited, and was so important for the growing legend about him. Rumor about London, particularly in Recusant circles, would be eagerly picking up every fragment of report from prison visits and prison gossip. But more was needed to satisfy the interest of sympathizers scattered over the country and abroad, especially after Campion's condemnation and his execution with two other priests at Tyburn on the first of December, 1581.

The fellow workers of Campion had already had experience of the prompt printing of hostile accounts of the execution of one of their number, Everard Haunce, the last day of the preceding July, accounts which flatly labeled him a traitor.[85] One was actually the work of a versatile Elizabethan poet and playwright, who had not only been an actor but was variously to distinguish himself as a writer of romances, pageants, plays, poems, and as a translator, Anthony Munday. He had been abroad as a student at the English College in Rome only a few years before, probably because, in his eagerness to get out of the print shop and see the world, he had embraced the invitation of a Catholic agent recruiting students for the seminaries on the Continent, although in this period the possibility of spying, particularly in view of Munday's later record, is not to be ruled out.[86] Now in the excitement over the coming of the English Mission, Munday obviously saw an opportunity, whether it was, as has been suggested, to make clear his own soundness as an English patriot,[87] or simply to make the most of inside information for literary purposes.

In view of the hostile attention which Campion had already received, similar accounts of his death might be expected. Indeed, the proclamation of the offenses of Campion and his companions which had been read at their execution, and which has sometimes been falsely attributed to Munday,[88] was printed promptly before the end of 1581.[89] The unknown author of this work complained of what was said "maliciously, falsely, and traiterously by some of the secret favourers of the said Campion, and other the said condemned Traitours, whispered in corners," that they had been executed for religion and not treason. That charge the *Advertisement* firmly rebutted, pointing out that the very efforts to "move people to change their Religion" were in themselves "offences very hainous, and seedes of sedicion not allowable by the Lawes of the Realme." But the author no less firmly reiterated that the "factes, whereof they were arraigned and condemned, were such as were in trueth high Treasons committed against her Majesties most Royal person, and against the ancient Lawes and Statutes of this Realme, which many hundred yeeres past were in force against like Traytours, and not for factes of doctrine or Religion, nor yet for offenses against any late or newe Statute."[90]

But however distressing this presentation of Campion's end might be to his friends and supporters, worse still was to come. *A Discoverie of Edmund Campion, and his Confederates, their Most Horrible and Traiterous Practises, against her Majesties Most Royall Person, and the Realme*, which Anthony Munday published on the twenty-ninth of January, 1582, is a small pamphlet, repetitious and not too well organized, but an epitome of the case against Campion. Munday put his credentials on the title page: "A.M. sometime the Popes Scholler, allowed in the Seminarie at Roome amongst them." As he complained in his address to the Council, Munday had had to suffer unjust attacks on his character for his efforts to expose these conspiracies;[91] so there was a note of self-justification in his book. There was a note of patriotic anxiety, too, for the only danger that could really befall this little island so singularly blessed of God was that "it prove false within itselfe."[92] There was, too, the constant excitement of the revelation of the Catholic conspiracy, as he promises in his address to the reader: ". . . read this Discourse, and thou shalt evidently see into the depthe of their secret and trayterous dealings." [93] But the supreme power of Munday's book is that it does a good deal more than satisfy curiosity about the enemy. It confirms the worst fears of all those who, from motives of sincere conviction, or prudence, or indifference, had committed themselves to the established order in its assertion that the English Mission had come to England to subvert the public in preparation for a foreign assault upon the Queen and her government.[94]

Munday was a master of the propagandist's art of making known fact corroborate his charge: "The like was put in practise in Ireland, through Doctor Saunders and other Traitours, who there joyned themselves together, under the Popes standard, to bring to passe their secret appointment in this Realme." [95] And to this manifest example was joined the effort of Sanders and Bristowe to defend the Pope's Bull against the Queen, and the Rebellion in the North.[96] So the case against Campion was reinforced by the reminder of all the various well-known efforts at violent Catholic resistance, and when at his trial Campion pleaded conscience when challenged as to whether the obedience he professed to the Queen would hold against the Pope's command, Munday triumphantly concluded that Campion recognized that the traitorous purposes that had brought him to England would not allow the direct answer which a good subject should have given.[97] And Munday found fresh confirmation for this alleged bad conscience of Campion in his behavior at his execution, a description of which he appended to his *Discoverie*.[98]

Clearly, this execution was recognized as an important occasion, for Munday notes the presence at the scene of "divers of her Majesties Honorable Counsell, with many honourable Personages, and Gentlemen of worship and good account, beside a multitude of people, not heer to be numbred." [99] At the scene of his execution, Campion declared himself innocent of the treasons of which he had been convicted.[100] Reminded of his offense to the Queen, he acknowledged her as his lawful Queen, but again, Munday, in his account of all this, contrived to reiterate his former insinuation when he commented that: ". . . there somewhat he drew in his woords to himselfe, whereby was gathered, that somewhat hee would have gladly spoken, but the great timeritie and unstable oppinion of his conscience, wherein he was all the time, even to the death, would not suffer him to utter it." [101] Munday did not scruple to say that fear and terror had seized Campion, but he felt it necessary, also, to note that "the outward protestations of this man, urged some there present to teares, not entring into conceyte of his inward hipocrisie." [102]

Obviously, that was one of the things that troubled Munday, the way in which at every stage of Campion's career his personality had made such a lasting impression. For the brilliance of Campion's Oxford reputation, Munday had a rather surprising explanation: "The learned . . . loathed his manners, yet looved the man, because Christian Charitie wylled them so to doo." [103] But he was more explicit in his effort to disparage the impression which Campion had made at his trial: "Nowe beeing brought unto a publique triall, it stoode him upon to argue somewhat of the prayse that had been given him: wherefore, in verie quaint and familiar eloquent gloses, he stoode uppon quirkes and fine devise of speeche, thinking, as he had deluded many before, so at that present, he might blinde the eyes of Justice, and acquite him selfe of his horrible treasons." And then he went to the heart of the matter: "With this continuall course of boldnesse and impudencie, Maister Campion and his fellowes would grant nothing, but stifflie denied everie cause." [104]

The effect of such a publication as this, however reassuring to the Elizabethan public in general, would only whet the determination of Campion's friends to get their side of the story before that same public. The result was the very small book that appeared early in 1582 without name of author, printer, place, or even date, *A True Reporte of the Death and Martyrdome of M. Campion Jesuite and Preiste, and M. Sherwin, and M. Bryan Preistes, at Tiborne the First of December 1581,* as the title page went on to explain, "Observid and written by a Catholike preist, which was present thereat." Actually, the little pamphlet was printed on a secret press in Smithfield. [105] The authorship of the book was ascribed to Stephen Vallenger, but he was only the editor, for as he explained: "Amongst the divers reportes of the behavior of M. Campion, M. Sherwin, and M. Bryan at their death (passing among freindes from hand to hand) I hapned upon one geven out as it seemeth by a Catholike priest who as it apereth pressed to observe and marke those dealings." This he apparently hurried to print without the priest's knowledge.[106] This priest has been identified as Thomas Alfield, who was on the same mission as the men whose deaths he described; indeed, he was to be executed himself in 1585 for his part in distributing copies of Allen's *True Sincere and Modest Defence of English Catholiques*, of which we shall hear more presently.[107]

The very opening of *A True Reporte* suggests the entirely practical approach of the author. After telling how he, a Catholic priest, pressed to see the spectacle, he continued: "Since which time, upon request of some of my fellows and brethren, I wrote those dealings, to answere and satisfie our adversaries generally, to content and comfort our persecuted brethren specially, and in part to diminish those sinister rumors which are raysed against these good men by a notable and most infamous libel, entituled, An Advertisement and defence for truth against her backbyters, and specially against the whispering favorers and colorers of Campions, and the rest of his confederates treasons." [108]

As for himself, the thing that obviously most concerned Alfield was to establish his credit as simply a faithful and reliable reporter of what had happened, for he appealed to some of his fellow witnesses for validation of his story. Whatever the effect of that appeal, it certainly gives us a very lively glimpse of the crowd of the indifferent curious that would gather with the deeply interested partisans about the Elizabethan scaffold:

Well here as I wil answere for myne owne soule before God I mynde to write sincerly and simply a truth concerning the behaviour of these men at their departure, wherin of myne owne faith and fidelitie in reporting I call witnes of those gentilmen who before the begining of this tragedie at Tiborne disputed of the motion of the Sunne from east to west which was violent and which was natural, at whose backes I staied the end of this pageant: I mynded this end, and they I know atended the same. This I do implie to remember those gentilmen of the manner, of the behaviour, meke, humble, constant and resolute of those honorable martirs, nowe no doubt daily intercessors for this our miserable countrie, not douting but that, as they were then charitably moved and affected with compassion, so now they wil truely give testimony of their innocencie and my fayth in relation.[109]

When Alfield addressed himself to the heart of his report, the execution of Campion, he wrote in a fashion that is reminiscent of some of the lives of More, which stressed the human excellence of the martyr as fresh argument for the merit of his cause. Indeed, in this panegyric Alfield deviated, for once, from the general simplicity of his narrative to the formal eloquence of the literary type, when he declared that "the frute of his lerning, vertue, and rare giftes, whiche as they were in his childhood here among us wonderful, so they were abrode, as in Italy, Germany, and Bohemia an honor to our country, a glasse and mirror, a light and lanterne, a paterne and example to youth, to age . . . "[110] But when it came to the crisis itself, then Alfield returned to his accustomed plainness: "This man (M. Campion I say) first mekely yelded himself and his carkasse to this butcherie, with such humility and corage, as moved most beholders to compassion and pity."[111] Indeed, as we shall see very shortly, Alfield had more to say of the sufferings of one of Campion's fellows, Briant, than of Campion's.

For the most part, Alfield was careful to stick to what he knew himself. Apparently he had gone ahead of the crowd to make sure of his place at the scaffold; so of what happened on the way he carefully labeled what he had to record hearsay: "Those speches he used in the way to divers calling and crying unto him, I leave (my selfe not able to make relation therof) to common report, or to that mans testimonie, who eyther for pity or affection wiped his face defiled with durt, as he was drawen most miserably through thick and thin, as the saying is, to the place of execution."[112] But at the scaffold it was a different story: "What he spake openly, that my meaning is to set down truly, my selfe beeing present and very nere, as hard by Syr Francis Knoles, the Lorde Howard, Syr Henry Lee and other Gentlemen then gathered there to see and heare him."[113]

Yet it would be a mistake to judge this narrator naïve, for he managed to get some of the report for which he could not personally vouch into the record anyway: "I wil omit, althogh it be very much material, his usage in time of imprisonment, his constant patience in his rackinges, and after his condemnation by report of some very nere to him, his five days fast from temporal and bodily sustenance, his abstinence from slepe and ordinary rest, which was before his death by credible reporte of some, continued two nightes, bestowed in meditation and prayer."[114]

Nor was he insensitive to that dramatic effect in which always

Campion was so instinctively skilled. For he went on to tell how, arrived at the scene of his execution, Campion "after some small pawse in the carte, with grave countenance and sweet voyce stoutly spake as followeth. *Spectaculum facti sumus Deo, Angelis, et hominibus* saying, These are the wordes of S. Paule, Englished thus: We are made a spectacle, or a sight unto God, unto his Angels, and unto men: verified this day in me . . ."[115] That quotation from Saint Paul is, of course, the classic for the martyr, having been used in ancient times by Origen in his exhortation to martyrdom.[116] It is not surprising that as Campion went forward in this text, he was interrupted by Sir Francis Knowles and the sheriffs, who were anxious to bring him to the point they wished, a confession of treason. But he protested his innocence, taking pains to explain that the secrets which, in a letter sent out of the Tower, he had promised not to disclose were not, as they had been misconstrued, matters of treason or conspiracy, but saying of Mass and other priestly duties, and he tried to clear one Richardson condemned about a book of his, saying that he was not the man.[117] Pressed for his opinion of the Bull of Pius Quintus excommunicating the Queen, "he gave no answere. But being asked whether he renounced the Pope, said he was a Catholike." He refused the invitation of a minister to pray with him, desiring his fellow Catholics to say a Creed for him in his agony. When he was urged to ask the Queen's forgiveness and pray for her, "He meekely answered: wherein have I offended her? In this I am innocent, this is my last speache, in this geve me credite, I have and do pray for her."[118]

Although there is no mistaking the characteristic accent of Campion in this modest account, still the story itself might be taken as the scenario for a whole series of executions in this period, and Alfield's for the classic account thereof. As so often happened in the crowds at Elizabethan executions, there were not wanting evidences of compassion. In his anxiety that he might be believed in his account of the death of these martyrs, Alfield appealed especially "unto divers of nobility and worship, unto those gallant and brave courtiers who beheld and hard the same, who pittied their innocency so punished, who commended their death so patiently sustained, who through pittye procured them favor, and prevented the bloudy purposes of some cruel tormenters," who, in other words, secured them the mercy of being hanged until dead or unconscious before being torn apart.[119] But this compassion was defeated in the case of Briant through the negligence of the hangman, and this misfortune gave Alfield his one chance for a touch of the old hagiographic marvel in his account of that unfortunate's death, "who after his beheading, himself dismembred, his hart bowels and intrels burned, to the gret admiration of some, being layd upon the blocke his bellye downward, lifted up his whole body then remayning from the grounde," but at that point Alfield's habitual caution reasserted itself: "and this I added upon report of others, not mine owne sight." [120]

After all, Alfield was not writing an edifying tale of ancient heroism. He was writing a defense of the honor of his comrades, to be passed from hand to hand, for he complained of the slanders that had been spread "to diminish the honour of their resolute departure and Martirdome, as that M Campion was timerous and fearfull, and that M Sherwin died a protestant, with other such false reportes." [121] And he was trying, also, to further the cause for which they had died, that "their resolute death for religion, for our faith, for the church, no doubt by Gods grace shall animat and strengthen us . . . And further may move her Majesties hart to have compassion, maye open her grave Counselors eyes to see our innocency, may alter our enemies and ill informers mindes to love and charitie, may stirre up the minds of al men inwardly and in conscience to consider the cause of our sufferance, affliction, and imprisonments, and give them such sense, reason, and religion, that they may acknowledge our undeserved calamities." [122] Loyally he ended his account with "God save the queene."

The generally business-like character of Vallenger's publication is maintained through the little essay that followed the story of the priest: "A caveat to the reader touching A,M his discovery," in which he attacked the credibility of Anthony Munday, who had already slandered the dead, pointing out that in Rome he "was charitably relieved, but never admitted in the seminary." [123] Before the book ended, however, the hagiographic level was regained in some verse, which he appended to the modest account of Campion, "The Complaynt of a Catholike for the death of M Edmund Campion." This composition was the work of Henry Walpole, who was converted by

Campion's death and was himself, after even greater sufferings, to be executed in 1595.[124] The blend of reassurance and defiance in this poem may be judged by a passage like the following:

> God knowes it is not force nor might,
>   not warre nor warlike band,
> Not shield and spear, not dint of sword,
>   that must convert the land,
> It is the blood by martirs shed,
>   it is that noble traine,
> That fight with word and not with sword,
>   and Christ their capitaine.[125]

It is not surprising that the affair of *A True Reporte* ended up in the Star Chamber, where Vallenger, blamed for the authorship, was condemned to the pillory with loss of both his ears and imprisonment for life.[126] But copies of the little book still passed from hand to hand, and men still talked. Clearly, something had to be done to counteract the impression which this report and the body of rumor that accompanied it had made on the public mind.

The first effort was to minimize the impression which Campion's complaints of torture had made. The issue was faced most directly in *An Answeare for the Time, unto that Foule and Wicked Defence of the Censure that was given upon M. Charkes Booke, and Meredith Hanmers*, published the following year: "As for *Campion's* racking, of which you so often speake, it was for treason, and not for religion. Wee are not to be charged with it, but his owne wickednesse, whome the Lorde founde out in his sinnes." [127] That that might prove a two-edged argument seems to have occurred to this unidentified writer, for he hastened to warn his opponents: "Neyther doeth this helpe your crueltie, that put not Heretikes to death, but Christians, and such as professe the Gospel of Christ against your cursed Idolatries." [128]

But more important from the point of view of the government of the time were the reports of the disputations which Campion had so eagerly sought on his arrival and which during his imprisonment in the Tower he had been accorded on limited terms. For he was not allowed to make any plea or defense of his own, but only to reply to the objections which his adversaries would bring against him. Nor was the situation improved by the context of torture. Yet Campion so bore himself in the successive disputations that his friends and supporters were heartened and even filled with such a pride of vindication that authority again felt it necessary to minimize the impression which he had made. The most important of the official efforts to this end was the publication on January 1, 1584, of *A True Report of the Disputation or rather Private Conference had in the Tower of London, with Ed. Campion Jesuite, the last of August, 1581 . . . Whereunto is joyned also a true report of the other three dayes conferences had there with the same Jesuite.* It would be hard to imagine anything more authoritative than the source of this report: "Set downe by the Reverend learned men themselves that dealt therein," Alexander Nowell, Dean of St. Paul's, and William Day, Dean of Windsor and afterward Bishop of Worcester.

In their address to the reader, Nowell and Day expressed themselves as at first of the opinion that since Campion's book had been confuted, and especially since the man was dead, there was no need of publishing their conference with him, but that his glorious conquest of them had been so much set forth in pamphlets that they had been much importuned to set forth the truth.[129] Nowell and Day clearly felt that it was not enough to emphasize Campion's intellectual defeat; there was, also, his manner to reckon with.[130] But their criticism of Campion's performance added very little to what Munday had already said of his behavior at his trial. And they would certainly have subscribed to the conclusion of *An Answeare for the Time* on the behavior of Campion and his companions: "As for protesting their innocency it was an aggravating of their sin and villany, that being so notoriously convicted by so many proofes, evidence and testimonies, they would not yet confess their offence against God and her Majestie."[131]

Seldom has the case against a martyr been presented so fully and so promptly. On the Catholic side an efficient summary of the Campion literature was published at Paris in 1585 by one James Laing, a Scotch controversialist in exile for his religion, in an account of the death of Campion and his companions which he appended to a life of Beza.[132] Laing was obviously interested in the disputes, emphasizing how well Campion had conducted himself in spite of his handicaps.[133] And he used the triumphant old term for Campion and his companions: "Omnes isti tres Iesu Christi fortissimi Athletae quos synagoga Sathane vincere non potuit, obtulerunt spiritus suos Deo."[134]

With so much attention thus focused on the English Mission of
1580, it is easy to see why such an eyewitness account as Alfield's
would be prized. How much more then a firsthand account of his
experience by a martyr himself! Such an account came into the hands
of the Jesuits on the Continent, and was made available to the popular
English market in an English translation of a French version of
Parsons' *De Persecutione Anglicana libellus, An Epistle of the Persecution of Catholickes in England*, published by G. T. at Douai, probably in 1582. This work, written in the characteristically vigorous style
of Robert Parsons, was itself not so much a martyrology as a protest
against persecution. But to it Parsons appended a letter of Alexander
Briant's that must have moved its first readers, who either looked
forward to the possibility of such a fate themselves, or, not expecting
such a fate, were yet the more awed by the sufferings of their champions. According to the translator's account, this letter was obtained
by some of the Catholics who were admitted into the Tower to hear
the Campion disputation, and then apparently managed in the confusion attending such an unwonted invasion to get into the cells of
some of the priests confined there.[135]

Briant was not a Jesuit, but he had become convinced, he said, that
in such a sacred congregation lay the right way to God, and he had
made a vow to give himself to the Society within one year after his
release.[136] Thomas Alfield considered Briant inferior in learning and
knowledge not only to Campion but to Sherwin as well, "yet equal
in patience, constancie, and humilitie . . ."[137] Briant clearly had
nothing of the brilliance, of the élan, of Campion, but he had his own
spiritual quality, that combination of strength and simplicity that
marks so many of the contemplatives. Briant was too modest to think
that anything in himself could explain the divine mercy. It was the
vow to join the Jesuits which God must have approved:

For in all my afflictions and tourments, he of his infinite goodnesse, mercifully
and tenderlie, did stand by and assiste me, comforting me in my trouble and
necessitie. . . . And this I say: that in the end of the torture though my hands
and feete were violently stretched and racked, and my adversaries fullfilled
their wicked lust, in practisynge their cruell tyranny upon my body, yet not-
withstanding I was with owt sense and feeling well nigh of all greefe, and
payne: and not so onlie, but as it were comforted, eased and refreshed by the
greeves of the torture by past, I continued still with perfect and present senses,
in quietnesse of hart, and tranquillitie of mynd.[138]

Such a passage gave, of course, the best encouragement to Briant's fellows. Its modesty would bring its courage within the realm of possibility, or at least conceivability, to the ordinary Christian. And the Jesuit with his confidence in his techniques of meditation would doubtless feel that here was fresh evidence of the validity of those techniques, even if Briant's contact with them were still limited.

Another inside view of the experience of the participants in the English Mission, this time less dramatic but more extensive, is to be found in the anonymous Latin diary of what happened to the Catholic prisoners in the Tower of London in the years 1580 to 1585, which was printed by Wolfgang Eder with his 1587 edition of Nicholas Sanders' history of the Anglican schism. Two pieces of information only does the unknown author give about himself, first, that he was a priest imprisoned in the Tower for all that period, and, second, that what he reported was what he had himself observed or gathered from report.[139]

Nothing could be more matter-of-fact than the author's approach to his subject as he opens his brief preface with a survey of the London prisons in which Recusants are confined, the names of which recur so often in the Recusant story: Westminster Gatehouse, Fleet, Newgate, Bridewell, the two Counters (Southwark and Wood Street), King's Bench, Marshalsea, White Lion, Clink, and the Tower.[140] Then only did he come to himself, summing up his personal experience of more than four years' imprisonment in the Tower with remarkable brevity.[141]

But he took pains to see that his reader had the necessary information about the scene so that he would understand the meaning of what he was going to report. He explained the distinctive feature of the Tower, the individual cells, each in constant charge of its own guard, with consequently no chance for that visiting that is so prized a privilege in prison or for any communication with the outside, unless by letter or message. From this cell the prisoner was brought to all the other places appointed for the grim routine of torture and examination.[142] The tortures he summed up under seven headings. The first was the pit, a subterranean dungeon, twenty feet deep, without any light. At the other extreme was the little cell in which one could not stand erect or lie at full length, which was appropriately known as "Little-ease." Then there was the rack, a wooden frame with rollers at each end to pull the limbs of a man in different directions.[143] More sinister-sounding was the fourth, "the Scavenger's daughter," an iron hoop to bend the arms, feet, and head of the victim into a circle. The fifth was the iron gauntlet for the torment of the hands. After these the sixth seems mild, manacles for the arms, and so does the seventh, iron fetters for the feet.[144] The diarist ended his preface by reminding the reader that what he reported was only what came to his notice, guarded separately from the others as he was. He hoped, however, that it would be enough to awaken the charity of the Christian reader to pray to God for their country so grievously afflicted.[145]

As for the actual diary itself, it reminds one of the entries made in a monastery calendar, out of which the ancient chronicles and histories originally evolved. It began with June 15, 1580, and another related event for June 18. For June 19 it gave a list of important Catholic prisoners from Ireland then in the Tower. It then skipped to December, with half-a-dozen entries for that month.[146] For the year 1582, to take a sample from the middle of the record, there are at least three entries each for four months, a smaller number for five, and none for the remaining three months.[147] For the closing year of 1585 there are only two entries, one for the deportation of June 21, which included the still anonymous diarist, presumably one of the modest unnamed "ten other priests" included in the total of twenty-one.[148]

Appropriately enough, the entries begin with an arrival, not, as one would have supposed, the author's own, but that of a young layman, William Tyrrwhit, on June 15, 1580. He was, however, a young man of rank, the eldest son of a man of importance, Sir Robert Tyrrwhit. The diarist had the usual Elizabethan sensitiveness to rank, enhanced by the natural eagerness of the persecuted to claim as much prestige as possible to make up for the obvious disadvantage in numbers. The cause of young Tyrrwhit's arrest was noteworthy, too — he was said to have assisted at Mass for his sister's wedding. Three days later his brother Robert was brought in on the same charge, in spite of the fact that he was gravely ill, and he died soon after.[149]

Perhaps the quietest records of arrivals were those which grieved the diarist most, those of the taking of his fellow priests and missioners, for he knew only too well how much every man counted in that little band. Those four simple words for April 7, 1582, "Thomas Alfildus presbyter capitur," [150] must have covered dismay. Sometimes the notice of capture carries a later addition of suffering endured, like that of July 15, 1584, "Thomas Vorthingtonus presbyter capitur, et in lacu detinetur ad menses duos, dies tres." [151] Both the diarist and Worthington were deported less than a year later, but even then neither could know that Worthington was going to live to write his own martyrology in 1601.[152] Sometimes the dismay must have come close to despair, as when the news came of such a seizure as that of July 22, 1581, when Campion and his companions were brought in as the result of Eliot's treachery.[153] Before the end, Campion was to shed his peculiar radiance over these sober pages as over everything he touched, but the taking of one of the two leaders on whom so many hopes had been pinned must have chilled many hearts within the walls of the Tower.

One of the most dramatic episodes was that which began on October 30, 1583, with the bringing to the Tower of John Somerville, son-in-law of Edward Arden, both gentlemen, on the charge of planning to kill the Queen. On the fourth of November, his confessor, the priest Hugh Hall, was brought in, and three days later Edward Arden himself.[154] On November 16, the women of the family, Mary Arden and her daughter Margaret Somerville, were brought in, with the girl Elizabeth Somerville, John's sister. The Arden story rushed to a swift conclusion in the diarist's pages. On November 24, Hugh Hall, the priest, was racked; the diarist does not say with what result. On December 16, Arden, Somerville, Hall, and Mary Arden were condemned to death. On the twenty-first of December, John Somerville, being hardly of sane mind, was transferred to another prison, and the following night he was found strangled; it was not known whether by himself or others. On the twenty-second, Edward Arden, protesting his innocence, was hanged.[155] The diarist, who seems to have been quite innocent of any romantic or sentimental interest, did not tell what happened to the bereaved women; neither did he give any further account of the priest Hall, unless, like himself, he was one of the anonymous ten deported in 1585.

There were moments of satisfaction, even of partisan triumph, to cheer these devoted fighters, such as the John Nichols episode in 1581. Nichols, a Protestant minister, had become a Catholic and gone to Rome. On his return from Rome he was seized and put in the Tower. So much the diarist recorded. Apparently a number of ministers came at once to the Tower to dispute with him. But on the day appointed for the disputation Nichols abjured his new faith and undertook to preach against his former coreligionists, and so was set at liberty. On February 5 the prisoners were forced to go to hear him preach, but some interrupted the course of what they considered his insults, and when the sermon was finished, there was an uproar of indignation.[156] It was a dangerous game — Thomas Cottam was said to have hastened his death by the freedom of his remarks when distinguished visitors from outside had come in to hear Nichols, but the diarist felt that in all this Nichols had been pretty much discredited.[157]

To men who lived in daily expectation of torture, there was, of course, something particularly encouraging in the reports of those who had valiantly withstood it. The young layman John Jetter, who had been seized on his return from France, is not otherwise known to history, but in September of 1582 he must have sent a thrill through the Tower. He had suffered the scavenger's daughter on the first and been put in the dungeon for eight days. Then he had been drawn out and racked almost to unconsciousness: "At the height of which torture when already it seemed as if he must yield up his spirit, he called upon the name of Jesus with extraordinary joy of countenance and laughed at his tormentors."[158]

From the point of view of martyrology the next step beyond the limited and basic accounts of Alfield and Briant and the diarist of the Tower is that taken by Cardinal Allen. The founder of the seminaries had always, as we have seen, shown himself alert to the needs of the Recusants, and resourceful in devising measures to meet them. So now he addressed himself to the situation created by the executions of Campion and his companions. The result was a much more extensive and systematic martyrological production, *A Briefe Historie of the Glorious Martyrdom of Twelve Reverend Priests Father Edmund Campion and his Companions*, published in the early autumn of 1582.[159]

Allen was not the first to attempt to gather together the stories of the Recusant martyrs as a group. Nicholas Sander or Sanders had already preceded him.[160] Sanders belonged to the older generation of Allen, having been born in 1530. Educated at Winchester and at New College, Oxford, he was promising enough to be offered the position of Latin Secretary to Queen Mary, which he declined to stay at Oxford.[161] He left England soon after the passage of the acts establishing the Elizabethan Settlement, and set out for Rome in the spring of 1559.[162] After his arrival at Louvain in 1564, he is said to have assumed the virtual leadership of the exiles there.[163] Sanders was, like Parsons, an enthusiastic controversialist. He had written on usury before he left England,[164] and afterward published a number of books dealing with the central religious issues of the day, notably, *De Visibili Monarchia Ecclesiae* in 1571. And he confirmed the suspicions that the latter book had raised in England[165] by his participation in the expedition to Ireland under the papal banner of 1579.[166] There he died in the spring of 1581.[167]

He was perhaps the first to gather together the stories of a number of the English Catholic martyrs, in the seventh chapter of his *De Visibili Monarchia*. More important from the point of view of martyrology was his account of the rise and growth of Anglicanism, his *De Origine ac Progressu Schismatis Anglicani*, which he seems to have written originally for his friends in exile. For the manuscript is said to have been well known in English circles abroad before his death in 1581. It was apparently at the urging of Parsons that Edward Rishton, one of the Douai priests who had been in the Tower, undertook to collect the manuscripts of this work of Sanders after his death and publish it at Cologne in 1585.[168] Sanders took a highly personal, not to say dramatic, view of his theme. The villain of his piece was Wolsey, and the divorce was the primary cause of the rupture in the relations between the Pope and England.[169] If Sanders was severe on the villains of the story, he was correspondingly enthusiastic about the heroes.[170] The work enjoyed a great success, being reprinted in 1586 and 1588, with translations into several foreign languages.[171] There is no question that Sanders' story helped to fix the image of the changes in England for a great many people on the Continent, but the fact that it was not translated into English until the nineteenth century reduced its possible influence among the author's own countrymen. Moreover, the martyrological interest of Sanders' book is incidental to the controversial history.

The honors, therefore, remain with Allen, for the purposes of his undertaking are those of the classic martyrologist. In a letter to Agaz-zari, the Jesuit Rector of the English College at Rome, of July 7, 1582, which J. H. Pollen printed in the introduction to his 1908 reprinting of this very rare work, Allen explained that he was writing his book in English first, because "our people desire this very much and send me information for it."[172] The core of Allen's book was, of course, the account of Alfield, from which he did not hesitate to reprint whole passages word for word. But he also had access to other materials from which he drew liberally, although we find him complaining in a letter of August, 1583, that he cannot publish details of his martyr stories because of the grave danger threatening Catholics whose rela-tions and activities might be so exposed.[173] In spite of that caution, however, he was able to fill in the background of the Campion story as Alfield, with his concentration on what he knew firsthand, could not. Allen, for example, gave an explanation, apparently not avail-able to Alfield, for Campion's asking forgiveness for the names he had mentioned, that on the rack "upon the commissioners' othes, that no harme should come unto them, he uttered some persons with whom he had been." [174] Interestingly, too, for anybody desirous of reconstructing the Recusant scene of the time, Allen gave a general account of Campion's activities from his landing at Dover on the day after Midsummer Day, 1580. It was symptomatic of the tensions and suspicions of that harassed world that the first gentleman to whose house in the country Campion was conducted upon his landing in 1580, when he learned that he was a religious man who had been long in foreign parts, would not admit him until he had been satis-fied on the question, "whether he meant not under coulor of religion to with draw her Majestie's subjects from their obedience." Not until Campion had convinced him that his motives were solely of religion would he support him.[175]

Campion was, of course, the star of Allen's account, but he included the deaths of a number of other martyrs, some of whom, like Filby, had been associated immediately with Campion, though they were to die later, others of whom, like Richardson and Cottam, were mem-bers of the same mission. But Allen did not confine himself to the more recent martyrs but went back to Cuthbert Mayne, who had died on November 29, 1577,[176] and Thomas Sherwood, executed on

February 7, 1578, who, so far as Allen could ascertain, was the first to be racked for his faith.[177]

Two years later Allen carried the martyr story forward in an anonymous publication, printed without place or date, the very title of which recalls the classic collection of saints' legends, *A True Sincere and Modest Defence, of English Catholiques that Suffer for Their Faith both at Home and Abrode: against a False, Seditious and Slanderous Libel intituled; The Execution of Justice in England.* This was, of course, first of all what the title said, an answer to William Cecil's famous defense of the treatment of Catholics in England, published anonymously in 1583. But it was also written, as Allen explained in his preface to the reader, "for the memorie and honour of such notable Martirs, as have testified the truth of the Catholique faith, by their pretious death. Which was an ancient Canon and custome of the primitive Church." [178] In this he added still further detail to the story of Campion, meeting incidentally some of the efforts of the negative witness to minimize the charges of torture.[179] But for the most part Allen moved swiftly over the stories of his martyrs, sometimes contenting himself with little more than a line: "And an honorable gentleman of an ancient familie, for onelie receyving the said blessed Priest into his house, remaineth condemned at this daye to perpetual prison and hath lost both landes and goodes of great importance for that fact," [180] or "We speake nothing . . . of the deathe of welneare twenty happie Catholiques at once, infected and pestered in Yorke prison, wher they perished by the unmercifulnesse of the protestantes, of whom by no pitiful complaintes they could obteine libertie or freshe aire for the saving their lives, without condescending to goe to their abhominable service." [181]

But in spite of the familiar *vera et sincera* of the martyrologist in the title, this work belongs not so much to martyrology as, like Parsons' and Sanders' books, to controversy. What Allen is trying to do is to make good the claim on his title page: "Wherin is declared, how unjustlie the Protestants doe charge Catholiques with treason: how untrulie they deny their persecution for Religion; and how deceitfullie they seeke to abuse strangers about the cause, greatnes, and maner of their sufferinges, with divers other matters perteining to this purpose."

Something of the same purpose inspired, at least in part, the publication, about a year before the appearance of this defense of Allen's, of what was to prove on the Catholic side the nearest approach to Foxe's *Book of Martyrs*. The first version of the *Concertatio Ecclesiæ Catholicæ in Anglia, adversus Calvinopapistas et Puritanos* was published at Trier, or Trèves, in 1583. There was no author's name on the title page, but the dedicatory address was signed by the initials T. C. and the name of the printer, Edmundus Hatotus.[182] In the course of that address the printer made clear that the author of the work was an English priest.[183] He has been identified by A. C. Southern as John Fen, the chaplain to Saint Ursula's convent of Austin canonesses in Louvain. He seems to have worked in collaboration with the Jesuit John Gibbon,[184] to whom Parsons had ascribed the work, although his name does not appear anywhere in it.[185]

The problem of authorship is not very important, however, for this work, even more than Foxe's book, though on a much smaller scale, is a compilation, in which not only the raw materials of historic record but still more, whole and finished works of history and controversy are reprinted more or less entire. As the title indicates, this is essentially a record of controversy. But it is controversy carried on not only by the usual methods of theological disputation but even more by the ministry and sufferings of those who gave their lives for their position on the points at issue. It is a story not only of trial but of triumph, the triumph of the martyr.

The book was, as the place of publication, the dedicatory address to John, Archbishop of Trèves and Archchancellor of the Holy Roman Empire, and, above all, the use of Latin suggest, an address to the international Catholic world. In that spirit the printer paid tribute to the relations, both ancient and more recent, between England and Germany,[186] noting especially how Edmund Campion, whose distinguished words and deeds are rehearsed in this work, had emulated those Englishmen of old who had brought the faith to Germany, by working in upper Germany for some years before he had met his death in his own country.[187]

Although the editors do go back to the first of the seminary priests to be executed, Cuthbert Mayne,[188] the heart of the book is really the mission of Parsons and Campion in 1580. Appropriately, in view of the international public, the story began with two of Campion's letters, the first to the Queen's Council announcing his mission, translated from English into Latin, and the other the letter which Campion sent to Everard Mercurian, the General of the Society of Jesus, after he had been in England for some months, giving an account of the situation there and the progress of his own labors; this, of course, in Campion's own Latin.[189] These letters are followed by his appeal to the English intellectual world, the *Rationes Decem*, again in his own Latin,[190] and Parsons' *De Persecutione Anglicana, Epistola*,[191] already referred to.[192] Then comes the heart of the book: *Vita et Martyrium Edmundi Campiani, diligenter collecta ex variis scriptis, tàm Anglicis quàm Latinis*.[193] After a miscellaneous group of victims[194] and a general defense of the martyrs comes another retraction of the John Nichols who had so outraged the prisoners in the Tower.[195] In view of the date of the dedication of the book, August 28, 1583,[196] the fact that the public confession of Nichols is dated February 20, 1583,[197] says a good deal for the effort of the authors to bring their story up to date, to say nothing of the relative speed of serious publication at that time.

The second part, which has its own dedication, dated September 2, 1583,[198] begins with the crucial edicts of Elizabeth against the Jesuits and the seminary priests,[199] and Cardinal Allen's justification of the seminaries and of the English Mission,[200] and his message of admonition and of consolation to the afflicted Catholics of England,[201] all in Latin, of course. Then the authors return to the martyrological theme, to record, in some lines of very fine print, the names of still other martyrs that have since come to hand. And they conclude with the report in the letters of three priests from the seminary of Rheims, working in England, that after the deaths of one group of these martyrs, they had been able to restore forty to the fold.[202] On this triumphant note the work ended.

This first version of the *Concertatio* was ambitious enough, but the edition of 1588 was even more imposing. The very physical appearance of the new version, both larger and thicker, suggested as much. This 1588 edition was also published at Trèves, or Trier, this time by the printer Henry Bock. The dedication to the Archbishop of Trèves, a new and expanded one, is signed by a new editor, Joannes Aquepontanus Anglus — John Bridgewater, a Jesuit.[203]

Something of a more business-like character in the expanded book is suggested at once by the substitution for the arms of the Arch-bishop of Trèves, on the obverse of the title page in the earlier edition, of a table of the numbers and ranks of those who under Elizabeth have fought the good fight at the cost of life, liberty, fortune, or exile.[204] This table is illuminating in its revelation of the incidence of the Elizabethan persecution among the four social classes: 467 *Ecclesiastici*, 106 *Academici*, 257 *Sæculares* (headed significantly enough by the Queen of Scotland), with, uncounted, "Laici inferioris ordinis plurimi," and *Fœminæ*, "the Countess of Northumberland and more than a hundred of other ranks."[205] Needless to say, not all of these so-called martyrs would survive any modern process of canonization, for the issues are often more mixed than this summary would suggest.

As one might expect, the part of the work which in substance re-mains closest to the earlier version is the first, containing Campion's letters,[206] and his *Rationes Decem*,[207] and Parsons' *De Persecutione Anglicana*.[208] Here, the new editor forsook the old plan, ending his first part. The reason is apparent in a marginal note beside the very brief explanation of the second part in the beginning of the book: "Historiae martyrum."[209] The center of the corresponding section of the earlier book, it will be remembered, was the martyrdom of Campion and his companions. That is still here in full in the new second part, but it has been almost engulfed by the mass of additional martyr stories, both before and after Campion. Some of these stories come from well-known sources like Nicholas Sanders' *De Visibili Monarchia* and *De Schismate Anglicano*.[210] But others would seem to be mainly the new editor's own composition, such as most of the stories of the martyrs for whom simply name, date, and place of suffer-ing were added in the note at the end of the 1583 volume.[211]

Bridgewater then added a number of new martyrs, some of whose names we have already encountered in the diary of the Tower.[212] He meant to end this second part of his book with the "martyrdom of the most fair and glorious Queen of Scots," based on Edward Rish-ton's continuation of Sanders' *De Schismate Anglicano*.[213] But, as was not surprising for an enterprise carried out in so fluid a situation, additional material came to hand which he felt clearly belonged with the foregoing. So he broke the sequence of signatures and inserted some twenty-four pages of the new material.[214]

At last Bridgewater returned to the interrupted course of his book with the third part, for which, in spite of the continuing pagination and signatures, he provided a separate title page. This section opens with the closing materials of what was in substance the first part of the first edition, the *Apologia Martyrum*, with its emphasis on the fact that the martyrs were persecuted for the sole cause of their adherence to the Catholic religion,[215] and the letters and public confession of John Nichols.[216] By this time, however, there were other apostates whose return might be exploited to counteract the effect of the use which the enemy had made of them. Since the last recantation was dated as recently as May 19, 1587, Bridgewater obviously kept this business of recovering the most scandalous of weak brethren well up-to-date.[217]

He then returned to the pattern of the second part of the first edition, with the two edicts of Queen Elizabeth against the Jesuits and seminary priests,[218] and the reply of Cardinal Allen, followed by his admonition and consolation to the afflicted Catholics,[219] which completed the first edition. But meanwhile, Allen's even more extensive *A True Sincere and Modest Defence, of English Catholiques that Suffer for Their Faith both at Home and Abrode: against a False, Seditious and Slaunderous Libel intituled; The Execution of Justice in England*, had been published without place or date (actually at Rouen in 1584).[220] This defense of the martyrs, with its extended argument of the Recusant case, was here presented in a Latin version of the original English, printed in full.[221] As if to reinforce Allen's plea, this was followed by the printing of the second chapter of the parliamentary legislation of 1585 against Jesuits and seminary priests.[222] But Bridgewater was not content to print this opprobrious material without adding a rebuttal of his own of the charge of treason, citing, for evidence, Parsons' *De Persecutione Anglicana*, and Allen's *Apologia pro Seminariis Anglorum*, and *Vitas Duodecim Præclarissimorum Martyrum*,[223] and still not sure he had done all he could, he went on to a very energetic, though briefer, arraignment of the statute as a whole, "Annotatio ad ipsa Saevissima Statuti Decreta." [224]

Finally he summed up the whole story in what was substantially a table of the martyrs of the period, gathered in part from this book and in part from the seventh book of Sanders' *De Visibili Monarchia*, the third book of his *De Schismate Anglicano*, and the diary of the

Tower attached to the 1587 edition of that book. He opened his roster with *Ecclesiastici et Academici*, listing his sufferers by years in the margin, beginning with the year 1560 and the eleven bishops, headed by Nicholas Heath, Archbishop of York and Chancellor of England, who died in prison, and he carried his tables down to 1587.[225] Turning then from the martyrological to the controversial, he added a brief list of notable controversialists against the English heretics, Allen, Sanders, Harding, and so on, and an index of those who suffered prison, loss of goods, exile, or death — not all, but as many as had come to the editor's notice.[226] And finally, he summed it all up in a closing address to the reader, listing altogether twelve hundred sufferers, of whom one hundred and forty-seven were martyrs. He added that he had no doubt that there were many more who had endured hardships for the faith.[227] With a scholarly care like Foxe's he appended an analytical index.[228]

The success of this compilation is attested by the fact that a third edition, dated 1594, survives, though it is only a reissue of some leftover sheets with a new title page.[229] The fact that it was in Latin denied the *Concertatio* any widespread direct influence upon the English public, Recusant or Protestant. But it did, of course, insure its currency on the Continent. There it would secure the sympathy and understanding so essential for the maintenance of the work of the English Mission. It would also redress the balance in Catholic circles and vindicate the credit of Englishmen. For however the English Mission might have fallen short in its practical effects of the high hopes of Allen or Parsons or Campion, it had certainly transformed an end-of-the-world prostration and surrender into a struggle not unworthy of comparison with the heroic memories of the ancient martyrs.

Every martyrology has its types and its patterns. The noble virgin of the *Legenda Aurea* will come readily to mind. And there was the beautiful young man, too, gallant and noble. Sometimes these two almost cast into the shade the more ancient hagiographic constants, the bishop and the ascetic, for they give the *Legenda Aurea* so much of its distinctive atmosphere of glamor and romance. Foxe had his types and his patterns, too; the learned and painful divine was clearly his favorite. So these martyrologies have their favorite heroes. They are mostly priests. There are, of course, other martyrs, laymen who sheltered and aided the fugitive missionaries, even, at times, women. But the typical hero is the priest, and though other orders make their contributions, and the secular priests more than bear their honorable share, still it is the order which Campion graced that in these years bears the palm, and his story may be taken as the classic pattern of that stage of the English Mission.

When one compares these stories with those of the *Legenda Aurea,* one becomes aware of certain shifts of emphasis that arise, partly from the concentration on certain types of character, but even more from the circumstances of the time. One thinks of the dramatic role which the theme of virginity played in the old stories, particularly the stories of the young women martyrs. The very nature of this persecution, as noted above, made it a predominantly masculine affair, even though there are some valiant women to be found in its roster. And the fact that the overwhelming majority of the men involved were priests meant that the issue hardly arose. But when it did arise, the change in the religious climate is nowhere more apparent than here. For the antimonastic literature had done its work very effectively. The authorities who questioned the youthful Geninges, who was executed in 1591, could not believe that it was possible for so good-looking a youth, who by reason of his profession was thrown into such intimate relations with young women, to preserve his chastity.[230]

Something of the same influence of the contemporary situation is to be seen in the field of asceticism. Especially among the saints of the desert in antiquity and the saints of the monasteries in the Middle Ages, asceticism had been one of the defining marks of sanctity. There is, of course, some evidence of that traditional asceticism among these martyrs. Allen records the possibility that Cottam had a hair shirt under his outer shirt when he was executed,[231] but in general the traditional signs of the ascetic life play little part in these stories. The reason is not far to seek. The very circumstances of the hard and laborious and perilous lives which these men had to lead made much of the traditional technique of mortification superfluous, if not an actual impediment to the work which they had to do. And the triumphs of endurance of the old ascetics, it must be confessed, paled a little beside the achievement of the men who endured creditably the best efforts of the Elizabethan examiner and executioner.

As for that other constant of the *Legenda Aurea*, the delighted and grateful emphasis on the marvelous and the miraculous, that survives in greater strength, though not untouched by the Zeitgeist. There is still something of the old hagiographic excitement in Allen's summary of Campion's story, "this marvellous tragedie, contening so many strang and divers acts, of examining, racking, disputing, treacheries, proditions, subornations of false witnesses." [232] And there is even a touch, too, of the old marvels in the story of Cuthbert Mayne being seen in contemplation at night with a strange light about him, [233] and at least one example of a possible miracle, reported with reserve. [234] But in general Allen, who is quite aware of the attacks on the *Legenda Aurea*, is cautious, and so are most of the reporters of these martyrdoms.

And in the place of these old elements had come other things characteristic of the time. First of these, and perhaps the most striking, was the stress on learning and on skill in controversy and in preaching. The pre-Henrician authorities had not been eager to encourage religious controversy. And they had clearly not considered preaching as more than one of the activities of the Church, among others. But the success of their adversaries forced their Elizabethan successors to change their ways. The very nature of the Elizabethan persecution, with its special concentration on the clergy, made imperative, as we have seen, the recruiting of their depleted ranks. And the very conditions of survival in an era of proscription made necessary the winning of men of means and of influence who could protect the priests and afford secret rallying places for the administration of the sacraments. That meant an intellectual line of attack, with resultant stress on controversy, oral and written. There were emotional and moral issues in the struggle, true enough, but the primary ones were, so far as the missionary was concerned, the intellectual ones. That is why he was so eager for the chance to dispute them with his adversaries in a fair field. It was a traditional technique of the battle with heresy, viewed from the other side, one of the constants of Foxe's *Book of Martyrs*. When the prospective martyr was given his chance, however meagre it might prove for lack of books or of prison-spent strength, or even as in Campion's case because of torture, then there was, as we have seen, great pride in the learning and eloquence of the champion, and great rejoicing in the discomfiture of the enemy. Often the controversial battle continued to the very gallows, and the desired recollection of the dying was shattered by the anxiety to make sure that every chance bystander and curiosity-hunter should have his opportunity to understand the cause which was about to be witnessed in blood.[235]

It is that almost business-like attitude that is so striking a feature of these stories. This is no matter of invoking ancient memories to flag the zeal of the world's unheroic latter end. Rather, the ancient situation has returned, and men have discovered afresh the meaning of their commitment. Now even the note of surprise so characteristic of the Henrician stories is pretty much absent, and there is relatively little of the appeal to pity. This is not a story of victims but of warriors. And though there are, as we have seen, passages of exultation in the martyr's victory over the adversary without, and over the common human frailty within, they do not set the prevailing tone. It is the business in hand that is the important thing, the recovery of the fallen-away, the winning, as time goes on, of those who have had no opportunity to hear the true gospel, the salvation of as many souls as possible, perhaps one day, the saving of England. These are reports from the middle of that battle, for the encouragement of those who are struggling, for the winning of those who may be persuaded that this is the true faith for which these men have so willingly given their lives. It is that battle here and now that is the main concern of the hagiographer, as of his subject, the martyr.

THE TRIUMPHS OF DEATH

Just as the execution of Campion in 1581 may be said to mark the culmination of one period in the history of the Elizabethan Recusants, so the execution of Robert Southwell in 1595 may be taken for the culmination of another. For like Campion, Southwell, though not the superior of the English Mission, is for his period the stellar figure, for his gifts, the leadership he takes, and the impression he makes — what might be called the personal legend. As in Campion, so in Southwell, a muted and repressed and shadowed world catches the spotlight in a singularly luminous personality.

But though the two men were so much alike in the role they played in a troubled history, they were two very different kinds of men, and in their differences they reflect some important differences in the periods they represent. Both were Jesuits, that is to say, among the most active and effective agents of the Catholic Reformation; both were devoted Englishmen, in nothing more English than in their chivalrous, even romantic, readiness to adventure all for what they believed the good of their country, and in their love of and power over the word. And yet there is a difference. In the brilliance of Campion one feels the full tide of the high Elizabethan genius, with all its optimistic energy and color and dramatic edge. In Southwell, for all his radiance and charm and versatility, there is something more withdrawn, more reflective, more solitary, more ecstatic; he belongs to a later, more complicated, more shadowed world. In the end we do not see him so clearly as Campion, but I am not sure that we may not know him better, for all that we are conscious of depths at which we can only guess. For he was not only a mystic but a poet.

He was never a courtier like Campion, nor did he ever have any hope of this world. Indeed, the scion of the highly connected East Anglian family, that like so many had founded its Henrician opulence on the dispossession of the monasteries and reared its gracious country seat against the shell of a ruined priory,[1] must early have learned to take his own lonely way. For as a schoolboy he gave up the security of his father's conformity for the loyalty to the old faith of some of his less successful relatives, and finally in 1576, when he was not yet fifteen, he left family and land both, for perilous schooling abroad.[2] And this inwardness must have been increased by certain obscure struggles over vocation,[3] perhaps occasioned by a tension between the fierce concentration of the potential mystic, who will have nothing less than God, and the poet, who, however cavalierly he may doff the world aside, cannot so easily tear himself free from his own self-awareness, his own passionate urgency. His seminary experience, too, particularly the stresses of his experience as a prefect in the English College in Rome at a time when the contentions perhaps inevitable to any institution of exiles came to a crisis,[4] must have confirmed this tendency of a sensitive spirit to seek its reinforcement within, an excellent preparation, of course, for the ministry of the hidden priest in the heart of London.

And there was something else in the basic make-up of the man that helped to form this remarkable suitability to the time and the task. In his way Southwell had quite as fine a mind as Campion's, with, for all its baroque emotional and imaginative involvement, the kind of edge indispensable to irony, even of the rather musing type, as his so often was. He had preëminently, too, as poet and prose writer, both the metaphysical power of organization, and the metaphysical power of revelation of the heart of the matter through a lightning flash of the continued reality in a momentary detail. There was something in Southwell beyond even Campion's reach, but he was narrower. He had given up the world earlier, and for all the practical efficiency with which he met the demands of his preëminence in the Recusant underground, for all the resourcefulness with which he embraced and even created opportunities of service to his cause, there is no reason to think that he ever changed his basic preoccupation. His was the kind of concentration needed for a desperate hope, a hope, it may be added, even more desperate than Campion's.

For it was not simply the intensification of the effort to eliminate recusancy, as represented by the Act of Persuasions (23 Eliz. 1, c. 1) of 1581, which made reconciliation with Rome high treason, and the Act of 1585 against Jesuits, seminary priests, "and other suchlike disobedient persons" (27 Eliz. 1, c. 2), which imputed high treason to every seminary priest or Jesuit in England for his mere presence there,[5] that made the Recusant plight so grave. Rather it was the apparent ratification which two events of that decade gave to the determination of the English government to equate resistance to the Elizabethan Settlement of religion with civil disloyalty. The first was the Babington plot for the armed release of the Queen of Scots, officially discovered in August of 1586, and the second was the coming of the Spanish Armada in 1588.

It is in the darkening shadows of the aftermath of one disaster and the foreshadowing of another that Southwell came to take up the work of Campion in July of 1586. It is significant of the changed time that the first literary fruit of the new mission was, so far as we can tell, no challenge or manifesto, but an epistle of comfort to the sufferers of persecution.

The epistle of consolation and encouragement to martyrdom is one of the classic types of martyrological literature, going back, as we have seen, to Christian antiquity.[6] In more recent times, both Fisher and More had made distinguished contributions to the genre, Fisher, as one might expect, in more general spiritual terms, More with more specific, even if veiled, allusions to the contemporary scene.[7] And later in the reign of Henry VIII, in 1544, a notable example had appeared on the Protestant side, *A Present Consolation for the Sufferers of Persecucion for Ryghtwysenes*, usually attributed to George Joye.[8] One may measure something of the new impulse which the English Mission gave to this genre by taking a look at a fairly traditional example published at Louvain by Thomas Hide, a priest resident on the Continent, probably primarily for the Catholic exiles, *A Consolatorie Epistle to the Afflicted Catholikes*.

For what was obviously the sharpest of his readers' griefs, the charge of disobedience to their prince, Hide offered the highest of all examples: "Was it not objected to Christes Apostles, that they contraried the senate and counselers?" And he went on to recall from Eusebius' history the example of Polycarp on swearing to Caesar and reviling Christ.[9] And of that ancient glory he claimed a portion for the present: "It is no lesse glorie to suffer martyrdome for the conservation of unitie, then it is, not to offer to idolles, yea rather it is a greater martyrdome, for in the one, eache man suffereth for him selfe, in the other eache man suffereth for the whole churche."[10]

Two years later William Allen published *An Apologie and True Declaration of the Institution and Endevours of the Two English Colleges, the One in Rome, the Other Now Resident in Rhemes: against Certaine Sinister Informations given up against the Same.*[11] To the six chapters of this spirited defense of the seminaries against the charges of the royal proclamations of July 15, 1580, and January 10, 1581, Allen added a seventh, "An Admonition and Comfort to the Afflicted Catholikes." In this address of comfort and encouragement to the Recusants suffering in England, Allen invoked the great memories of the ancient martyrs to whom his predecessors in this genre, Saints Polycarp and Cyprian, had addressed their admonitions and exhortations, and compassion warmed his habitual eloquence to a brilliance not unworthy of his models.[12]

Southwell's *Epistle of Comfort* was first written, as he explained in his address to the reader, for "an especiall frende" of his (identified by Henry More, the seventeenth-century historian of the English Province of the Society of Jesus, as the faithful wife of the imprisoned Philip, Earl of Arundel,[13] who had given Southwell shelter),[14] and then revised for wider circulation.[15] A reference in the text, "You have laboured to suppresse us this 29 years,"[16] usually taken to refer to the imprisonment in 1558 of Bishop White of Winchester, who had praised Mary in his sermon at her funeral for rejection of the Royal Supremacy,[17] would put the composition of this work soon after Southwell's arrival in England, in 1587. The survival of an undated copy of this work with "Imprinted at Paris" on the title page, but printed on English paper, has led to the suggestion that the first edition was actually printed on the private press which Southwell is known to have had at Arundel House.[18]

Like his predecessors, Southwell began with a reminder of the tradition: "It hath bene alwayes a laudable custome in Gods Church, for such, as were afflicted in time of persecution, not onlye, by continuall prayer, and good works, but also by letters, and bookes, to comfort one another." [19] But this note of immemorial dignity soon warmed when he went on to the motive of his work, "to shew my reverent affection towardes Gods prisoners," whom he reminded of the Fathers' honorable title of "designed martyrs," with a reference in the margin to Tertullian's *Ad Martyres*.[20] He then proceeded quite systematically in the ensuing chapters to enumerate the grounds of consolation "to those that suffer in Gods quarell." [21] The first is a large and general one, namely, that the very fact of the persecution shows that they are out of the Devil's power and recognized by him as "sheepe of Gods flocke." He went on to sustain this reassurance with quotations from Scripture, both the Old and the New Testament, and from the Fathers, led by Saint Cyprian for the earlier, and Saint Bernard, for the later.[22] The second consolation is equally classic, "Whome God loveth, he chastiseth," [23] this time, again, with abundant scriptural and patristic warrant.

The normal disposition of the sixteenth century was to see in such a situation as was now that of England, from the Catholic point of view, a particular and specific judgment for specific and particular sins. It is interesting to find Southwell, who had so much to say, and so feelingly, of the cruelty of the persecutors, arguing against this view: "I beseeche them that shall reade this booke, that they be not terrified, by these adversities, but rather deme those thinges which have happened, to be rather to the amendment, then destruction of our nation: . . . for God dealeth not with us, as with other nations, whose sinnes he leaveth to the laste daye, to be punished together." [24] This same patriotic concern inspired a letter of August 31, 1588, to the Father General, now the Spaniard Claudio Aquaviva, in which Southwell was clearly anxious to make sure that the name of his people was not tarnished with the imputation of cruelty as a result of the executions that followed the Armada: "Meanwhile your Paternity should regard the situation in this light. The constancy of the Catholics is such as is always admired in a people naturally inclined to piety, but the fury and cruelty of the enemy is not to be regarded as a disgrace on the nation, but as the outcome of the pestilent heresy, which does violence not only to religion, but to the laws and restraints of nature. Thus the virtue of the former will appear more attractive, the ignorance of the latter more deserving of pity." [25]

The third ground of consolation offered was no less classic, namely, that the suffering for a good cause is an imitation of Christ's example and the ratification of the sufferer's claim to the title of Christian, again reinforced with copious citations from Scripture and the Fathers.[26] Then Southwell went on to remind his readers of the equally traditional positions that suffering best fits the conditions of man's life [27] and that even the sufferings of the Recusants are but slight in respect of man's deserts.[28]

Finally, in the sixth chapter, he came to "the principall drift" of his discourse, and the gist of that he presented at once pithily and directly: "First the cause which you defend, is the onlye true and Catholike religion, that which impugneth you is erroneous, and blasphemous heresye," [29] and he proceeded with summary vigor to epitomize the history of both.[30] He then resumed the larger view in his reassurances in the seventh chapter that the state of the persecuted was honorable because of the cause,[31] and these reassurances he still further reinforced in the eighth with the reminder not only of the honor of their state here but of its pledge of glory to come.[32] In the ninth chapter he faced the ultimate end: "And now to drawe to the ende of your conflicte, for your final comfort I put you in mynd of a moste comfortable thing, that if you be putt to death in this cause of the Catholike fayth, your death is Martyrdome." [33] The preacher himself was to put his text to the test in less than a decade. Now in the contemplation of that prospect he contented himself with quoting Richard White's comment on the detailed rehearsal of the torments of the traitor's death, the smiling, "And all this is but one death." [34] And he went on to cite examples, heathen and Christian alike, to prove his thesis that in a good cause torments are tolerable.[35] For always there is the final comfort: "If we dye in this cause, our pitcher is broaken over the fountayne, where the water is not loste, but onlye returned thether, from whence it was firste taken." [36]

But death was far from the sum of the Recusants' anxieties, or their comforter's. The one test of loyalty to their country that would satisfy their oppressors was the very one they could not give, the surrender of their faith to their loyalty. The resulting suspicion of treason to men for whom loyalty was an especially prized virtue was the bitterest feature of their lot. Even for that Southwell tries to bring his stern assuagement:

Let our adversaryes therefore loade us with the infamous titles of traytours, and rebels, as the *Arians* did in the persecution of the *Vandals*, and as the *Ethnicks* were wonte to call Christians *Sarmentitios, and semiasios*, because they were tyed to halfpeny stakes, and burnte with shrubbes: So lett them drawe us uppon hurdles, hange us, unbowel us alyve, mangle us, boyle us, and sett our quarters upon their gates, to be meate for the byrdes of the ayre, as they use to handle rebles: we wil aunswere them as the Christians of former persecutions have done. *Hic est habitus victoriae nostrae, hec palmata vestis, tali curru triumphamus, merito itaque victis non placemus.* Such is the manner of our victorye, such our conquerous garment, in such chariotes doe we triumph.[37]

In the eleventh chapter he invoked the immemorial glory of the martyrs [38] and the never-failing profit they bring to the Church.[39] But now against this splendid vision of the martyrs he set in the twelfth chapter those who could not rise to this high destiny, the schismatics (or conforming Catholics), and the lapsed.[40] Like Saint Cyprian, returning to his flock after the first great persecution in the middle of the third century,[41] he was too concerned about bracing the weak to the demands of a time of persecution for tenderness to the renegade: "O how unhappy are they, that for the saving of goods, credite temporall authority, or such worldly respects, forsake these so glorious and divine honours, and purchase a most lamentable and ignominious stile." [42]

Nor was it any time for patience with those who might plead less ignoble motives, such as the parental solicitude that made certain professing Catholics shrink from exposing their children to the penalties that threatened nonconformity. Before them he held up the examples of the mother of the Maccabees, and of Saint Felicitas, and other heroines of a sterner pattern, underscoring the contrast between such heroic figures and "parentes of our dayes, who as thoughe theyre children were nothing but fleshe and bloode, and bodyes with-out soules, pamper them in all sensuall delight, and feare nothinge more, then that theyre soules should be in the state of grace, and members of the Catholicke Churche." [43]

For the issue of truth was the supreme one. As he asked in the thirteenth chapter, "Howe is it possible for them to have the trueth of martirdome, that wante the trueth of Christe?"[44] and he reminded his readers that not only the heretics but the Jews and the Gentiles, as in India, had their devotees who died gladly for their "dreames" and "fables."[45] Yet Southwell could not help wondering at the Anabaptists, even as his Protestant predecessors had wondered at the courage of those whom all men despised as mad and dangerous fanatics: "Yet dye they in defence of these damnable Paradoxes, and that with such pertinacye, as thoughe they had bodyes of steele, that felte no payne or tormente."[46]

As for those who have died for the true faith, it is impossible to exaggerate the measure of their felicity: "For first all the comfortes, joyes, and delightes that are here scattered in divers creatures, and contryes all the bewtye and comlynesse that any worldlye thinge here hath, shalbe there united and joyned together in every Sayncte, without any of these imperfections, wher-withal they are here coped."[47] This relatively sober summary was followed, it is true, by a classic description of the jeweled heaven of the Apocalypse,[48] but there can be no question of the real center for the man who concluded this brilliant passage with the simple sentence: "Finallye, in the syghte of God we shall have the fulnesse of felicity."[49] For Southwell this was not some divine far-off event of which he was dreaming, but the most present of immediate realities. As he was later to write in his epistle of consolation to the Sackvilles for the loss of their mother, *The Triumphs over Death*, first published after his own death, in 1595: "Let God strippe you to the skinne, yea to the soule, so hee stay with you himselfe. . . . Thinke him enough for this world, that must be all your possession for a whole eternity."[50]

It was his confidence in the privilege of martyrdom that made it possible for him in the fifteenth chapter, the second last, to challenge, even to taunt, the persecutors: "Consider now O you that persecute us, what harme you doe us: yea to what tytles and glory you preferre us, by putting us to death."[51] It was not only the unintended good to their victims that Southwell urged. It was even more the futility: "Our prisons preach, our punishmentes converte, our dead quarters and bones confound youre heresye: You have laboured to suppresse us this 29. yeares: and yet of our ashes spring others, and our deade bones, as *Ezechiell* prophesied, are come to be *exercitus grandis*, a huge army."[52] Indeed, the very obloquy heaped upon them drew men to embrace the same fate, for "odyous and untolerable crueltye, breedeth when it is practised upon malefactoures, terroure, feare, and horroure of the wicked fruites, for whiche they are punished: Yett in the faythfull, and vertuous, the same bitter tormentes practised upon them, worke the pleasante and goodlye fruites of salvation, not onlye moste acceptable unto God, but able to allure mens harts to taste of the same."[53] And he went on to warn of the judgments of God on the persecutors of the innocent, invoking both ancient and modern examples. Of these latter the most dramatic, not surprisingly, concerned the death of Campion. He retailed briefly the story of Judge Aleph at the martyr's condemnation, pulling off his glove to find it unaccountably bloody, and his death soon after,[54] and he then suggested with dramatic forbearance two other "tokens of Gods indignation": "I omit the wonderful stay and standing of the Thames the same day that Father Campian and his companye were martyred to the great marvayle of the Cittizens and maryners. I omit the lyke staye of the ryver Trente about the same tyme";[55] but he had made his point.

Yet this touch of the marvelous was but incidental. It was the spiritual triumph that was the important thing. In the end it was on the good wrought in the realm of England for the martyrs and their cause that he was most insistent and most eloquent:

And as a cunninge imbroderer havinge a peece of torne or fretted velvet for his ground, so contryveth and draweth his worke, that the fretted places beinge wroughte over with curious knottes or flowers, they farr excell in shew the other whole partes of the velvet: So God being to worke upon the grounde of our bodyes, by you so rente and dismembred, will cover the ruptures, breaches, and wounds, which you have made, with so unspeakable glory, that the whole partes which you lefte shalbe highlye beautifyed by them. And as the paperer of olde rotten shreddes, often times gathered out of uncleane dunghils, by his industrie maketh so fyne, white, and cleane paper, that it is apte to receyve anye curious drawinge, paynting, or limminge: so oure scattered partes by you cast in to dunghils, he will restore to such puritye and perfection, that they shalbe more capable of his glorious ornamentes, then they were before.[56]

In his final chapter of conclusion, the sixteenth, Southwell returned to his main purpose, the encouragement of the suffering Catholics. And that final encouragement he opened with the reminder to them to "remember who sayd unto you *Feare you not my little flocke*," and he went on to cheer them with the prophecy that the time would come when the prisons and places of their execution would be resorts of devotion.[57] He fortified his own plea for perseverance with an eloquent passage from the beloved Saint Bernard,[58] who was to cheer his own final solitude,[59] and he concluded with a request for the prayers of those imprisoned, perhaps the final proof of his confidence in the state of his audience. And with no less tact he closed at last with a line from the thirtieth chapter of Isaiah, "In silence and hope shalbe your strength." [60] So ended what may fairly be counted the most impressive Recusant contribution to the classic martyrological type of the encouragement to martyrdom. That it continued to be valued by those for whom it was written is evidenced by the fact that it was reprinted after Southwell's death, in 1605, in 1616,[61] and possibly in 1608.[62]

But impressive as is this contribution of Southwell's to a timeless genre, it is surpassed for topical interest by a work which he was to compose some four years later. Indeed, it may well be claimed that the greatest document of the martyrological literature of the Recusants in this period is Southwell's *An Humble Supplication to Her Majestie*. This work was composed toward the end of the year 1591, some half-dozen months or so before his capture and the end of his active missionary career. The occasion was the publication of the royal proclamation of October 18, 1591, the most extensive of the anti-Jesuit proclamations in the Dyson collection: "By the Queene, *A Declaration of Great Troubles pretended against the Realme by a number of Seminarie Priests and Jesuits, sent, and very secretly dispersed in the same, to worke great Treasons under a false pretence of Religion, with a provision very necessary for remedy thereof. Published by this her Majesties Proclamation.*" The authors of this publication, fearing a massing of greater forces than ever before against England, accused the Pope of having

practised with certaine principall seditious heads, being unnatural subjects of our kingdom (but yet very base of birth) to gather together with great labors upon his charges, a multitude of dissolute yong men, who have partly for lacke of living, partly for crimes committed, become Fugitives, Rebelles, and Traitors, and for whom there are in Rome, and Spaine, and other places certaine receptacles made to live in, and there to be instructed in Schoole pointes of sedition, and from thence to be secretly and by stealth conveyed into our Dominions, with ample authoritie from Rome, to moove, stirre up, and perswade as many of our subjects as they dare deale withall, to renounce their naturall allegeance due to us and our Crowne, and upon hope by a Spanish Invasion to be enriched and endowed with the possessions and dignities of our other good subjects; . . . And though these maner of Popish attempts, have bene of long time used, yet in some sort also they have bene impeached, by direct execution of lawes against such traitors for meere treasons, and not for any poynts of religion, as their fautours would color falsely their actions, which are most manifestly seene and heard at their arraignements how they are neither executed, condemned, nor endited, but for high treasons, affirming amongst other things, that they will take part with any army sent by the Pope against us and our Realme. And of this that none do suffer death for matter of religion, there is manifest proofe in that a number of men of wealthe in our realme professing contrary religion, are knowen not to be impeached for the same, either in their lives, landes, or goodes, or in their liberties, but onely by payment of a pecuniary summe, as a penalty for the time that they do refuse to come to Church, which is a most manifest course to satisfie the slanderous speeches and Libelles of the Fugitives abroade.

The proclamation then went on to describe how the Jesuits came in from abroad "by secrete Creekes, and landing places, disguised, both in their names and persons," and how they proceeded to the universities and houses of law and the houses of the great for shelter. In order to stop this invasion, the Queen ordered people of all degrees to make and keep a register of all the persons admitted within the last year into their households, with information as to each man's origins, how he had lived before this, and where he had been for the last year, and whether he attended divine service according to the laws of the land, and to have this ready to show to the commissioners appointed to look into such matters, if question should arise. And if in the making of this record, they should find any doubtful people, they were to send them to the proper authority for questioning, on pain of being punished as "abettors and mainteiners of traitors." [63]

Southwell was by no means the only Jesuit to reply to those charges of treason. A year later Robert Parsons, under the pseudonym of Andreas Philopatrus, published a Latin reply that was an overt attack not only on Cecil, a familiar target of Parsons, but on the Queen as well: *Elizabethæ Angliæ Reginæ Hæresin Calviniam Propugnantis, Sævissimum in Catholicos sui regni Edictum . . .* [64] Unfortunately this reply coupled an attack on the Queen's treatment of Catholics with an attack on her treatment of the King of Spain, a coupling which doubtless appealed to the public for a Latin book published at Lyons, but which did nothing to help Catholics in England. The approach of Southwell was, from the opening of his treatise, very different. This was to be seen not only in the address of the supplication which might be taken purely as matter of form, "Most mighty and most mercifull, most feared and best beloved Princesse," but in its invocation of the traditional assumption of the innocence of the sovereign deceived by bad counselors: "The due respect that everyone carieth to your gratious person, acquitteth you in their knowledg from any meaning to have falshood masked under the vaile of your Majestie." [65] Later we shall have occasion to examine the implications of that approach for Southwell's basic position, but for the present the important thing is that it set the tone of the appeal within the framework of unquestioned loyalty to the Queen.

In no way did this, however, diminish the vigor of Southwell's attack upon the main heads of the arraignment of his colleagues in the proclamation. To the stinging charge of being unnatural subjects, he argued: "If then, as we esteeme it [the Catholic faith] at a higher rate then our owne lives, believing that out of it neither god can be truly honoured, nor any soule saved; soe if we seeke with our deepest perills to plant it in our Realme, and to winne soules from misbeliefe unto it, we thinke that we owe a most sincere and *naturall* love unto our Cuntrie: (for even by *Christs* owne testimony, noe mans Charity reacheth to any higher point then to yeald his life for the benefitt of his Friends.)." [66] On the charge of sedition often leveled against the English colleges at Douai and Rome he was even pithier: "It was noe *Sedition* for many in Queene Maryes tyme to be harboured in *Geneva*, mayntained then by those that now enveigh against us." [67] To the contemptuous references to the base social origins of the refugees, he retorted that "in the small number of the Catholique priests of our Nations, (which reacheth not to the tenth of the Protestant Ministery) there are very neare as many, yea happily more gentlemen, then in all the other Clergy of the whole Realme." [68] And to the charge that the seminarists were "a multitude of dissolute yong men" who were driven from their country by "a Conscience guilty of crimes committed," he pointed out that "the very age of the greater parte (they going over very yonge) is a warrant to acquitt them from any such offence as should force them to flie their Cuntrie." [69] And for the accusation that sedition was the study of the institutions abroad, Southwell revealed his characteristically urbane orientation when he claimed for their studies none but "the common end that all men shoote at: namely, to obtaine such knowledg as might be an ornament to our function, a help to our Conversation, and a benefit to our Cuntry." [70]

As for the more serious charges that the seminary priests came to seduce the Queen's subjects to the support of the King of Spain (a charge which a book like Parsons' would do nothing to disprove), he pointed out how few, and how "well watched" and "ill provided," they were for any such action, and he went on from reasonable probability to argue from experience: "And what better Advocate can pleade for us in this Cause, then your Majesties owne experience, who in the last attempt of the King, found none more forward to doe all duties, or liberall to stretch their habilities, then Catholiques were in your Highnes defence." [71] There was a special appeal, too, to the Queen's own sympathies in Southwell's account of the suspected oaths of ordination: "And as for Oathes and promises in receaving holy Orders, we neither take nor plight any, but one Common to the Priests of all Nations, which is a solemne Vowe of perpetuall Chastity, a thing rather pleasing then offensive to a vertuous *Queene*, who hath for her self made Choise of a single life." [72]

But the real interest of this document from the martyrological point of view was not so much in Southwell's defense of his fellows as in his picture of the situation of the Recusants. Even to give that was under the circumstances a task of no mean delicacy: "It hath byn alwaies the Pollicy of our Adversaries, to keep us aloofe from revealing our unjust oppressions, least they should enclyne your Majesties mercy to pitty us: And they fore-arme your Hignes with soe hard Informations against us, that they make our very sute for lenity seeme an offensive motion." [73] It is clear from this that Southwell's basic premise was that the Queen could not know what was going on. So he took up first the bitterest issue of all, that of taking the part of an army of the Pope against the realm, the so-called Bloody Question. He thought it most unlikely that any Catholics had expressed such an intention, "unles it were pressed out of some fraile tongue by force of torture." [74]

He assumed that it was because the Catholics were so neglected by their superiors "that contrary to the Course of all Christian Lawes we are by the extreamest tortures forced to reveale our very thoughts."

And here it was that Southwell underscored what must for the priest have been the most difficult feature of these "odious Interrogatories," as the bewilderment over Campion's reported admissions [75] would suggest: "We are compelled to accuse those whom our Conscience assureth us to be Innocent, and to cause their overthrowes by our Confessions, to whose soules we were Pastors, and they the Fosterers of our bodies; and if we doe not, because without untruth or Injury we cannot answere, we are so unmercifully tormented, that our deaths, though as full of panges as hanging drawing and unbowelling us quick can make them, are unto us rather remedies then further revenges, more releasing then increasing our miseries." [76]

As for the description of the physical detail of that torture, even Foxe hardly surpasses Southwell in that grim genre. The passage of which the beginning was given above went on with bitter particularity:

Some are hanged by the hands, eight or nyne, or twelve howers together, till not only their witts, but even their sences faile them; and when the soule, weary of so painfull an harbour, is ready to depart, they apply Cruell Comforts, and revive us, only to Martyr us with more deaths; for eftsoones they hang us in the same manner, tyring our eares with such questions, which either we cannot, because we know not, or without damning our soules we may not satisfie. Some are whipped naked soe long and with such excesse, that our enemies unwilling to give Constancy her right name, sayd, that noe man without the help of the Divell could with such undauntednes suffer soe much. . . . Some have bene watched and kept from sleepe, till they were past the use of reason, and then examined upon the advantage, when they could scarcely give accompt of their owne names. Some have bene tortured in such parts, as is almost a torture to Christian eares to heare it; let it then be judged what it was to Chast and modest men to endure it, the shame being no lesse offensive to their mynds then the paine (though most excessive) to their bodies . . . What unsufferable Agonies we have bene put to upon the Rack, it is not possible to expresse, the feeling so farr exceedeth all speech. [77]

To do justice to the literary power of the passage above, it must be remembered that although Southwell was to know the full measure of the torture described above, when he wrote this passage he had only the vicarious experience of the accounts of other sufferers, to the preservation and circulation of which he had been devoted ever since he worked on the newsletters of his Society in his Roman days, [78] and which during his years in England he was to go on collecting and forwarding in letters to his superiors. [79]

In all martyrological accounts the physical sufferings of the martyrs have received most attention because they are the most readily conceivable to the ordinary human being, to say nothing of the most dreaded. But it may be questioned if, as efficient instruments of repression, they have been so effective as certain others. The Elizabethan age was not, to the modern eye at least, very sophisticated in its appreciation of the economic factors in social life. In theoretic discussions it usually analyzed what would today be regarded as economic predicaments in terms of personal morality. But in the realm of practice, as distinguished from theory, the government of Cecil knew how to apply economic pressure with intelligence and effectiveness. On the crucial matter of church attendance the lay Recusant was struck by the Statute of 1585 with provisions which Southwell described as follows: "For first there are 20. pounds by the moneth exacted of such as are able to pay it, after the rate of 13 moneths by the yeare (an account unusuall in all other Causes) as the Lawes commonly read, printed, and practised doe witnes. And multitudes of the unabler sort of Catholiques daily feele, that all their goods and two third parts of their lands are seized on for their Recusancy, that cannot yearly pay 13. score pounds for the same." [80]

It was an age when the privileges of rank and wealth were more openly taken for granted than was to be true later; so their infringement attracted an attention that was usually neglected in the case of what that age would have called the "baser sort." But just as Southwell in his undertaking to speak for all of his coreligionists had not confined himself to what was most immediate to his consciousness, the sufferings of the missionary priests, so now he moved beyond the burdens of the rich and the great, which have usually received more attention, to the much obscurer matter of the sufferings of the humble: "Yea and this Law hath bene so violently executed, that where poore Farmers and Husbandmen had but one Cow for themselves and many Children to live upon, that for their Recusancy hath bene taken from them. And where both Kine and Cattell were wanting, they have taken their Coverletts, sheetes, and blanquetts from their bedds, their victualls and poore provision from their howses, not sparing so much as the very glasse of their windowes, when they found nothing ells to serve their turnes withall." [81]

Comprehensive and eloquent as was Southwell's presentation of the sufferings of the Recusants at the opening of the last decade of the sixteenth century, from the point of view of the historical problem of the meeting of the changes of the century by the adherents of the old faith, his handling of the problem of religious and patriotic loyalty was quite as important. It was most clearly expressed in what he had to say of what the Catholics of the time called the "Bloody Question"—what would they do if the Pope should send an army against England? Before Campion and Parsons left for the English Mission, the Jesuits had, as we have seen, obtained an interpretation of the Bull of 1570 that would make it possible for the Catholic, for the time at least, to combine civil loyalty to his Queen with steadfastness in his religion.[82] Of course, that solution, even if it had seemed dependable, would have gone against the strong integrating tendencies which we have already noted in the England of the time. The activities of Sanders in Ireland,[83] as Campion and Parsons realized when they first learned of them,[84] made that solution seem most undependable, and by Southwell's time the later activities of Allen and Parsons had done nothing to reassure anybody.[85]

Campion had clearly succeeded in meeting the suspicions of some at least of these English Catholics who did not wish to see their religious loyalties exploited for the political purposes of any foreign interest. But if we can trust the accounts of his execution, even the sympathetic ones, he rather eluded than met the issue.[86] Now Southwell, in his turn, was anxious to lift the burden of shame from the minds of his coreligionists who, like most men in all ages, regarded traitors with a horror that is still current, and rebels with a horror no less, even if it is a horror less instinctive among the heirs of various seventeenth- and eighteenth-century revolutions. That burden was a heavy one. For to the mind of the time, it was hard to conceive of any settlement of the religious problem but one Church for the whole nation. Failure to accept that Church was treason. When, therefore, Thomas Hemerford, in 1584, in answer to the usual question of what he would do if the Pope should send an army into England, tried to discriminate between political and religious grounds, "That in case they were sent in respect of the Pope's own person, then he would holde with the Queen; but if it were sent to suppresse heresy or to restore the land to the catholick faith, then he would holde with the Pope,"[87] he made a distinction that had little meaning for most of his contemporaries, and he announced a policy that seemed to his adversaries to confirm their worst fears and substantiate their most drastic charges.

In the course of his gathering-up of martyr stories, particularly those of his own order, Southwell could hardly have failed to think long and deeply on the most publicized of all, one, moreover, involving a type of man for whom he would naturally have an especial sympathy, that of Campion. Now in his address to the Queen he came to grips with it quite clearly and directly in the conclusion of the description of the torture of the priests by their interrogators. Such tortures were employed "of purpose to wring out of us some odious speeches which may serve at our Arraignements for stales to the people to make them imagine greater matters then can be proved; wheras neither ill meaning, nor truth, but torture only was guide of the tongue that spake them, which in soe hard Conflicts of flesh and bloud, with soe bitter Convulsions, is apt to utter any thing to abridge the sharpnes and severity of paine." [88] It was characteristic of Southwell that with his reasonable expectation that he might be called upon to endure torture himself he never minimized its impact. There was in him none of that rather cavalier expectation of superhuman heroism sometimes found in those who never expect to come any closer to the test than the judge's seat or the amateur's study. "Such undoubtedly," he went on,

were the words alleaged of taking parte with any Army of the Popes against the Realme, if ever they issued out of any Priests mouth: or ells they were spoken by some unskillfull Lay man, that not knowing how to answere such Captious questions, and for reverence to the Chiefe Pastor of gods Church, not daring to say he would fight against him, had rather venture his life by saying too much, then hazard his Conscience in not answering sufficient. But the Ignorance of one must not measure the meaninge of all, whom knowledg of our duties teacheth answeres farr different from this, and maketh us ready to defend your Realme, as the Catholique subjects of your Majesties Auncestors, or any other Prince were, are, or ever shalbe. [89]

Here Southwell enunciated sharply and clearly the point of view which would seem to have been Campion's, that justice could be done to both the claims of Christ and of Caesar, that a man could be loyal to both Pope and Queen. In the details of explication, that position would involve discriminations more delicate than would appeal to the men in power, who were trying to make the Elizabethan Settlement secure in the only way that age knew, by enforcing conformity. It would involve discriminations, too, hardly congenial to some of the political enterprises of Allen or Parsons, whom Southwell tried to defend from the charges of the proclamation. Ultimately, in its foundations it rested on a claim to what Southwell eloquently called "soule-rights," [90] and to the inquisitor pressing for proof of his fears, there is always something exasperating in the plea of conscience, so baffling to his conviction, so elusive of his compulsion.

A man who tries to make such discriminations runs a risk in any age, often enough drawing those whom he would reconcile into agreement on one subject alone, his own unsoundness. In the sixteenth century such a man stood very little chance. His government killed Southwell before he could publish his *Supplication*, and after his death some of his fellow Recusants, with government connivance, published it in a cause which he could hardly have countenanced. The Appellant controversy is a very complicated business, in which suspicion of the Jesuits and distrust of Continental politico-religious intrigues undoubtedly played a part, as did the psychology of the old priest against the new, to say nothing of the classic rivalries between seculars and regulars and among the various orders. The appointment of Archpriest George Blackwell in 1598 was designed to compose these perilous divisions but, in view of his relations to the Jesuits, actually inflamed them, and a group of secular priests who had questioned his authority and been in turn accused by him of schism appealed to Rome in 1600. The government was not slow to see the possibilities of such divisions, and apparently accepting the Appellants' claim that they were more loyal than the Jesuits, allowed a group of the Appellants to go to Rome in 1601.[91]

The publication of Southwell's *Supplication* in 1600 with a false date of 1595 on the title page was a move in this Appellant struggle against the Jesuits, with which Southwell, a loyal member of his order, could have had no sympathy. Indeed, Garnet, the Jesuit superior of the time, had persuaded Blackwell to forbid its publication.[92] And the rigor with which the publication was suppressed and those immediately responsible for its publication punished by the government indicates that there was no doubt in the official mind as to the danger of the work.[93]

It has been suggested that there was something not unlike the Gallicanism of the French Church implicit in Southwell's position,[94] but, I think, without warrant. His position was essentially that of the Recusants who, straining their penalty-depleted resources, went out to defend their Queen against the Armada in 1588. And it was the position of the priests who at their execution as traitors continued to pray for Queen or King.[95] Southwell was himself in this tradition when, on the last day of December, 1591, he concluded his *Supplication* with a prayer for the Queen's temporal and eternal happiness.[96]

If Southwell felt any loneliness on that last day of December, it was nothing compared to the loneliness he was to know when, on June 26, 1592, he was betrayed into the hands of one of the most avid of the Elizabethan priest-hunters, Richard Topcliffe.[97] He had, as we have seen, made a careful study of the torments which a man of his calling might look forward to, but his expectation was to be exceeded. At his trial more than two and a half years later he is reported to have summed up his experience briefly: "I am decayed in memorie with long and close imprisonment, and I have bene tortured ten times. I had rather have indured ten executions. I speak not this for my self, but for others." [98] And yet he seems to have emerged from that ordeal not only without any rumor of yielding or weakness but with a firm and serene confidence that enabled him to play the last act of his life with a wholeness and sureness of devotion that impressed even the crowd that had come for the spectacle of his agony. Indeed, one of the most generous tributes ever paid a martyr by one of his opponents is recorded by Thomas Leake, a fellow priest, in the comment which the Lord Mountjoy was reported to have made on Southwell's end: "I cannot judg of his religion; but pray God, whensoever I die, that my soule may be in no worse case than his." [99]

Any martyrologist might hesitate to particularize the vehicle of the grace that enabled a young man in his early thirties to come so well out of such an ordeal. But the Jesuits in England and in Rome would have little doubt as to its identity. Indeed, that was very much the ground on which the unknown editor of the 1622 Saint-Omer edition of *A Short Rule of Good Life* commended that work to the reader: "But because thou shouldest not be ignorant, of the way by which this valiant Champion of Christ, arrived unto so happie a Countrey, he himselfe hath left behinde him for thy benefite, and even amongst the least of his fruitfull labours, for the good of soules, had designed to publish unto the world, the description of this most gainefull voyage to heaven." [100] This book, exactly what the title implies, began with the foundation of a good life, the consideration of the purpose and end of man's creation, [101] and on that foundation the author proceeded to take up the Christian's duty to God, neighbor, and self. [102] In its basic organization the book proceeded conventionally enough, but the general temper was humane, as may be seen in the following: "I must procure to goe neatlie and handsome in my attire, agreablie to my calling, and to avoide all kind of indecency which breedeth dislike and contempt, and dooth rather offend, than please God." [103] Like Parsons' *Book of Resolution*, though on a more modest scale, it was to make its way in two distinct versions, under both Catholic and Protestant auspices. [104]

But the technique of development is the Ignatian one, first the consideration, and then various "affections" that follow therefrom. There are not many references to contemplation in these lives, but that is a consequence of circumstances rather than of attitude. There was not much room for consideration of the techniques of contemplation in the conscience-torn and pursuivant-harassed world which Southwell described in his letter to Agazzari on December 22, 1586, with its conclusion: "Every priest here is useful, especially those who are well skilled in moral theology and controversy. The other departments of sacred learning, though they may occasionally gratify the curious, are seldom called for amongst us." [105]

On the other hand, if there were ever men who needed the steady serenity which is one of the by-products of contemplation, it was these. Some degree of approach to contemplation was, indeed, within the scope of the basic Jesuit undertaking. For however modest human prudence might make the members of the Society as to their own personal resources, there was one resource of their order which they never failed to extol when they had the chance, and that was the method of meditation of their founder, the *Spiritual Exercises*. It was something which they not only used themselves, but commended to a wide variety of contemporary needs and predicaments.

In one sense there was, as we have seen, nothing particularly original about the *Spiritual Exercises*. Meditation had been the mainstay of the religious life for centuries, giving to prayer body and direction, to preaching and controversy scope and depth. The exploration of what might be called the inner life of man had been one of the pre-occupations of Christian psychology from Saint Augustine down, and the great contemplatives of the Middle Ages, like Bernard of Clairvaux and the Victorines, had applied to the immemorial accumulations of Christian thought and feeling their own very considerable genius for intellectual organization. And yet just because the enterprise was so traditional a one, and for the religious orders so organic a one, there emerged in the crisis of the sixteenth century two problems of great importance.

The first was the problem of communication, always present, of course, in the effort to transfer tradition across the succession of the generations, but especially acute in any period of accelerated change like that of the sixteenth century, and in any period of broadening involvement like that made possible by the invention of printing. The second was the problem of adaptation to the circumstances of the context of spiritual life, always urgent in the very effort to survive of any institution like the Church. Concern about both problems was apparent in the modifications which both defenders and assailants of the old order and reformers of various stripes made in the popular aid to English devotional life, the Primer, earlier in the century. Here the example of Richard Whitford, monk of Syon, and translator of the first printed English edition of the *Imitation of Christ*, is particularly instructive. A friend of More and Erasmus, he had moved in the highest circles in his earlier years.[106] But he had a very good notion, too, of the magnitude of the spiritual challenge presented by the rise of the new middle classes. He translated into the vernacular the popular devotional classic usually ascribed to Thomas à Kempis, the *Imitation of Christ*. This he did with such a command not only of the popular language but still more of the psychology of the time that his translation ran through some seven editions in the next quarter-century.[107] But even Richard Whitford, extraordinarily skillful as he was in carrying a great master of the meditative life across the barriers of time and language, did not offer in his popular prayer books and devotional guides a solution for the problem of the techniques of meditation. He provided for meditation, and he stressed the importance of meditation, but he either did not see the necessity of instruction in techniques or, with the blindness of the most intelligent professional in facing the lay public, he took it for granted that the man who could profitably meditate would find the way.[108] His successors on the Reforming side, from the circumstances of their habit of mind and experience free of his monastic assumptions, solved the problem by giving it up and providing either set forms of meditation or instructional types of prayers that supplied the gap.[109] In either case the problem remained.

It is at this point that the originality of Ignatius of Loyola becomes apparent. For he addressed himself to the problem of technique with the vigor with which he addressed himself to any practical problem. It may well be that the fact that he had come relatively late to the religious life made it easier for him to remember the difficulties of mastering the art of meditation. But more important, probably, was his capacity, the capacity of genius in any field, to absorb by a process of intellectual osmosis whatever in the forward-moving forces of his time would meet his need. The next century was to see the triumph of a new spirit of systematic organization that, while it might achieve its most sensational triumphs in the field of man's natural environment, was nevertheless to include the mind of man in its operations.[110] Ignatius of Loyola was a part of that movement; the traditional character of the materials upon which he operated rather veiled the fullness of his anticipation of what was most characteristic of the seventeenth century. But for the sixteenth century he provided what was so much needed, a scheme of directions as to how to proceed, that began at the beginning and with perfectly clear and pedagogically continuous steps led the novice to the height of the difficult art of meditation.

The basic scheme of the *Spiritual Exercises* of Saint Ignatius of Loyola is too well known to need any but the briefest recapitulation here: the preparatory prayer; the two preludes, the first, a composition of place, the second, a petition for the spiritual fruit desired from that meditation; then the core of the intellectual undertaking, the systematic point-by-point meditation on some divine truth to bring it home to heart and imagination and so fire the will with love of God; followed by a colloquy with one of the Persons of the Trinity, the saints, the Virgin, or even one's self, this last a culminating exercise of the affections and will.[111]

Simple as that scheme is, it gives the man who has mastered it a wholeness and integrity of orientation that will enable him to face a hostile world with a confidence and steadiness possible only to the man who knows that he has within his own spirit unfailing access to a world that will outlast any with which he is confronted. Ignatius understood, too, what one may call the positive side of the sixteenth-century predicament. It was not the first time that men had found the possibilities of life on this earth good. But in the sixteenth century the possibilities of enjoying life on this earth were intensified by the quickening of sense and imagination that the Renaissance brought and were made more widely available by the growing prosperity of the Western world. Certain inhibitions had been removed, too, by the growing secularization of culture, particularly in the arts. One might take a dim view of these things, and many did. In view of some of the excesses of the Renaissance, rejection was a not illogical response, and it was tried by a Borgia, among others.[112] But there was also the possibility of transformation, of conversion rather than destruction.

But this way took understanding of human nature, and that Ignatius of Loyola had; and it is part of his strength that he held on to it even in his regeneration. For luxury appeals not only to the senses but to the imagination; and art, the purest distillation of the impulse to luxury, adds the passions. And the passions, like the tree of life itself, have their own organic continuity. Southwell, the most gifted of Ignatius of Loyola's English pupils in this field, in the dedicatory epistle to *Marie Magdalens Funeral Teares*, published in London toward the end of 1591, expressed the Ignatian solution in a sentence: "Passions I allow, and loves I approve, onely I woulde wishe that men would alter their object and better their intent."[113]

The choice of Mary Magdalene, the penitent Mary Magdalene, for his meditations in itself demonstrates Southwell's responsiveness to his age. Nothing needs to be added to what has already been said about the fascination of the most famous of fair penitents for the repentant but only half-converted sensuality of the time. The story of Mary Magdalene had held a prominent place in Christian letters from the beginning, but it was peculiarly congenial to the Counter-

Reformation mood of self-reproachfulness.[114] Pious tearfulness was in fashion, too, after the Council of Trent, as is seen in such poems as Erasmo di Valvasone's *Le Lagrime della Maddallena*.[115]

It was apparently in response to a friend's request, as he explained in his dedicatory epistle, that Southwell undertook *Marie Magdalens Funeral Teares*.[116] He then went on to explain, also, the reason for his choice of this particular aspect of the Magdalene's life: "And among other glorious examples of this Saints life, I have made choise of her Funeral Tears, in which as shee moste uttered the great vehemency of her fervent love to Christ, so hath she given therein largest scope to dilate uppon the same: a theame pleasing I hope unto your self, and fittest for this time." [117] It is characteristic of Southwell that the gaudy past of Mary Magdalene was quite forgotten when he opened his meditation. Only the episodes that bring her into the Gospel story, the tearful anointing of Christ's feet, and the recalling to life of her dead brother, and finally her choice of the better part at her new Master's feet,[118] were recalled, and not even the memory of any other love but one survived in the woman who shed the tears of the title.

But a good deal more than Scripture was involved in the composition of this, one of the best-known and most characteristic of Southwell's works, and fortunately we have more evidence than we usually do in Southwell's case as to the history of that composition. Southwell's nineteenth-century editor, Grosart, called attention to a manuscript in the library of Stonyhurst College containing a first draft of this work and another manuscript containing a few short devotional treatises in Italian, the sixth of which Southwell had clearly translated and expanded into the *Teares*. This was a treatise described as "Le infrascripte cose sono cavate dal libro de sancto bonaventura et chiamase stimulus amoris." [119]

As a matter of fact, this homily is more commonly attributed to Origen. It was so attributed in an edition printed for William Menyman in London in the early sixteenth century,[120] and in a Continental edition printed about a century later,[121] which we shall examine in more detail presently. This pseudo-Origen homily must have been popular in this period. In addition to these two Latin versions at either end of the century, there also survives an English translation printed by R. Wolfe in London in 1565. In the earlier Latin edition there seems to be no question of the ascription to Origen; in the later, challenge is implied in the phrase "Origeni hactenus adscripta."

That there is some relation between the Italian version and the first draft of Southwell's handling of the story seems reasonable from the passages which Pierre Janelle prints in his discussion of this point,[122] but it would take a very detailed comparison of the three works involved to determine whether these relations amount to more than a common source. There seems to me no doubt about two points: that the Italian version, described and excerpted by Janelle, is a rendering of the Latin homily ascribed to Origen, and that whatever Southwell's possible indebtedness to it, he had also from the beginning access to the Latin original. This is apparent from the fact that the opening phrase of his first attempt at a translation of it, which Janelle thought indicated that Southwell "meant to read it as a sermon on some feast day," [123] since it was evidently not found in the Italian (as it is not found in the London version of 1504), is the actual beginning of the Latin version which Joannes Croesslius dedicated on May 6, 1604, to Maria, Archduchess of Austria, and published with some meditations of Thomas à Kempis.[124] A comparison of Southwell's work with this shows that the supposed homily of Origen furnished the skeleton on which Southwell freely molded the full flesh of his meditation. This is clear in the very opening of the composition:

In præsenti solennitate locuturi auribus vestræ charitatis, dilectissimi, amor venit ad memoriam, quomodo beata Maria Magdalena Dominum nostrum super omnia diligendo, discipulis fugientibus, eum ad mortem euntem sequebatur, ac veri amoris indefinenter plorans à monumento non recedebat. Maria enim (ut ait Evangelista) stabat ad monumentum foris plorans. Audivimus, fratres, Mariam ad monumentum foris stantem, audivimus et plorantem: videamus, si possumus, cur staret, videamus et cur ploraret. Profit nobis et illius stare, profit et illius plorare.[125]

In his rendering of this opening passage Southwell dropped the sermon preface and plunged directly into his meditation: "Emongst other mourneful accidents of the passion of Christ, that love presenteth it selfe to my memory, with which the blessed *Mary Magdelen* loving our Lord more than her life, followed him in his journey to his death, attending uppon him when his Disciples fledde, and being more willing to die with them, then they to live without him." [126]

But the expansive character of Southwell's treatment is soon apparent. The Origen homily certainly did justice to the emotional implications of the crucial moment when Mary Magdalene turned and saw Jesus and did not know him: "Dixit ei Jesus, Mulier quid ploras? et quem quæris? O desiderium animæ eius, cur interrogas eam, quid ploras, et quem quæris? Ipsa paulo ante coram oculis suis cum magno dolore cordis sui viderat spem suam suspendi in ligno: et tu numc dicis, Quid ploras?"[127] But Southwell went beyond his original in the amplification and the intensification of the emotional impression:

. . . and therefore as hee seemeth unto thee so like a stranger, hee asketh this question of thee, O woman why weepest thou, whom seekest thou?

O desire of heart, and onely joy of her soule, why demandest thou why shee weepeth, or for whome she seeketh? But a while since she saw thee hir onely hope hanging on a tree, with thy head full of thornes, thy eies full of teares, thy eares full of blasphemies, thy mouth full of gall, thy whole person mangled and disfigured, and doest thou aske her why she weepeth?[128]

However, Southwell can be quite as sparing as his original, as may be seen in what he makes of the ending of the work:

Audeo tibi confidenter promittere, si in fide ad monumentum cordis tui steteris, si plorando Iesum quæsieris, et quærendo perseveraveris, si te cum humilitate inclinaveris, si exemplo Mariæ nullam consolationem de Iesu nisi Iesum recipere volveris: ipso revelante ipsum invenies, et ipsum cognosces: ita ut non sit necesse ab aliis quærere ubi sit Iesus, sed tu magis indicabis eum, nuncians aliis. Quia vidi Dominum, et haec dixit mihi: Cui est honor, et gloria cum patre, et spiritu sancto in secula seculorum, Amen.[129]

Here Southwell stays very close to his original, probably because this is the point of the whole meditation:

Thus preparing thee with diligence, comming with speede, standing with high lifted hopes, and stouping with inclined hart: if with *Marie* thou cravest no other solace of Jesus but Jesus himselfe, he will answere thy teares with his presence, and assure thee of his presence with his owne wordes, that having seene him thy selfe, thou maiest make him known to others: saying with *Marie*, I have seene our Lord, and these thinges he said unto me. Laus Deo.[130]

But although Southwell took the work of another for the body of his homily, there is no question of the warmth of feeling with which he invested it. It was the love of Mary Magdalene in the context of the Passion that was the theme of Southwell's meditation. And that love he did not hesitate to array in its characteristic movements and preoccupations with the other loves of man, viewed on their nobler and more imaginative levels. Of the action that precipitated the narrative, Mary's bringing spices to embalm her Master's body, he observed that "though all had beene done that shee could devise, and as wel as shee could wishe, yet unlesse she were an Actor it would not suffice, sith love is as eager to be uttered in effects, as it is zealous in true affection."[131] And on the question of whether Mary had Christ present in her heart when she went seeking him in the the tomb, he reminded himself: "In true lovers every part is an eie, and every thought a looke, and therefore so sweet an object among so many eies, and in so great a light, could never lie so hidden but love would espie it."[132] The very terms in which he described Mary's grief for her Beloved were indebted to the terms in which the love poets of the time were wont to define their love griefs: "But drawing into her minde all pensive conceites, shee museth and pineth in a consuming languor, taking comfort in nothing but in being comfortlesse."[133] But this was no disinterested panegyric, even on divine love. The end of all the exploration of Mary's love was still the call to action: "O christian soule take *Mary* for thy mirrour, follow her affection that like effectes may follow thine."[134]

If one did not know that this work went a good deal further back than Ignatius, one would say that it is a fine example of Ignatian influence. And even though the basic conception and organization of the meditation so clearly predate the *Spiritual Exercises*, one may still find the influence of the actual literary milieu in which Southwell was working, in the often highly emotional terms in which he developed the given theme. For he used practically every device of contemporary rhetoric to bring his reader into as close relationship with the expanded Biblical scene as possible; indeed, to carry him into a direct participation in its experience. For example, on Mary's encounter with the angels, given first with the brevity of the scriptural text, he enlarged at leisure, addressing himself to Mary as if he were indeed there with her, and presumably his readers, too: "O *Mary*, thy good hap exceedeth thy hope, and where thy last sorrow was bred, thy first succour springeth. Thou diddest seeke but one, and thou hast found two. A dead body was thy errand, and thou hast light upon two alive. Thy weeping was for a man, and thy tears have obtained Angels." [135] Sometimes, he even pretended to enter into an argument with Mary, as when she was made to exclaim, *"They have taken away,* O unfortunate worde," and he retorted, *"O afflicted woman,* why thinkest thou this word so unfortunate?" and then he went on to suggest a series of possibilities, of which the first was: "It may be the Angels have taken him more solemnly to entombe him, and sith earth hath done her last homage, happily the Quires of heaven are also descended to defray unto him, their funerall duties." [136] And he was at no less pains to explain, addressing himself to Jesus, why Mary may have failed to recognize Him and thought Him the gardener: "Shee thought to have found thee, as shee left thee, and shee sought thee as shee did last see thee, being so overcom with sorrow for thy death, that shee had neither roome nor respite in her mind, for anie hope of thy life, and being so deepely interred in the grief of thy buriall, that she could not raise her thoughtes to any conceite of thy resurrection." [137]

But in this development of the psychological possibilities South-well did not lose sight of the homely details of the physical presenta-tion of the scene, so important in the Ignatian tradition. Perhaps the finest example of this is his argument with Mary's wonder if some-body had stolen her Master's body away: "Would any theefe think-est thou have bin so religious, as to have stollen the body and left the clothes? yea, would he have beene so venturous, as to have staied the unshrowding of the corse, the well ordering of the sheets, and fold-ing up the napkins? Thou knowest that mirrhe maketh linnen cleave as fast, as pitch or glue: and was a theefe at so much leisure, as to dissolve the mirrhe and uncloath the dead?" [138]

For one reader, at least, the Mistress D. A. to whom the work was dedicated, Dorothy Arundel, daughter of Sir John Arundel of Lan-herne, the appeal was effective, for she was to leave the wealth and splendor of her father's house and die a Benedictine nun at Brus-sels. [139] To a later generation, such a meditation will not seem as interesting as Southwell's poetry, but its reprinting in 1592, and after its author's death, in 1602, 1607, and 1609, [140] shows that it appealed to something deep in the feeling of the time, even in circles that would have repudiated Southwell's faith.

As for the poetry, it, too, springs from the same habit of medita-tion. For the very form of the dramatic lyric in the title poem of the first collection of Southwell's verse, published after his death in 1595, "Saint Peters Complaynt," involves a highly emotional exploration of an experience only briefly hinted at in the simple Biblical account of the cock crowing and Saint Peter going out weeping. Here again Southwell was inspired by an Italian predecessor, Luigi Tansillo, whose *Le Lagrime di San Pietro* he had actually begun to translate but gave up to make his own poem on the same theme.[141] In a sense, this poem is the masculine version of the feminine tears of the Magdalene. For it was in the prime masculine virtue, courage, that the chief of the apostles had failed — "Giant in talke, like dwarfe, in triall quaild."[142] But Peter faced his fear and asked himself what had caused it, and found the answer in a false estimate of life:

> Ah life, the maze of countlesse straying waies,
> Open to erring steps, and strow'd with baits,
> To winde weake sences into endlesse strayes,
> A loofe from vertues rough unbeaten straights;
> A flower, a play, a blast, a shade, a dreame,
> A living death, a never turning streame.[143]

And then he realized that already he had begun to see how misguided he had been when Christ looked upon him:

> In time, ô Lord, thine eyes with mine did meete,
> In them I reade the ruines of my fall:[144]

It is doubtless the series of stanzas on the eyes of Christ, in which almost every possible figure of speech for eyes, ever used by poets, sacred or profane, was exploited that moved the emulation of the poets of the time:

> These blazing Comets, lightning flames of love,
> Made me their warming influence to know;
>
> .   .   .   .
> O living mirrours, seeing whom you shew,
> Which equall shadows worths with shadowed things:
>
> .   .   .   .
> O Pooles of Hesebon, the bathes of grace,
> Where happy spirits dive in sweet desires:
>
> .   .   .   .
> O Sunnes, all but your selves in light excelling,
> Whose presence, day, whose absence causeth night,
>
> .   .   .   .
> O gracious spheres, where love the Center is,
> A native place for our selfe-loaden soules:[145]

But the end of all this catalogue of ingenious hyperbole is still dramatic:

> Twice *Moses* wand did strike the stubborne rocke,
> Ere stony veynes would yeeld their christall blood:
> Thy eyes, one looke serv'd as an onely knocke,
> To make my hart gush out a weeping flood.[146]

And elaborate as is this long meditation on the eyes of Christ, in which each impulse of the inflamed imagination brings out some fresh appreciation of the reality the frightened man had forgotten in his fear, it would be hard to conceive of anything simpler and more direct than the final summary of Peter's realization of the full measure of his betrayal:

> At sorrowes dore I knockt, they crav'd my name;
> I aunswered one, unworthy to be knowne;
> What one, say they? one worthiest of blame.
> But who? a wretche, not Gods, nor yet his owne.
> A man? O no, a beast; much worse, what creature:
> A rocke: how cald? the rocke of scandale, Peter.[147]

So great was the interest in Southwell's work that the year of his death saw the publication of an unlicensed edition of *Saint Peters Complaint, with Other Poems,* by another London publisher, John Wolfe,[148] possibly, as its very incomplete state suggests, hurried out to anticipate the licensed one of Gabriel Cawood discussed above, and then later in the year a more complete edition by Wolfe.[149] The success of these two publications must have been considerable, for later in the same year of 1595 a second volume of verse, titled *Mæoniæ, or Certaine Excellent Poems and Spirituall Hymnes: Omitted in the Last Impression of Peters Complaint,* appeared with the title-page explanation, "beeing needeful thereunto to be annexed, as being both Divine and Wittie," and this time giving the poet credit so far as the initials, "R. S." [150] In his address to the Gentlemen Readers, the printer spoke gratefully of the "kind admiration shown Complaint of holie Peter," and went on to justify his publication of the additional poems: "Having these poems in hands I thought it a charitable deede to give them life in your memories, which else should die in an obscure sacrifice, gently embrace them, gentle censurers of gentle indevors." [151] Apparently this venture was successful, too, for a second edition was brought out that same year.

That Southwell's contribution to the religious literature of his country was appreciated is demonstrated in the most effective way possible, by the continued publication of his work after his death. We have seen how *Marie Magdalens Funeral Teares* continued to be reprinted throughout and even beyond our period. So did *Saint Peters Complaynt, with Other Poems*, new editions appearing in London in 1597, 1599, 1602, 1607–9(?), and 1615. As in the case of the earlier work, there were Continental editions of this too, and it went on being reprinted in the seventeenth century. There was even an edition in Edinburgh about 1599.[152]

The relation of an artist's politics to his art is not an easy matter even for the twentieth century. It was no easier for the sixteenth. John Trussell, the versifier who addressed the reader in the 1595 edition of *The Triumphs over Death*, was certainly not tactful in what he had to say of the possible objections of "Bible-bearing hypocrites," but he came to the heart of the matter when he pleaded with his readers: "I wish them weigh the words, and not who writes."[153] It is a tribute to an element in the sixteenth-century English temper not always apparent in this history that that seems to have been precisely what a sufficient number of readers were able to do, at least enough to make it worthwhile for the publication to continue.

True, the printers of *Mœoniæ* seem to have exercised some care in the selection of material. In the case of the cycle on Mary and her Son, poems on "The Death of Our Ladie" and "The Assumption of Our Lady" found in manuscripts were not included.[154] On the other hand, the close rendering of Saint Thomas Aquinas' great Corpus Christi hymn, *Lauda Sion salvatorem*, is kept, under the cautious title, *A Holy Hymne*.[155]

This record of republication, in view of what was well known about the end of the author, is impressive enough in itself. But there is another type of tribute which deserves attention in our estimate of the contemporary reaction to Southwell, and that is the tribute of direct imitation, by men who could have no sympathy for his religious position. The influence of Southwell's distinctive style upon succeeding poets is now generally recognized. It is significant, then, that some of the earliest examples of this more direct and complete imitation involved not Southwell's poetry but his prose. In the year of his death, an anonymous prose meditation on the same segment of scriptural story as he had treated in *Marie Magdalens Funeral Teares*, styled *Marie Magdalens Love*, was published with the verse *A Solemne Passion of the Soules Love*, in London.[156] This has been ascribed, with reason, not to a preacher but to a lay religious poet and pamphleteer, Nicholas Breton.[157] Breton followed Southwell in the detailed analysis of the emotional situation, but he was always preoccupied by the moral significance of its implications, as may be seen in what he has to say of Mary's weeping:

Nowe Marie it is saide, stood weeping not crying: now there are teares of subtilty, called crocodiles teares, which are said to mourne and weepe, till they can bring their praie within the compasse of their calles, and then they overthrow them, sting them to death and then feede upon them: so may I say, are the teares of a harlot . . . thus did not Mary, for the body was dead as shee thought, that shee wept for, the earth had no eyes to behold her teares, nor did she see any man, that she could think to deceive with her weeping: no, no, her hart was too full of sorrowe for the deade, to thinke to deceive any living.[158]

In other words, for Breton the warmth of feeling is always leashed firmly to the hortatory purpose, and this is the more remarkable in that Breton was not a clergyman or preacher, but a religious poet and journalist, cultivating one of the most popular sectors of the literary field of his day. And this was still true of the much less extensive treatment of the same theme in a work published two years later that is certainly Breton's, *Auspicante Jehova. Maries Exercise*, in which the episode of Mary Magdalene at the tomb was but one of a series of illustrations of God's mercies as revealed in the histories of some scriptural "women in his especiall favour," offered for the contemplation of Breton's readers.

But it is not hard to see the influence of Southwell's enthusiasm for contemplation in the address to the readers in which Breton explains both his approach to his subject and his purpose in this book.

Ladies and Gentlewomen, so it is, that having passed some partes of the world, and beholding the stately pallaces of divers princes, after my returne into my native country, finding the contemplative life, the most neere unto Angelical nature, and no contemplation so comfortable as the mercies of god, the first fruicts whereof, and the never ending Glory of the same, are no where so apparant as in the historie of the holy scriptures . . . and reading in this divine historie of the excellencie of Gods love, and among many of his elected, of some women in his especiall favour, I could not but acquaint your good

mindes, with the memory of their names, and such matter touching them
as you may and will (I hope) applie to your comfort.[159]

And there are unmistakable echoes of Southwell in such passages
as the following from the prayer on Mary at the tomb:

I reed oh Lord of Mary Magdalens great grace, who being a great sinner yet
by a great repentance, received a great measure of thy mercy: in sorrow she
sought thee, in humility she loved thee, and in love she found thee: yea, alive
shee loved thee, dead, shee mourned for thee, buried she sought thee, and risen
she found thee: sweetly was shee blessed, that having once beegon to seeke thee
could never leave till shee found thee, and having once found thee, did so
deerely love thee that in the depth of hir love, shee had no joie to live from
thee: sweet Jesu, so give me grace to seeke thee, . . .[160]

But the appeal of Southwell's verse with its novelties of tone and
style probably explains why even the Mary Magdalene material was
handled more in his spirit by the poets than the prose writers. A very
good example is the anonymous *Marie Magdalens Lamentations for
the Losse of Her Master Jesus*, published in London, just at the turn
of the century, in 1601.[161] The form which the unknown poet chose
is the measure of Southwell's "Saint Peters Complaynt." Unlike
Southwell, he began directly and immediately with Mary's lamentations. The opening stanzas, therefore, seem rather flat in their emotional summary of the situation which Southwell had developed
with question and answer, and description and speculation, very
much as the Origen meditation had. But once past this fresh introduction and into the central matter of Mary's lamentation, then the
relation of this work to Southwell's becomes apparent, as may be
seen in the way in which the poet expanded the first sentence of
Mary's address to the tomb in Southwell's prose: "O sweet Tombe
of my sweetest Lord, while I live I will staie by thee: when I die,
I will cleave unto thee: neither alive nor dead, will I ever be drawne
from thee,"[162] into a whole stanza:

> O life-containing Tombe of my dead Lord,
> From thee no chaunce shall hale me hence away,
> Ile linger here while death doth life affourd,
> And being dead, my twining armes shall stay,
>   And cleave unto thee; nor alive or dead
>   Will I be drawne from where my Lord is laid.[163]

In general, the unknown poet knew a poetic possibility when he
saw it, but he was hardly able to sustain it. Fortunately the frame-

work of *Marie Magdalens Funeral Teares*, resting as it did on the sure ground of Scripture, helped to keep this later work moving forward so that it is, surprisingly, a good deal more than a mosaic.

So much has been made of the vogue of the Mary Magdalene theme in this period, especially of Southwell's handling of it, that it is easy to forget that his penitent Saint Peter also enjoyed the tribute of imitation. For the lamentation of the weeping Peter afforded another model for the kind of penitential expansion that appealed especially to the mood of the close of the century, in so many quarters.

The anonymous *Saint Peters Ten Teares* of 1597 shows the possibilities of the genre very well. The unknown poet must have been aware of Southwell's work. For he chose the lamentation form of "Saint Peters Complaynt" and the basic symbol of tears that Southwell had used in his Magdalene meditation. He used, too, the verse form of Southwell, the six-line iambic pentameter stanza with the alternating rhyme quatrain closed by a couplet. He even picked up one of the most interesting tendencies of Southwell's pattern, that of making a unit of the first two lines of the quatrain, and another unit of the third and fourth, for the most part only glanced at in Southwell, and developed them systematically, and, it must be confessed, rather obviously. The general temper and tone of the work is what one would expect from its obvious preoccupation with sound doctrine, but there is also a freshness of psychological exploration that goes beyond the usual preacher's zeal, as in the following development of the theme of Christ's looking at Peter:

> O glorious starres, me thinks you are his eyes,
>   That staind with pittie to behold my paine:
> All things are his that burnish thus the skyes,
>   his matchlesse selfe amongst them dooth remaine.
>   O then but looke on *Peters* lamentations,
> As thou doost note the wickednesse of nations.
>
> If I but sleepe I dreame of thy divinenesse,
>   O let me sleepe and never wake againe:
> For once awake, such is our sinfull blindnesse,
>   wee cannot see the purenesse of the same.
> Or els dissolve me I may ever dwell,
> To view that beautie which no toung can tell.[164]

Fancy and emotion are firmly leashed by the preoccupation with doctrine, but they are by no means stifled.

The appeal of this weeping-Peter theme even carried over into a work in which the whole career of Peter was but a part of a full-dress treatment of the apostles as a group, William Broxup's *Saint Peters Path to the Joyes of Heaven*, of 1598. The title-page description makes clear that a good deal more than the exploitation of a penitential theme was intended here: "Wherein is described the frailtie of Flesh, the power of the Spirit, Sathans subtiltie, and the Soules salvation, as also the Election, Lives and Martyrdome of the twelve Apostles." Broxup's work is a more ambitious one than those we have been looking at, from the point of view of what might be called historical research, because for the details of Peter's life he cited in the margin, in addition to the evangelists and the Acts, such authorities as Eusebius and Jerome.[165] But the weeping note was still firmly emphasized, as in Peter's adjuration to his fellow sinners:

> Flie fast to Christ, and imitate my teares,
> If sight thereof, affright thy soule with feares.
>
> .   .   .   .
>
> Then let thy teares, for sinne in streames arise,
> Till death damme up the welsprings of thy eyes.
>
> Such pearled deaw, allureth God to grace.[166]

The influence of this type of lamentation of the repentant sinner went beyond Peter in another of these poems about the turn of the century. Gervase Markham used the form, this time for Saint John, in *The Teares of the Beloved* of 1600. He used, too, the stanza of Southwell, and some of his imagery, and he came closer than did most of his fellow imitators to catching something of the dramatic variety and interest of Southwell's approach to his scriptural material, both in prose and verse. For example, at the memory of Christ's bloody sweat, the beloved disciple broke into tears that recall Mary Magdalene's:

> Ye silver drops, that from my eyes thus streame,
> Crossing that colour, brinish as ye be!
> My Lords were red; for forc't with paines extreame,
> He ventured life, from death to set us free.
>   His bitter pangs, what pen or wit can tell?
>   My Lord indured th'extreame paines of hell.[167]

In a certain sense one may say that this literature of lamentation is another example of the wheel coming full circle. One of the grounds of attack on the old handling of scriptural story earlier in the century, as, say, in the famous *Meditations of St. Bridget,* was that it distracted from the scriptural lesson by its emotional embellishment.[168] It is clear that by the end of the century interest in this sort of emotional embellishment had returned, at least in certain quarters. It may well have been a consequence of the exploration of emotion, to say nothing of exploitation of emotion, in the great lyrical development of Elizabethan poetry. It may, also, be a part of that growing interest in human psychology, in what goes on within the mind and heart of man, that was to be so striking a feature of English literature, as of European literature in general, around the turn of the century. But whatever it was, this interest in the exploration of the psychology behind the generally simple and objective account of Scripture is noteworthy, and, viewed historically, it is not the least of the ironies of a period that was rich in ironies.

As we shall see presently, Southwell's was by no means the only answer to the problem of finding a fresh and more accessible approach to the materials of Scripture, but clearly his achievement had an appeal that reached across not only the difference of belief, but even the perhaps more formidable barriers to emotional and imaginative acceptance. That it did is apparent in these imitations, as in the continuing republication after his death.

It was from the beginning a more limited and a more desperate hope than Campion's that brought Southwell to England, and even of that he was destined to be disappointed. The memory of his direct action, of his ministry, and of its end was to endure, with the indestructible magnetism of the martyr, but its influence was to remain in the immediate circumstances limited. In the fruit of his own solitary but by no means uncompanioned or unsustained meditations he was to achieve a wider and more immediate response, and a lasting influence. And here his career may be taken as an epitome of the Recusant situation in the last decade of the sixteenth century.

And, to go beyond the limits of our period and the limits of the Jesuits, it is surely not without significance that perhaps the most notable figure of the age of hidden and even buried life that was in

the new century to succeed the culminating disaster of the English
Mission, the Gunpowder Plot, with Father Garnet's involvement
therein, was to be a great contemplative, the Benedictine Augustine
Baker. Here again, Southwell, who in so many respects sums up
the movement begun by Campion and his companions and its seeming failure, looks to the future with the prophetic certainty of one
who was never quite in time anyway.

CONTINUING CLASSICS
AND EMERGENT TYPES

for the hagiographic story of the later years of the sixteenth century it is the Recusant sector of the English scene that yields the richest returns, for the obvious reason of opportunity. But when we turn to the problem of the continuation of traditional types and the emergence of new types, or new versions of old types, the situation is from the literary point of view, at least, quite different. Here it is the Established Church that claims attention, for any activity in this area is interesting in view of the earlier revolt against the saint's legend, and some developments are important for their fruits in the immediate future. The major part of this chapter will be concerned, therefore, with developments in the Church of England.

But before we turn to them, we should note briefly for the historical context that this is in the Catholic world one of the great ages of traditional hagiographic writing. The very effort to give reality to spiritual commitment in a time when the insufficiency of social conformity and private mediocrity had been so abundantly demonstrated would alone have assured that. But, as we have seen in Southwell's work, the whole baroque effort to convert the resources of art to the service of religion found in the lives of the saints rich material for its distinctive techniques of exploitation, and so reinforced the traditional interest in the genre. Interestingly enough, one of the notable early sixteenth-century contributions to this hagiographical revival had been produced in England, Richard Whitford's translation into

English of the Martyrology of Salisbury Use, which Wynkyn de Worde published in 1526.[1] Whitford's example was followed almost a century later by the priest John Wilson, in *The English Martyrologe*, which he published in 1608 with an appended catalogue of those who had suffered for the Catholic cause since Henry's breach with Rome down to that time, the whole dedicated to the Catholics of England for their consolation.[2]

Obviously, after Whitford's time the real public for the traditional hagiography was on the Catholic Continent. This public responded with enthusiasm to the eight volumes of the first great mid-century collection, which the Venetian Aloysius Lippomanus, bishop, successively, of Modena, Verona, and Bergamo, published from 1551 to 1560, the *Historiae de Vitis Sanctorum*. The busy Bishop of Verona arranged his materials pretty much as they came to hand, a technique hardly conducive to any systematic plan.[3] This lack of order was remedied by the Carthusian Lawrence Sauer, better known by his Latin name of Surius, who arranged his materials by months, and brought out his six folio volumes, dedicated to Pius V, in the years from 1570 to 1575. The work of Lippomanus had not been distinguished by much evidence of the critical spirit. Surius not only added new lives to Lippomanus' collection; he did some weeding-out of dubious elements in the old stories, and some correcting of the style of his originals in the light of the taste of his day.[4] The great success of Surius' work in the sixteenth and seventeenth centuries gave wide circulation not only to the imaginative creations of a Gregory of Tours but to such masterpieces as the lives of Saint Hilary of Poitiers by Fortunatus,[5] of Saint Felix of Nola by Bede,[6] of Saint Antony the Abbot by Athanasius,[7] and of Saint Paula by Jerome.[8]

The extensive and quite serious work of Surius, with the more limited Spanish *Flos Sanctorum* of the Dominican Alfonso Villegas, and the more purely edifying *Flos Sanctorum* of the Spanish Jesuit Pedro de Ribadaneyra,[9] unquestionably gave fresh life to the hagiographic genre in the Catholic world. The Recusant exiles on the Continent were, of course, quite aware of this treasure, and translations from this material played a large part in the extensive vernacular literature issued in the early seventeenth century at the Recusant publishing centers on the Continent, for the Englishmen in exile and for smuggling into England. But this effort, much as it deserves and will repay further investigation, lies outside the necessary chronological limits of this study.

The more imaginative and emotional type of hagiographic writing, such as we have encountered in the seriously meditative work of Southwell and his imitators, should be noticed again, because it does find its way into English in this period in a more popular and even romantic form that reminds us of the ancient connection between the hagiographic romance and the Greek romance, which had enjoyed such a revival in the secular literature of the sixteenth century.[10] The remarkable complexity of taste revealed in this genre is especially apparent in the handling of the lives of scriptural figures, like the expected Saint Mary Magdalene in I. or J. C.'s stanzaic account of *Saint Marie Magdalens Conversion*, printed without indication of place in 1603, and the much less expected study of Saint John in *Our Ladie hath a New Sonne*, published anonymously at Douai in 1595. But even more curious is the romanticizing of the central transaction of the New Testament in *Palestina* by Robert Chambers, a young priest of the English College of Rome, which was printed at Florence in 1600. This was dedicated to the Virgin Mary, "to our most gracious and sovereign lady and princess, whose dowery is little England and the largest heavens her fairest inheritance," [11] in a tribute which the author modestly described as "but a harsh discourse of a sometime happie countrey."[12]

This work opens with a glowing picture of the heavenly Jerusalem and then goes on to make an extraordinary translation of the Christian story into the terms of romance. An Emperor deputed his son to a shameful death. The motive was the son's love for an adopted daughter, who, enchanted by her own folly, had become most misshapen and ugly. Interestingly enough, this enchantment had been wrought by her eating an apple. The enchanter had been the "chiefest" under the lord and master, and for vengeance had won the love of the Emperor's daughter, to the extent that she had paid attention to his blandishments. The son decided to take the same nature of which his sister was made, except for her perverseness.[13] Thereupon Chambers proceeded to give a colorfully expanded account of the birth and early life of Christ up to his thirteenth year and the beginning of his public ministry.[14] The account closes with a brief reference to the end of the story. In other words, we have here a highly romantic account of the fall and the redemption of man that recalls such a medieval romantic treatment of the same basic spiritual material as the "example" in the *Ancrene Riwle* of the King who wooed a lady in distress, and when she disdained his suit, died for her.[15]

Not only is there a great emphasis on the part of the Virgin in this romance, but throughout, the bare scriptural outline of the major events is developed not only with considerable analysis of thought and feeling but with extended descriptions of places and often elaborate expositions of incidental circumstances. A good example is the passage on the housekeeping at Nazareth:

But how can it be that the virgine should bee an inheretrix, and to no small revenewes, and yet bee forced to live upon her sonnes labour? (for *Joseph* lived not many yeares after his returne from *Egipt*) it seemeth a very inconvenient thing, that without any necessitie either she should give from her selfe all that she had, or he be subject both to evill words and waste usage. To this some do easily make this answere, that the virgine enjoyed what her parents had before, although after her sonne shewed himselfe unto the world, both he and she forced themselves to live uppon the charitie of others, lest in counselling others to sell all which they had, and give it to the poore if they would follow him, hee might justly have beene challenged for preaching one thing, and practising another.[16]

The pedagogical habit of mind revealed in this passage is apparent, also, in various incidental explanations, for example, of the Olympic and the Roman games, to show how the Gentiles honored false gods,[17] and of the Jewish laws of pedigree, with careful consideration of different theories about their interpretation, to demonstrate that Christ was of the princes of Judah,[18] and, above all, of the ceremonies of the observance of the "Phese or passeover," and other feasts of the Jews, as a preparation for the familiar story of the finding of the child Jesus in the Temple.[19]

But for all these explanations, the lyric note is not wanting in the more purely edifying passages, as when the author expatiates happily on the name of Jesus: "But the name it selfe discloseth some secret mysterie. For who is not deaf, and hath not his eares filled with a most sweete sound, when hee heareth this holy name *Jesus*? Who is not dumbe, and hath not his mouth flowing with a most sacred sweetnes, when hee soundeth this holy name *Jesus*? who is not dead, and hath not all his senses furnished with a straunge delight, when hee apprehendeth the name of *Jesus*? who is not damned, and hath not his soule deified, by an infinite goodnes when hee engraveth this holy name *Jesus*?"[20] In such a work as this the Recusant hagiographer for a little while escaped from the grim preoccupations of his beleaguered fellow countrymen and entered into the freer and more exuberant contemplations of the, at this point at least, happier baroque world.

And here too, ironically enough, he reached some common ground with his Anglican colleague, who was also exploring the romantic possibilities of the rejected saint's life. One may judge this sixteenth-century English revival of the saint's life from more than one point of view. There is no question of the passion of the time for romance, and it may well be that the purveyors of pious literature for the masses saw in some yielding to this taste a means of redirecting the imaginative activity of the public. Nor should we forget that a similar motivation had played its part in the making of the *Legenda Aurea* in the first place. But this sixteenth-century effort does indicate some relaxation of the sober literalism that had inspired so much of the campaign against the saint's legend earlier in the century. There can be no question of the popular interest in some such development. Campion's opponent, Meredith Hanmer, in the introduction to the translations of the ancient ecclesiastical histories he published in 1577, was eloquent on the happy state of England under Queen Elizabeth, but he was much less complacent on the popular reading tastes of the time:

Many nowe adayes had rather reade the stories of *Kinge Arthur*: The monstrous fables of *Gargantua*; the Pallace of Pleasure; The Diall of Princes, where there is much good matter: The Monke of Burie full of good stories; Pierce Ploweman: the tales of Chaucer where there is excellent wit, great reading and good decorum observed, the life of *Marcus Aurelius* where there are many good Morall precepts: the familiar and golden Epistles of *Antonie Guevarra* where there is both golden witt and good penning: The pilgremage of Princes well penned and Clerckly handeled: Reinard the Fox: Bevis of Hampton: the hundred mery tales: *skoggan: Fortunatas*: with many other infortunate treatises and amorous toies wrytten in Englishe, Latine, Frenche, Italian, Spanishe, but as for bookes of divinitie, to edifie the soule, and instructe the inwarde man, it is the least part of their care.[21]

Indeed, an even more formidable foe was already apparent to observers of more exacting temper than Hanmer's. In the preface to the reader of a book which we shall look at shortly, a work, like Hanmer's, offered to patronage of high rank, Henry Holland well defined the new danger: "The divell in elder ages in the blinde Papacie fed blinde soules with fables, and idle Friers inventions" (as we have seen, the regular view, for the time, of the ancient hagiography). But he went on to claim that "now men's wits bee refined, they can no more feede on such drie stubble. He [the Devil] feedes daintie eares with choise of wordes, and uncleane hearts with the unchast and wanton lovesongs of Italian poetrie." [22]

Clearly it would take something more than the tales of ancient martyrs which Meredith Hanmer hopefully offered, to meet this situation; and there were sixteenth-century writers who took the course of their despised predecessors. It is perhaps not surprising that one of the earliest of these efforts was John Partridge's rehandling of the Eustace legend, one of the popular themes of both romancers and hagiographers in the Middle Ages.[23] Probably the fact that Eustace was a hunter had something to do with this. At any rate it is his story which John Partridge chose, very much as at the beginning of the century Henry Bradshaw had turned to the saint's life for the entertainment and edification of merchants and other "secular people" in the long evenings of the English winter.[24] Partridge dedicated his 1566 version of the story to the Worshipful Arthur Dwabene, Merchant Adventurer. Certainly, Partridge proved himself more knowledgeable with regard to merchants when he chose Eustace rather than the beautiful queen turned nun whom Bradshaw had selected for his earlier effort. For the emphasis is upon valor and action in the very title of *The Worthie Hystorie of the Most Noble and Valiaunt Knight Plasidas, otherwise called Eustas, Who, was Martyred for the Profession of Jesus Christ.* It is true that Partridge offers Placidus as an example of what, he said, Democritus had called "the chiefeste beste" among all human types, "a pacient man in miserie." [25] But Placidus is represented in the proper romantic guise as excelling in martial feats, and equipped with a wife "of glistering hew." There is a Renaissance touch in the fact that he and his wife are devoted to study, and that their recreations are hunting, chess, and speculation.[26] The purely religious end of the book is managed with an almost debonair brevity, which may be due to Partridge's concern with a good story, but more probably to the limitations of his verse. as may be judged by the following account of what happened when Placidus tried to take a huge buck with lofty horns:

> The mighty God in Skyes above,
> his servant did him make.
> And out from cloudes he called to him,
> his Idolles to detest:
> Which by and by fel in a swoune,
> And so he left the beast.[27]

As God had predicted,[28] Satan did certainly annoy the converted Placidus. After he and his wife Thespis and their children were baptized, Satan opened his attack by slaying the sheep and cattle of his victim. Placidus was brought to poverty, and his pretended friends spoiled and sacked his house. So he and his family took ship to leave the country.[29] The master of the ship was smitten with the beauty of Thespis, and when Placidus was unable to pay their fare, he seized her.[30] Misfortune pursued the bereft husband on land. When he tried to cross a stream with the children, a wolf seized the youngest child and a lion the eldest. (The children were, however, rescued, by herdsmen from the lion, and by plowmen from the wolf.)[31] Placidus then went to a neighboring town, where he secured a job keeping sheep. Meanwhile, the lustful shipmaster as he tried to take possession of Thespis had been struck dead, and the faithful wife had reached land and settled down to live as a widow for fifteen years.[32] With Placidus out of the way, enemies began to disturb Rome, and the King sent knights to seek Placidus, whom Placidus received in his house. Through an old wound on his head, he was recognized, and went with them. Taking over the defense of Rome, Placidus ordered each town to send him two lusty men for service, and so the town where his two sons were living sent them as their contribution. Because of the nobleness of their manner (one of the old medieval romantic touches), Placidus put them at his own table. It then chanced that they attacked the town where Thespis was living, and when the town was won, the boys repaired to the hostelry which their mother was now keeping. The mother, overhearing them talking of the past, recognized them, and after their happy reunion went to Placidus to see about their returning to Rome, and recognized him, too.[33] Thereupon they all proceeded to Rome, where one would have thought that the end would be happiness forever, but

Hadrian commanded Placidus to adore the idols in thanks for the victory, and Placidus refused. Then Hadrian gave orders that Placidus and his family should be devoured by a lion in a church, but the lion lay down at their feet like a dog. So Hadrian directed that they be put in a brazen ox to die:

> The Oxe with flame is thorow hote,
>   and they are put therein:
> And joyfully in Christ they all,
>   to sing do then beginne.
> Thus ended they their mortall race,
>   their file was at an ende:
> That we may so indure good Lorde,
>   to us thy mercy sende.[34]

Thus the appropriate martyrological lesson was drawn at the end, but the interest of the great bulk of the story is purely romantic adventure.

An even more preposterous example of the romanticizing of the saint's legend is the retelling of the popular Alexius story by George Pettie in *A Petite Pallace of Pettie His Pleasure*, which Richard Watkins printed in London in 1576. The young Alexius persuaded to virginity the wife whom he had married against his will, and then forsaking her and all the wealth of his father's house, went on pilgrimage, until at last he settled in a distant land to live in great poverty. Miraculously discovered by the Virgin's image, after many adventures he returned home in disguise to beg from his parents and to suffer the abuse of their servants. On the approach of death he wrote out the story of his life to be read after he was dead. This legend had been a popular one in England, as in other countries, during the Middle Ages.[35] For his highly euphuistic collection of romantic retellings of ancient stories of love and passion, dedicated to the "gentle Gentlewomen Readers" of his day,[36] Master George Pettie radically changed the motivation and the balance of the saint's legend. Indeed, at first sight it looks as if the story of Alexius were introduced as an example to justify the not especially spiritual observation that "no man is so surely setled in any estate, but that fortune may frame alteration." [37] But it is soon clear that the theme immediately involved is the familiar Elizabethan debate between learning and love, with Alexius at first maintaining the classic ascetic view of women and marriage, but soon yielding like an obedient son to his father's wishes and applying himself no less diligently to the acquisition of an understanding of love.[38] The fruit of this effort was a panegyric on women, which he presented to his wife, a work of a character sure to please Pettie's audience but hardly to be paralleled in any saint's legend.[39] But some shadow of the original point of view, though hardly of the story, returns when Alexius discovers that "there is satietie of all things." [40] It is perhaps fitting to the emotional climate of this version of the story that Alexius expresses his new resolution in terms of the classic text of the Song of Songs: "No, let me first seeke my beloved, who is gon downe into his garden to the beds of his spicerie to gather up Lilies, and then shall I know how to love my earthly beloved as I ought to doe." Not surprisingly, in view of the context, the rest of Alexius' story is compressed into a brief paragraph, noting the facts of separation from wife, friends, and country, and ending with the bare report that Alexius "spent the remaindour of his life in pilgrimage and travel." [41]

But entertaining as these romantic revivals of the saint's legend are, they were to prove much less enduring than Richard Johnson's *The Most Famous History of the Seaven Champions of Christendome*, published first in 1596 and dedicated to Lord Howard in terms that suggest, not so much the continuing veneration of the saints, but rather the enduring fame of the heroes: "a Historie of the seaven Champions of Christendome, whose names to this day is held in great estimation through Europe." [42] The seven champions are, of course, Saint George of England, Saint Denis of France, Saint James of Spain, Saint Anthony of Italy, Saint Andrew of Scotland, Saint Patrick of Ireland, and Saint David of Wales, in other words, the patron saints either of the neighboring kingdoms or of the leading regions or countries of Christendom. But the description that follows their listing on the title page is very different from what one would expect of the patron saint: "Shewing their Honorable battailes by Sea and Land: their Tilts, Jousts, and Turnaments for Ladies; their Combats with *Giants, Monsters*, and *Dragons: their* adventures in forraine Nations: their *Inchauntments in the holie Land: their* Knighthoods, Prowesse, and Chivalrie, in Europe, Affrica, and Asia, with their victories against the enemies of Christ." In other words, this is a great romantic collection of magic tales and chivalric adventures, exploiting folk heroes, and foreign travel, with, it must be admitted, but a very dim aura of endeavor for the Christian cause.

Johnson ostensibly disclaims the popular favor when in his address to the reader he says that "only the censure of the conceited I stand unto, that is the marke I aim at," [43] but his techniques are eminently those of the popular romancer. Saint George, for instance, is given a local habitation — he was born at Coventry. His mother dreamed that she conceived of a dragon. She was cast into a deep sleep, her womb cut with razors, and Saint George taken, with an image of a dragon on his breast, a bloody cross on his right hand, a golden garter on his left leg.[44] Kalyb, the enchantress, stole the infant and for fourteen years kept him in an enchanted cave, offering him every delight, for she was covetous of his love. He longed for martial adventure, but agreed to yield to her on condition that he be the sole governor of the enchanted cave. So she took him to a castle where the six other champions were prisoners. There she gave him the swiftest steed and the strongest armor in the world, and, also, a silver charming rod, which George used promptly to imprison Kalyb in a rock and release the other champions.[45] After staying in Coventry for nine months and erecting a sumptuous monument over Saint George's mother, the seven champions set forth on their adventures. First among these, of course, was that of the King's daughter and the dragon in Egypt.[46]

Johnson's handling of the adventures of Saint George reminds one of Caxton's *Golden Legend*. There is the same delight in color and splendor. Indeed, on occasion Johnson can strike the authentic note of Renaissance magnificence, as in the description of King Ptolemy's preparation for the coming of Saint George:

Then Ptolomie commaunded everie street of the Cittie to be hung with rich Arras and Embroitered Tapestry, and likewise provided a sumptueus Charriot of gold, the wheeles and other timber worke of the purest Ebonie, the covering thereof was made of purple silke, cross barrde with staves of gold; Likewise a hundred of the Noblest Pæres of Egipt, attired in crimson Velvet and white, mounted on milke white coursers with rich Caparison attended the comming of Saint George.[47]

But Johnson has homeliness, too, and a certain delight in practical ingenuity and resourcefulness that recalls some of the contemporary tales of the clever apprentice. Above all, he has a very clear and fast-moving narrative line that is well illustrated by his account of the famous combat between Saint George and the dragon:

Thus weltred he from his hideous denne, and fiercly assailed the sturdy Champion with his burning winges, that at the first encounter, hee had almost felled him to the ground, but the Knight nimbly recovering him selfe gave the Dragon such a thrust with his speare, that it shivered in a thousand peeces, whereat the furious Dragon so fiercely smote him with his venemous tayle, that downe fell man and horse, in which fall two of St. George's ribs were sore brused, but yet stepping backward, it was his chaunce to leape under an Oringe tree, which tree had such pretious vertue, that no venemous worme durst come within the compasse of the braunches, nor within seaven foote thereof, where this valiant Knight rested himselfe untill he had recovered his former strength: who no sooner feeling his spirits revived, but with an eger courage smote the burning Dragon under his yellow burnisht bellie with his trustie sworde Askalon, whereout came such abundance of venome that it sprinkled upon the Champion's Armour, whereby immediatly through the impoysoned strength of the venome his Armour burst in twaine, and the good knight fell into a greevous and dead sound, that for a time he lay breathles, but yet having that good memorie remayning that he tumbled under the branches of the Oringe tree; in which place the Dragon could proffer him no further violence . . .

Then kneeled hee downe and made his divine supplication to heaven, that God would send him (for his dear deare sonnes sake) such strength and agility of body as to slay the furious and tirrable monster, which beeing done, with a bold and couragious heart he smote the Dragon under the wing, where it was tender without scale, wher by his good sworde Askalon with an easie passage went to the verie hilts through both the Dragon's heart, liver, bone and blood, whereout issued such abundance of purple gore, that it turned the grasse which grewe in the valley into a crimson colour, and the ground which before partched through the burning stinch of the Dragon, was now drenched with overmuch moysture which voyded from his venemous bowels, where at last for want of blood, and long continuance in fight, the Dragon yielded his vitall spirits to the mercy of the conquering Champion.[48]

It is hardly surprising that so lively and so versatile a work as this should have continued to enjoy favor long after our period.[49]

Moreover, there was clearly an interest in Saint George as the champion of England; the very primacy that he, "the English knight," [50] assumed in the *History of the Seaven Champions of Christendome* is an undoubted reflection of national pride. That mingling of piety and patriotism characterizes the most serious use of the figure of Saint George in the literature of this period, in the first book of

Spenser's *Faerie Queene*, the fable of which Mrs. Josephine Waters Bennett has well described as "a conflation of the St. George Legend with the second half of the Revelation of St. John." [51] In that fable, as Mrs. Bennett points out, "St. George, representative of the true-born Englishman, is the symbol of religion on earth." [52]

But it was not until the more sympathetic period of the High Anglican movement of the next century that even the theme of Saint George might be treated as straight hagiography, as in Tristram White's rather baroque poem of 1614, *The Martyrdome of Saint George of Cappadocia*. The printer, William Barley, commended his venture with a double appeal to patriotism and to social prestige in the subtitle, "Titular Patron of *England*, and of the most Noble Order of the Garter," and he dedicated it to Mr. George Shilliton, Justice of the Peace, "the Kings Receiver for *Yorke-shire*," and one of the chief clerks of the Court of Star-Chamber. [53] And to make doubly sure, he added a second dedication on the obverse of the first, to "all the noble, honourable, and worthy bearers of the name of George in Great Britain" and to all other lovers of Saint George's name and virtues. [54]

It is thoroughly in keeping with this romantic revival of the saint's legend in the later sixteenth century that that extraordinary medieval collection of classical stories, saints' lives, oriental wonder tales, pseudo history, folk tales of varying levels, and romantic stories of almost every description, all elaborately moralized, the *Gesta Romanorum*, should also have enjoyed a new lease of life. With the *Legenda Aurea*, the *Gesta Romanorum* had been, it will be remembered, one of the sources of John Mirk's famous late medieval collection of homilies for preachers, *The Festial*. An old vernacular version of something less than half the stories of the *Gesta Romanorum*, somewhat altered and modernized, had been printed by Wynkyn de Worde in the opening decades of the sixteenth century, and then apparently pretty much forgotten. But in 1577 an Elizabethan man of letters, Richard Robinson, took it in hand, still further modernized the form of the work and published it, "perused, corrected, and bettered," as "a record of Ancyent Historyes, intituled in Latin *Gesta Romanorum*." This publication must have met with great success, for apparently some six editions of this work were printed by Thomas East between 1577 and 1601. [55]

The treatment of some episodes in Robinson's version of the *Gesta Romanorum* reminds one of Robert Chambers' *Palestina*. The whole handling of sacred themes in romantic symbolism is a very interesting development of the times, a far cry indeed from the earlier sixteenth-century attack on the legends of the saints. But however engaging this romantic hagiographic development may be from the literary point of view, it must not be allowed to overshadow the serious use of the saint's and martyr's life, so important for this period. The very success of these revivals of the hagiographic romance must have not only seemed dubious to serious critics of contemporary literary taste like Hanmer, but must also have brought home to purveyors of edifying literature the need for some safer substitute for the exciting literary fare which the natural man of the sixteenth century craved. The obvious substitute would be the story of the Biblical hero, for he brought the reassurance of God's Word. And if he came from the Old Testament, so much the better, for he was less likely then to be involved in the extravagances of the *Golden Legend*. Caxton, as we have seen, had already in his first edition of the *Golden Legend* set the example in his addition to the traditional materials of the *Legenda Aurea* of "the storyes of the byble," thirteen in number, and all from the Old Testament, beginning with Adam and including Moses and Judith, among others.[56]

The crucial word "saint" is actually used in the title of John Marbecke's book of 1574, *The Lyves of Holy Sainctes, Prophetes, Patriarches, and Others, Contayned in Holye Scripture*, but there is a clear note of caution in the further explanation on the title page: "contayned in holye Scripture, so farre forth as expresse mention of them is delyvered unto us in Gods worde." Clearly, Marbecke was thinking of a very popular audience because in his dedication to Lord Burghley he expressed a wish that the fruits of his gleanings might "be bestowed amongest the mainye, and simple sorte of the reast of the Christian flocke."[57] In his commendations of his book to the Christian reader there was a note of civic as well as religious purpose when he reminded him that the wisest of the pagan philosophers were convinced that man "was framed of Nature such an excellent Creature as he is, to that ende, that he myght employ those singular gifts wherewith he is beautifyed . . . not onely to his owne private commoditie, but also to the profite of his Countrie, and others."[58]

Marbecke had not by any means forgotten the Reformers' case against the saints' lives, because he went on to reassure his reader that his book "is of God, and his holy Saintes, and therefore to be reverenced: collected out of Scripture, and therefore no vaine fable." [59] These lives were arranged in alphabetical order for easy reference and embellished with engraved portraits, some in classical costume, some in a generally Oriental type of dress, and some in a modified version of the armor and garb of the time.

The use of the Bible for the heroic example of human virtue and God's grace to sustain it is illustrated, also, by Thomas Hudson's translation of G. Saluste du Bartas' *The Historie of Judith in Forme of a Poeme*, printed at Edinburgh in 1584. In the dedication to James VI, King of Scotland, Hudson explained that the actual undertaking of this translation was the result of a literary discussion at the Scottish Court in which Hudson had claimed that it was possible to translate something as exquisite as the poetry of Du Bartas "succintlie, and sensibly in our owne vulgar speech." [60] But a less sophisticated audience was clearly envisaged in the cautious reprinting of an explanation of the title in "The Argument": "This History is entituled by the name of Judith, because it conteines the narration of her great vertues, and for that the Lord used her as an instrument for the deliverance of his people," [61] and in the notes at the end of the book, which identify, among others, Abraham as "Father of the Jews or the faithful," Aurora as "the morning," Bacchus as "Wyne or drunkennes," and "Monark" as "One sole gouvenour." [62]

Hudson was quite aware, too, of the possibility that the rash might be led astray by admiration for the slayer of Holofernes, for he took the precaution of reprinting Du Bartas' own admonition to the reader, "to attempt nothing without a cleare and indubitable vocation of God against those whom he hath erected above us." [63] But if perhaps not too sophisticated, the audience for whom this work was designed was clearly a sober and godly one, as is suggested by the description of Judith's rearing by her father Merari:

> He taught her not to reade inventions vaine,
> As fathers dayly do that are prophaine:
> But in the holy scriptures made her reade,
> That with her milke she might even sucke the dreade
> Of the most high.[64]

Judith's husband, Manasses, was worthy of her, for he was "the whole support / And chiefe conforter of the godly sorte" in their community.[65] It was only natural, then, that when thirst threatened their city, the weeping Judith should seek help in the Scriptures. There it was that she chanced to read the story of Ahud [66] and took the decision that led to the saving of the city and her enshrinement among the heroines of Israel.

By the end of this period the Old Testament saint's life was well enough established as a literary type to command the interest of a poet of merit, Michael Drayton, whose *Moyses in a Map of his Miracles* was published in 1604. One at least of the friends who wrote prefatory verses for the book, Sir John Beaumont, was aware of the hagiographic significance of the undertaking,

> See how ingrate forgetfulnesse
>   Circles us round with dangers,
> That all the Saints whom God doth highly blesse,
>   To us are strangers.[67]

The tone and temper of Drayton's own poem may be judged from the opening lines:

> Girt in bright flames, rapt from celestiall fire,
> That our unwearied faculties refine,
> By zeale transported boldly we aspire
> To sing a subject gloriouslie divine:
> Him that of mortals only had the grace,
> (On whom the Spirit did in such power descend)
> To talke with God face opposite to face,
> Even as a man with his familiar friend.[68]

There is a problem of proportion in this work. A great deal of detail is lavished on the account of Moses' early perils and rescue by Pharaoh's daughter, with a fairly full development of the anguish of his mother at the prospective loss of her son.[69] There is a romantic glow, too, to the picture of the princely young Moses:

> For *Zipora* a Shepheards life he leades,
> And in her sight deceaves the subtill howres,
> And for her sake oft robes the flowrie meades.
> With those sweet spoiles t'enrich her rurall bowres.[70]

And there is something of the old *Golden Legend* splendor when the Israelites came to Sinai:

> Where as the people in a wondrous fright
> (With hearts transfixed even with frosen blood)
> Beheld their Leader openly in sight
> Passe to the Lord, where he in glory stood.
> Thunder and lightning led him downe the aire,
> Trumpets celestiall sounding as he came,
> Which strooke the people with astounding feare.[71]

But Drayton was still cautious about the hagiographic emphasis, in his closing account of the death and burial of Moses:

> Who being dissolv'd the Angels did interr
> Neere to *Bethpeor* in the valied ground,
> But yet so secret kept his Sepulcher,
> That it by mortall never should be found.
> Lest that his people (if the place were knowne)
> (Seeing by him the myracles were done,
> That ever to Idolatrie were prone,)
> Unto his bones a worshipping should runne.[72]

This concern about idolatry is the probable reason why, on the whole, the hagiographic writers of the period were more wary of the New Testament saint, unless they were caught up by some such half-religious, half-literary influence as Southwell's. Even then, Nicholas Breton, for example, in *Marie Magdalens Love* in 1595, took pains to explain Mary Magdalene's answering the angels' question about her weeping:

Now some perhaps will have a Jerk at this peece of Scripture, to pray to the Saintes ere they come to Christ: because she talked with the Aungels ere shee came to Christ himselfe; but let those overseene wittes looke a little better into the matter: First the Aungels came but to the grave, and seeing her there weeping, they asked her but a question in these words, woman? *Why weepest thou?* she saide *they have taken away my Lorde, and I knowe not where they have laid him*: Here is no praier made unto them, though they were Aungels, but she onelie answered their question, and so ended their talke; so if the Saints will come and speake to them; let them aunswere their questions and have no more to doe with them: for surely God will better appeare unto them in his mercie, then aunswere them by his Saintes, if they could deliver him any message; but let these blinded people take heede that these mistaken Saints prove not Divels that by illusions lead them not from God, and his mercie, to their utter confusion both of bodie and soule.[73]

But, as we have seen in the lamentation literature written under the inspiration of Southwell, there was for all this caution about idolatry a real interest in the more extended, more contemplative, more emotional development of episodes in the Gospel story. It even came, within certain limitations, to include the mother of Christ. The campaign against the emphasis which had been placed on Mary in the old order had been one of the most vigorous of the sixteenth-century Reforming efforts and one of the most successful. It is very interesting, therefore, that around the turn of the century there should come a revival of attention to the mother of Christ in this new hagiographic literature. It may have seemed to these writers simply a logical extension of the interest in Mary Magdalene and Peter and the other apostles. But it may, also, be that the poet moving forward in the exploitation of this highly popular field became aware of the fact that no figure could be more humanly appealing than the mother of Christ.

Even so, the anonymous *The Song of Mary the Mother of Christ*, published in London in 1601, is a curious work for this time. The title suggests the classic lamentation of the Virgin, or the type of emotionally charged complaint in the Southwell tradition with which we are familiar. But the emphasis of this work is very different, as the subtitle suggests, "Containing the story of his life and passion." For the purpose of this poem is to tell the story of Christ's life with appropriate lessoning. The distinctly cautious treatment of the Virgin is apparent even when the poet has as it were handed the poem over to her:

> But yet in me, farre more then all the rest,
> Thy love ô Lord and glory doth appeare:
> Extolling her, that was the very least,
> The onely Sonne our Saviour for to beare.
> And lodge within so lowe and straite a roome,
> The Judge of all, in dreadfull day of doome!
>
> .   .   .   .
>
> My Lord, my God, my Saviour and my King,
> Myne onely Sonne, ô Saints and Angels sing.
>
> .   .   .   .
>
> Thou onely Sonne of God, Father of might,
> Maker of me and all, the well of grace:
> Fountaine of love, eternall Sonne of light,
> Because my Sonne; and falling on her face,
> Repeating this full oft (with musique sweet)
> She did adore and kisse our Saviours feete.[74]

Having thus reassured the Protestant concern about overemphasis
in this image of the Virgin kneeling at her son's feet, the poet allowed
a little more of the human touch in the mother's description of the
scene in Bethlehem:

> The time expyr'd, in *Bethlem* thou wert borne,
> Where, in a Crib Upon a locke of hay,
> Twixt Oxe and Asse, thou Lord didst thinke no scorne
> Swadled in cloutes, thy mother should thee lay.
> O sacred Lord! sweet Sonne, what should I call?
> My God, my babe, my blisse, and all in all.[75]

But the picture of Christ's hidden life in Nazareth is redolent of the
sixteenth-century ideal of sober piety:

> But I indeed was witnes with mine eye,
> I saw his deeds and wrote them in my brest:
> His modest cheare, his deep humility,
> His heavenly talke, devoyd of idle jestes.
> His instant prayer and contemplation hye.
> Declaring well his God head was so nye.
>
> .   .   .   .
>
> The morning still in lamentation spent,
> The day divided into equall space:
> What prayer mist, to humble worke was bent,
> Who made the heavens and earth a wondrous case.
> And hard for haughty mindes to understand,
> Doth worke with *Joseph*, with his Axe in hand.[76]

After all, these hagiographic materials from the Bible were appealed to in the first place for purposes of moral illustration, very
much in the old medieval homily style, and very much in the manner,
too, of the contemporary Catholic guide to the devout life. For example, when Robert Parsons came to expand his *Book of Christian
Exercise* into *The Christian Directory*, he inserted between what had
earlier been the third chapter of the second part, on love of the world,
and the fourth chapter, on presumption against God's mercy, a new
chapter, titled "Examples of True Resolution in the two former
Pointes: of Suffering for Christ, and Contemning the World."[77]
These were the ancient Christian martyrs, beginning with the apostles
and their immediate disciples like Saints Ignatius and Polycarp, and
going on to the victims of the great persecutions of the pagan emperors, and finally of the ancient heretics.[78] Richard Robinson did very

much the same thing on a smaller scale, using scriptural characters for illustration in *The Vineyarde of Vertue*. This work presented, in the words of the title-page description, "XXXII. most excellent plants of fruitful vertue: In most beautiful and blessed maner environing the true elect Churche of God upon earth." Robinson's technique of development of his basic figure is traditional enough, every "plant" receiving its distinctive definition, "testimonie," and examples. For instance, the first plant is defined as follows: "True knowledge of God, is, when we understand and acknowledge the Essence, that is to say, the beeing, or rather the majestie, dietie, and humanitie of the eternall and incomprehensible God, and the efficacie of his heavenly will, first revealed by Christe Jesus his onely Sonne, preached and taught unto his Apostles by the lawe and Gospel, and by this miraculous power of the holy Ghost, actually testified unto the holy Prophets and Patriarkes, and unto his Apostles." [79] This definition is supported by a collection of relevant scriptural texts, and then for examples the Three Wise Men journeying from the East, Moses, Joshua, David, Esdras, Tobias, Esther, and Job.[80]

From the point of view of what might be called hagiographic safety, the next period after that of Scripture would be the first age of the Church, that time of primitive purity to which the Protestant Reformers so wistfully looked back. Of course, invocation of the memory of this first period involved a good deal more than moral example and spiritual inspiration. It also gave opportunity for that reinforcement of contemporary position from history that all parties in this most controversial of ages eagerly sought. We have already seen how Foxe used Primitive Church history. A little more than a dozen years later, Meredith Hanmer published *The Auncient Ecclesiasticall Histories of the First Six Hundred Years after Christ,* translations from the Greek of Eusebius, Socrates, and Evagrius. Something of the traditional devotional character which the reading of the saint's life had had earlier is recognized in his address to Elizabeth, Countess of Lincoln, a member of Elizabeth's Court: "Wherefore in so godly a place, to be so vertuously disposed at vacant times, as to reade these auncient histories wilbe a commendation unto your honor, an encrease of knowledge, a confirmation of the faith, a maintenance of the zeale, and a lively beholdinge of Christ Jesus in his members." [81] Apparently Hanmer did not mind the miracles that were wrought by the faithful in the time of Saint Irenaeus, as reported by Eusebius in his fifth book,[82] but he made some very nice distinctions when it came to Eusebius' account of some images of the time, especially the image of the woman cured of the bloody flux: ". . . that there were such images resembling Christ and the woman (monuments of memorye and not of superstition) . . . we cannot denye, insomuch that many doe testifie of the same, some by heare saye, and some other that they sawe it. Yet thus much we may note with Eusebius in the same chapter, that the originale erection of these and such like images was derived from the Gentiles, who of a heathenishe custome were wont to adore such as of olde tyme had benefitted them with the setting up of their pictures for monuments in remembraunce of them."[83] And of Julian's tearing down an image and putting his own in its place, which the lightning then broke, Hanmer explains, "This God did not that he was pleased at the setting up of pictures, but in token of his wrath and displeasure against Julian for so dispiteful a deede."[84] And when it came to the question of the duration of this first age of the Church, in which things that would later be suspect could still be recognized, however cautiously, Hanmer took essentially Foxe's position, stopping with Evagrius at the year 595, "leaving the times following (which are wonderfully corrupted) to such as are disposed to discourse of them."[85]

As Hanmer was doubtless quite aware, there were many so disposed. For the memory of ancient history could be used to cast fresh obloquy upon later persecutors of what the sixteenth-century Protestant would regard as worthy foreshadowings of his own position, by identifying them with the pagan emperors and other persecutors of the faithful, whom all abhorred. The effort of Foxe to establish a Protestant history of Christianity was, thus, to receive direct and continuing reinforcement in contemporary Church histories and books of martyrdom from the pens of Continental Protestant leaders, and the Anglican writer could find a larger setting for the local experience in such a survey as that of Heinrich Bullinger of the history of the persecutions suffered by the true Church. This work of the great Continental Reformer was translated by Thomas Twine, and, as *Tragedies of Tyrantes*, published with a dedication to Matthew, Archbishop and Primate of England, in London in 1575. The very title-page description makes the sweep of the work clear, and also its motivation: "The Tragedies of Tyrantes, Exercised upon the church of God, from the birth of Christ unto this present yeere, 1572, Containing the causes of them, and the just vengeance of God upon the authours, Also some notable comfortes and exhortations to pacience." The translator in his address to "the loving Reader" not only reminded him that "the Crosse is companion to the woorde of God," but on that basis he proceeded to put the classic case for the book of martyrdom: "In respect wherof, for the better stay of the weaker sort, many excellent wel learned men have in foretimes written Bookes of Martyrdome, to no smale comfort of the Churche and hartening of the faithfull to continue patiently and stedfastly in their calling, and profession of Christ." [86]

Bullinger went back of the beginning of the Christian Era to include the heroes of the Old Testament, on the ground "that all the Sainctes and holy men whiche lived before, and after the comming of Christe, were all one people, and united into one bodye, and into one Church under one head, and that they have one only and eternal saviour and *Messias*, Jesus Christe." [87] So the persecutions which Moses endured at the hands of Pharaoh, and, after him, the prophets in Judah and Israel, may be counted as part of the history of the persecutions for the "ryght fayth." [88] Then with Herod's slaying of the Innocents, Bullinger was launched on the more usual version of the Christian martyrological story. [89] So he ran through the earliest persecutions and on through the familiar series of the persecutions of the Roman emperors and the Vandals. [90] The nineteenth persecution, the longest and most grievous of all, was that by the followers of Mohammed, whom Bullinger did not scruple to call "the wicked hypocrite, and most craftie verlet." [91] As for Saracen and Turkish persecutions, Bullinger recognized that there were those who would call these wars rather than persecutions, since the Church in the case of the Roman emperors did not defend itself but "wyllyngly and paciently submitted it selfe to al miserie and death." [92] To this objection Bullinger retorted, as one would expect him to, "that before times their was farre more integritie and veritie of doctrine as wee have shewed before then now in our age accustomably is taught or received in the Churche of *Rome*." Yet he concluded that the persecutions by the Saracens and the Turks "are in verye deede and may bee tearmed persecutions of the Christian relygion," and went on to compare the Turkish persecutions in particular to the captivities into

which the Assyrians and Babylonians led away "the auncient people
of God." [93] But though he was willing to call Christians all whom
the Turks "for the names sake" persecuted, he took pains to explain
that "neither by any meanes therby are the errours of the Romish
Churche excused." But contemplating the Turkish persecution and
remembering the ancient prophecies like Daniel's of the sharpness
of the last persecution, Bullinger gave it as his opinion that the final
judgment was not far off. [94] The twentieth and last "Tragical Act,
or persecution," was the "Papisticall." Bullinger's is the classic Protestant history of the popes, [95] ending with present persecutions in Higher
and Lower Germany, Scotland, England, Spain, Italy, and other regions, but chiefly France. [96]

As for the explanation of persecution, Bullinger went back to Job
to remind his readers that "Persecutions are sent to the Church by
the just judgment of god." He then refined that generalization: "God
sendeth persecution unto sutch, as ought to bee the people of God,
and partly also are indeede, and so are named: but are not so innocent,
pure, and holly, as of duetie they should bee," [97] a fairly safe description of Christians in any age. And for comfort in persecution he offered such reflections as that the faithful "by persecutions are advanced
unto greter things." [98] Then he addressed himself to the task of answering the complaint of the faithful about the prosperity of the
ungodly, with assurance of the evil fates of persecutors, drawing forth
"out of most credible histories certen examples." Those examples begin with Pharaoh, and range through the kings of Judah and Israel,
and the people of Babylon, to Antiochus, King of Syria. [99] As for those
who have persecuted the Church since the death of Christ, he covers
a wide range, beginning with Herod and ranging through the emperors like Nero and Domitian and Diocletian, Mohammed and the
disasters of the end of the Saracen empire, to the popes, of whose
troubles he says, "Moreover, God raised adversaryes moste mightie
Kinges, and Emperours agaynste the Popes, who wyth great gravitie
and authoritie wythstoode them, and accused them." [100]

Bullinger's book was sweeping enough, but even larger in its undertaking was a French work which toward the end of this period was
translated to satisfy the popular interest in Church history which Foxe
had so much encouraged. It is *The Estate of the Church*, which
Simon Patrick translated out of French into English and published

in London in 1602. Again the title-page addition indicated the scope of the enterprise: "With the discourse of times, from the Apostles untill this present: Also of the lives of all the Emperours, Popes of Rome and Turkes: As also of the Kings of Fraunce, England, Scotland, Spaine, Portugall, Denmarke etc. With all the memorable accidents of their Times." Although the name of the author did not appear on the title page, it was given in the dedicatory address to Sir William Wray of Glentworth (Lincoln), by the translator, as "I. Crispinus"[101] — Jean Crespin, the great French Protestant martyrologist. Born at Arras early in the sixteenth century, Crespin had been a lawyer, but had adopted the ideas of the Reform and finally taken refuge in Geneva, where he established a printing press to help spread those ideas. Here in 1554 he published his famous *Le Livre Des Martyrs*, covering the martyr story from John Hus to that year.[102] Here, too, he published in 1564 *État de l'Église des le temps dès apôtres jusqu'a 1560, avec un Receuil des troubles advenus sous les rois Francois II et Charles IX*.[103] After his death in 1572 the history was brought down by other hands to the date of this edition which Patrick translated in 1601.[104]

Actually, Crespin's work is very different from Foxe's. It is more in the nature of an expanded chronicle, covering pretty much the history of the known world, or at least so much of the known world as impinged upon European consciousness, with a dominating but by no means exclusive emphasis upon religion, from the Protestant point of view. (The account of the changes in England at the accession of Mary is headed "The Historie of the revolt of England.")[105] Only rarely does Crespin, in his concentration on major events, yield to the temptation of developing a good story. Perhaps the most dramatic instance is the story of the end of Pope Alexander VI, "fearefull, and with manifest tokens of the just judgment of God." Poisoned by the wine which he had designed for one of his cardinals, the Pope sent a servant to his wardrobe for a book of magic to determine his end. There the terrified man "sawe a certaine person sit in the Popes Chaire there, who was altogether like unto his maister." Not surprisingly, he returned to the Pope, who gave him time to recover his courage and then sent him back. This time the apparent Pope asked the trembling man what brought him there, and when he managed to answer that he came to get a certain garment for the Pope, "the divell being then in the Chaire, making an horrible noise said, what Pope? I am the Pope." The next day the Devil in the likeness of a carrier or lackey came and demanded admittance to the chamber in which the dying Pope lay. Although the company drew back, they apparently heard the argument between the Devil and Alexander as to the length of the papal term which the Devil had promised. For all the Pope's pleas, the Devil refused to change his arithmetic, and "even as Sathan went and departed from the place, in like manner also with great cries, sighes, and fearfull sobbes, the Popes soule (as it were following his steppes) dislodged and miserably departed from his body." [106]

From the point of view of the ordinary reader, the swift pageant of all of these years, even if confirmatory of Crespin's thesis that all things are continually in change, must have proved bewildering had it not been for two kinds of helps provided in this English version. The first of these are the marginal comments and guides, such as *"John de Salisburie* a true Doctor" against a summary of his criticism of "the wickednes of Popes and Cleargie," [107] or "Persecution against the faithful" against an account of the Paris edicts of 1542 against the Lutherans.[108] More important, however, are the sentences in italics interposed here and there in the middle of the page to bring home to the reader the significance of what he has just read. For example, after an account of some third-century heretics: *"There are at this day certaine Anabaptistes which say that when man dyeth, his soule sleepeth until the day of judgement, which is an execrable heresie."* [109] Against the very brief account of the effort of Pope Pelagius II to reduce the number of Prefaces in the Mass there is both a marginal notation, "An heape of superstitions," and an italicized sentence following: *"Yet this is nothing in respect of the abhominations which by succession of time came into the Masse."* [110]

But the interest of this book is not confined to religion. It may have been the fascination of the common enemy that prompted some very extensive accounts of the often lurid happenings within the realm of the Turk. For example, the strangling of Mustapha by his father, Sultan Solyman, in the year 1553 undoubtedly "came wel" for the Christians whom Mustapha had persecuted, but the story of the harem intrigues that led up to it is told in what is for the scale of this book considerable detail, so that the effect of the account is more on

the romantic than the moralizing side.[111] And it is not without significance that the chronicle ends with a quite secular event, which
aroused a great deal of interest in London at the time, the reception
of the ambassadors from Moscow at the Court of Queen Elizabeth
on the fourteenth of October, 1600.[112]

But however engaging these traditional revivals and imitations are,
it would be a mistake to think of the hagiographic development of
this period as in any sense confined to the retrospective. Actually, the
classic hagiographical development was taking place in England
very much as it had in antiquity. The recording of the lives of the
martyrs was being followed by the writing of the lives of the confessors and the great leaders of the movement of conversion to Reforming principles. It might be argued that some of these latter really
belong to the Puritan tradition rather than the Anglican, and in a
sense that is true. But it should never be forgotten that what might
be called the Puritan movement was still firmly within the Church
of England; indeed, its promoters were still hopeful of dominating
that institution. Although it is true that the great collections of the
lives of the Puritan ministers are going to come later with, notably,
the publications of Samuel Clarke in the years between 1646 and
1683,[113] the pattern of the Puritan saint's life is already apparent in
the life of Calvin which his great disciple, Theodore Beza, dated
from Geneva August 19, 1564, and which promptly appeared in an
English translation by I. S. in London before the end of that year.
This is, as one would expect from its date, an interesting transitional
document, illustrating some of the transformations that the old hagiographic type had already undergone. Actually, this work is not a
full-dress biography, but a preface to Calvin's *Commentaries upon
the Book of Josua*, published after his death, but the English printer
chose to publish it separately in a little book with a purpose that is
at once clear in his address to the reader: "Friend Reader, I offer
unto thee this present gathering or summe, contayning the Lyfe and
Death of the Faithful servant of God, Maister John Calvin: by the
which thou shalt see marvellous examples of the assaultes, that he
hath endured for the Doctrine of the Sonne of God, and also what
assistance God doth give to his, when his honor and glorye commeth
in question." [114]

As might be expected from one who, like Beza, had shared his master's active life of controversy, the battle note is strong in his account of the man whom he considered not only a servant of God but God's "champion" in "the quarell of the Lord." It is appropriate, then, that Beza should begin his account with his hero's "doctrine," defined in terms of the enemies against whom he maintained it. Among these enemies that incurred the judgment of God in a fashion that should make clear the nature of the ultimate contest between God and Satan were the Anabaptists, the Apostate Carol, the monster Servetus, the monk Bolseck, "filthy and stincking to every man that hath any good understanding," and the "glorious Cardinall Sadolet." [115] It is only after Beza had disposed of this rabble that he undertook the classic account of the family and education of his hero: "Hee was alway of a singular good wit, and above all other things of a very good conscience, enimy to vices, and greatly given to the service of God, as men did then call it." [116] His legal studies at the desire of his father [117] gave a fresh twist to the usual clerical story. But the great turning point came when Calvin on his way back from Italy passed through Geneva: "But the Lord being even then willing to prepare a way to his so great goodnesse as his pleasure was to bestowe upon his Church by the meane of him, did put in the heart of the sayde Farel to staye him." When Calvin left Geneva, he went to Strasbourg, where he set up a French church, and "therein did establish Ecclesiasticall discipline in such sort, as the Almaignes could never yet attaine unto, for their Churche, even to this very day." [118] But no less exciting than Calvin's triumphs were the retributions that overtook those responsible for his trials: "In the mean time the Lord did execute his judgements at Geneva, punishing certaine which being in the place of Syndique .1538. were the cause of the banishement of Calvin and Farel, in such sort as one of them beyng gyltie of a sedition, and thinking to save himself thorow a window, did all burst himselfe, an other of them having committed a murder, was by order of justice beheaded, the other twaine being convinced of certain untrouth against the state of the towne, fledde awaye and were condemned in their absence." [119]

So Calvin returned to Geneva in 1541 to frame "an order of Ecclesiasticall Discipline, which hath alwayes since continued there firmely, albeit Satan and hys adherentes have employed all theire forces to abolishe it." But this accomplishment was possible only because of labors that might truly be called heroic, for "beside that he preached continually every daye in the weeke, and most commonly, and as often as he was able, hee preached twice every Sonday: hee did reade divinitie three times in a weeke: hee made declaration in the Consistorie or as it were a whole lesson every Friday, in conference of the Scripture which we call Congregation, and did continue this order thorowly without interruption untill his death, and in dede never did fayle so much as once, except it were by extreme sicknesse." [120] Something of the old admiration for asceticism comes into the account of Calvin's personal habits: "As touching his ordinary life and dyet, every man can witnesse that it was so temperate, that there was never excesse in it, no more was there of nigardise, but a commendable meane, saving that he had alwayes to small regarde to his health, being contented for the space of many yeares with one repast in .xxiiii. houres, and never receiving any thing betwene his meales . . . Being of so smal a dyet, he slept very litle." [121]

But the controversial note bore hard on the hagiographic when Beza undertook to defend his master against the charges of his enemies. To those who blamed Calvin for a passion to rule, Beza asked, "with whom did hee ever strive for the first or the seconde place, when men have not given unto him that which the gifts and graces that God had given him did require?" [122] As for the charge of cruelty, he cited the fact that only one man was put to the fire, Servetus, who "for the chiefe and principall of all his wickednesses, would never neyther repent in giving place to the truth, wherby hee had bene so often times convinced, nor shewe any token of conversion." [123]

On the other hand, Beza went into great detail as to the various diseases that in the end afflicted his master and carried him off, but not until he had made an exemplary will, testifying to the little profit in a worldly sense he had made of his opportunities, and had made a deathbed appearance at the Friday-night-before-Pentecost supper of his fellow ministers. It seems almost superfluous to add that the body was accompanied to the common churchyard by "the greatest part" of the town, all lamenting. [124]

But though from the point of view of the English public there could be no serious contender for leadership in the Reform to compare with Calvin, there were many others whose services were gratefully remembered. Here it will be recalled that the formal biography had been preceded in the hagiographic development by the panegyric delivered as part of the commemoration of the anniversary of the martyr's death.[125] Now the Protestant victory made possible such a tribute for those who had contributed to it in the area of its triumph, and close ties with Reformers in other lands widened the field of potential interest. A very good example is the oration on the life and death of Hyperius which was delivered in "a solemne assemblie of all the States of the Citie of Marpurge" by Wygandus Orthlius, and which John Ludham, Vicar of Weathersfield, translated into English and published with his translation of Hyperius' *The Practice of Preaching, otherwise called The Pathway to the Pulpit,* in London in 1577. This oration, basically a tribute to an academic, had been delivered at Marburg more than a dozen years before, on February 27, 1564, where the orator could properly say that all of his audience had lost "a most worthie companion, many . . . a most excellent Scholemaster," and otherwise pay tribute to him as the "chiefe and principall Divine of our Churches." [126] There was reason, however, for English interest in Hyperius, because he had been at Cambridge at the expense of Erasmus' patron, Lord Mountjoy, when the execution of Cromwell and the Edict against Strangers had made it seem wise for him to leave. He was on his way to Strasbourg when he stopped at Marburg in 1541 to wait for his books, and presently he settled down there to teach, publicly the Holy Scriptures and privately the liberal sciences.[127]

The style of the panegyrist is sober enough, but even so one gets a picture of a zealous and careful teacher:

As for the forme and maner of preaching in the Schole, with what great laboure, I pray you, with what great paynfulness did he order it? He prescribed common places, which he thought most needeful to be handeled: he corrected the Sermons written by Studentes, before they were recited: he hearde also them that were appoynted to preach, before they should openly come into the Church: to the intent that if anythinge were amisse either in their voyce, or in their gestures, that also might be amended.

.   .   .   .

There was in him besides all these thinges, a most diligent meditation touching the reforming of Churches, wherein he was occupied day and night. For he coveted greatly to revoke the people of our nation to the paterne of the primityve Church.

It adds to the attractiveness of the portrait, too, to learn that Hyperius "so behaved himselfe in all places and towarde all men, that his maner seemed not onely pleasaunt to the learned, but also most sweete and delectable to the rude and ignoraunt." It is interesting again that here, as in Beza's life of Calvin, there is a very full description of the last illness, with emphasis upon the completion of the testimony: "And truely the very first day of Februarie, wherin also he departed, all his talke was altogether in this, that he might testifie unto those whom he saw present: that he remayned even to the last gaspe constant and inflexible in that profession of fayth and doctrine, which he so many years had professed in the *Scole*." [128] This emphasis upon fidelity to doctrine even to the end is apparently a very precious thing to the Reforming hagiographer of the time.

The biography prefaced to the collected works is, of course, another one of the classic genres of both sacred and profane tribute. A notable example of this period is that of the distinguished Puritan minister Richard Greenham. It may be the fact that Henry Holland, author of this life, dedicated this work to the Lary Margaret, Countess of Cumberland, and the Lady Katherine, Countess Dowager of Huntington, that made him, like Meredith Hanmer, mindful of Court taste.[129] Especially interesting is Holland's explanation of the evil of the times: "The cause why mens hearts are hardned now adaies, may be this in part, because they see as great gifts of learning, tongues, and civill life in papists, and heretikes, as in Gods true servants" [130] — an unusually candid admission, one may add, for a period in which assumed commitment to evil generally overshadowed in the eyes of the judicious every other aspect of personality. We have seen how the panegyrist of Hyperius emphasized the important theme of preaching. Henry Holland in his tribute concentrated even more firmly on the delicate art of the cure of afflicted souls, one may add, one of the great preoccupations of the preacher of the time: "This reverend man of God M. Greenham, was a man in his life time of great hope, and could have given best rules for this unknowne facultie: for that the Lorde by his good knowledge and experience, restored many from unspeakable torments, and terrors of minde of which some are asleepe in Christ, and as yet living not a few." [131] Again, there was a stress on graciousness: "In his holy ministrie, he was ever carefull to avoide all occasions of offence, desiring in all things to approve himselfe as the minister of Christ. . . . He was the speciall instrument and hand of God to bring many, both godly and learned, to the holy service of Christ, in his ministrie, and to restraine, and to reduce not a few from schisme and error, striving alwaies to retaine such in obedience of lawes, and preciously to esteeme and regard the peace of the Church and people of God." [132] As a whole, this modest sketch of Holland's has both pattern and point, dealing, as it does, with a matter of great interest to those who took their religion seriously at the end of the sixteenth century and the beginning of the seventeenth, and that is the suffering of the tender conscience. It is certainly worthy of note as the precursor of a good many Puritan tributes of the next century.

One may see a fuller realization of these tendencies in a ministerial biography of only a slightly later period. Although the fact that it was not printed until the nineteenth century precluded any popular influence, there is still something highly representative of the emerging hagiographic pattern at the end of our period in the manuscript account of "The Life and Death of Master William Whittingham, Dean of Durham, who departed this life, Anno Domini 1579, June 10," written by a "Student of the Temple, about 1603." [133] Whittingham was one of the progenitors of what we might call the more aggressive Puritan movement of the early years of the seventeenth century. Consequently, this account of his life is really the story of a Puritan martyr of the sixteenth century, who had fought the Prayer Book men at Strasbourg in the days of exile, and who, in spite of his willingness to compromise on what he had considered nonessentials, had been persecuted by his opponents even after the victory of the Reform.

The author of this life was clearly a trusted friend of his subject, for when in 1576 the Earl of Leicester, through a common friend, urged Whittingham to come to Court, with promise of either the see of York or the see of Durham, which were then vacant, Whittingham sent his letter declining the proffered honor on the score of health to this man, then a student at the Temple, for delivery to the courtier.[134] Now a quarter of a century later, the deepening of the Puritan struggle for a pure Reformed Church had clearly sharpened the interest of this unknown early seventeenth-century writer in the victim of an earlier generation, and there is no question of the sympathy with which he detailed Whittingham's difficulties.

As a Scholar of Brasenose, Fellow Probationer of All Souls, and Fellow of Christ Church, William Whittingham already had a distinguished academic career behind him when in 1550 he set out for

Italy. But on the way he providentially fell sick and so missed that country "from which few return the godlier," as his biographer put it. So he stayed for several years in France, where he married, and then went to Germany and Geneva. Returning at the end of Edward's reign, and seeing the turn in religious affairs at the accession of Mary, he went abroad again, presently joining the English Protestant refugees at Frankfurt. There he took an active part in the controversies in the English Church of that city over the forms of the Edwardian Church, and when agreement was clearly impossible, he was one of the convinced admirers of the Discipline of Geneva who retired to that city.[135]

There, at the insistence of Calvin, Whittingham, who had evidently prepared himself for a diplomatic career, succeeded John Knox in the ministry of the English Church. He also took his part in the preparation of what became the Geneva Bible, remaining there for a year and a half after the accession of Elizabeth, to finish the translation.[136]

After his return to England, Queen Elizabeth took advantage of his foreign experience and of his command of French for a couple of missions abroad, where his valor and his skill alike commanded admiration. Out of this experience came his preferment to the deanery of Durham.[137] There he took an active part in allaying the troubles of that region, and as his biographer says: "For eight or nine years after, Master Whittingham lived in the great love and liking of his neighbors, for his affability, and bountiful hospitality, which was in such a proportion, as it is marvelled even to this day [1603], how the naked Deanery alone, for he had no more, could support his expenses."[138]

But the close of his life was troubled with vexation over his defense of the liberties of his church against the Archbishop of York. Unfortunately for Whittingham, the see of York, for which he had declined to be considered, fell to an old opponent of his, Edwin Sandys, who had made one of the party that had carried the day for the Edwardian Prayer Book at Frankfurt and so caused Whittingham to go to Geneva.[139] When, therefore, Sandys claimed rights of visitation over the cathedral of Durham, Whittingham had every reason to fear that his enemy might challenge the measures he had taken for the order of that church. At any rate, he resisted the Archbishop's visitation claim on the ground that it violated the liberties of the church of Durham, which he had sworn to defend.[140] The recent publication abroad, in 1575, of a highly partisan English account of the troubles at Frankfurt, generally believed to be by Whittingham, would not have done anything to give present authority any confidence in Whittingham. And the fact that his ordination had been according to the form of Geneva and not of England, added to some question of his academic degrees, apparently made possible a challenge to his competence for his office.[141] Clearly, Whittingham's biographer felt that his hero had been unjustly treated by those who had urged trivial objections for partisan reasons.[142]

Whittingham would seem to be a good example of the sixteenth-century Puritan who was ready to conform in what he thought minor matters, such as vesture, but not in what he thought essential matters of principle. He seems, too, to have had a great interest in church music, as well as skill in it: "And concerning Singing in the Church, Master Whittingham did so far allow of that, as he was very careful to provide the best Songs and Anthems that could be got out of the Queen's Chapel, to furnish the Quire withal: himself being skilful in music." [143] The ex-diplomat who went to Geneva had not by any means surrendered the tastes of a cultivated man. He seems, too, to have taken very seriously the duties of his office, going so far at one time as to teach in the grammar school for three or four hours a day for want of a competent schoolmaster, and above all, providing the preaching by which men of his sympathy so preëminently set store.[144]

The story ends in the classic fashion for the minister not a martyr, with a detailed account of "his so long languishing sickness; how he passed it over; and what was the manner of his death." What his biographer considered the malice of Archbishop Sandys and his other adversaries still pursued him, "as would not afford him a time of rest from their vexation, to die in." Apparently, Whittingham now shunned company, finding all he needed in the Bible on his bed. But even then he did not neglect his responsibility for his household, for the unknown biographer concludes his account with the following picture of the dying man:

Sometimes, in his sickness, he would call all his servants, which were many, to come into his Chamber; and would exhort them, for an hour together, to the fear of GOD: and privately would call them, by one and by one, and tell them of such faults as he had suspected them to be guilty of, and admonish them to leave them; shewing withal that he had been too indulgent or negligent towards them, in not carrying a stricter hand over them. For this he did now find as great a burden in conscience as for any other sins that he could remember; and did verily think that that negligence towards them, had as much drawn these his late afflictions and crosses upon him as any other his sins whatsoever.[145]

There is in all these early lives of Puritan ministers a certain note of urgency. After all, these were men in a position very different from that of Meredith Hanmer. For whatever the latter thought of the way in which the members of the Church of England were making use of their opportunities, he was quite sure that theirs was the best order which men had ever known for the worship of God. The Puritan not only had no such assurance; quite to the contrary, he was harried by a real anxiety over the catastrophic risks which the Church of England was running in its dallying on the road to a more perfect reformation. For that reason, the Puritan minister's life still kept something of the atmosphere of the early martyrological accounts. Throughout, the emphasis is highly functional and topical, even controversial.

The situation is, of course, quite different when it comes to the lives of the bishops of the Anglican Church, even of one like Jewel, whose survival of the Marian persecution would certainly qualify him for the status of confessor. In ancient times the lives of the bishops had been an important expression of the martyrological effort of the Christian community because the bishop played so important a part in the organization of its resistance in time of persecution. The very position of the bishop in the English establishment gives his life, therefore, an institutional significance, particularly in these early formative years of the new order. In all this there is, moreover, a controversial element, as in most things religious in this period; indeed, this is going to be true of English religious biography for a long time. Modern studies of Walton, for instance, have shown that back of his apparent naïveté was a very definite position, and that on matters which were much controverted.[146] But already in the earliest lives of the Anglican bishops one feels, also, that sense of what is established, what should be taken for granted, in other words, the tacit confidence of the Church of England.

Indeed, the basic lines of the Anglican bishop's life may be said to have been laid down in the first example, Laurence Humphrey's Latin life of Bishop John Jewel, published by John Day in 1573 with a dedicatory epistle to Matthew Parker, Archbishop of Canterbury, and Edwin Sandys, Bishop of London.[147] The fact that this work was published in Latin of course limited its circulation and its popular influence. It was given much wider availability and, therefore, influence in 1609, when Daniel Featley's very effective condensation and translation was appended to the John Norton edition of Jewel's works. It will be easier to do justice to the biographical quality of Humphrey's work in the Featley version, because the translator has, so to speak, dug out the body of the life from the matrix of sermons, letters, and summaries of controversies in which it was imbedded in the Latin.

But the fuller version of Humphrey has some features to which Featley was obviously not able to do justice, which are of interest to our study. The "Prolegomena seu *Præfatio*" is one example, for in it Humphrey discussed the problem of honoring the martyrs and saints. After presenting what he considered the extremes on this question, he took up what he believed was a middle ground: "*Etsi vero ut illi superiores* non debemus esse superstitiosi, nec ut isti posteriores furiosi, tamen esse possumus officiosi, ut media quædam via et regia et divina et æquabilis teneatur, quòd defunctis honores debiti non denegentur."[148] Humphrey also set forth his scheme more formally than Featley's later version would indicate: "*Erunt autem* huius Tragicocomoediæ (sic enim vita humana rectè dici potest) quinque Actus præcipui, et primus quasi rudimenta et initia pueritiæ, secundus Academiæ studia, Tertius exilium, Quartus reditum et Episcopatum, Quintus mortem et ultimam vitæ catastrophen, ubi omnes mundi cives iussit valere et plaudere, continebit."[149] In such a scheme of organization the indebtedness to the plan of the classic saint's life is, of course, quite apparent. The "Carmina et Epitaphia" at the end are interesting, too, written as they are in Latin, Greek, and Hebrew, by such well-known figures of the time as, among others, Alexander Nowell, Tobie Mathew, Thomas Bodley, John Rainolds, George Buchanan the Scot, and John Foxe.[150]

In itself, Daniel Featley's *The Life of the Worthie Prelate and Faithfull Servant of God John Jewel sometimes Bishop of Sarisburie,* prefaced to John Norton's 1609 publication of the works of Jewel,[151] is a very fine thing, a worthy forerunner of the episcopal biographies of Walton, later in the century. But for our purposes the most interesting aspect is the influence of the traditional saint's life, even of the repudiated *Golden Legend*, in this life of the great champion of the Church of England.

The opening of the story is cautious enough from the hagiographical point of view: "If rare and admirable qualities of our Ancestors do deserve a thankfull acknowledgement of posteritie, then most deservedlie ought the singular natural endowments and supernaturall graces of this reverend Prelate live and flourish in perpetual memory: by whom as an especiall meanes the sincere religion we now professe received much vigor and strength after her long suppression in the time of superstition." But the old etymological passion of the *Golden Legend* peeps out in a reminder of the way in which the distinctive quality of such heroes as Augustine and Gregory was revealed in their names, and the author's own contribution to the tradition: "There lies a great treasurie in names, so heere grace in *John*, and eminent perfection in *Jewel.* . . . His Mothers name was *Bellamie*, composed of beauty and love, which name he caused to be engraven in his signet." [152] The biographer devoted a good deal of space, relatively, to the education of his hero, with emphasis on "his singular promptnes of wit and industrie"; especially did he dwell on his career at Oxford, where his tutor prophesied, "Surely *Pauls* Crosse will one day ring of this boy." Featley enthusiastically followed his hero's career from Merton College to Corpus Christi, recounting the brilliant success of his "Humanitie Lecture," his intimacy with Peter Martyr, his preaching at Sunningwell, "whither . . . he went on foot at least once every fortnight," his preaching at Oxford, and later his controversies with Harding.[153] The admiration of the biographer deepened into compassion when he came to the expulsion of Jewel from his college and "the tragicall events ensuing; first when looking every houre to be delivered up to the cruell Butcher Boner, and to be slaughtered at his shambles, he went on foot in a snowie Winters night towards *London*, and was in the way found by *Bernet, Latimers* servant, starved with colde, and faint with wearinesse, lying on the ground panting and labouring for life, or rather for death, and afterwards being fled from his native soil, he wan-

dred beyond the sea, disappointed of all friends and meanes to procure him so much as a lodging." [154] But in this summary of his hero's
troubles Featley had got ahead of himself, for he soon returned to
Jewel's taking refuge at Broadgates Hall, and the very satisfactory
evidence of his old college's discovery of its loss, including Dean
Wright's rebuke of their pride in having, alone of all the colleges,
kept their church treasure and ornaments, with the observation that
they had wilfully lost one treasure, "farre more precious than any
of them." The university chose Jewel to be her orator, and he wrote
the congratulatory letter to Queen Mary. But soon after, "the Inqui-
sition caught him, urging upon him subscription under paine of
proscription and horrible tortures," and Jewel, "having no other
counsellers in this heavie encounter than horror without, and frailtie
within," yielded.[155]

Featley would naturally have preferred to omit this, but decided
that "the truth of love must not prejudice love of truth, and, I verily
thinke, the wisdome of God, who draweth good out of mans evill
so ordered this matter." He then invoked the memory of notables,
from Saint Augustine to Cranmer, who had had occasion to repent
of various types of weakness and won honor in the expression of
their repentance. Jewel apparently seized the first opportunity of
a sermon in Frankfurt to confess his weakness and so won fresh
honor of his audience, and Featley took this occasion to call attention to the good Protestant who would not stoop to sophistry or
equivocation. And he gave a glowing account of the service of Jewel,
mostly in the house of Peter Martyr, to the English exiles. [156]

The "happy Catastrophe" of the story with the accession of Elizabeth not only brought Jewel back to England, but to a bishopric, the
bishopric of Salisbury. Of his conduct in that high place, Featley
gives what was to be the classic Anglican picture of a good bishop:
"The memorie of his assiduitie in preaching, carefulnesse in providing Pastours, resolutenesse in reforming abuses, bountie in relieving
the poore, wisdome in composing litigious strifes, equitie in judging
spirituall causes, faithfulnesse in keeping, and sincerity in bestow-
ing Church-goods, is as an ointment powred out and blowen abroad
thorow the Diocesse of *Sarum* by the breath of every mans commendation." His daily routine in his almost monastic household
with its delight in the "scholasticall warres betweene yoong scholars,

whom he maintained at his table," was suggested pleasantly. [157] Then the author devoted himself to a fuller account of two especially note-worthy qualities of his hero: "his memorie of things past, and presage of things to come." Of the first he recalled that "he could repeat faithfully any thing he had penned, as he had penned it, after once reading; and therefore usually at the ringing of the bell began to commit his sermons to heart." This was not merely the gift of nature, but of art, an art which he "professed to teach others." Memorable, too, was his "divination," shown especially, as so often by the saints, in his foreseeing of the time of his own death. Indeed, "the super-naturall motions of Gods spirit within him, in the end became, as it were, naturall, *in fine velociores*, and the last endevours of grace in him were most vehement," so that he nearly died preaching. "Such was the life and death of B. Jewel, a most worthy trumpet of Christs glorious Gospell." [158]

Quite understandably, the institutional note was even stronger in the first of the archiepiscopal lives, Josselin's life of Parker. But one must also remember in approaching this life that it was quite in keeping with the ancient traditions of the genre that some particular spiritual value or principle should be demonstrated or promoted in its emphasis. It was, in fact, to Archbishop Parker's eagerness to demonstrate the continuity of the teaching and government of the Church of England that we owe the writing of his life, probably by his Latin secretary, John Josselin, and its first publication in a rather free English translation. Josselin assisted Parker in the prepara-tion of his *De Antiquitate Britannicæ Ecclesiæ et Privilegiis Ecclesiæ Cantuariensis*, privately printed by John Day in 1572. [159] The enthu-siastic account of the seventieth archbishop, headed "Matthaeus," was apparently printed at the end of a few copies of the original publica-tion of the *De Antiquitate*. [160] The suggestion that it is the work of Josselin is confirmed by the fact that this history of Archbishop Par-ker is also found in one manuscript of the *Historiola Collegii Corporis Christi*, which Josselin composed at Parker's direction. [161]

It must have been this version which was freely translated in *The Life off the 70. Archbishopp of Canterbury Presentlye Sittinge Eng-lished, and to be added to the 69, lately Sett forth in Latin*, published without printer or place in 1574. The relation is indicated not only in the title at the top of the first page of the book, "*Historiola*, A

litle storye of the actes and life of Mathew now, Archbishoppe of
Canterb.," but also by the opening sentences: "Nowe sithens we
have declared many thinges which we thought specially worthye
of rehersall concerning the state off Corpus Christi coll. and the actes
of certain masters therof: it remaineth that we drawe out the narration a little longer for the fore said Mathew Parker his sake of
whom we have hitherto spoken those things which he onely did for
the amplifying and commoditie off the said colledge off the which
he was mayster." [162]

What follows is the classic account of the subject's family, education, and launching upon his career, in this case his license as a
preacher in the Southern Province in 1533.[163] His success in this
popular preaching brought him to the favor of King Henry, Queen
Anne, and Edward VI, "All which princes bestowed on him very
large, and plentifull Rewards for his diligence," a judgment which
the author proceeded to make good by an account of the benefices
which his hero now received. And, characteristically, he proceeded
to show what good use he made of his fortune in benefiting his
various charges, as for instance in building a school and providing
a stipend for a schoolmaster in the village of Stoke.[164] Parker lost all
his benefices in the second year of Mary, for various reasons, but
especially for his marriage to "a woman very chaste and well manered
and that did greatly reverence her husband," a sad understatement
for a woman who must have been uncommonly charming and intelligent and gifted.[165] For the rest of Mary's reign "he lurked se-
creatlye" within a friend's house, occupying himself in study, and
rejoicing in what would but for the danger have been the kind of
life he most desired. When at the accession of Queen Elizabeth he
was invited to become Archbishop of Canterbury, he refused "often
times." [166] Josselin speaks very briefly of Parker's consecration "with
out any blemishe or spott off olde wives superstitions and unprofyt-
able cerimonies off the Romishe Pope," and of his consecrating
more bishops in his first years than any of his predecessors, because,
as Josselin notes, all but one of the bishops created in Queen Mary's
reign "withhelde their consent from the Religion established in the
generall assemblie of all estates and orders." [167] But Josselin is even
more summary in his picture of Parker as the perfect pattern of archiepiscopal behavior, just mentioning

how wisely he behaved him therin for those yeeres that are past, with general allowance, consent, and favour of all Good men, how discretly also in so great diversitie and dissention off judgementes, how uprightly and sincerely in other mens matters and controversies, with how great gentilnes and patience in other mens wrath and displeasure, with what forbearing and sufferance towardes the evill that he mighte winne them, with what godlines in reconciling the stomakes of gentilmen and determining their controversies, how lothe he was that contumeliously they should drawe eche other unto the law, lastly how often his voice was heard to sound owt off the holy pulpittes, as well off his cathedral churche, as the churches off other meane townes and villages, especially in this his old age, in his weake and crazed state off bodie, in the middest off so great busines, and in thes contagious and pestilent times, all thes thinges I will leave as matters untouched, because ther are verie many which without me by the vew off his manners, and tried trade off his life, are able to report thes and many thinges moo.[168]

The truth is that this was not what engaged Josselin's interest. Rather, he concentrated on Parker's generosity in financial matters, and his restoration of the buildings of his see of Canterbury, and his magnificent hospitality in the restored palace of the archbishops.[169]

It is not surprising that Josselin should stress these aspects of Parker's activity, because he had apparently approached his hero from the point of view of the beautifying and enriching of Corpus Christi College, Cambridge. But he was no less enthusiastic about Parker's interest in historical studies, especially anything touching the history of the Church of England, and his pains to provide the churches with the Scriptures. The fitting culmination of this care of Parker's for history and piety was his provision of a tomb for himself of black marble, as a reminder when living of his "uncertaine estate," and when dead, "as a testimonie to his posteritye, what principall place by the bountye off his Prince he obteyned in Christ his common welthe." [170]

The picture that emerges from Josselin's account is a clear and enthusiastic one, and that in spite of the hostile motive of the actual publication of his work. For there is no question that the motive of this publication was unfriendly to Parker and all that he stood for. That motive is at once apparent in the suggestion printed in the middle of the title page: "This numbre off seventy is so compleat a number as it is great pitie ther shold be one more: but as Augustin was the first, so Mathew might be the last." And throughout the text it is all too apparent in the marginal comments, as, for example, against the account of Parker's preaching "everie where" the note: "He that Preacheth every where preachethe no where"; against the account of his benefices: "Charges livinges enoughe for one man. But he shewed betymes, what game he loved. Paule sayethe they seke there owne not the thinges which belonge to Christe Jesus. Philip. 21";[171] against the account of his repairing of churches in his see: "Turne mine eyes from beholding vanity. Psal. [1]19."; and against the report of the Archbishop's giving of feasts: "whose god is their belly. Phil. 3.19."[172] Some of these notes are even mocking, as against the account of the Queen's preferring of him to Canterbury: "Yow shot at a Good marcke,"[173] and against the explanation of why the archbishop has the key three times in his arms: "O deepe divinitie, th[e] archbishope hath three keies because Christ saide pasce, pasce, Nay rather because he locketh up the Kingdome of heaven soe fast by holdinge out of minesters that might preache the worde, and keapinge in of idell and ignoraunt that can doe nothinge, that hardlie doth anie man enter thearin."[174]

As for the Archbishop's great work in writing the history of his predecessors, the editor, in the address "To the Christian reader" that follows the life, made his attitude clear: "thauncientye off thenglishe Church is but a vizard for that wormeaten Church of Caunterbury, to maske under, the bolder to boast hir off her lovers."[175] As for the monsters, not men, who had held that see, he was clearly shocked to see stamped in print "such a succession of Idolaters, conjurers, canonized traitors, and rebells as that sea hathe yelded."[176] And the translator justified his own enterprise by saying that the Latin life of Parker came out of the same shop, the copy being written by, he thinks, his secretary. And if it was not possible to spare the world the printing of "such a legend off Canterbury tales" as the foregoing, he thought it some compensation that they would not go "undisgraced, and untaxed by one of the meanest off the Laitie."[177] This is certainly one of the liveliest of the many efforts of the time to advance one's own views by the marginal comment on a respected text of one's opponents. This hostile presentation of Josselin represents what might be termed the Puritan view of the see of Canterbury.

For the Anglican we have, fortunately, a popular English history in *A Catalogue of the Bishops of England, since the First Planting of Christian Religion in This Island, together with a briefe History of their lives and memorable actions, so neere as can be gathered out of antiquity,* published in London in 1601, by Francis Godwin, the Subdean of Exeter. The very title suggests both the emphasis on continuity and the delight in remembering noble lives of service that were so to inspire Walton. The motives for this publication are set forth with engaging candor, not to say naïveté, in the author's address to the reader. Especially appealing is the half-apologetic admission: "I cannot deny, but my delight in the study of histories and antiquities, hath beene somewhat greater, then was needfull for a man that had dedicated himself and his labours unto the service of Gods church in the Ministery. Which fault acknowledging in my selfe, and being unable wholy to amend (*trahit sua quemque voluptas,* and I would to God that were the woorst might be said of me) I endevoured long since in some sort to reforme the same by restrayning my selfe within the compasse of such antiquities, as seemed to concerne but ecclesiasticall causes or persons."[178]

As for the presentation of the fruits of those studies, he had, of course, no thought that in "matters ecclesiaticall" he could add anything to "that large and painefull worke of Master *Foxe,*" but he did think he had something to contribute from his own long labors "concerning ecclesiaticall persons."[179] Actually, it is quite clear from what follows that he very much wished to redress the balance in certain current controversies over ecclesiastical matters, and that in a direction that would certainly appeal more to Walton than to Foxe: "For it is not to be denied, that the most part of the Chroniclers and historiographers of our age, have borne a hand hard ynough at least upon the Prelates and Cleargy of former times, every where like *Chams,* discovering the nakednes of these fathers, but seldome or never indevouring with *Sem* to hide the same, much lesse affoording unto them any honorable mention never so well deserved." The results of this treatment have been rather different from what these writers could, or perhaps should, have intended:

For in the vulgar sort (which distinguish not so easily betweene persons and things) it bred a conceit, not onely that the men were wicked, and so their doctrine corrupt (although I know the consequence to be weake) but also their functions and callings to be utterly unlawful and Antichristian, which opinion once received in the minds of the multitude, gave occasion of divers plots, coloured with the plausible shew of reformation, but indeed principally ayming at the goods and revenues of the church, the temporall rewards of learning; which being once taken away, what confusion is like to follow, we may easily see by the effects it bringeth foorth elsewhere . . .[180]

The fact that the author thought it wise to avoid any suspicion of flattery of the living or the friends and posterity of the recently dead, takes away from the value of the work for contemporary biography. But it is interesting to note what Godwin makes of some of the controversial figures of the past. Of these the most crucial is, of course, Thomas à Becket, the thirty-eighth in the succession of Canterbury. Godwin began with impressive simplicity and perhaps an unexpected touch of patriotic pride: "Since the Conquest never any English man obtained this Archbishopricke before *Thomas Becket*." Godwin was quite emphatic, too, on the subject of Becket's talents, using such adjectives as "subtile" and "discrete" and "painefull" and "industrious." He repeated the familiar charges as to Becket's easily falling into the luxurious ways of the King's Court, and he pointed out that the "king little thinking what a snake he nourished in his bosome," did everything for his advancement. He described, too, Becket's change after his consecration as archbishop — "he altered all the whole course of his life; became so grave, so austere, and so devout in all outward shewe, as he seemed quite another man." All this might arouse suspicion as to whether Godwin had not given away too much to his enthusiasm for the past. If there was any danger of that, he returned promptly enough to the present in his summary of the difficulties between the King and Becket: "The Cleargy of those times bare themselves so bold upon the privileges of the Church, whereby, in crymes never so haynous they claymed to be exempted from the judgment of temporall courts; as, dayly infinite outrages were committed by Cleargy men." [181]

In spite of the temptations to drama, Godwin dealt briefly with the climax of his story, showing the knights "breathing out terrible threats, and he [Becket] continuing still the same man without yeelding one jotte." The murder itself was handled briefly: "At evening prayer time the same day, they came suddenly into the church with their swords drawn, crying, Wheres the Traytor, Wheres the Traytor? The Archbishop who was then going up the steps toward the quire, hearing the noyse, turned backe unto them, and every one of the fower striking mainely at him, upon the third or fourth greice of those steps was slaine." Comparatively more detail is given to the terms of penance which were imposed upon the King, and the whole account ends with the not entirely unambiguous sentence: "All this (such were those times) the king was faine to performe." [182]

But Godwin did allow one of Becket's successors, Edmund Rich, to keep the title of Saint denied to Thomas, perhaps because of the terms in which the last years of his life are summed up: "Being thus continually vexed, thwarted, and disgraced, he departed into voluntary exile, and there bewailing the misery of his countrey, spoyled and wasted by the tyranny of the Pope, spent the rest of his life in continuall teares." [183]

In general, the history of the bishops of Rochester is presented more summarily than that of Canterbury (in his address to the reader, Godwin had already referred to the difficulties of collecting information on certain sees).[184] So the brief summary of the career of the most famous of the incumbents of that see against the marginal notation of the year 1504 is actually longer than that of many of his colleagues: "65. *John Fisher*, Doctor of Divinitie. For denying to acknowledge the kings supremacy in ecclesiasticall matters, he was executed on Tower Hill June 22. *1535.* being made Cardinall about a moneth before. His head was set on London bridge, and his body buried in Barking churchyard." [185]

More representative of Godwin's general approach is his account of Archbishop Parker. The tact of both subject and author is well indicated in Godwin's account of what might be termed the first stage of the future Archbishop's official progress: "His first preferment was the deanry of Stoke, which he obtained by the favor of Queene *Anne Bulleyn* whose Chaplaine he was . . . After the death of that noble Lady King *Henry* her husband tooke him for his Chapleine, in which place he also served King *Edward* his sonne." [186] Godwin then gives a summary of Parker's "many other good ecclesiasticall promotions," culminating in his deprivation for marriage under Queen Mary. "That terrible fire being extinguished that consumed so many zealous and learned men, and the Archbishopricke left void by the death of Cardinall *Poole*," Parker succeeded to it.[187] For the fifteen years and five months of his incumbency, Godwin concentrated on his beneficences to education, the founding of a grammar school at Rochdale in Lancashire, the procurement of scholarships for his own college, Corpus Christi, at Cambridge, as well as an addition to its library, and gifts of books, plate, church patronage, and land. Perhaps the most touching of these benefactions was his gift of a sum for the maintenance of a fire in the hall of the college from Allhalloweentide to Candlemas. Parker, also, provided for the preaching of sermons in Rogation week in five churches of Norfolk, and plate and an annual gift for the poor of the city to Norwich, his birthplace. To Gonville and Caius College and to Trinity Hall he gave books and plate, and to the University of Cambridge, books. Besides other charities he gave generously to the repair of his palaces at Canterbury and at Lambeth. This emphasis on Parker's beneficence to education is, of course, the best answer to those whose designs on the wealth of the bishoprics Godwin had already noted. But it is pleasant to see that for all his concern about the present dangers threatening the Church, Godwin gave the final and most emphatic place in his account to what was closest to his own heart: "But above anything I may not forget his great care of preserving antiquities, unto which his care we are beholding for most of our ancient histories, that but for him were even upon the point utterly to perish." [188] Godwin was a loyal and devoted son of his Church in his time, but he was not without critical sense. For example, he qualified his account of the wealth Stephen Gardiner left behind him with the parenthetical phrase, "if *Bale* say true." [189] But he began his history of the bishops of Oxford with the story of the beautiful Frideswide, who had resolved on a monastic life, and fleeing from an importunate lover of rank ("some say he was a king"), prayed for help. The lover, Godwin cautiously observes, "(as the story saith) was miraculously stricken blind." Upon her praying, he recovered his sight. [190]

It is pleasant to know that Godwin's efforts were appreciated. His book appeared in 1601; on the fifth of October of that year, he was nominated by the Queen to the see of Llandaff, elected on the fourteenth of the same month, confirmed on the twentieth of November, and two days later consecrated in Henry VII's chapel at Westminster, [191] a happy consummation for one of his tastes, both ecclesiastical and antiquarian. An enlarged and improved edition of his catalogue, published in 1615 with a dedication to King James I, seems to have proved no less popular, and equally efficacious in advancing his career, this time with his translation to the see of Hereford on November 10, 1617. The degree of this promotion may be measured by comparing the valuation of the two sees, which as usual Godwin put at the end of his account of the incumbents. That of Llandaff was £154/14/1;[192] that of Hereford £768/10/10,[193] a very impressive advance.

But there is something in that last detail that suggests not so much an anticipation of Walton and his rather innocent enthusiasm for the hierarchy, as a foreshadowing of the eighteenth-century Establishment. It is a very institutional, not to say careerist, conclusion to an ancient history, but whatever suggestions one may be tempted to draw from it, Godwin's book certainly has that ambivalent quality that so much of the literature of the sixteenth century had in this field, as in every other.

The story of the saint's and martyr's life in England is, of course, but an episode in a larger story that one may say begins with the printing of Caxton's translation of the *Legenda Aurea* in 1483 and ends, perhaps, with the publication in 1616, some fifteen years after Godwin's history, of the first of the Bollandists' works of what might be called scientific hagiography, Rosweyde's *Vitæ Patrum*.

But between the world of the *Legenda Aurea* and the beginning of the modern *Acta Sanctorum* stretches the sixteenth century. Characteristically, in this field, as in others, though the changes were often dramatic and final enough, in fact the past did not cease to be entirely operative at once, and new forms often displayed fascinating reminiscences of old. There were curious survivals, too, and in these one often learns a good deal of that tension between change and continuity that is so marked a feature of this age. One learns, too, a little more of how men confront the cataclysms, large and small, of history, not inappropriate treasure-trove from the martyr story, and from whatever point of view one approaches this shifting scene, one is rewarded with some great episodes of human devotion and resolution. With all we know today of the often shabby maneuverings of greed and ambition behind so many of the religious controversies and struggles of the period, it is well to be reminded that there were also men on both sides for whom the religious issue was the only one that mattered. And in our own time of sudden and baffling changes, it is not without relevance to remember how, on another dark and confused scene, a generous spirit, finding himself almost alone against his world, could look beyond the imminent scaffold to that other realm in which he trusted that he and the judges who had just condemned him "may yeat hereafter in heaven meerily all meete together, to our everlasting salvacion." [194]

REFERENCE MATTER

NOTES

Chapter I

1 H[ippolyte] Delehaye, *The Legend of the Saints, an Introduction to Hagiography*, trans. V. M. Crawford (London, 1907), p. 11.
2 James Edward Sherman, *The Nature of Martyrdom* (Paterson, N.J., 1942), pp. 3–4.
3 Edelhard L. Hummel, *The Concept of Martyrdom according to St. Cyprian of Carthage* (Washington, D.C., 1946), pp. 3–4.
4 A. J. Festugière, *La Sainteté* (Paris, 1942), p. 70.
5 Paul Allard, *Dix Leçons sur le Martyre* (Paris, 1907), pp. 44–45.
6 See E. C. E. Owen, General Introduction to *Some Authentic Acts of the Early Martyrs* (London: SPCK, 1933), pp. 19–20, and H[enri] Daniel-Rops, *The Church of Apostles and Martyrs*, trans. Audrey Butler (London and New York, 1960), pp. 359–60.
7 See Hippolyte Delehaye, *Les Origines du Culte des Martyrs* (Bruxelles, 1912), p. 1.
8 See Owen, *Some Authentic Acts of The Early Martyrs*, p. 16.
9 Allard, *Dix Leçons sur le Martyre*, pp. 152 ff.
10 See, e.g., *The Acts of the Pagan Martyrs, Acta Alexandrinorum*, ed. Herbert A. Musurillo (Oxford, 1954), p. 237; Festugière, *La Sainteté*, pp. 61 ff.
11 Owen, *Some Authentic Acts of the Early Martyrs*, p. 88. See Festugière, *La Sainteté*, p. 124.
12 Delehaye, *Les Origines du Culte des Martyrs*, p. 11.
13 Matt. x. 28.
14 Owen, *Some Authentic Acts of the Early Martyrs*, p. 107.
15 Rom. viii. 16–18.
16 *The Epistles of St. Clement of Rome and St. Ignatius of Antioch*, trans. James A. Kleist (Ancient Christian Writers, No. 1 [Westminster, Md., 1949]), p. 54.
17 *Ibid.*, pp. 55–56.
18 *Ibid.*, pp. 81–82.
19 *Ibid.*, p. 54.
20 *The Writings of Quintus Sept. Flor. Tertullianus*, trans R. S. Thelwall and Dr. Holmes (Ante-Nicene Christian Library), I (Edinburgh, 1872), 1.
21 Origen, *Prayer, Exhortation to Martyrdom*, trans. John J. O'Meara (Ancient Christian Writers, No. 19 [Westminster, Md., and London, 1954]), p. 10.
22 *Ibid.*, pp. 143–57.
23 *Ibid.*, pp. 158 ff.
24 *Ibid.*, pp. 168 ff.
25 *Ibid.*, p. 195.
26 St. Cyprian, *The Lapsed, The Unity of the Catholic Church*, trans. Maurice Bévenot (Ancient Christian Writers, No. 25 [Westminster, Md., and London, 1957]), p. 31.
27 *Ibid.*, pp. 13–14.
28 *Ibid.*, pp. 16–23.
29 *Ibid.*, p. 23.
30 *Ibid.*, pp. 32–42.
31 René Aigrain, *L'Hagiographie: ses*

sources, ses méthodes, son histoire (Paris, 1953), pp. 208 ff.

32 Owen, *Some Authentic Acts of the Early Martyrs*, p. 15.

33 Hippolyte Delehaye, *Les Passions des Martyrs et les Genres Littéraires* (Bruxelles, 1921), p. 11.

34 *The Epistles and the Martyrdom of St. Polycarp*, trans. James A. Kleist (Ancient Christian Writers, No. 6 [Westminster, Md., 1948]), p. 100.

35 Owen, *Some Authentic Acts of the Early Martyrs*, p. 79.

36 *Ibid.*, p. 81.

37 *Ibid.*, p. 91.

38 *Ibid.*, p. 34.

39 *Ibid.*, pp. 80–84.

40 *Ibid.*, pp. 36–39.

41 *Ibid.*, p. 117.

42 Eusebius Pamphili, *Ecclesiastical History*, trans. Roy J. Deferrari (The Fathers of the Church, No. XIX [New York, 1953]), Introduction, I, 6–9.

43 *Ibid.*, I, 28.

44 *Ibid.*, I, 35–36.

45 *Ibid.*, I, 233 ff.

46 *Ibid.*, I, 282.

47 See, e.g., *ibid.*, II, 3.

48 *Ibid.*, II, 163 ff.

49 *Ibid.*, II, 186 ff.

50 *Ibid.*, II, 288.

51 *Ibid.*, II, 14.

52 *Ibid.*, II, 199–200.

53 Owen, *Some Authentic Acts of the Early Martyrs*, p. 15.

54 Friedrich von Hügel, *The Mystical Element of Religion as Studied in Saint Catherine of Genoa and Her Friends* (London, 1909), I, 219.

55 Delehaye, *The Legends of the Saints*, pp. 111–15.

56 F. Homes Dudden, *The Life and Times of St. Ambrose* (Oxford, 1935), I, 313.

57 V. L. Kennedy, *The Saints of the Canon of the Mass* (Città del Vaticano, 1938), p. 77; Delehaye, *Les Origines du Culte des Martyrs*, p. 40.

58 Martin R. P. McGuire, "The Christian Funeral Oration," Introduction to *Funeral Orations by Saint Gregory Nazianzen and Saint Ambrose* (New York, 1953), pp. vii–xxi.

59 Josef A. Jungmann, *The Early Liturgy: To the Time of Gregory the Great*, trans. Francis A. Brunner (Notre Dame, Ind., 1959), pp. 185–86.

60 Delehaye, *Les Origines du Culte des Martyrs*, p. 120.

61 *Ibid.*, p. 135.

62 Dudden, *The Life and Times of St. Ambrose*, I, 49; and A. D. Nock, *Conversion: The Old and the New in Religion from Alexander the Great to Augustine of Hippo* (Oxford, 1933), pp. 83 ff.

63 C. Grant Loomis, *White Magic, an Introduction to the Folklore of Christian Legend* (Cambridge, Mass., 1948), pp. 103 ff.

64 Delehaye, *Les Origines du Culte des Martyrs*, p. 139.

65 *Ibid.*, p. 110.

66 Hippolyte Delehaye, *L'Oeuvre des Bollandistes, 1615–1915* (Bruxelles, 1920), pp. 59–60.

67 Delehaye, *Les Origines du Culte des Martyrs*, p. 90.

68 Dudden, *The Life and Times of St. Ambrose*, I, 298 ff.

69 Kennedy, *The Saints of the Canon of the Mass*, p. 79.

70 Aigrain, *L'Hagiographie*, pp. 13 ff.

71 *Ibid.*, p. 126.

72 *Ibid.*, p. 166.

73 Delehaye, *The Legends of the Saints*, pp. 2, 68; Aigrain, *L'Hagiographie*, p. 243.

74 Sherman, *The Nature of Martyrdom*, p. 193.

75 Delehaye, *The Legends of the Saints*, p. 92.

76 Charles W. Jones, *Saints' Lives and Chronicles in Early England* (Ithaca, N.Y., 1947), p. 61.

77 Delehaye, *Les Origines du Culte des Martyrs*, pp. 111 ff.

78 Kennedy, *The Saints of the Canon of the Mass*, pp. 79–82.

79 Aigrain, *L'Hagiographie*, p. 20.

80 Delehaye, *Les Origines du Culte des Martyrs*, pp. 19–20.

81 *Ibid.*, pp. 116–17.

82 Aigrain, *L'Hagiographie*, p. 34.

83 *Ibid.*

84 *Ibid.*, pp. 294 ff.

85 *The Book of Paradise, being the Histories and Sayings of the Monks and Ascetics of the Egyptian Desert*, by Palladius, Hieronymus, and Others, trans. E. A. Wallis Budge (London, 1904), I, 134 ff.

86 *Ibid.*, pp. 173 ff.

87 *Ibid.*, p. 568.
88 *Ibid.*, p. 309.
89 *Ibid.*, pp. 563–64.
90 Aigrain, *L'Hagiographie*, p. 162.
91 Sherman, *The Nature of Martyrdom*, p. 74.
92 Aigrain, *L'Hagiographie*, p. 246.
93 St. Athanasius, *The Life of Saint Antony*, trans. Robert T. Meyer (Ancient Christian Writers, No. 10 [Westminster, Md., 1950]), p. 11.
94 Charles W. Kennedy, *Early English Christian Poetry* (New York, 1952), pp. 111 ff.
95 *Ibid.*, pp. 169 ff.
96 *St. Brandan: A Medieval Legend of the Sea*, ed. Thomas Wright (Percy Society, No. XIV [London, 1844]).
97 Adamnan, *Life of Saint Columba*, ed. William Reeves (Edinburgh, 1874); Donald A. Stauffer, *English Biography before 1700* (Cambridge, Mass., 1930), p. 8.
98 *The Works of Sir Thomas Malory*, ed. Eugène Vinaver (Oxford, 1947), II, 847 ff.
99 "Vita sancti Martini," in *Sulpicii Severi Libri qui Supersunt*, ed. Karl Halm (Corpus Ecclesiasticorum Latinorum, Vol. I [Vindobonae, 1866]), pp. 107 ff.
100 St. John Damascene, *Barlaam and Ioasaph*, trans. G. R. Woodward and H. Mattingly (Loeb Classical Library) (London and New York, 1914), pp. 198 ff.
101 [St. Bonaventura], "Life of Saint Francis," in *"The Little Flowers" and the Life of Saint Francis with the "Mirror of Perfection,"* introd. Thomas Okey (London, 1917).
102 B. Raymond de Capoue, *Vie de Sainte Catherine de Sienne* (Paris, 1877).
103 John of Salisbury, "Vita Sancti Thomae Cantuarensis Archiepiscopi et Martyris," in *Materials for the History of Thomas Becket, Archbishop of Canterbury*, ed. James Craigie Robertson (Rerum Britannicarum Medii Aevi Scriptores, Vol. II [London, 1876]), p. 317.
104 Heinrich Günter, *Die Christliche Legende des Abendlandes* (Heidelberg, 1910), pp. 49 ff.
105 J. A. MacCulloch, *Medieval Faith and Fable* (London, 1932), p. 6; P. Saint-yves, *En Marge de la Légende Dorée: songes, miracles et survivances* (Paris, 1930), p. viii.
106 Jones, *Saints' Lives and Chronicles in Early England*, pp. 2–3.
107 Aigrain, *L'Hagiographie*, pp. 32 ff.
108 *Venerabilis Bedae Opera Quae Supersunt Omnia, Nunc Primum in Anglia . . .* , ed. J. A. Giles (London, 1863), III, 317.
109 Aigrain, *L'Hagiographie*, p. 51.
110 *Ibid.*, pp. 58–64.
111 *Ibid.*, p. 91.
112 Joseph B. Collins, Introduction to *The Roman Martyrology* (Westminster, Md., 1946), p. vi.
113 Aigrain, *L'Hagiographie*, pp. 17 ff.
114 *Ibid.*, pp. 103–105.
115 Albert Poncelet, "Le Légendier de Pierre Calo," *Analecta Bollandiana*, XXIX (1910), 5–7.
116 *Ibid.*, p. 14.
117 Aigrain, *L'Hagiographie*, pp. 67–68.
118 Jacobus de Voragine, *The Golden Legend*, trans. and adapted by Granger Ryan and Helmut Ripperger (London and New York, 1941), Part I, Foreword, p. v.
119 Teodor de Wyzewa, *La Légende Dorée* (Paris, 1925), p. vi.
120 Ryan and Ripperger, Foreword to *The Golden Legend*, pp. v–vi.
121 Wyzewa, *La Légende Dorée*, p. x.
122 Ryan and Ripperger, Foreword to *The Golden Legend*, p. vi.
123 Jacobus Jan Zuidweg, *De Werkwijze van Jacobus de Voragine in de Legenda Aurea* (Oud-Beijerland, 1941), p. 9.
124 Ryan and Ripperger, Foreword to *The Golden Legend*, p. viii.
125 Zuidweg, *De Werkwijze van Jacobus de Voragine*, p. 147.
126 Pierce Butler, *Legenda Aurea — Légende Dorée — Golden Legend: A Study of Caxton's Golden Legend with Special Reference to its Relations to the Earlier English Prose Translation* (Baltimore, Md., 1899), p. 7.
127 Zuidweg, *De Werkwijze van Jacobus de Voragine*, p. 154.
128 Ryan and Ripperger, Foreword to *The Golden Legend*, pp. xii–xiii.
129 Zuidweg, *De Werkwijze van Jacobus de Voragine*, pp. 151–53.
130 *Ibid.*, pp. 147–48.

131 Robert Francis Seybolt, "The 'Legenda Aurea,' Bible, and 'Historia Scholastica,' " *Speculum*, XXI (1946), 339–42.

132 John Mirk, *The Festyvall* (London: Wynkyn de Worde, October 23, 1532), sig. A2.

133 *Ibid.*

134 Gordon Hall Gerould, *Saints' Legends* (Boston and New York, 1916), p. 200.

135 Delehaye, *L'Oeuvre des Bollandistes*, p. 121.

136 Stauffer, *English Biography before 1700*, p. 20.

137 Rudolf Kapp, *Heilige und Heiligenlegenden: Studien zum 16. und 17.*

138 *Jahrhundert*, I (Halle Saale, 1934), 48 ff.

138 Delehaye, *Les Origines du Culte des Martyrs*, p. 468.

139 Delehaye, *The Legends of the Saints*, pp. 111 ff.

140 *Ibid.*, p. 11.

141 Karl Young, *The Drama of the Medieval Church* (Oxford, 1933), II, 307 ff.

142 Émile Mâle, *L'Art Religieux du XIIIᵉ Siècle en France* (Paris, 1898), p. 338.

143 John M. Mecklin, *The Passing of the Saint* (Chicago, [1941]), p. 82.

144 Mâle, *L'Art Religieux du XIIIᵉ Siècle*, p. 349.

Chapter II

1 Henry R. Plomer, *William Caxton (1424–1491)* (London, 1925), pp. 18–19.

2 Nellie Slayton Aurner, *Caxton, Mirrour of Fifteenth-Century Letters* (Iowa City, 1926), pp. 23–24.

3 *Ibid.*, pp. 26–27.

4 *Ibid.*, p. 27.

5 Plomer, *William Caxton*, pp. 51–57.

6 *Ibid.*, p. 80.

7 *Ibid.*, p. 153.

8 George Parker Winship, *William Caxton and His Work* (Berkeley: Book Arts Club, 1937), p. 23.

9 Plomer, *William Caxton*, pp. 162–63.

10 Winship, *William Caxton and His Work*, p. 22.

11 *Ibid.*, p. 18.

12 Pierce Butler, *Legenda Aurea — Légende Dorée — Golden Legend: A Study of Caxton's Golden Legend with Special Reference to its Relations to the Earlier English Prose Translation* (Baltimore, Md., 1899), p. 35.

13 Sister Mary Jeremy, "The English Prose Translation of *Legenda Aurea*," *Modern Language Notes*, LIX (1944), 181–82.

14 Sister Mary Jeremy, "Caxton's *Golden Legend* and Varagine's *Legenda Aurea*," *Speculum*, XXI (1946), 212–14.

15 *The Golden Legende* (Westmestre: Wylyam Caxton, November 20, 1483), sigs. e4ᵛ ff.

16 Charles C. Butterworth, *The Literary Lineage of the King James Bible, 1340–1611* (Philadelphia, 1941), pp. 52–53.

17 *The Golden Legende*, sig. g7.

18 Butterworth, *The Literary Lineage of the King James Bible*, pp. 54–55.

19 *Ibid.*, p. 52.

20 *The Golden Legende*, sig. g6ᵛ.

21 E. Gordon Duff, *Fifteenth Century English Books* (Oxford: The Bibliographical Society, 1917), p. 114.

22 *The Golden Legende* (Westmestre: Wyllyam Caxton, May 20, 1493), sigs. F1ᵛ–2.

23 Two extra sheets (or four pages), of which the first only is signed sig. F1, have been put in between sig. e8ᵛ and sig. f1. The first completes "The Dedication of the chirche," sigs. F1–1ᵛ; the second carries the first two pages of *The Life of saynt Andrewe*, sigs. [F] 2–2ᵛ. The insertion is reflected in the foliation, too, which proceeds normally through "The Dedication of the chirche," folio xliv; then *The Life of saynt Andrewe* begins folio xl again, and proceeds to xli, and quite normally then to xlii.

24 I am indebted to Mrs. Elizabeth North McCutcheon for kindly checking the British Museum editions for me.

25 *The Golden Legende* (Westminster: Wynkyn de Worde, 1498), sigs. Aa1–Gg6.

26 Sister Mary Jeremy, "Caxton's *Golden Legend* and Varagine's *Legenda Aurea*," p. 215.

27 Colophon, *The Golden Legende* (1483), sig. gg4ᵛ.

28 *The Golden Legende* (1493), sigs. e2ᵛff. All the ensuing references are to this edition.

29 *Ibid.*, sig. C2^v.
30 *Ibid.*
31 *Ibid.*, sig. o4^v.
32 *Ibid.*, sig. f6^v.
33 *Ibid.*, sig. B4.
34 *Ibid.*, sigs. A3–3^v.
35 *Ibid.*, sigs. Q3–3^v.
36 *Ibid.*, sigs. Q3^v–4.
37 *Ibid.*, sig. Q4^v.
38 *Ibid.*, sigs. Q4^v–5.
39 *Ibid.*, sig. N2.
40 *Ibid.*, sigs. v3–3^v.
41 *Ibid.*, sig. p2^v.
42 *Ibid.*, sig. o7^v.
43 *Ibid.*, sig. D7.
44 *Ibid.*, sig. n7^v.
45 *Ibid.*, sig. m8.
46 *Ibid.*, sigs. R2^v–3.
47 *Ibid.*, sig. l7^v.
48 *Ibid.*, sig. p3.
49 *Ibid.*, sig. m3.
50 *Ibid.*, sig. q4^v.
51 *Ibid.*, sig. M4.
52 *Ibid.*, sig. E3.
53 *Ibid.*, sig. x3.
54 *Ibid.*, sig. 92^v.
55 *Ibid.*, sig. n4.
56 *Ibid.*, sig. l1.
57 *Ibid.*, sig. n1.
58 *Ibid.*, sigs. r7^v–8.
59 *Ibid.*, sig. m4^v.
60 *Ibid.*, sig. m8^v.
61 *Ibid.*, sigs. &6–8^v.
62 *Ibid.*, sig. T5^v.
63 *Ibid.*, sig. T6.
64 *Ibid.*, sig. n4.
65 *Ibid.*, sigs. s6–6^v.
66 *Ibid.*, sigs. k8, n4, for instance
67 *Ibid.*, sigs. R2^v–3^v.
68 *Ibid.*, sig. C2.
69 *Ibid.*, sig. C3^v.
70 *Ibid.*, sig. n7.
71 *Ibid.*, sig. l4^v.
72 *Ibid.*, sig. X2^v.
73 *Ibid.*, sig. M8^v.
74 *Ibid.*, sig. x2.
75 *Ibid.*, sigs. r5^v–6.
76 *Ibid.*, sig. G5.
77 *Ibid.*, sigs. z2–3.
78 *Ibid.*, sigs. M4–4^v.
79 *Ibid.*, sigs. H6–7.
80 *Ibid.*, sigs. &1–2^v.
81 *Ibid.*, sigs. Y3^v–7.
82 *Ibid.*, sigs. dd7–8.
83 *Ibid.*, sigs. E3^v–4^v.
84 *Ibid.*, sig. ē1^v.

85 *Ibid.*, sigs. s2–2^v.
86 *Ibid.*, sig. N3.
87 *Ibid.*, sig. A7.
88 *Ibid.*, sigs. k2^v–3.
89 *Ibid.*, sig. &2^v.
90 *Ibid.*, sigs. Y2–3.
91 *Ibid.*, sig. r8^v.
92 *Ibid.*, sig. s4^v.
93 *Ibid.*, sigs. p7–7^v
94 *Ibid.*, sig. L7.
95 *Ibid.*, sig. V3.
96 *Ibid.*, sig. V1^v.
97 *Ibid.*, sig. V5.
98 *Ibid.*, sig. f6.
99 *Ibid.*, sig. r7.
100 *Ibid.*, sig. v3^v.
101 *Ibid.*, sig. l7.
102 *Ibid.*, sig. 93.
103 *Ibid.*, sigs. t3^v–4.
104 *Ibid.*, sig. p7^v.
105 *Ibid.*, sig. O2.
106 *Ibid.*, sigs. O2^v–3^v.
107 *Ibid.*, sig. r8.
108 *Ibid.*, sig. p4^v.
109 *Ibid.*, sig. t1^v.
110 *Ibid.*
111 *Ibid.*, sig. T8^v.
112 *Ibid.*, sig. N6^v.
113 *Ibid.*, sigs. m4^v–5.
114 *Ibid.*, sigs. n1–1^v.
115 *Ibid.*, sig. s1.
116 *Ibid.*, sig. S6^v.
117 *Ibid.*, sig. V5.
118 *Ibid.*, sig. cc2.
119 *Ibid.*, sig. M4.
120 *Ibid.*, sigs. aa3^v–4.
121 *Ibid.*, sig. k7^v.
122 *Ibid.*, sig. x3.
123 *Ibid.*, sig. z5^v.
124 *Ibid.*, sig. S1.
125 *Ibid.*, sigs. o8–8^v.
126 *Ibid.*, sig. m7.
127 *Ibid.*, sig. p4.
128 *Ibid.*, sig. &8.
129 *Ibid.*, sig. M8^v.
130 *Ibid.*, sig. aa5^v.
131 *Ibid.*, sig. o5.
132 *Ibid.*, sig. R7.
133 *Ibid.*, sig. x8^v.
134 *Ibid.*, sig. l2^v.
135 *Ibid.*, sig. m7.
136 *Ibid.*, sig. z3^v.
137 *Ibid.*, sig. y2^v.
138 *Ibid.*, sig. x3^v.
139 *Ibid.*, sig. K4^v.
140 *Ibid.*, sig. O2^v.

141 *Ibid.*, sig. s3.
142 *Ibid.*, sig. bb6^v.
143 *Ibid.*, sig. t3^v.
144 *Ibid.*, sig. m8^v.
145 *Ibid.*, sigs. P7–Q1^v.
146 *Ibid.*, sig. 94^v–6.
147 *Ibid.*, sigs. bb6^v–7^v.
148 *Ibid.*, sigs. l 3^v–4.
149 *Ibid.*, sig. k7.
150 *Ibid.*, sig. &4.
151 *Ibid.*, sigs. n6–6^v.
152 *Ibid.*, sig. 96.
153 *Ibid.*, sig. P7.
154 *Ibid.*, sig. m3^v.
155 *Ibid.*, sigs. C1^v–2^v.
156 *Ibid.*, sigs. S2–2^v.
157 *Ibid.*, sig. p5^v
158 *Ibid.*, sig. I2.
159 *Ibid.*, sigs. H4–5^v.

160 *Ibid.*, sig. y3^v.
161 Sister Mary Jeremy, "Caxton's *Golden Legend* and Varagine's *Legenda Aurea*," pp. 220–21.
162 See, e.g., Caxton's prologue to "Le Recueil des Histoires de Troyes" of 1476, reprinted in W. J. B. Crotch, ed., *The Prologues and Epilogues of William Caxton* (EETS, O.S., No. CLXXVI [London, 1928], p. 4.
163 See, e.g., Caxton's epilogue to Book VII of the 1482 edition of *Polycronicon*, in Crotch, *Prologues and Epilogues of William Caxton*, p. 68.
164 See, e.g., Caxton's prologue to the 1487 edition of "The Book of Good Maners," in Crotch, *Prologues and Epilogues of William Caxton*, pp. 99–100.
165 *The Golden Legende*, sigs. N5^v–6.

Chapter III

1 F. S. Ellis, Introduction to *The Golden Legend; or, Lives of the Saints as Englished by William Caxton* (London, 1900), I, x.
2 Charles C. Butterworth, *The Literary Lineage of the King James Bible, 1340–1611* (Philadelphia, 1941), pp. 56–58.
3 *Ibid.*, pp. 61–62.
4 Quoted in Philip Hughes, *The Reformation in England*, II (London, 1954), 103.
5 *The Golden Legende*, trans. William Caxton (Westmestre: Wyllyam Caxton, May 20, 1493), sig. e5.
6 Jacques Douillet, *What Is a Saint?* trans. Donald Attwater, *Twentieth Century Encyclopedia of Catholicism*, XLVI (New York, 1958), 85.
7 *Ibid.*, p. 87.
8 V. L. Kennedy, *The Saints of the Canon of the Mass* (Città del Vaticano, 1938), p. 7.
9 Douillet, *What Is a Saint?* p. 87.
10 *Ibid.*, p. 88.
11 Philip Hughes, *A History of the Church* (New York, 1949), II, 379.
12 See Helen C. White, *The Tudor Books of Private Devotion* (Madison, Wis., 1951), pp. 58–66.
13 *Hore Beatissime Virginis Marie ad Legitimum Sarisburiensis Ecclesie Ritum* (Paris: à Francisco Regnault, 1527), sigs. R8–S1.

14 René Aigrain, *L'Hagiographie: ses sources, ses méthodes, son histoire* (Paris, 1953), pp. 62ff.
15 Jacobus de Voragine, *The Golden Legend*, trans. and adapted by Granger Ryan and Helmut Ripperger (London and New York, 1941), Part I, Foreword, p. xii.
16 *The Republic*, in *The Dialogues of Plato*, trans. B. Jowett (Oxford, 1924), III, 60–75.
17 Desiderius Erasmus, *In Praise of Folly* (London, 1951), pp. 88–92.
18 Geoffrey Chaucer, *Complete Works*, ed. F. N. Robinson (Boston, 1933), pp. 26–27, 179–81, 186–87.
19 John Foxe, *Actes and Monuments* (London: John Day, March 20, 1563), sig. *3.
20 Reginald Pecock, *The Repressor of Over Much Blaming of the Clergy*, ed. Churchill Babington (London, 1860), I, 156–57.
21 See Louis Bouyer, *Erasmus and the Humanist Experiment* (London, 1959), pp. 16 ff.
22 Herbert Weisinger, "The Renaissance Theory of the Reaction against the Middle Ages as a Cause of the Renaissance," *Speculum*, XX (1945), 461–67.
23 See, e.g., Juan Luis Vives, *On Education (De Tradendis Disciplinis)*, trans. Foster Watson (Cambridge, 1943),

pp. 248–49, and Rudolf Kapp, *Heilige und Heiligenlegenden: Studien zum 16. und 17. Jahrhundert*, I (Halle Saale, 1934), 115 ff.

24 Henry Bett, *Nicholas of Cusa* (London, 1932), p. 51.

25 Desiderius Erasmus, *A Dialoge or Communication of Two Persons* (n.p., n.d. [1536–37]), sigs. A1–2ᵛ.

26 *Ibid.*, sigs. A2ᵛ–3.

27 *Ibid.*, sigs. A3–6.

28 *Ibid.*, sig. B1ᵛ.

29 *Ibid.*, sigs. B2–2ᵛ.

30 *Ibid.*, sigs. B2ᵛ–3.

31 *Ibid.*, sigs. B3ᵛ–4.

32 *Ibid.*, sigs. D5–5ᵛ.

33 *Ibid.*, sigs. D5ᵛ–6.

34 *Ibid.*, sigs. E6–6ᵛ.

35 *Ibid.*, sigs. E7–7ᵛ.

36 *Ibid.*, sigs. D8–E1.

37 *Ibid.*, sigs. E1–1ᵛ.

38 *Ibid.*, [no sig.] 1ᵛ–2.

39 Erasmus, *Ten Colloquies*, trans. Craig R. Thompson (Library of Liberal Arts) (New York, 1957), p. 60.

40 *Ibid.*, Thompson, Introduction, pp. xxvi–xxvii.

41 John Calvin, *A Very Profitable Treatise, . . . ,* trans. Steven Wythers (London: Rouland Hall, 1561), sig. A8.

42 *Ibid.*, sigs. A2–3ᵛ.

43 *Ibid.*, sig. H7.

44 See C. Grant Loomis, *White Magic, an Introduction to the Folklore of Christian Legend* (Cambridge, Mass., 1948), p. 3, and H[enri] Daniel-Rops, *The Church of Apostles and Martyrs*, trans. Audrey Butler (London and New York, 1960), pp. 520–21.

45 J. D. Mackie, *The Earlier Tudors 1485–1558* (Oxford, 1952), p. 372.

46 *Ibid.*, pp. 400–401.

47 Foxe, *Actes and Monuments*, sigs. Ss1 ff.

48 *Ibid.*, sig. HH3.

49 *Articles devised by the Kynges Highnes Majestie, to stablyshe Christen Quietnes and Unitie amonge us* (n.p., 1536), sigs. [A]2–2ᵛ.

50 *Ibid.*, sig. C4ᵛ.

51 *Ibid.*, sig. D1.

52 *Ibid.*, sigs. D1ᵛ–2.

53 *Injunctions gyven by Thauctoritie of the Kynges Highnes to the Clergie of this his Realme* (London: Thomas Berthelet, 1536), [no sigs.] 2–2ᵛ.

54 Henry de Vocht, *The Earliest English Translations of Erasmus' Colloquia, 1536–1566* (Louvain and London, 1928), p. xliv.

55 Erasmus, *A Dialoge or Communication of Two Persons*, sigs. +2–3ᵛ.

56 *Ibid.*, sig. +4.

57 *Ibid.*, sigs. +4ᵛ–5ᵛ.

58 *Ibid.*, sigs. +6–6ᵛ.

59 Foxe, *Actes and Monuments*, sig. HH4ᵛ.

60 Mackie, *The Earlier Tudors*, p. 395.

61 *The Institution of a Christen Man* (London: Thomas Berthelet, 1537), sig. a4ᵛ.

62 *Ibid.*, sigs. P1–1ᵛ.

63 *Ibid.*, sig. P2ᵛ.

64 Mackie, *The Earlier Tudors*, p. 396.

65 *Injunctions for the Clerge* (London: [T. Berthelet?], 1538), s. sh. fol.

66 *A Litel Treatise ageynste the Mutterynge of Some Papistis in Corners* (London: Thomas Berthelet, 1534), sig. A2.

67 *Ibid.*, sigs. A7ᵛ–8.

68 Millar Maclure, *The Paul's Cross Sermons, 1534–1642* (University of Toronto Department of English Studies and Texts, No. VI [Toronto, 1958]), p. 40.

69 *Ibid.*, pp. 30–31.

70 *A Necessary Doctrine and Erudition for any Chrysten man, set furth by the Kynges Majestye of Englande, . . .* (London: Thomas Berthelet, May 29, 1543), sigs. A2–2ᵛ.

71 *Ibid.*, sigs. L1ᵛ–2.

72 *A Necessary Doctrine and Erudition for any Chrysten Man, . . .* (London: John Mayler, 1543), sig. T4ᵛ.

73 *Ibid.*, sig. B1.

74 *Ibid.*, sig. F1ᵛ.

75 *Ibid.*, sig. D3ᵛ.

76 *Ibid.*, sig. D7.

77 Mackie, *The Earlier Tudors*, pp. 510 ff.

78 A famous series of Passion prayers ascribed to Saint Bridget of Sweden.

79 *Certayne Sermons or Homilies, appoynted by the Kynges Majestie* (London: Richard Grafton, 1547), sig. K1.

80 Charles C. Butterworth, *The English Primers (1529–1545)* (Philadelphia, 1953), pp. 11–17.

81 *Ibid.*, pp. 20–46.

82 See White, *Tudor Books of Private Devotion*, Chap. VI.

83 Henry Offley Wakeman, rev. S. L. Ollard, *An Introduction to the History of the Church of England* (London, 1927), pp. 266–67.

84 *The Booke of the Common Prayer and Administracion of the Sacramentes, and other Rites and Ceremonies of the Churche: after the Use of the Churche of England* (London: Edouardi Whitchurche, March 7, 1549), sig. [leaf] 1.

85 *Ibid.*, sig. [leaf] 1ᵛ.

86 *Ibid.*, sigs. A3 ff.

87 *Ibid.*, sigs. 2A1 ff.

88 *Ibid.*, sigs. x1–y2.

89 *Ibid.*, sig. ¶2ᵛ.

90 *Ibid.*, sig. ¶6.

91 Wakeman, *Introduction to the History of the Church of England*, pp. 284–85.

92 *Ibid.*, pp. 302–3; Henry Gee, *The Elizabethan Prayer-Book and Ornaments* (London, 1902), pp. 128 ff.

93 Wakeman, *Introduction to the History of the Church of England*, pp. 284–86.

94 *Ibid.*, p. 304.

95 Hughes, *The Reformation in England*, II, 347.

96 *Ibid.*, pp. 236–43.

97 *Articles to be enquired of in the Visitation, in the First yeere of the Raign of our most dread Soveraign Ladie Elizabeth . . . 1559* (London: Robert Barker, 1600), sig. A2.

98 *Ibid.*, sigs. A2ᵛ–3.

99 *Ibid.*, sig. A3ᵛ.

100 *Ibid.*, sig. B1ᵛ.

101 *Proclamation against Breakinge or De-*

facing of Monumentes of Antiquitie, beyng set up in Churches or other Publique Places for Memory, and not for Supersticion (London: Richarde Jugge and John Cawood, Sept. 19, 1560).

102 *The Bible and Holy Scriptures conteyned in the Olde and New Testament* (Geneva: Rouland Hall, 1560), sig. **4.

103 *Ibid.*, sigs. **2–2ᵛ.

104 *Ibid.*, sig. **2ᵛ.

105 Butterworth, *The Literary Lineage of the King James Bible*, p. 165.

106 *Ibid.*, pp. 187–88.

107 *Ibid.*, pp. 163–65.

108 *The Seconde Tome of Homelyes* (London: Richard Jugge and John Cawood, 1563), sigs. Dd4 ff.

109 *Ibid.*, sigs. Dd4–Ff4.

110 *Ibid.*, sig. Ff3.

111 *Ibid.*, sig. Ii1ᵛ.

112 *Ibid.*, sig. Ii3ᵛ.

113 *Ibid.*, sigs. Kk1–Mm1ᵛ.

114 *Ibid.*, sig. Mm2ᵛ.

115 *Ibid.*, sigs. Nn2ᵛ–Oo1.

116 *Ibid.*, sigs. Pp1–1ᵛ.

117 *Ibid.*, sigs. Rr3–Ss4ᵛ.

118 *Ibid.*, sigs. Yy1–2ᵛ.

119 *Ibid.*, sigs. Yy3ᵛ–4.

120 Pierre Janelle, *The Catholic Reformation* (Milwaukee, 1951), p. 99.

121 Hippolyte Delehaye, *L'Oeuvre des Bollandistes, 1615–1915* (Bruxelles, 1920), pp. 8 ff.

Chapter IV

1 Edward Halle, *The Union of the Two Noble and Illustrate Famelies of Lancastre and Yorke . . . with All the Actes done in Bothe the Tymes of the Princes, Bothe of the One Linage and of the Other . . .* (London: Richard Grafton, 1548), sigs. PPP2–2ᵛ.

2 J. D. Mackie, *The Earlier Tudors, 1485–1558* (Oxford, 1952), p. 334.

3 Philip Hughes, *The Reformation in England*, I (London, 1950), Chap. II, "Ecclesia Anglicana."

4 *Ibid.*, pp. 164–67.

5 Henry de Vocht, *Acta Thomae Mori: History of the Reports of His Trial and Death with an Unedited Contemporary Narrative* (Louvain, 1947), pp. 37–40.

6 *Ibid.*, pp. 59–68.

7 *Ibid.*, pp. 145–63.

8 *Ibid.*, pp. 59 ff., 105 ff.

9 Thomas Stapleton, *The Life and Illustrious Martyrdom of Sir Thomas More, Formerly Lord Chancellor of England. Part III of "Tres Thomae," printed at Douai, 1588*, trans. Philip E. Hallett (London, 1928).

10 De Vocht, *Acta Thomae Mori*, pp. 110 ff.

11 R. W. Chambers, Introduction, "The Continuity of English Prose from Alfred to More and his School," in Nicholas Harpsfield, *The Life and Death of Sʳ Thomas Moore, knight, sometymes Lord high Chancellor of England*, ed.

Elsie Vaughan Hitchcock (EETS, O.S., No. CLXXXVI [London, 1932]), p. ccii.

12 Quoted in Chambers, "The Continuity of English Prose," p. xlv.

13 Halle, *The Union of the Two Noble Famelies of Lancastre and Yorke*, sig. PPP4.

14 *Ibid.*, sigs. PPP4–4ᵛ

15 *Ibid.* sig. PPP4ᵛ.

16 Fr[anciscus] van Ortroy, ed., *A Treatis Contayninge the Lyfe and Maner of Death of that Most holy Prelat and Constant Martyr of Christ John Fysher Byshop of Rochester and Cardinale of the Holy Church of Rome*, in *Vie du Bienheureux Martyr Jean Fisher Cardinal, Évêque de Rochester (†1535): Texte Anglais et Traduction Latine du XVIᵉ siècle*, Extrait des *Analecta Bollandiana*, X (1891), et XII (1893) (Bruxelles, 1893), p. 361.

17 *Passio XVIII. Carthusianorum in regno Angliæ . . .* , in *Historia Aliquot Nostri Saeculi Martyrum* (Moguntiae: Franciscus Behem, 1550), sigs. D3ᵛ–R5.

18 Dom Maurice Chauncy, *The History of the Sufferings of Eighteen Carthusians in England, Who Refusing to Take Part in Schism, and to Separate Themselves from the Unity of the Catholic Church, were Cruelly Martyred*, trans. a Professed Member of the London Charter House (London and New York, 1890).

19 E. Margaret Thompson, *The Carthusian Order in England* (London: SPCK, 1930), pp. 346–52.

20 Chauncy, *The Sufferings of Eighteen Carthusians*, p. xv.

21 Editor's Introduction, *ibid.*, p. xi.

22 David and Gervase Mathew, *The Reformation and the Contemplative Life* (London, 1934), pp. 101–2.

23 Chauncy, *The Sufferings of Eighteen Carthusians*, p. 46.

24 *Ibid.*, pp. 48–49.

25 *Ibid.*, p. 18.

26 *Ibid.*, pp. 54–55.

27 *Ibid.*, p. 27.

28 *Ibid.*, pp. 66–68.

29 *Ibid.*, pp. 1–7.

30 *Ibid.*, p. 20.

31 *Ibid.*, p. 9.

32 *Ibid.*, p. 18.

33 Hughes, *The Reformation in England*, I, 40 ff.

34 Chauncy, *The Sufferings of Eighteen Carthusians*, pp. 14–16.

35 *Ibid.*, p. 27.

36 *Ibid.*, p. 19.

37 *Ibid.*, pp. 57–58.

38 Elizabeth Shirley, "The Life of Our Rev. Old Mother Margaret Clement," in *The Troubles of Our Catholic Forefathers Related by Themselves*, First Ser., ed. John Morris (London, 1872), pp. 27 ff.

39 Chauncy, *The Sufferings of Eighteen Carthusians*, p. 24.

40 *Ibid.*, p. 31.

41 *Ibid.*, p. 32.

42 *Ibid.*, p. 73.

43 *Ibid.*, pp. 37 ff.

44 *Ibid.*, p. 77.

45 *Ibid.*, pp. 71–72.

46 Van Ortroy, *The Lyfe and Death of John Fysher*, pp. 82 ff.

47 *Ibid.*, pp. 4–7.

48 Tho[mas] Baily, D.D., *The Life and Death of that Renowned John Fisher Bishop of Rochester* (London: n.p., 1655).

49 Van Ortroy, *The Life and Death of John Fysher*, pp. 18 ff.

50 *Ibid.*, pp. 77–81.

51 *Ibid.*, pp. 87–90.

52 *Ibid.*, pp. 96–106.

53 See, for example, Sir Thomas More, *A Dialoge of Comfort against Tribulacion* [London: Richard Tottel, Nov. 18, 1553], sigs. A3ᵛ–4, H2ᵛ.

54 John Fyssher, *A Spirituall Consolation . . . to hys sister Elizabeth* (n.p., n.d.), sigs. B3ᵛ–4.

55 *Ibid.*, sig. B5ᵛ.

56 Van Ortroy, *The Lyfe and Death of John Fysher*, pp. 339–40.

57 William Roper, *The Lyfe of Sir Thomas Moore, knighte*, ed. Elsie Vaughan Hitchcock (EETS, O.S., No. CXCVII [London, 1935]), p. 73.

58 De Vocht, *Acta Thomae Mori*, p. 106.

59 *Ibid.*, p. 124.

60 For example, Van Ortroy, *The Lyfe and Death of John Fysher*, p. 276; Roper, *The Lyfe of Sir Thomas Moore*, p. 94.

61 Marcelle Auclair, *Saint Teresa of Avila*, trans. Kathleen Pond (New York, 1953), pp. 10–11.

62   Baily, *The Life and Death of John Fisher*, sig. A4.

63   Stapleton, *The Life and Martyrdom of Sir Thomas More*, p. 22.

64   *Ibid.*, p. 167.

65   Roper, *The Lyfe of Sir Thomas Moore*, pp. 20–21.

66   More, *A Dialoge of Comfort*, sig. O3ᵛ.

67   Stapleton, *The Life and Martyrdom of Sir Thomas More*, p. 215.

68   Van Ortroy, *The Lyfe and Death of John Fysher*, pp. 91–92.

69   Roper, *The Lyfe of Sir Thomas Moore*, p. 11.

70   Mackie, *The Earlier Tudors*, p. 360.

71   Van Ortroy, *The Lyfe and Death of John Fysher*, pp. 321 ff.

72   Stapleton, *The Lyfe and Martyrdom of Sir Thomas More*, p. 192.

73   Van Ortroy, *The Lyfe and Death of John Fysher*, pp. 159–61.

74   *Ibid.*, p. 166.

75   *Ibid.*, pp. 101–27.

76   *Ibid.*, p. 124.

77   *Ibid.*, p. 102.

78   *Ibid.*, p. 124.

79   *Ibid.*, pp. 315–16.

80   *Ibid.*, pp. 358, 374.

81   *Ibid.*, pp. 18 ff.

82   *Ibid.*, p. 46.

83   *Ibid.*, pp. 278–79.

84   *Ibid.*, pp. 83–96.

85   *Ibid.*, pp. 96–148.

86   *Ibid.*, pp. 149–91.

87   *Ibid.*, pp. 191–318.

88   *Ibid.*, pp. 318–34.

89   *Ibid.*, pp. 335–51.

90   *Ibid.*, pp. 177–78, 217–20.

91   *Ibid.*, pp. 357–58.

92   *Ibid.*, pp. 373–74.

93   *Ibid.*, pp. 224–27.

94   *Ibid.*, pp. 381–93.

95   *Ibid.*, p. 341.

96   *Ibid.*, pp. 82–83.

97   *Ibid.*, pp. 337–42.

98   *Ibid.*, pp. 346–47.

99   *Ibid.*, pp. 349–50.

100   For example, Stapleton, *The Life and Martyrdom of Sir Thomas More*, p. xiii.

101   Erasmus, *The Epistles*, trans. Francis Morgan Nichols, III (London, 1918), 387–401.

102   See above, p. 98.

103   Stapleton, *The Life and Martyrdom of Sir Thomas More*, pp. 214–15. See also R. S. Sylvester and D. P. Harding, eds., *Two Early Tudor Lives*: *Cavendish's Wolsey and Roper's More* (New Haven and London, 1962), p. xv.

104   See, e.g., Roper, *The Lyfe of Sir Thomas Moore*, pp. 55–56.

105   *Ibid.*, p. 3.

106   *Ibid.*, pp. 30–31.

107   Van Ortroy, *The Lyfe and Death of John Fysher*, p. 46.

108   See, e.g., Donald A. Stauffer, *English Biography before 1700* (Cambridge, Mass., 1930), p. 63.

109   Roper, *The Lyfe of Sir Thomas Moore*, p. 3.

110   *Ibid.*, p. 103.

111   *Ibid.*, pp. 102–3.

112   *Ibid.*, p. 102.

113   *Ibid.*, p. 3.

114   *Ibid.*, e.g., pp. 11–12.

115   *Ibid.*, pp. 39, 51–52.

116   *Ibid.*, pp. 48–49.

117   *Ibid.*, pp. 25–26.

118   *Ibid.*, pp. 45–47.

119   *Ibid.*, pp. 6, 76.

120   *Ibid.*, pp. 28–29.

121   *Ibid.*, p. 100.

122   *Ibid.*, pp. 50–51.

123   *Ibid.*, p. 26.

124   *Ibid.*, p. 35.

125   *Ibid.*, p. 21.

126   *Ibid.*, pp. 58–59.

127   Quoted by Chambers, "The Continuity of English Prose," p. clvii. See also Pearl Hogrefe, *The Sir Thomas More Circle* (Urbana, Ill., 1959), esp. pp. 253–56.

128   Roper, *The Lyfe of Sir Thomas Moore*, p. 5.

129   *Ibid.*, pp. 94–95.

130   *Ibid.*, p. 96.

131   *Ibid.*, p. 103.

132   Quoted by Chambers, "The Continuity of English Prose," p. xlvi.

133   *Ibid.*, p. xlvii.

134   De Vocht, *Acta Thomae Mori*, pp. 37 ff.

135   Chambers, "The Continuity of English Prose," pp. l–li.

136   Harpsfield, *The Life and Death of Sʳ Thomas Moore, knight*, pp. 80–81.

137   *Ibid.*, p. 74.

138   *Ibid.*, p. 212.

139   *Ibid.*, p. 207.

140   *Ibid.*, pp. 217–18.

141   R. W. Chambers, "Life and Works of

Nicholas Harpsfield," in Harpsfield, *The Life and Death of Sr Thomas Moore, knight*, pp. clxxxix–cxcii.

142 *Ibid.*, p. cciv.
143 Harpsfield, *ibid.*, pp. 209–13.
144 For example, *ibid.*, p. 71.
145 *Ibid.*, p. 72.
146 *Ibid.*, pp. 133–34.
147 *Ibid.*, p. 81.
148 Hallett, Translator's Preface, Stapleton, *The Life and Martyrdom of Sir Thomas More*, p. xi.
149 Stapleton Preface, *ibid.*, p. xiii.
150 *Ibid.*, p. xvi.
151 *Ibid.*, pp. xiv–xvi.
152 *Ibid.*, p. 9.
153 *Ibid.*, p. 43.
154 *Ibid.*, p. 10.
155 *Ibid.*, p. 82.
156 *Ibid.*, p. 77.
157 *Ibid.*, pp. 99–111.
158 *Ibid.*, pp. 112 ff.
159 *Ibid.*, p. 145.
160 *Ibid.*, p. 146.
161 *Ibid.*, p. 215.
162 *Ibid.*, p. 1.
163 *Ibid.*, p. 2.
164 *Ibid.*, p. 9.
165 *Ibid.*, p. 66.

166 *Ibid.*, pp. 70–72.
167 *Ibid.*, p. 81.
168 *Ibid.*, p. 158.
169 *Ibid.*, p. 196.
170 *Ibid.*, p. 212.
171 *Ibid.*, pp. 213–14.
172 *Ibid.*, pp. 218–26.
173 *Ibid.*, p. 215.
174 Ro. Ba., *The Lyfe of Syr Thomas More, Sometymes Lord Chancellor of England*, ed. Elsie Vaughan Hitchcock and P. E. Hallett, with additional notes and Appendices by A. W. Reed (EETS, O.S., No. CCXXII [London, 1950]), p. 14.
175 Hitchcock, Introduction to Ro. Ba., *ibid.*, pp. xi–xvii.
176 Ro. Ba., *ibid.*, p. 9.
177 *Ibid.*, p. 10.
178 *Ibid.*
179 *Ibid.*, p. 11.
180 *Ibid.*, p. 113.
181 *Ibid.*, p. 273.
182 *Ibid.*, p. 35.
183 *Ibid.*, pp. 263–64.
184 Stapleton, *The Life and Martyrdom of Sir Thomas More*, pp. 71–72.
185 Ro. Ba., *The Lyfe of Syr Thomas More*, pp. 260–61.

Chapter V

1 Philip Hughes, *The Reformation in England*, I (London, 1950), 368, n. 3.
2 J. F. Mozley, *John Foxe and His Book* (London: SPCK, [1940]), p. 118.
3 *Ibid.*, pp. 12–18.
4 *Ibid.*, pp. 20–25. See also Gordon Rupp, *Six Makers of English Religion, 1500–1700* (London, 1957), pp. 54–55.
5 Mozley, *John Foxe and His Book*, pp. 29–31.
6 *Ibid.*, pp. 39 ff.
7 *Ibid.*, pp. 118–19.
8 *Ibid.*, pp. 119–21.
9 *Ibid.*, pp. 122–23.
10 *Ibid.*
11 Thomas Brice, *A Compendious Register in Metre*, . . . (London: Jhon Kyngston for Richard Adams, 1559).
12 *Ibid.*, sigs. A3–3^v.
13 *Ibid.*, sig. A7^v.
14 *Ibid.*, sigs. B3^v–4.
15 *Ibid.*, sigs. C2 ff.
16 *Ibid.*, sigs. B5^v–6.
17 *Ibid.*, sig. C2.

18 *Ibid.*, sig. D5.
19 *Ibid.*, sig. B4.
20 Mozley, *John Foxe and His Book*, pp. 128–30.
21 John Foxe, *Actes and Monuments* . . . (London: John Day, March 20, 1563).
22 *Ibid.*, sigs. *2–2^v.
23 *Ibid.*, sigs. *3–6^v.
24 See above, pp. 86–88.
25 Foxe, *Actes and Monuments*, sigs. *3–5^v.
26 *Ibid.*, sig. *4.
27 *Ibid.*, sig. *5^v.
28 *Ibid.*, sigs. *5–5^v.
29 *Ibid.*, sig. *3.
30 *Ibid.*, sig. *4.
31 See Helen C. White, *The Tudor Books of Private Devotion* (Madison, Wis., 1951), pp. 76, 120–21; and above, pp. 86–88.
32 Foxe, *Actes and Monuments*, sigs. B1–2.
33 *Ibid.*, sigs. B4^v–5^v.

34 *Ibid.*, sigs. B5ᵛ–6ᵛ.
35 *Ibid.*, sigs. B5ᵛ–6.
36 *Ibid.*, sig. B6.
37 *Ibid.*, sig. B6ᵛ.
38 *Ibid.*, sigs. B3–4.
39 *Ibid.*, sig. NNNN2ᵛ.
40 *Ibid.*, sig. NNNN8ᵛ.
41 Mozley, *John Foxe and His Book*, pp. 86–91. See also Rupp, *Six Makers of English Religion*, pp. 61–62.
42 Foxe, *Actes and Monuments*, sig. N6.
43 *Ibid.*, sig. OOOO1.
44 *Ibid.*, sig. LL1.
45 *Ibid.*, sig. QQ1.
46 *Ibid.*, sig. O1.
47 *Ibid.*, sig. FF4.
48 *Ibid.*, sig. Yy4ᵛ.
49 *Ibid.*, sig. DDD3.
50 *Ibid.*, sig. HHh6.
51 *Ibid.*, sig. YYy1.
52 *Ibid.*, sig. KK5.
53 *Ibid.*, sigs. PP4ᵛ–5.
54 *Ibid.*, sig. MMm2.
55 *Ibid.*, sig. Ss6ᵛ.
56 *Ibid.*, sig. Tt2.
57 *Ibid.*, sigs. AA2ᵛ–3.
58 *Ibid.*, sig. BB5.
59 *Ibid.*, sig. CC1.
60 *Ibid.*, sig. QQ1.
61 *Ibid.*, sig. MMm1.
62 *Ibid.*, sig. MMMM1ᵛ.
63 *Ibid.*, sigs. NNNN3–3ᵛ.
64 *Ibid.*, sig. NNNN2ᵛ.
65 *Ibid.*, sigs. Vv7–7ᵛ.
66 *Ibid.*, sigs. MMM5–5ᵛ.
67 *Ibid.*, sig. DDD5ᵛ.
68 *Ibid.*, sig. Tt2ᵛ.
69 *Ibid.*, sig. Yy3.
70 *Ibid.*, sig. SSS3ᵛ.
71 *Ibid.*, sig. MMm1.
72 *Ibid.*, sig. OO5.
73 *Ibid.*, sig. PP3ᵛ.
74 See *ibid.*, sigs. NNNn6, R2ᵛ–3, Kk1ᵛ, Pp5ᵛ–6.
75 *Ibid.*, sigs. MMM4ᵛ–5.
76 *Ibid.*, sig. OOOo3ᵛ.
77 *Ibid.*, sig. YYy1ᵛ.
78 *Ibid.*, sig. Tt3.
79 *Ibid.*, sigs. BB6, Vv7.
80 *Ibid.*, sigs. CCC5–5ᵛ.
81 *Ibid.*, sig. Vv8ᵛ.
82 *Ibid.*, sig. Xx3ᵛ.
83 *Ibid.*, sigs. Xx1ᵛ–2. See also William Wilkinson, *A Confutation of Certaine Articles delivered unto the Familye of*

Love (London: John Daye, 1579), sigs. [hand] 3–3ᵛ, [hand] 4ᵛ.
84 Foxe, *Actes and Monuments*, sig. EEEE6.
85 *Ibid.*, sig. FF4.
86 *Ibid.*, sig. OO3ᵛ.
87 *Ibid.*, sig. AA4ᵛ.
88 *Ibid.*, sig. BB1.
89 *Ibid.*, sig. Rr4.
90 *Ibid.*, sig. HHHh2.
91 *Ibid.*, sig. NN4ᵛ.
92 *Ibid.*, sig. CC1.
93 *Ibid.*, sig. CC3.
94 *Ibid.*, sigs. HHHh1ᵛ–2.
95 *Ibid.*, sig. C4ᵛ.
96 *Ibid.*, sig. Ii6.
97 *Ibid.*, sig. LL2.
98 *Ibid.*, sig. CC3ᵛ.
99 *Ibid.*, sigs. CC2ᵛ–4ᵛ.
100 *Ibid.*, sig. DDD6.
101 *Ibid.*, sig. Ii5ᵛ.
102 *Ibid.*, sig. PP3.
103 *Ibid.*, sig. NNN2ᵛ.
104 *Ibid.*, sig. HHH3ᵛ.
105 *Ibid.*, sig. II3ᵛ.
106 *Ibid.*, sigs. Xx3ᵛ–5ᵛ.
107 *Ibid.*, sig. DDDD4.
108 *Ibid.*, sigs. BB6–FF3.
109 *Ibid.*, sigs. XXx5–5ᵛ.
110 *Ibid.*, sig. HHHH4.
111 *Ibid.*, sig. VVV4.
112 *Ibid.*, sig. CCC2.
113 *Ibid.*, sigs. FFFF6–GGGG1.
114 *Ibid.*, sigs. GGG3–3ᵛ.
115 *Ibid.*, sig. BBB2ᵛ.
116 *Ibid.*, sig. GGGg5.
117 *Ibid.*, sig. AAAA6.
118 *Ibid.*, sig. EEEE6ᵛ.
119 *Ibid.*, sig. EEEE6.
120 *Ibid.*, sig. DDD6.
121 *Ibid.*, sig. VVVv1.
122 *Ibid.*, sig. BBB2ᵛ.
123 *Ibid.*, sig. FFF4ᵛ.
124 *Ibid.*, sig. GGGg5ᵛ.
125 *Ibid.*, sig. Pp6ᵛ.
126 *Ibid.*, sig. VVVv5.
127 *Ibid.*, sig. Xx3.
128 *Ibid.*, sig. EEEE1ᵛ.
129 *Ibid.*, sig. SSSs1ᵛ.
130 *Ibid.*, sig. SSSs2.
131 *Ibid.*, sig. CCC4.
132 *Ibid.*, sig. CCC3ᵛ.
133 *Ibid.*, sig. BBB2ᵛ.
134 *Ibid.*, sig. MMM6ᵛ.
135 *Ibid.*, sig. AAA2ᵛ.
136 *Ibid.*, sig. GGGg4ᵛ.

137 *Ibid.*, sig. SSSs2.
138 *Ibid.*, sig. EEEE1ᵛ.
139 *Ibid.*, sig. LLL5ᵛ.
140 *Ibid.*, sig. GGGg5.
141 *Ibid.*, sig. BB2ᵛ.
142 *Ibid.*, sig. PPPP1ᵛ.
143 *Ibid.*, sig. PPPP3.
144 *Ibid.*, sig. HHHH4.
145 *Ibid.*, sig. K6.
146 *Ibid.*, sig. VVv4ᵛ.
147 *Ibid.*, sig. MMMM1ᵛ.
148 *Ibid.*, sig. MMMM2.
149 *Ibid.*, sigs. MMMM6 ff.

150 *Ibid.*, sig. MMMM6ᵛ.
151 *Ibid.*, sig. MM5ᵛ.
152 *Ibid.*, sigs. VVVv2ᵛ–3.
153 *Ibid.*, sig. B6.
154 Leslie M. Oliver, "The Seventh Edition of John Foxe's *Acts and Monuments*," *Papers of the Bibliographical Society of America*, XXXVII (1943), 245–48.
155 Mozley, *John Foxe and His Book*, p. 147.
156 Oliver, "The Seventh Edition of Foxe's Acts and Monuments," pp. 243–46.
157 *Ibid.*, p. 243.

Chapter VI

1 John Foxe, *Actes and Monuments* . . . (London: John Day, March 20, 1563), sigs. B1–1ᵛ.
2 *The Auncient Ecclesiasticall Histories of the First Six Hundred Yeares after Christ, wrytten in the Greeke tongue by three learned Historiographers, Eusebius, Socrates, and Evagrius,* . . . translated out of the Greeke tongue by Meredith Hanmer (London: Thomas Vautrollier, 1577), sig. A1.
3 Eusebius Pamphili, *Ecclesiastical History*, trans. Roy J. Deferrari (The Fathers of the Church, No. XIX [New York, 1953]) I, 233ff.
4 *Liber preclarissimi religiosi fratris Jacobi de Voragine ordinis predicatorum de Vitis Sanctorum* (Venetiis: per Christoforum Arnoldum, 1477), sig. a1.
5 Foxe, *Actes and Monuments*, sig. C4.
6 William Haller, "John Foxe and the Puritan Revolution," in Richard Foster Jones et al., *The Seventeenth Century: Studies in the History of English Thought and Literature from Bacon to Pope* (Stanford, 1951), p. 213.
7 Foxe, *Actes and Monuments*, sigs. C3ᵛ–4.
8 *Ibid.*, sig. C4.
9 *Ibid.*, sigs. C4–4ᵛ.
10 *Ibid.*, sigs. C4ᵛ–6.
11 *Ibid.*, sig. **I*ᵛ [an interpolated leaf].
12 *Ibid.*, sig. K1.
13 *Ibid.*, sigs. S5ᵛ ff.
14 *Ibid.*, sigs. Ii5ᵛ–6.
15 *Ibid.*, sig. Ii7.
16 *Ibid.*, sig. PP6.
17 *Ibid.*, sigs. PP6ᵛ ff.
18 *Ibid.*, sigs. LLl1 ff.
19 *Ibid.*, sig. NNNN2ᵛ.

20 *Ibid.*, sig. C1.
21 *Ibid.*, sig. LL3.
22 *Ibid.*, sig. B5.
23 *Ibid.*, sigs. OOO1–1ᵛ.
24 *Ibid.*, sig. Qq1ᵛ.
25 *Ibid.*, sig. C5ᵛ.
26 *Ibid.*, sigs. E1ᵛ–2ᵛ.
27 *Ibid.*, sig. D6.
28 *Ibid.*, sig. E1ᵛ.
29 *Ibid.*, sigs. E3–3ᵛ.
30 *Ibid.*, sig. EEE1.
31 *Ibid.*, sigs. I1–1ᵛ.
32 *Ibid.*, sig. FF5.
33 *Ibid.*, sigs. *I4–5.
34 *Ibid.*, sigs. Ss6–6ᵛ.
35 *Ibid.*, sig. AA2ᵛ.
36 *Ibid.*, sig. PP5ᵛ.
37 *Ibid.*, sig. AA4ᵛ.
38 *Ibid.*, sigs. BB6ᵛ–CC1.
39 *Ibid.*, sig. CC1.
40 *Ibid.*, sigs. CC3–3ᵛ.
41 *Ibid.*, sigs. MMm1–1ᵛ.
42 *Ibid.*, sigs. PPPp5ᵛ–6.
43 *Ibid.*, sig. YYYy2.
44 Gordon Rupp's suggestion that Foxe has borrowed from the "Magdeburg Centuries" of Flaccius Illyricus [and others] "the view of history in terms of the rise and overthrow of Anti-Christ" is deserving of further study; see Gordon Rupp, *Six Makers of English Religion, 1500–1700* (London, 1957), p. 71.
45 Foxe, *Actes and Monuments*, sigs. SS1–2ᵛ.
46 *Ibid.*, sigs. QQQQ1–VVVV4.
47 *Ibid.*, sigs. SSSS1.
48 *Ibid.*, sigs. TTTT1ᵛ–2.
49 *Ibid.*, sig. HH1ᵛ.
50 *Ibid.*, sig. HH6.
51 *Ibid.*, sig. LL1.

52 *Ibid.*, sig. Yy2ᵛ.
53 *Ibid.*, sigs. PPp1ᵛ–QQq4ᵛ. See also sigs. MMm3ᵛ–NNn2ᵛ.
54 *Ibid.*, sig. Yy6.
55 *Ibid.*, sig. Mm1.
56 *Ibid.*, sig. NN5.
57 *Ibid.*, sig. Yy5.
58 *Ibid.*, sigs. Ii5ᵛ–KKk1.
59 *Ibid.*, sig. LLl1.
60 *Ibid.*, sig. LLl3ᵛ.
61 *Ibid.*, sig. LLl6ᵛ.
62 *Ibid.*, sigs. GG6ᵛ–HHH1.
63 *Ibid.*, sig. EEE1ᵛ.
64 *Ibid.*, sig. O1.
65 *Ibid.*, sig. O4ᵛ.
66 *Ibid.*, sig. HHH5.
67 *Ibid.*, sig. PP6ᵛ.
68 *Ibid.*, sigs. DDD1–1ᵛ.
69 *Ibid.*, sig. OOOO6ᵛ.
70 *Ibid.*, sigs. B4ᵛ–5ᵛ.
71 *Ibid.*, sig. B5ᵛ.
72 *Ibid.*, sig. Ll1ᵛ.
73 *Ibid.*, sig. Rr2ᵛ.

74 *Ibid.*, sig. Vv7ᵛ.
75 *Ibid.*, sigs. PP4ᵛ–5.
76 *Ibid.*, sig. VV5.
77 *Ibid.*, sig. BBB1.
78 *Ibid.*, sig. AAAA4.
79 *Ibid.*, sig. I6ᵛ.
80 *Ibid.*, sig. PPPp3ᵛ.
81 *Ibid.*
82 *Ibid.*, sig EEEe6.
83 *Ibid.*, sigs. Ll1ᵛ–2.
84 See, e.g., *Politique Discourses, treating of the Differences and Inequalities of Vocations, as well Publique, as Private,* trans. Aegremont Ratcliffe (London: for Edward Aggas, 1578), sig. A3ᵛ.
85 Foxe, *Actes and Monuments,* sigs. EEEE3–3ᵛ.
86 Haller, "John Foxe and the Puritan Revolution," p. 218.
87 Foxe, *Actes and Monuments,* sig. KK5.
88 *Ibid.*, sigs. KK5–LL1.
89 Haller, "John Foxe and the Puritan Revolution," p. 210.

Chapter VII

1 J. D. Mackie, *The Earlier Tudors, 1485–1558* (Oxford, 1952), p. 395.
2 Thomas Gilbart, *A Declaration of the Death of John Lewes, a Most Detestable and Obstinate Hereticke, Burned at Norwich the xviii, daye of September 1583 aboute Three of the Clocke in the Afternoone. To the Tune, of John Carelesse* (London: Richard Jones, October 8, 1583).
3 Conyers Read, *Mr. Secretary Cecil and Queen Elizabeth* (New York, 1955), p. 129.
4 Henry Offley Wakeman, rev. S. L. Ollard, *An Introduction to the History of the Church of England* (London, 1927), pp. 300 ff; A. F. Scott Pearson, *Church and State* (Cambridge, 1928), p. 54.
5 Wakeman, *Introduction to the History of the Church of England,* p. 304; Read, *Mr. Secretary Cecil,* pp. 132–33.
6 Millar Maclure, *The Paul's Cross Sermons 1534–1642* (University of Toronto Department of English Studies and Texts, No. VI [Toronto, 1958]), pp. 57 ff.
7 Evelyn May Albright, *Dramatic Publication in England, 1580–1640* (New York and London, 1927), pp. 60 ff.

8 *A Proclamation for Bringing into the Realme of Unlawfull and Seditious Bookes* (London: Richard Jugge and John Cawood, March 1, 1568), in *A Booke containing All Such Proclamations as were published during the Raigne of the late Queene Elizabeth,* collected . . . by Humfrey Dyson (London: Bonham Norton and John Bill, 1618), pp. 305–7.
9 *A Proclamation made against Seditious and Traiterous Bookes, Billes, and Writinges* (London: Richard Jugge and John Cawood, July 1, 1570), in Dyson, *Proclamations,* pp. 139–40.
10 Martin Haile, *An Elizabethan Cardinal, William Allen* (London, 1914), pp. 4–6, 11.
11 *Ibid.*, pp. 34, 58.
12 *Ibid.*, pp. 77–78; Philip Hughes, *The Reformation in England,* III (London, 1954), 283–90. For the view that the seminary at Douai only gradually assumed this character, see Pierre Janelle, *The Catholic Reformation* (Milwaukee, 1951), p. 318.
13 Haile, *An Elizabethan Cardinal,* p. 119.
14 B. J. Kidd, *The Counter-Reformation, 1550–1600* (London: SPCK, 1933), p. 214.

15 Philip Hughes, *Rome and the Counter-Reformation in England* (London, 1944), p. 185.
16 *Ibid.*, pp. 220–21.
17 *Ibid.*, p. 190.
18 *Ibid.*, pp. 195 ff.
19 *Ibid.*, p. 165.
20 *Ibid.*, p. 182.
21 Haile, *An Elizabethan Cardinal*, p. 179.
22 Hughes, *Rome and the Counter-Reformation*, p. 181.
23 L. Hicks, *Letters and Memorials of Father Robert Parsons, S.J.*, (Catholic Record Society, Vol. XXXIX [London, 1942]), ix.
24 For example, [Robert Parsons], *A Declaration of the True Causes of the Great Troubles, Presupposed to be Intended against the Realme of England* (n.p., 1592), sigs. A2, B6.
25 R[obert] Parsons, *A Brief, and Cleere Confutation of a New, Vaine, and Vaunting Challenge made by O. E. Minister, unto N. D.* (n.p., 1604), sigs. +7ᵛ, ++1ᵛ-2.
26 See Helen C. White, *English Devotional Literature (Prose) 1600–1640* (Madison, Wis., 1931), pp. 143 ff.
27 Hicks, *Parsons*, p. 61.
28 *Ibid.*, p. 83.
29 See Arthur J. Hawkes, "The Birchley Hall Secret Press," *The Library*, N.S. VII (1926–27), 138; A. F. Allison and D. M. Rogers, review of A. C. Southern, *Elizabethan Recusant Prose: 1559–1582*, in *The Library*, 5th Ser., VI (1951), 50–51; Hicks, *Parsons*, pp. xxxi–xxxix.
30 Hicks, *Parsons*, p. xxxii.
31 [Robert Parsons], *A Brief Discours contayning certayne Reasons why Catholiques refuse to goe to Church* (Doway: John Lyon, 1580), sigs. ‡2–‡‡8ᵛ.
32 *Ibid.*, sig. A1.
33 *Ibid.*, sigs. A5ᵛ-6.
34 *Ibid.*, sigs. I4ᵛ-5.
35 Kidd, *The Counter-Reformation, 1550–1600*, p. 214.
36 *The Historie of Ireland*, collected by Meredith Hanmer, Edmund Campian, and Edmund Spenser (Dublin: Societie of Stationers, 1633), sigs. ¶4–4ᵛ.
37 Richard Simpson, *Edmund Campion: A Biography* (London, 1896), p. 1.
38 *Ibid.*, p. 2.

39 *Ibid.*, pp. 4–12.
40 *Ibid.*, p. 21.
41 *Ibid.*, pp. 28–34.
42 *Ibid.*, pp. 72–74.
43 Meredith Hanmer, *The Great Bragge and Challenge of M. Champion a Jesuite, commonlye called Edmunde Campion . . . confuted and aunswered* (London: Thomas Marsh, 1581), sig. C4.
44 Evelyn Waugh, *Edmund Campion* (London, 1947), p. 118.
45 *Ibid.*, pp. 121 ff.
46 William Charke, *An Answere to a Seditious Pamphlet lately cast abroade by a Jesuite, with a Discoverie of that Blasphemous Sect* (London: Christopher Barker, December 17, 1580), sig. A3.
47 Hicks, *Parsons*, pp. xiii–iv.
48 Charke, *An Answere to a Seditious Pamphlet*, sig. C2.
49 *Ibid.*, sig. C4.
50 M. M. Knappen, *Tudor Puritanism: A Chapter in the History of Idealism* (Chicago, 1939), pp. 239, 261.
51 Hanmer, *The Great Bragge*, sig. A3.
52 *Ibid.*, sig. F2ᵛ.
53 Edmund Campion, *Ten Reasons proposed to his Adversaries in the Name of the Faith and presented to the Illustrious Members of Our Universities* (London, 1914), pp. 10–11.
54 Hanmer, *The Great Bragge*, sig. H2.
55 John Keltridge, *Two Godlie and Learned Sermons, appointed and preached, before the Jesuites, Seminaries, and Other Adversaries of the Gospel of Christ in the Tower of London . . . May 7 and 21, 1581* (London: Richard Jones, [1581]), sig. ¶1ᵛ.
56 *Ibid.*, sig. ¶4.
57 Hicks, *Parsons*, pp. xxxi–xxxii, xxxvii–xxxviii; A. F. Allison and D. M. Rogers, *A Catalogue of Catholic Books in English Printed Abroad or Secretly in England, 1558–1640*, in *Biographical Studies*, Vol. III, No. 3 (Bognor Regis, 1956), p. 165.
58 William Whitaker, *Ad Rationes Decem E. Campiani, Responsio* (London: T. Vautrollier for T. Chard, 1581).
59 William Whitaker, *Responsionis ad Decem illas Rationes quibus fretus E. Campianus Defensio* (London: T. Vautrollier for T. Chard, 1581).

60 *Edmundi Campiani Jesuitae Rationes Decem . . . Guilielmi Whitaker . . . Responsio* (Antverpiae: Aegidius Radaeus, 1582).

61 John Dury, *Confutatio responsionis Guilielmi Whitakeri ad Rationes Decem* (Parisiis, 1582).

62 William Whitaker, *Responsionis ad Decem Rationes quibus fretus E. Campianus Defensio* (London: H. Midleton for T. Chard, 1583).

63 William Whitaker, *An Answere to the Ten Reasons of Edmund Campian the Jesuit*, trans. Richard Stocke (London: Felix Kyngston for Cuthbert Burby and Edmund Weaver, 1606).

64 *Ibid.*, sig.)(4^v.

65 *Ibid.*, sigs. B4–4^v.

66 *Ibid.*, sig. Ss4.

67 Hanmer, *The Great Bragge*, sig. H1.

68 Whitaker, *An Answere to Campian*, trans. Stocke, sig. B1^v.

69 *Ibid.*, sig. D1.

70 *Ibid.*

71 *Ibid.*, sig. B1.

72 Hicks, *Parsons*, p. xxxiii.

73 [Robert Parsons], *A Brief Censure uppon Two Bookes written in Answere to M. Edmonde Campions Offer of Disputation* (Doway: John Lyon, 1581), sig. D8.

74 *Ibid.*, sig. E1.

75 William Charke, *A Replie to a Censure written against the Two Answers to a Jesuites Seditious Pamphlet* (London: Christopher Barker, 1581), sig. M5^v.

76 *An Answeare for the Time, unto that Foule and Wicked Defence of the Censure, that was given upon M. Charkes Booke, and Meredith Hanmers . . .* (London: Thomas Dawson and Tobie Smith, 1583).

77 George Ellyot, *A Very True Report of the Apprehension and Taking of that Arche Papist Edmond Campion the Pope his Right Hand . . .* (London: Thomas Dawson, 1581), sig. A3.

78 *Ibid.*, sig. A4^v.

79 *Ibid.*, sigs. B1–2^v.

80 *Ibid.*, sigs. B2^v–3.

81 *Ibid.*, sigs. B3^v–C1^v.

82 Hicks, *Parsons*, pp. 92–93.

83 *Diarium Rerum Gestarum in Turri Londiniensi*, in Nicholas Sanders, *De Origine ac Progressu Schismatis Anglicani* (Ingolstadii: ex officina Typo-

graphica Wolfgangi Ederi, 1587), sig. Aa3^v.

84 See Simpson, *Edmund Campion*, pp. 352–53; Waugh, *Edmund Campion*, pp. 65–66.

85 M. S., *The Araignement, and Execution of a Wilfull and Obstinate Traitour, named Everalde Ducket, alias Hauns* (London: John Charlewood and Edward White, 1581), and [Anthony Munday], *A True Report, of the Araignement and Execution of the Late Popishe Traitour, Evered Haunce* (London: Henrie Bynneman, 1581).

86 Celeste Turner, *Anthony Mundy, an Elizabethan Man of Letters* (University of California Publications in English, Vol. II [Berkeley, 1928]), p. 13; A. C. Southern, *Elizabethan Recusant Prose, 1559–1582* (London and Glasgow, [1950]), p. 281.

87 Turner, *Anthony Mundy*, p. 53.

88 *Ibid.*, p. 57; Simpson, *Edmund Campion*, p. 452.

89 *An Advertisement and Defence for Truth against her Backbiters, and especially against the Whispring Favourers, and Colourers of Campions, and the rest of his Confederats Treasons* (n.p., 1581).

90 *Ibid.*, sigs. A2^v–3.

91 A[nthony] M[unday], *A Discoverie of Edmund Campion, and his Confederates, their Most Horrible and Traiterous Practises, against her Majesties Most Royall Person, and the Realme* (London: for Edwarde White, January 29, 1582), sigs. A3^v ff.

92 *Ibid.*, sig. B7^v.

93 *Ibid.*, sigs. A7–7^v.

94 *Ibid.*, sig. A6^v–7.

95 *Ibid.*, sig. B3^v.

96 *Ibid.*, sig. B6.

97 *Ibid.*, sig. E5^v.

98 *Ibid.*, sigs. F7–G4.

99 *Ibid.*, sig. F7^v.

100 *Ibid.*, sig. F8.

101 *Ibid.*, sig. F8^v.

102 *Ibid.*, sig. G1^v.

103 *Ibid.*, sig. G2.

104 *Ibid.*, sig. C5^v.

105 Southern, *Elizabethan Recusant Prose*, p. 279.

106 [Thomas Alfield], *A True Reporte of the Death and Martyrdome of M. Campion Jesuite and Preiste, and M.*

Sherwin, and M. Bryan Preistes, at Tiborne the First of December *1581*
([London: Richard Verstegan, 1581]),
sig. A1.

107 John Hungerford Pollen, ed., *Unpublished Documents relating to the
English Martyrs, Vol. I, 1584–1603*
(Catholic Record Society, Vol. V [Lon-
don, 1908], pp. 112–20.

108 [Alfield], *A True Reporte*, sig. A4ᵛ.

109 *Ibid.*, sigs. B2–2ᵛ.

110 *Ibid.*, sigs. B3ᵛ–4.

111 *Ibid.*, sig. B4.

112 *Ibid.*

113 *Ibid.*, sigs. B4–4ᵛ.

114 *Ibid.*, sig. B4ᵛ.

115 *Ibid.*, sigs. B4ᵛ–C1.

116 Origen, *Prayer, Exhortation to Martyrdom*, trans. John J. O'Meara (Ancient
Christian Writers, No. 19 [Westmin-
ster, Md., and London, 1954]), p. 158.

117 [Alfield], *A True Reporte*, sig. C1ᵛ.

118 *Ibid.*, sigs. C2–2ᵛ.

119 *Ibid.*, sig. D2ᵛ.

120 *Ibid.*

121 *Ibid.*, sigs. A2–2ᵛ.

122 *Ibid.*, sig. D4.

123 *Ibid.*, sigs. D4ᵛ–E1.

124 Augustus Jessopp, *One Generation of a
Norfolk House: A Contribution to
Elizabethan History* (London, 1879),
pp. 100–101, 281–82.

125 [Alfield], *A True Reporte*, sig. G1ᵛ.

126 Southern, *Elizabethan Recusant Prose*,
pp. 279–80.

127 *An Answeare for the Time, unto that
Foule and Wicked Defense of the Censure*, sig. C1ᵛ.

128 *Ibid.*, sig. D1ᵛ.

129 [Alexander Nowell and William Day],
*A True Report of the Disputation or
rather Private Conference had in
the Tower of London, with Ed. Campion Jesuite, the last of August, 1581*
(London: Christopher Barker, January 1, 1584), sig. A2.

130 *Ibid.*, sig. C3ᵛ.

131 *An Answeare for the Time, unto that
Foule and Wicked Defence of the Censure*, sig. B2ᵛ.

132 *De vita et Moribus Theodori Bezae,
omnium haer[e]ticorum nostri temporis facilè principis . . . cui adiectus
est libellus, de morte Patris Edmundi
Campionis, et aliorum quorundam
Catholicorum, qui in Anglia pro fide*

Catholica interfecti fuerunt primo die
Decembris. Anno domini. *1581*, au-
thore Jacobo Laignæo (Parisiis: apud
Michaelem de Roigny, 1585), sigs.
G8ᵛ ff.

133 *Ibid.*, sig. H5 ff.

134 *Ibid.*, sig. I6ᵛ.

135 [Robert Parsons], *An Epistle of the
Persecution of Catholickes in England*
(Doway: G. T., [1582?]), sig. L6.

136 *Ibid.*, sig. L8ᵛ.

137 [Alfield], *A True Reporte*, sig. D2.

138 [Parsons], *An Epistle of the Persecution*, sig. M1.

139 *Diarium Rerum Gestarum in Turri
Londiniensi*, sig. Aa7.

140 *Ibid.*, sig. Aa3ᵛ.

141 *Ibid.*, sigs. Aa3ᵛ–4.

142 *Ibid.*, sig. Aa4.

143 *Ibid.*

144 *Ibid.*, sig. Aa4ᵛ.

145 *Ibid.*

146 *Ibid.*, sigs. Aa5–5ᵛ.

147 *Ibid.*, sigs. Aa7ᵛ–8ᵛ.

148 *Ibid.*, sig. Bb2.

149 *Ibid.*, sig. Aa5.

150 *Ibid.*, sig. Aa8.

151 *Ibid.*, sig. Bb2ᵛ.

152 Thomas Worthington, *Relation of Sixtene Martyrs Glorified in England in
Twelve Monethes* (Doway: the Widow
of James Boscard, 1601).

153 *Diarium Rerum Gestarum in Turri
Londiniensi*, sig. Aa6ᵛ.

154 *Ibid.*, sig. Aa8ᵛ.

155 *Ibid.*, sig. Bb1.

156 *Ibid.*, sig. Aa5ᵛ.

157 *Ibid.*, sig. Aa6.

158 *Ibid.*, sig. Aa8ᵛ.

159 Southern, *Elizabethan Recusant Prose*,
p. 272.

160 Thomas McNevin Veech, *Dr. Nicholas
Sanders and the English Reformation,
1530–1581* (Louvain, 1935), p. 1.

161 *Ibid.*, pp. 5–12.

162 *Ibid.*, p. 23.

163 *Ibid.*, p. 57.

164 *Ibid.*, p. 89.

165 *Ibid.*, p. 296.

166 *Ibid.*, pp. 259–61.

167 *Ibid.*, p. 288.

168 *Ibid.*, p. 234.

169 *Ibid.*, pp. 244–46.

170 Nicholas Sander, *Rise and Growth of
the Anglican Schism*, trans. David
Lewis (London, 1877), pp. 313–14.

171 Veech, *Dr. Nicholas Sanders*, pp. 234–37.

172 William Allen, *A Briefe Historie of the Glorious Martyrdom of Twelve Reverend Priests, Father Edmund Campion and His Companions*, ed. J. H. Pollen (London, 1908), p. ix.

173 *Ibid.*, pp. x–xi.

174 *Ibid.*, p. 3.

175 *Ibid.*, p. 8.

176 *Ibid.*, p. 106.

177 *Ibid.*, p. 119.

178 [William Allen], *A True Sincere and Modest Defence, of English Catholiques that Suffer for Their Faith both at Home and Abrode* ([Rouen, 1584]), sig. *3ᵛ.

179 *Ibid.*, sig. A8.

180 *Ibid.*, sig. A1ᵛ.

181 *Ibid.*, sig. A7ᵛ.

182 *Concertatio Ecclesiæ Catholicæ in Anglia, adversus Calvinopapistas et Puritanos* (Augustæ Trevirorum: apud Edmundum Hatotum, 1583), sig. A6ᵛ.

183 *Ibid.*, sig. A2.

184 Southern, *Elizabethan Recusant Prose*, pp. 47–48.

185 Pollen, *Unpublished Documents relating to the English Martyrs*, p. 143.

186 *Concertatio Ecclesiæ Catholicæ* (1583), sigs. A3ᵛ–4.

187 *Ibid.*, sig. A5ᵛ.

188 *Ibid.*, sig. A8.

189 *Ibid.*, sigs. B1–5ᵛ.

190 *Ibid.*, sigs. B6–E7ᵛ.

191 *Ibid.*, sigs. E8–K4ᵛ.

192 See above, p. 224.

193 *Concertatio Ecclesiæ Catholicæ* (1583), sigs. K5–T7ᵛ.

194 *Ibid.*, sigs. S4ᵛ–Z2ᵛ.

195 *Ibid.*, sig. Z3.

196 *Ibid.* sig. A6ᵛ.

197 *Ibid.*, sig. Z6.

198 *Ibid.*, sig. a2ᵛ.

199 *Ibid.*, sigs. a3ᵛ–8.

200 *Ibid.*, sigs. a8–k5ᵛ.

201 *Ibid.*, sigs. k6–l7ᵛ.

202 *Ibid.*, sigs. l7ᵛ–8.

203 *Concertatio Ecclesiæ Catholicæ in Anglia adversus Calvinopapistas et Puritanos sub Elizabetha Regina* (Augustæ Trevirorum: Henricus Bock, 1588), sigs.)(2–4ᵛ.

204 *Ibid.*, sig.)(1ᵛ.

205 *Ibid.*

206 *Ibid.*, sigs. A1–4.

207 *Ibid.*, sigs. A4ᵛ–E3.

208 *Ibid.*, sigs. E3ᵛ–K4.

209 *Ibid.*, sig.)(5ᵛ.

210 See, for examples, *ibid.*, sigs. L1ᵛ–3 and N1.

211 *Ibid.*, sigs. Aa4ᵛ–Ii2ᵛ.

212 *Ibid.*, sigs. Ll1–Mm3ᵛ.

213 *Ibid.*, sigs. Ddd1–Eee2ᵛ.

214 *Ibid.*, sigs. A1–E3.

215 *Ibid.*, sigs. Fff2–Kkk1.

216 *Ibid.*, sigs. Kkk1–4.

217 *Ibid.*, sigs. Kkk4ᵛ–Mmm4ᵛ.

218 *Ibid.*, sigs. Nnn1–3.

219 *Ibid.*, sigs. Nnn3–Xxx3ᵛ.

220 Southern, *Elizabethan Recusant Prose*, pp. 386–87.

221 *Concertatio Ecclesiæ Catholicæ* (1588), sigs. a1–ee3ᵛ.

222 *Ibid.*, sigs. ee3ᵛ–ff3ᵛ.

223 *Ibid.*, sigs. ff4–4ᵛ.

224 *Ibid.*, sig. *1.

225 *Ibid.*, sigs. *1ᵛ–***1ᵛ.

226 *Ibid.*, sigs. ***2ᵛ–*****1.

227 *Ibid.*, sig. *****1.

228 *Ibid.*, sigs. *****1ᵛ–******2ᵛ.

229 Pollen, *Unpublished Documents relating to the English Martyrs*, p. 144.

230 *The Life and Death of Mr. Edmund Geninges, Priest* (S. Omers: Charles Boscard, 1614), sig. K1ᵛ.

231 Allen, *A Briefe Historie*, p. 83.

232 *Ibid.*, p. 18.

233 *Ibid.*, p. 106.

234 *Ibid.*, p. 116.

235 *Ibid.*, p. 62.

Chapter VIII

1 Christopher Devlin, *The Life of Robert Southwell, Poet and Martyr* (London, New York, Toronto, 1956), p. 3.

2 Pierre Janelle, *Robert Southwell the Writer* (Clermont-Ferrand, 1935), p. 6.

3 Devlin, *Southwell*, pp. 27 ff.

4 *Ibid.*, pp. 58 ff.

5 David Mathew, *Catholicism in England, 1535–1935* (London and New York, 1936), p. 46.

6 See above, pp. 8–9.

7 See above, pp. 108–9, 112, 121–22, 125.

8 G[eorge] J[oye], *A Present Consolation for the Sufferers of Persecucion for*

Ryghtwysenes (n.p., September, 1544).

9 Thomas Hide, *A Consolatorie Epistle to the Afflicted Catholikes* (Louvaine: John Maes for John Lion, 1579), sig. B4.

10 *Ibid.*, sig. D2.

11 William Allen, *An Apologie and True Declaration of the Institution and Endevours of the Two English Colleges, the One in Rome, the Other Now Resident in Rhemes* . . . (Mounts in Henault [Rheims: John Fogny], 1581). See A. C. Southern, *Elizabethan Recusant Prose, 1559–1582* (London and Glasgow, [1950]), pp. 381–83.

12 Allen, *An Apologie and True Declaration of the Institution of the Two English Colleges*, sigs. P5ᵛ–6.

13 Janelle, *Robert Southwell the Writer*, p. 147.

14 Devlin, *Southwell*, p. 134.

15 [Robert Southwell], *An Epistle of Comfort, to the Reverend Priestes, and to the Honorable, Worshipful, and Other of Laye Sort restrayned in Durance for the Catholicke Fayth* (Paris, n.d. [Douai? 1604?]), sig. A2.

16 *Ibid.*, sig. Aa6.

17 Philip Hughes, *The Reformation in England*, III (London, 1954), 16.

18 Janelle, *Robert Southwell the Writer*, p. 147.

19 [Southwell], *An Epistle of Comfort*, sig. A4.

20 *Ibid.*

21 *Ibid.*, sig. A5.

22 *Ibid.*, sigs. A5 ff.

23 *Ibid.*, sigs. B4ᵛ ff.

24 *Ibid.*, sigs. B8–8ᵛ.

25 John Hungerford Pollen, ed., *Unpublished Documents relating to the English Martyrs, Vol. I, 1584–1603* (Catholic Record Society, Vol. V [London, 1908]), p. 328.

26 [Southwell], *An Epistle of Comfort*, sigs. D1ᵛ ff.

27 *Ibid.*, sigs. F2 ff.

28 *Ibid.*, sigs. G8 ff.

29 *Ibid.*, sig. K5.

30 *Ibid.*, sigs. K7 ff.

31 *Ibid.*, sig. M6.

32 *Ibid.*, sig. N4.

33 *Ibid.*, sig. P1.

34 *Ibid.*, sig. Q4ᵛ.

35 *Ibid.*, sigs. Q5 ff.

36 *Ibid.*, sig. R1ᵛ.

37 *Ibid.*, sig. R6.

38 *Ibid.*, sigs. S2ᵛ ff.

39 *Ibid.*, sigs. S8ᵛ ff.

40 *Ibid.*, sig. X8ᵛ.

41 St. Cyprian, *The Lapsed, The Unity of the Catholic Church*, trans. Maurice Bévenot (Ancient Christian Writers, No. 25 [Westminster, Md., and London, 1957]), p. 3.

42 [Southwell], *An Epistle of Comfort*, sig. X8ᵛ.

43 *Ibid.*, sigs. Y6–7ᵛ.

44 *Ibid.*, sig. Z7ᵛ.

45 *Ibid.*, sigs. Z7ᵛ ff.

46 *Ibid.*, sig. &1ᵛ.

47 *Ibid.*, sigs. &5–5ᵛ.

48 *Ibid.*, sig. &6.

49 *Ibid.*, sig. &7ᵛ.

50 R[obert] S[outhwell], *The Triumphs over Death* (London: V[alentine] S[ims] for John Busbie, 1595), sig. E1ᵛ.

51 [Southwell], *An Epistle of Comfort*, sig. Aa5.

52 *Ibid.*, sig. Aa6.

53 *Ibid.*, sig. T5.

54 *Ibid.*, sig. Bb3.

55 *Ibid.*, sig. Bb3ᵛ.

56 *Ibid.*, sigs. Bb4–4ᵛ.

57 *Ibid.*, sig. Cc5ᵛ.

58 *Ibid.*, sig. Cc7ᵛ.

59 Devlin, *Southwell*, p. 290.

60 [Southwell], *An Epistle of Comfort*, sig. Cc7ᵛ.

61 James H. McDonald, *The Poems and Prose Writings of Robert Southwell, S.J.: A Bibliographical Study* (Oxford: for the Roxburghe Club, 1937), pp. 115–16.

62 Janelle, *Robert Southwell the Writer*, p. 310.

63 By the Queene, *A Declaration of Great Troubles pretended against the Realme by a Number of Seminarie Priests and Jesuits,* . . . (London: Christopher Barker, October 18, 1591), in *A Booke containing All Such Proclamations as were published during the Raigne of the late Queene Elizabeth*, collected . . . by Humfrey Dyson (London: Bonham Norton and John Bill, 1618) pp. 305–7.

64 Andreas Philopatrus, *Elizabethæ Angliæ Reginæ Hæresin Calviniam Pro-*

pugnantis, Sævissimum in Catholicos sui regni Edictum (Lugduni: apud Joannem Didier, 1592).

65 Robert Southwell, *An Humble Supplication to her Majestie*, ed. R. C. Bald (Cambridge, 1953), pp. 1–2.

66 *Ibid.*, pp. 3–4.

67 *Ibid.*, p. 4.

68 *Ibid.*, p. 7.

69 *Ibid.*, pp. 7–11.

70 *Ibid.*, p. 13.

71 *Ibid.*, p. 14.

72 *Ibid.*, p. 30.

73 *Ibid.*, p. 25.

74 *Ibid.*, p. 33.

75 See above, p. 214.

76 Southwell, *An Humble Supplication*, pp. 33–34.

77 *Ibid.*, p. 34.

78 Devlin, *Southwell*, pp. 52–53.

79 *Ibid.*, pp. 172 ff.

80 Southwell, *An Humble Supplication*, pp. 42–43.

81 *Ibid.*, p. 43.

82 Philip Hughes, *Rome and the Counter-Reformation in England* (London, 1944), p. 258.

83 David Mathew, *The Celtic Peoples and Renaissance Europe* (London and New York, 1933), pp. 175 ff.

84 Hughes, *Rome and the Counter-Reformation*, p. 260.

85 See Hughes, *The Reformation in England*, III, 320 ff.

86 For example, see above, p. 255.

87 Pollen, *Unpublished Documents relating to the English Martyrs*, p. 62.

88 Southwell, *An Humble Supplication*, p. 35.

89 *Ibid.*

90 *Ibid.*, p. 28.

91 Hughes, *Rome and the Counter-Reformation*, pp. 295 ff.

92 Bald, Introduction to Southwell, *An Humble Supplication*, p. xiv.

93 *Ibid.*, pp. xiii–xv.

94 *Ibid.*, p. xxii.

95 See Christopher Devlin, "The Patriotism of Robert Southwell," *The Month*, N.S., Vol. X, No. 5 (1953), pp. 345–54.

96 Southwell, *An Humble Supplication*, p. 46.

97 Devlin, *Southwell*, pp. 278 ff.

98 "Leake's Relation of the Martyrdom of Father Southwell," in Pollen, *Unpublished Documents relating to the English Martyrs*, p. 335.

99 *Ibid.*, p. 337.

100 [Robert Southwell], *A Short Rule of Good Life* (S. Omers: J. Heigham, 1622), sig. A3ᵛ.

101 *Ibid.*, sigs. A8 ff.

102 *Ibid.*, sig. B6ᵛ.

103 *Ibid.*, sig. E4.

104 Louis L. Martz, *The Poetry of Meditation* (New Haven and London, 1954), p. 204.

105 Pollen, *Unpublished Documents relating to the English Martyrs*, p. 318.

106 Edward J. Klein, Introduction to *The Imitation of Christ*, trans. Richard Whitford (New York and London, 1941), p. xiv.

107 *Ibid.*, p. lviii.

108 Helen C. White, *The Tudor Books of Private Devotion* (Madison, Wis., 1951), pp. 157–61.

109 *Ibid.*, pp. 164 ff.

110 See Basil Willey, *The Seventeenth Century Background* (London, 1934), Chap. V.

111 St. Ignatius of Loyola, *The Spiritual Exercises*, trans. W. H. Longridge (London and Oxford, 1950), pp. 52–58.

112 St. Francis Borgia, third general of the Society of Jesus.

113 [Robert Southwell], *Marie Magdalens Funeral Teares* (London: J. [Wolfe] for G. C[awood], 1591), sig. A3ᵛ.

114 Janelle, *Robert Southwell the Writer*, p. 189; Martz, *The Poetry of Meditation*, p. 191.

115 Janelle, *Robert Southwell the Writer*, pp. 189–90.

116 [Southwell], *Marie Magdalens Funeral Teares*, sig. A3.

117 *Ibid.*, sig. A3ᵛ.

118 *Ibid.*, sigs. C1–3ᵛ.

119 Janelle, *Robert Southwell the Writer*, p. 184.

120 *Omelia Origenis de Beata Maria Magdalena* (London: ad rogatum Magistri Will'm Menyman socii collegii Ricardi Whityngton, [1504?]).

121 *Dialogismus sive Colloquium D. Mariæ Magdalenæ cum Christo Domino redivivo, Origeni hactenus adscripta homilia; studio nunc M. Joan. Cræsellii*

... *Soliloquiis Thomæ à Kempis merità adjuncta* (n.p., n.d. [1604?]).

122 Janelle, *Robert Southwell the Writer,* pp. 184–89.

123 *Ibid.,* p. 185.

124 *Dialogismus sive Colloquium D. Mariæ Magdalenæ,* sig. A2.

125 *Ibid.,* sig. A3.

126 [Southwell], *Marie Magdalens Funeral Teares,* sig. B1.

127 *Dialogismus sive Colloquium D. Mariæ Magdalenæ,* sig. B1.

128 [Southwell], *Marie Magdalens Funeral Teares,* sig. G3ᵛ.

129 *Dialogismus sive Colloquium D. Mariæ Magdalenæ,* sig. B5ᵛ.

130 [Southwell], *Marie Magdalens Funeral Teares,* sigs. K4–4ᵛ.

131 *Ibid.,* sig. B3.

132 *Ibid.,* sig. C4.

133 *Ibid.,* sig. C6ᵛ.

134 *Ibid.,* sig. K2ᵛ.

135 *Ibid.,* sig. B8.

136 *Ibid.,* sig. E5ᵛ.

137 *Ibid.,* sigs. G7ᵛ–8.

138 *Ibid.,* sig. D8.

139 Janelle, *Robert Southwell the Writer,* p. 59.

140 McDonald, *Writings of Robert Southwell,* pp. 109–10.

141 *Ibid.,* pp. 144–47.

142 [Robert Southwell], *Saint Peters Complaynt, with Other Poems* (London: J. R. for G. C. [James Roberts for Gabriel Cawood], 1595), sig. B1.

143 *Ibid.,* sig B2.

144 *Ibid.,* sig. C2ᵛ.

145 *Ibid.,* sigs. C3ᵛ–4ᵛ.

146 *Ibid.,* sig. D1.

147 *Ibid.,* sig. E2ᵛ.

148 [Robert Southwell], *Saint Peters Complaint, with Other Poems* (London: John Wolfe, 1595).

149 McDonald, *Writings of Robert Southwell,* pp. 73–76.

150 R[obert] S[outhwell], *Mœoniæ, or Certaine Excellent Poems and Spirituall Hymnes* (London: Valentine Sims for John Busbie, 1595).

151 *Ibid.,* sig. A2ᵛ.

152 McDonald, *Writings of Robert Southwell,* pp. 81–90.

153 S[outhwell], *The Triumphs over Death,* sig. A3ᵛ.

154 Janelle, *Robert Southwell the Writer,* pp. 162–63.

155 S[outhwell], *Mœoniæ,* sigs. C4–D1.

156 [Nicholas Breton], *Marie Magdalens Love* (London: John Danter for William Barley, 1595).

157 See Jean Robertson, Introduction to *Poems by Nicholas Breton* (Liverpool, 1952), p. lxvi.

158 [Breton], *Marie Magdalens Love,* sigs. E2ᵛ–3.

159 Nicholas Breton, *Auspicante Jehova. Maries Exercise* (London: Thomas Este, 1597), sigs. A3–3ᵛ.

160 *Ibid.,* sig. D2ᵛ.

161 *Marie Magdalens Lamentations for the Losse of Her Master Jesus* (London: Adam Islip for Edward White, 1601).

162 [Southwell], *Marie Magdalens Funeral Teares,* sig. D6.

163 *Marie Magdalens Lamentations for the Losse of Her Master Jesus,* sig. B2.

164 *Saint Peters Ten Teares* (London: G. Simson for W. Jones, 1597), sig. A4ᵛ.

165 W[illiam] B[roxup], *Saint Peters Path to the Joyes of Heaven* (London: Felix Kingston, 1598), sig. A4ᵛ.

166 *Ibid.,* sig. C3.

167 J. M. [Gervase Markham], *The Teares of the Beloved* (London: Simon Stafford for John Browne, 1600), sig. B3.

168 White, *Tudor Books of Private Devotion,* pp. 226–27.

Chapter IX

1 René Aigrain, *L'Hagiographie: ses sources, ses méthodes, son histoire* (Paris, 1953), p. 325.

2 J[ohn] W[ilson], *The English Martyrologe* ([St. Omer], 1608), sig. *2.

3 Aigrain, *L'Hagiographie,* p. 326.

4 *Ibid.*

5 *De Probatis Sanctorum Historiis . . .* collectis per F. Laurentium Surium

Carthusianum, Tom I (Coloniæ Agrippinæ: apud Gervinum Calenium et hæredes Quentelios, 1570), sig. Y6ᵛ.

6 *Ibid.,* sigs. Cc4 ff.

7 *Ibid.,* sig. Ii5ᵛ.

8 *Ibid.,* sig. Nnn6.

9 Aigrain, *L'Hagiographie,* p. 328.

10 A. D. Nock, *Conversion: The Old and the New in Religion from Alexander*

the Great to Augustine of Hippo (Oxford, 1933), p. 198.

11 R[obert] C[hambers], *Palestina* (Florence: Bartelmew Sermatelli, 1600), sig. #3.

12 *Ibid.*, sig. ¶3.

13 *Ibid.*, sigs. A4–B1.

14 *Ibid.*, sig. Cci^v.

15 *The English Text of the Ancrene Riwle* (Cotton MS. Nero A. XIV), ed. Mabel Day (EETS, O.S., No. CCXXV [London, 1952]), pp. 177 ff.

16 C[hambers], *Palestina*, sigs. Aa3–3^v.

17 *Ibid.*, sigs. P2^v–3.

18 *Ibid.*, sigs. R1–4.

19 *Ibid.*, sigs. Y4^v–Aa1^v.

20 *Ibid.*, sig. P2.

21 Meredith Hanmer, trans., *The Auncient Ecclesiasticall Histories . . . of Eusebius, Socrates, and Evagrius* (London: Thomas Vautrollier, 1577), sig. *3.

22 Richard Greenham, *The Works of . . .* , examined, corrected, and published by H[enry] H[olland] (London: Felix Kingston for Ralph Jacson, 1599), sigs. A4–4^v.

23 Gordon Hall Gerould, *Saints' Legends* (Boston and New York, 1916), p. 134.

24 [Henry Bradshaw], *The Lyfe of Saynt Radegunde* (London: Rycharde Pynson, [1521?]), sigs. a3–3^v.

25 John Partridge, *The Worthie Hystorie of the Most Noble and Valiaunt Knight Plasidas, otherwise called Eustas, Who, was Martyred for the Profession of Jesus Christ* (London: Henrye Denham for Thomas Hacket, 1566), sigs. ¶2–2^v.

26 *Ibid.*, sigs. A1–1^v.

27 *Ibid.*, sigs. A2^v–3.

28 *Ibid.*, sig. A7^v.

29 *Ibid.*, sigs. B1–2^v.

30 *Ibid.*, sigs. B3–4.

31 *Ibid.*, sigs. B5–5^v.

32 *Ibid.*, sigs. B8–C1.

33 *Ibid.*, sigs. C6–D1.

34 *Ibid.*, sigs. D3.

35 See, for example, "The Legend or Life of St. Alexius, in Four Versions from Six Manuscripts," in *Adam Davy's 5 Dreams about Edward II, The Life of St. Alexius, . . .* ed. from Laud MS. 622 (Bodleian) F. J. Furnivall (EETS, O.S., No. LXIX [London, 1878]).

36 George Pettie, *A Petite Pallace of Pettie His Pleasure*, ed. Herbert Hartman (London, 1938), p. 3.

37 *Ibid.*, p. 249.

38 *Ibid.*, pp. 256–57.

39 *Ibid.*, pp. 260 ff.

40 *Ibid.*, p. 269.

41 *Ibid.*, p. 270.

42 [Richard Johnson], *The Most Famous History of the Seaven Champions of Christendome* (London: for Cuthbert Burbie, 1596), sig. A3.

43 *Ibid.*, sig. A4.

44 *Ibid.*, sigs. B1^v–3.

45 *Ibid.*, sigs. B3^v–4^v.

46 *Ibid.*, sigs. C3–3^v.

47 *Ibid.*, sig. D1^v.

48 *Ibid.*, sigs. C4–D1.

49 Gerould, *Saints' Legends*, pp. 318–20.

50 [Johnson], *The Seaven Champions of Christendome*, sig. D1^v.

51 Josephine Waters Bennett, "Genre, Milieu, and the 'Epic-Romance,' " in *English Institute Essays, 1951*, ed. Alan S. Downer (New York, 1952), p. 111.

52 *Ibid.*, p. 117.

53 Tristram White, *The Martyrdome of Saint George of Cappadocia* (London: T. [Snodham] for William Barley, 1614), sig. A1.

54 *Ibid.*, sig. A1^v.

55 Sidney J. H. Herrtage, ed., *The Early English Versions of the Gesta Romanorum* (EETS, E.S., No. XXXIII [London, 1879, reprinted 1932]), p. xxiii.

56 *The Golden Legende* (Westmestre: Wylyam Caxton, November 20, 1483), sigs. e4^v ff.

57 John Marbecke, *The Lyves of Holy Sainctes, Prophetes, Patriarches, and Others, Contayned in Holye Scripture* (London: [H. Denham and R. Watkins], 1574), sig. A3^v.

58 *Ibid.*, sig. A4.

59 *Ibid.*, sig. A5^v.

60 Guillaume de Saluste du Bartas, *The Historie of Judith in Forme of a Poeme*, trans. Thomas Hudson (Edinburgh: T. Vautroullier, 1584), sig. A2^v.

61 *Ibid.*, sig. A8.

62 *Ibid.*, sigs. H2^v–3^v.

63 *Ibid.*, sig. A5^v.

64 *Ibid.*, sig. E4.

65 *Ibid.*, sig. E6^v.

66 *Ibid.*, sigs. D8–8^v.

67 Michael Drayton, *Moyses in a Map of His Miracles* (London: Humfrey Lownes for Thomas Man the Younger, 1604), [no sig.] 2.
68 *Ibid.*, sig. A1ᵛ.
69 *Ibid.*, sigs. A3ᵛ–B3ᵛ.
70 *Ibid.*, sig. D2ᵛ.
71 *Ibid.*, sig. I3ᵛ.
72 *Ibid.*, sigs. M1–1ᵛ.
73 [Nicholas Breton], *Marie Magdalens Love* (London: John Danter for William Barley, 1595), sigs. E4–4ᵛ.
74 *The Song of Mary the Mother of Christ* (London: E. Allde for William Ferbrand, 1601), sigs. A4ᵛ–B1.
75 *Ibid.*, sig. B1.
76 *Ibid.*, sig. B3ᵛ.
77 R[obert] P[arsons], *The Christian Directory* (n.p., 1607), sigs. Y7 ff.
78 *Ibid.*, sigs. Y7ᵛ ff.
79 Richard Robinson, *The Vineyarde of Vertue* (London: Thomas Dawson, [1579?]), sig. B1.
80 *Ibid.*, sigs. B1ᵛ–2.
81 Hanmer, *The Auncient Ecclesiasticall Histories . . . of Eusebius, Socrates, and Evagrius*, sig. *2ᵛ.
82 *Ibid.*, sig. G6.
83 *Ibid.*, sig. L6ᵛ.
84 *Ibid.*, sig. M1.
85 *Ibid.*, sig. E5ᵛ.
86 Heinrich Bullinger, *The Tragedies of Tyrantes, Exercised upon the Church of God*, trans. Thomas Twine (London: W. How for A. Veale, 1575), sigs. A2–2ᵛ.
87 *Ibid.*, sig. C6ᵛ.
88 *Ibid.*, sig. D3ᵛ.
89 *Ibid.*, sigs. D5 ff.
90 *Ibid.*, sigs. E1–K8.
91 *Ibid.*, sig. L1.
92 *Ibid.*, sigs. M8ᵛ–N1.
93 *Ibid.*, sig. N1.
94 *Ibid.*, sigs. N2–3ᵛ.
95 *Ibid.*, sigs. N4ᵛ ff.
96 *Ibid.*, sigs. P7ᵛ ff.
97 *Ibid.*, sigs. Q1–2ᵛ.
98 *Ibid.*, sig. Q7ᵛ.
99 *Ibid.*, sigs. R3ᵛ–6ᵛ.
100 *Ibid.*, sigs. T1ᵛ–4.
101 [Jean Crespin], *The Estate of the Church*, trans. Simon Patricke (London: Thomas Creede, 1602), sig. A2.
102 F. Pijper, *Martelaarsboeken* (s-Gravenhage, 1924), pp. 5–7.
103 *Biographie Universelle* (Paris, 1813), X, 243.
104 [Crespin], *The Estate of the Church*, sig. B1.
105 *Ibid.*, sig. Nn4.
106 *Ibid.*, sigs. Ii7–8.
107 *Ibid.*, sig. Y8ᵛ.
108 *Ibid.*, sig. Ll7.
109 *Ibid.*, sig. F1.
110 *Ibid.*, sig. N4.
111 *Ibid.*, sigs. Nn1–2ᵛ.
112 *Ibid.*, sig. Zz5ᵛ.
113 Donald A. Stauffer, *English Biography before 1700* (Cambridge, Mass., 1930), p. 84.
114 Theodore de Beza, *A Discourse . . . Conteyning in Briefe the Historie of the Life and Death of Maister John Calvin*, trans. I. S. (London, 1564), sig. A2.
115 *Ibid.*, sigs. A4–6ᵛ.
116 *Ibid.*, sig. B4.
117 *Ibid.*, sigs. B4–4ᵛ.
118 *Ibid.*, sigs. B6–7.
119 *Ibid.*, sigs. B7ᵛ–8.
120 *Ibid.*, sigs. B8ᵛ–C1.
121 *Ibid.*, sigs. C2ᵛ–3.
122 *Ibid.*, sigs. C3ᵛ–4.
123 *Ibid.*, sig. C8.
124 *Ibid.*, sigs. D2ᵛ–E3.
125 See above, p. 14.
126 Andreas Hyperius [Gerardus], *The Practise of Preaching*, trans. John Ludham (London: Thomas East, 1577), sigs. Bb1–1ᵛ.
127 *Ibid.*, sigs. Bb4–5ᵛ.
128 *Ibid.*, sigs. Bb8ᵛ–Cc1ᵛ.
129 Greenham, *Works*, sig. A2.
130 *Ibid.*, sig. C6ᵛ.
131 *Ibid.*, sigs. A4ᵛ–5.
132 *Ibid.*, sig. A5ᵛ.
133 "The Life and Death of Master William Whittingham, Dean of Durham," ed. M. A. Everett Green, in William Whittingham, *A Briefe Discourse of the Troubles at Frankfort, 1554–1558 A.D.*, ed. Edward Arber (London, 1907), pp. 1–17.
134 *Ibid.*, pp. 11–12.
135 *Ibid.*, pp. 1–2.
136 *Ibid.*, pp. 2–4.
137 *Ibid.*, pp. 4–5.
138 *Ibid.*, pp. 10–11.
139 *Ibid.*, p. 12, Arber's note.
140 *Ibid.*, p. 12.

141 *Ibid.*, pp. 13–14.
142 *Ibid.*, p. 15.
143 *Ibid.*, p. 9.
144 *Ibid.*, p. 10.
145 *Ibid.*, pp. 16–17.
146 For example, Frederic E. Pamp, Jr., "Walton's Redaction of Hooker," *Church History*, XVII (1948), 95–116.
147 Laurence Humphrey, *J. Juelli Episcopi Sarisburiensis Vita* (London: apud J. Dayum, 1573), sigs. +2 ff.
148 *Ibid.*, sigs. B1–2ᵛ.
149 *Ibid.*, sig. B3.
150 *Ibid.*, sigs. Mm3ᵛ–Qq2ᵛ.
151 John Jewell, *The Works of . . . and a Briefe Discourse of His Life* [by D. Featley] (London: J. Norton, 1609), sigs. ¶¶1–6ᵛ.
152 *Ibid.*, sig. ¶¶1.
153 *Ibid.*, sigs. ¶¶1ᵛ–2.
154 *Ibid.*, sigs. ¶¶2–2ᵛ.
155 *Ibid.*, sigs. ¶¶2ᵛ–3.
156 *Ibid.*, sigs. ¶¶3–4.
157 *Ibid.*, sigs. ¶¶4–5.
158 *Ibid.*, sigs. ¶¶5–6.
159 Edith Weir Perry, *Under Four Tudors, being the story of Matthew Parker sometime Archbishop of Canterbury* (London, 1940), p. 242.
160 *Ibid.*, pp. 305–6.
161 John Josselin, *Historiola Collegii Corporis Christi*, ed. John Willis Clark for the Cambridge Antiquarian Society (Octavo Publications No. XVII [Cambridge, 1880]), p. 51.
162 [John Josselin], *The Life off the 70. Archbishopp of Canterbury Presentlye Sitting* ([Zurich: C. Froschauer?], 1574), sig. A2.
163 *Ibid.*, sig. A2ᵛ, and W. M. Kennedy, *Archbishop Parker* (London, 1908), p. 35.

164 [Josselin], *The Life off the 70. Archbishopp of Canterbury*, sigs. A2ᵛ–3.
165 *Ibid.*, sigs. A4ᵛ–5; see also Perry, *Under Four Tudors*, pp. 72 ff.
166 [Josselin], *The Life off the 70. Archbishopp of Canterbury*, sigs. A4ᵛ–5.
167 *Ibid.*, sigs. B3–4ᵛ.
168 *Ibid.*, sigs. A6–6ᵛ.
169 *Ibid.*, sigs. A7–B2.
170 *Ibid.*, sigs. C1–3.
171 *Ibid.*, sigs. A3–3ᵛ.
172 *Ibid.*, sigs. A7ᵛ–B1ᵛ.
173 *Ibid.*, sig. A5ᵛ.
174 *Ibid.*, sig. B8.
175 *Ibid.*, sigs. C4–D1.
176 *Ibid.*, sig. E2.
177 *Ibid.*, sigs. E5–6ᵛ.
178 F[rancis] G[odwin], *A Catalogue of the Bishops of England, since the First Planting of Christian Religion in This Island* (London: for George Bishop, 1601), sig. A3.
179 *Ibid.*
180 *Ibid.*, sigs. A2–2ᵛ.
181 *Ibid.*, sigs. D5ᵛ–6ᵛ.
182 *Ibid.*, sig. E1ᵛ.
183 *Ibid.*, sig. F2ᵛ.
184 *Ibid.*, sigs. A4–4ᵛ.
185 *Ibid.*, sig. Dd1ᵛ.
186 *Ibid.*, sig. K1.
187 *Ibid.*
188 *Ibid.*, sig. K1ᵛ.
189 *Ibid.*, sig. O1ᵛ.
190 *Ibid.*, sig. Dd2.
191 *The Dictionary of National Biography* (Oxford, 1937–38), VIII, 56–57.
192 G[odwin], *A Catalogue of the Bishops of England*, sig. Ee7.
193 *Ibid.*, sig. Bb7.
194 William Roper, *The Lyfe of Sir Thomas Moore, knighte*, ed. Elsie Vaughan Hitchcock (EETS, O.S., No. CXCVII [London, 1935]), p. 96.

BIBLIOGRAPHY

Primary

The Acts of the Pagan Martyrs, Acta Alexandrinorum. Edited by Herbert A. Musurillo. Oxford, 1954.

Adamnan. *Life of Saint Columba*. Edited by William Reeves. Edinburgh, 1874.

An Advertisement and Defense for Truth against her Backbiters, and especially against the Whispring Favourers, and Colourers of Campions, and the rest of his Confederats Treasons. N.p., 1581.

[Alfield, Thomas]. *A True Reporte of the Death and Martyrdome of M. Campion Jesuite and Preiste, and M. Sherwin, and M. Bryan Preistes, at Tiborne the First of December 1581*. [London: Richard Verstegan, 1581.]

Allen, William. *An Apologie and True Declaration of the Institution and Endevours of the Two English Colleges, the One in Rome, the Other Now Resident in Rhemes, . . .* Mounts in Henault [Rheims: John Fogny], 1581.

―――. *A Briefe Historie of the Glorious Martyrdom of Twelve Reverend Priests, Father Edmund Campion and His Companions*. Edited by J. H. Pollen. London, 1908.

[Allen, William]. *A True Sincere and Modest Defence, of English Catholiques that Suffer for their Faith both at Home and Abrode*. [Rouen, 1584.]

The Ancrene Riwle, The English Text of. Cotton MS Nero A. XIV. Edited by Mabel Day. (Early English Text Society, O.S., No. CCXXV.) London, 1952.

An Answeare for the Time, unto that Foule and Wicked Defence of the Censure, that was given upon M. Charkes Booke, and Meredith Hanmers. . . . London: Thomas Dawson and Tobie Smith, 1583.

Articles devised by the Kynges Highnes Majestie, to stablyshe Christen Quietnes and Unitie amonge us. N.p., 1536.

Articles to be enquired of in the Visitation, in the First yeere of the Raign of our most dread Soveraign Ladie Elizabeth . . . 1559. London: Robert Barker, 1600.

349

Athanasius, St. *The Life of Saint Antony.* Translated by Robert T. Meyer. (Ancient Christian Writers, No. 10.) Westminster, Md., 1950.

The Auncient Ecclesiasticall Histories of the First Six Hundred Yeares after Christ, wrytten in the Greeke tongue by three learned Historiographers, Eusebius, Socrates, and Evagrius, . . . translated out of the Greeke tongue by Meredith Hanmer. London: Thomas Vautrollier, 1577.

Ba., Ro. *The Lyfe of Syr Thomas More, Sometymes Lord Chancellor of England.* Edited by Elsie Vaughan Hitchcock and P. E. Hallett, with additional notes and Appendices by A. W. Reed. (Early English Text Society, O.S., No. CCXXII.) London, 1950.

Baily, Tho[mas]. *The Life and Death of That Renowned John Fisher Bishop of Rochester.* London: [no printer], 1655.

Bede, The Venerable. *The History of the Church of England.* Translated by Thomas Stapleton. Antwerp: John Laet, 1565.

———. *Venerabilis Bedae Opera Quae Supersunt Omnia, Nunc Primum in Anglia.* . . . Edited by J. A. Giles. 12 vols. London, 1863.

Beza, Theodore de. *A Discourse . . . Conteyning in Briefe the Historie of the Life and Death of Maister John Calvin.* Translated by I. S. London, 1564.

The Bible and Holy Scriptures conteyned in the Olde and New Testament. Geneva: Rouland Hall, 1560.

[Bonaventura, St.]. "Life of Saint Francis," in *"The Little Flowers" and the Life of Saint Francis with the "Mirror of Perfection."* Introduction by Thomas Okey. London, 1917.

A Booke containing All Such Proclamations as were published during the Raigne of the late Queene Elizabeth, collected . . . by Humfrey Dyson. London: Bonham Norton and John Bill, 1618.

The Booke of the Common Prayer and Administracion of the Sacramentes, and other Rites and Ceremonies of the Churche: after the Use of the Churche of England. London: Edouardi Whitchurche, March 7, 1549.

[Bradshaw, Henry]. *The Lyfe of Saynt Radegunde.* London: Rycharde Pynson, [1521?].

[*St. Brandan: A Medieval Legend of the Sea.* Edited by Thomas Wright. (Percy Society, No. XIV.) London, 1844.

Breton, Nicholas. *Auspicante Jehova. Maries Exercise.* London: Thomas Este, 1597.

[Breton, Nicholas]. *Marie Magdalens Love.* London: John Danter for William Barley, 1595.

Brice, Thomas. *A Compendious Register in Metre,* . . . London: Jhon Kyngston for Richard Adams, 1559.

B[roxup], W[illiam]. *Saint Peters Path to the Joyes of Heaven.* London: Felix Kingston, 1598.

Bullinger, Heinrich. *The Tragedies of Tyrantes, Exercised upon the Church of God.* Translated by Thomas Twine. London: W. How for A. Veale, 1575.

Calvin, John. *A Very Profitable Treatise,* . . . Translated by Steven Wythers. London: Rouland Hall, 1561.

Campian Englished, or a Translation of the Ten Reasons, . . . N.p., [1632].

Campion, Edmund. *Ten Reasons proposed to his Adversaries in the Name of the Faith and presented to the Illustrious Members of Our Universities.* London, 1914.

Caxton, William, trans. *The Golden Legende.* Westmestre: Wylyam Caxton, November 20, 1483.

——. *The Golden Legende.* Westmestre: Wyllyam Caxton, May 20, 1493.

——. *The Golden Legende.* Westminster: Wynkyn de Worde, 1498.

Certayne Sermons or Homilies, appoynted by the Kynges Majestie. London: Richard Grafton, 1547.

C[hambers], R[obert]. *Palestina.* Florence: Bartelmew Sermatelli, 1600.

Charke, William. *An Answere to a Seditious Pamphlet lately cast abroade by a Jesuite, with a Discoverie of that Blasphemous Sect.* London: Christopher Barker, December 17, 1580.

——. *A Replie to a Censure written against the Two Answers to a Jesuites Seditious Pamphlet.* London: Christopher Barker, 1581.

Chaucer, Geoffrey. *Complete Works.* Edited by F. N. Robinson. Boston, 1933.

Chauncy, Dom Maurice. *The History of the Sufferings of Eighteen Carthusians in England, Who Refusing to Take Part in Schism, and to Separate Themselves from the Unity of the Catholic Church, were Cruelly Martyred.* Translated by a Professed Member of the London Charter House. London and New York, 1890.

Concertatio Ecclesiæ Catholicæ in Anglia, adversus Calvinopapistas et Puritanos. Augustæ Trevirorum: apud Edmundum Hatotum, 1583.

Concertatio Ecclesiæ Catholicæ in Anglia adversus Calvinopapistas et Puritanos sub Elizabetha Regina. Augustæ Trevirorum: Henricus Bock, 1588.

The Copie of a Double Letter sent by an Englishe Gentilman from beyond the Seas, to his Frende in London, containing the true advises of the cause, and maner of the death, of one Richard Atkins, executed by Fire in Rome, the seconde of August 1581. N.p., n.d.

[Crespin, Jean]. *The Estate of the Church.* Translated by Simon Patricke. London: Thomas Creede, 1602.

Crotch, W. J. B., ed. *The Prologues and Epilogues of William Caxton.* (Early English Text Society, O.S., No. CLXXVI.) London, 1928.

Crypian, St. *The Lapsed, The Unity of the Catholic Church.* Translated by Maurice Bévenot. (Ancient Christian Writers, No. 25.) Westminster, Md., and London, 1957.

——. *The Writings of Cyprian, Bishop of Carthage.* Translated by Robert Ernest Wallis. (Ante-Nicene Christian Library.) 2 vols. Edinburgh, 1876–80.

Diarium Rerum Gestarum in Turri Londiniensi, in Nicholas Sanders, *De Origine ac Progressu Schismatis Anglicani.* Ingolstadii: ex officina Typographica Wolfgangi Ederi, 1587.

Drayton, Michael. *Moyses in a Map of His Miracles.* London: Humfrey Lownes for Thomas Man the Younger, 1604.

Du Bartas, Guillaume de Saluste. *The Historie of Judith in Forme of a Poeme.* Translated by Thomas Hudson. Edinburgh: T. Vautroullier, 1584.

Dury, John. *Confutatio responsionis Guilielmi Whitakeri ad Rationes Decem.* Parisiis, 1582.

Edmundi Campiani Jesuitæ Rationes Decem . . . Guilielmi Whitakeri . . . Responsio. Antverpiæ: Aegidius Radaeus, 1582.

Ellyot, George. *A Very True Report of the Apprehension and Taking of that Arche Papist Edmond Campion the Pope his Right Hand. . . .* London: Thomas Dawson, 1581.

The Epistles of St. Clement of Rome and St. Ignatius of Antioch. Translated by James A. Kleist. (Ancient Christian Writers, No. 1.) Westminster, Md., 1949.

Erasmus, Desiderius. *A Booke called in Latyn Enchiridion Militis Christiani and in Englysshe the Manuell of the Christen Knyght.* London: Wynkyn de Worde for Johan Byddell, Nov. 15, 1533.

———. *A Dialoge or Communication of Two Persons.* N.p., n.d. [1536–37].

———. *The Epistles.* Translated by Francis Morgan Nichols. Vol. III. 3 vols. London, 1901–18.

———. *In Praise of Folly.* London, 1951.

———. *Ten Colloquies.* Translated by Craig R. Thompson. (Library of Liberal Arts.) New York, 1957.

Eusebius Pamphili. *Ecclesiastical History.* Translated by Roy J. Deferrari. (The Fathers of the Church, No. XIX.) 2 vols. New York, 1953.

Foxe, John. *Actes and Monuments. . . .* London: John Day, March 20, 1563.

Fyssher, John. *A Spirituall Consolation . . . to hys sister Elizabeth.* N.p., n.d.

[Gerardus], Andreas Hyperius. *The Practise of Preaching.* Translated by John Ludham. London: Thomas East, 1577.

Gilbart, Thomas. *A Declaration of the Death of John Lewes, a Most Detestable and Obstinate Hereticke, Burned at Norwich the xviii, daye of September 1583 aboute Three of the Clocke in the Afternoone. To the Tune, of John Carelesse.* London: Richard Jones, October 8, 1583.

G[odwin], F[rancis]. *A Catalogue of the Bishops of England, since the First Planting of Christian Religion in This Island.* London: for George Bishop, 1601.

Greenham, Richard. *The Works of Richard Greenham.* Edited by H[enry] H[olland]. London: Felix Kingston for Ralph Jacson, 1599.

Halle, Edward. *The Union of the Two Noble and Illustrate Famelies of Lancastre and Yorke . . . with All the Actes done in Bothe the Tymes of the Princes, Bothe of the One Linage and of the Other. . . .* London: Richard Grafton, 1548.

Hanmer, Meredith. *The Great Bragge and Challenge of M. Champion a Jesuite, commonlye called Edmunde Campion . . . confuted and aunswered.* London: Thomas Marsh, 1581.

Harpsfield, Nicholas. *The Life and Death of Sᵣ Thomas Moore, knight, sometymes Lord high Chancellor of England.* Edited by Elsie Vaughan Hitchcock. (Early English Text Society, O.S., No. CLXXXVI.) London, 1932.

Hide, Thomas. *A Consolatorie Epistle to the Afflicted Catholikes.* Lovaine: John Maes for John Lion, 1579.

The Historie of Ireland. Collected by Meredith Hanmer, Edmund Campian, and Edmund Spenser. Dublin: Societie of Stationers, 1633.

Hore Beatissime Virginis Marie ad Legitimum Sarisburiensis Ecclesie Ritum. Paris: à Francisco Regnault, 1527.

Humphrey, Laurence. *J. Juelli Episcopi Sarisburiensis Vita.* London: ap. J. Dayum, 1573.

Ignatius of Loyola, St. *The Spiritual Exercises.* Translated by W. H. Longridge. London and Oxford, 1950.

Injunctions for the Clerge. London: [T. Berthelet], 1538.

Injunctions gyven by Thauctoritie of the Kynges Highnes to the Clergie of this his Realme. London: Thomas Berthelet, 1536.

The Institution of a Christen Man. London: Thomas Berthelet, 1537.

Jacobus de Voragine. *The Golden Legend.* Translated and adapted by Granger Ryan and Helmut Ripperger. London and New York, 1941.

——. *Liber preclarissimi religiosi fratris Jacobi de Voragine ordinis predicatorum de Vitis Sanctorum.* Venetiis: per Christoforum Arnoldum, 1477.

Jewell, John. *The Works of . . . and a Briefe Discourse of His Life* [by D. Featley]. London: J. Norton, 1609.

John Damascene, St. *Barlaam and Ioasaph.* Translated by G. R. Woodward and H. Mattingly. (Loeb Classical Library.) London and New York, 1914.

John of Salisbury. "Vita Sancti Thomae Cantuarensis Archiepiscopi et Martyris," in *Materials for the History of Thomas Becket, Archbishop of Canterbury.* Edited by James Craigie Robertson. (Rerum Britannicarum Medii Aevi Scriptores, Vol. II.) London, 1876.

[Johnson, Richard]. *The Most Famous History of the Seaven Champions of Christendome.* London: for Cuthbert Burbie, 1596.

Josselin, John. *Historiola Collegii Corporis Christi.* Edited by John Willis Clark for the Cambridge Antiquarian Society. (Octavo Publications, No. XVII.) Cambridge, 1880.

[Josselin, John]. *The Life off the 70. Archbishopp of Canterbury Presentlye Sittinge.* [Zurich: C. Froschauer?], 1574.

J[oye], G[eorge]. *A Present Consolation for the Sufferers of Persecucion for Ryghtwysenes.* N.p., September, 1544.

Keltridge, John. *Two Godlie and Learned Sermons, appointed and preached, before the Jesuites, Seminaries, and Other Adversaries of the Gospel of Christ in the Tower of London . . . May 7 and 21, 1581.* London: Richard Jones, [1581].

Laing, James. *De vita et Moribus Theodori Bezae, omnium haer[e]ticorum nostri temporis facilè principis . . . cui adiectus est libellus, de morte Patris Edmundi Campionis, et aliorum quorundam Catholicorum, qui in Anglia pro fide Catholica interfecti fuerunt primo die Decembris. Anno domini. 1581.* Parisiis: apud Michaelem de Roigny, 1585.

"The Legend or Life of St. Alexius," in *Adam Davy's 5 Dreams about Edward II, The Life of St. Alexius. . . .* Edited from Laud MS 622, Bodleian, by F. J. Furnivall. (Early English Text Society, O.S., No. LXIX.) London, 1878.

The Life and Death of Mr. Edmund Geninges, Priest. S. Omers: Charles Boscard, 1614.

A Litel Treatise ageynste the Mutterynge of Some Papistis in Corners. London: Thomas Berthelet, 1534.

Malory, Sir Thomas. *The Works of Sir Thomas Malory.* Edited by Eugene Vinaver. 3 vols. Oxford, 1947.

Marbecke, John. *The Lyves of Holy Sainctes, Prophetes, Patriarches, and Others, Contayned in Holye Scripture.* London: [H. Denham and R. Watkins], 1574.

Marie Magdalens Lamentations for the Losse of Her Master Jesus. London: Adam Islip for Edward White, 1601.

M[arkham], J. [Gervase]. *The Teares of the Beloved.* London: Simon Stafford for John Browne, 1600.

Martin, Gregorie. *A Treatise of Schisme, Shewing, that al Catholikes ought in any wise to abstaine altogether from heretical Conventicles. . . .* Duaci: apud Johannem Foulerum, 1578.

Mirk, John. *The Festyvall.* London: Wynkyn de Worde, October 23, 1532.

More, Sir Thomas. *A Dialoge of Comfort against Tribulacion.* [London: Richarde Tottel, Nov. 18, 1553].

M[unday], A[nthony]. *A Discoverie of Edmund Campion, and his Confederates, their Most Horrible and Traiterous Practices, against her Majesties Most Royall Person, and the Realme.* London: for Edwarde White, January, 25, 1582.

[Munday, Anthony]. *A True Report, of the Araignement and Execution of the Late Popishe Traitour, Evered Haunce.* London: Henrie Bynneman, 1581.

A Necessary Doctrine and Erudition for any Chrysten Man. . . . London: John Mayler, 1543.

A Necessary Doctrine and Erudition for any Chrysten man, set furth by the Kynges Majestye of Englande. . . . London: Thomas Berthelet, May 29, 1543.

[Nowell, Alexander, and William Day]. *A True Report of the Disputation or rather Private Conference had in the Tower of London, with Ed. Campion Jesuite, the last of August, 1581.* London: Christopher Barker, January 1, 1584.

Origen. *Prayer, Exhortation to Martyrdom.* Translated by John J. O'Meara. (Ancient Christian Writers, No. 19.) Westminster, Md., and London, 1954.

Origen, ascribed to. *Dialogismus sive Colloquium D. Mariæ Magdalenæ cum Christo Domino redivivo, Origeni hactenus adscripta homilia; studio nunc M. Joan. Cræssellii . . . Soliloquiis Thomæ à Kempis meritò adjuncta.* N.p., n.d. [1604?].

———. *Omelia Origenis de Beata Maria Magdalena.* London: ad rogatum Magistri Will'm Menyman socii collegii Ricardi Whityngton, [1504?].

Our Ladie hath a New Sonne. Dowaie: [no printer], 1595.

Palladius, Hieronymus, and others. *The Book of Paradise, being the Histories and Sayings of the Monks and Ascetics of the Egyptian Desert.* Translated by E. A. Wallis Budge. 2 vols. London, 1904.

Parsons, R[obert]. *A Brief, and Cleere Confutation of a New, Vaine, and Vaunting Challenge made by O. E. Minister, unto N. D.* N.p., 1604.

[Parsons, Robert]. *A Brief Censure uppon Two Bookes written in Answere to M. Edmonde Campions Offer of Disputation.* Doway: John Lyon, 1581.

[Parsons, Robert]. *A Brief Discours contayning certayne Reasons why Catholiques refuse to goe to Church.* Doway: John Lyon, 1580.

P[arsons], R[obert]. *The Christian Directory.* N.p., 1607.

[Parsons, Robert]. *A Declaration of the True Causes of the Great Troubles, Presupposed to be Intended against the Realme of England.* N.p., 1592.

[Parsons, Robert]. *A Defence of the Censure gyven upon Two Bookes of William Charke and Meredith Hanmer Mynysters, whiche they wrote against M. Edmond Campian Preest, of the Societie of Jesus, and against his Offer of Disputation.* N.p., 1582.

[Parsons, Robert]. *An Epistle of the Persecution of Catholickes in England.* Doway: G. T., [1582?].

Partridge, John. *The Worthie Hystorie of the Most Noble and Valiaunt Knight Plasidas, otherwise called Eustas, Who, was Martyred for the Profession of Jesus Christ.* London: Henrye Denham for Thomas Hacket, 1566.

Passio XVIII. Carthusianorum in regno Anglie, . . . , in *Historia Aliquot Nostri Saeculi Martyrum.* Moguntiae: Franciscus Behem, 1550.

Pecock, Reginald. *The Repressor of Over Much Blaming of the Clergy.* Edited by Churchill Babington. 2 vols. London, 1860.

Pettie, George. *A Petite Pallace of Pettie His Pleasure.* Edited by Herbert Hartman. London and New York, 1938.

Philopatrus, Andreas [Robert Parsons]. *Elizabethæ Angliæ Reginæ Hæresin Calviniam Propugnantis, Sævissimum in Catholicos sui regni Edictum.* Lugduni: apud Joannem Didier, 1592.

Plato. *The Republic,* in *The Dialogues of Plato,* translated by B. Jowett. 5 vols. Oxford, 1924.

Politique Discourses, treating of the Differences and Inequalities of Vocations, as well Publique, as Private. Translated by Aegremont Ratcliffe. London: for Edward Aggas, 1578.

Polycarp, St. *The Epistles and the Martyrdom of St. Polycarp.* Translated by James A. Kleist. (Ancient Christian Writers, No. 6.) Westminster, Md., 1948.

A Proclamation against Breakinge or Defacing of Monumentes of Antiquitie, beyng set up in Churches or other Publique Places for Memory, and not for Supersticion. London: Richarde Jugge and John Cawood, Sept. 19, 1560.

Raymond de Capoue, B. *Vie de Sainte Catherine de Sienne.* 2 vols. Paris, 1877.

Robinson, Richard. *A Record of Ancient Histories, entituled in Latin: Gesta Romanorum.* London: Thomas Snodham, [1610?].

———. *The Vineyarde of Vertue.* London: Thomas Dawson, [1579?].

Roper, William. *The Lyfe of Sir Thomas Moore, knighte.* Edited by Elsie Vaughan Hitchcock. (Early English Text Society, O.S., No. CXCVII.) London, 1935.

[Roper, William]. *The Mirrour of Vertue in Worldly Greatnes. Or the Life of Syr Thomas More Knight.* Paris: [no printer], 1626.

S., M. *The Araignement, and Execution of a Wilfull and Obstinate Traitour, named Everalde Ducket, alias Hauns.* London: John Charlewood and Edward White, 1581.

Saint Peters Ten Teares. London: G. Simson for W. Jones, 1597.

Sander, Nicholas. *Rise and Growth of the Anglican Schism.* Translated by David Lewis. London, 1877.

The Seconde Tome of Homelyes. London: Richard Jugge and John Cawood, 1563.

Shirley, Elizabeth. "The Life of Our Rev. Old Mother Margaret Clement," in *The Troubles of Our Catholic Forefathers Related by Themselves.* First Ser., edited by John Morris. London, 1872.

Smith, Richard "The Life of the Lady Magdalen Viscountess Montague," in *An Elizabethan Recusant House,* edited by A. C. Southern. London, 1954.

The Song of Mary the Mother of Christ. London: E. Allde for William Ferbrand, 1601.

[Southwell, Robert]. *An Epistle of Comfort, to the Reverend Priestes, and to the Honorable, Worshipful, and Other of Laye Sort restrayned in Durance for the Catholicke Fayth.* Paris, n.d. [Douai?, 1604?].

Southwell, Robert. *An Humble Supplication to her Majestie.* Edited by R. C. Bald. Cambridge, 1953.

[Southwell, Robert]. *Marie Magdalens Funeral Teares.* London: J. [Wolfe] for G. C[awood], 1591.

S[outhwell], R[obert]. *Mœoniæ, or Certaine Excellent Poems and Spirituall Hymnes.* London: Valentine Sims for John Busbie, 1595.

[Southwell, Robert]. *Saint Peters Complaint, with Other Poems.* London: John Wolfe, 1595.

[Southwell, Robert]. *Saint Peters Complaynt, with Other Poems,* London: J. R. for G. C. [James Roberts for Gabriel Cawood], 1595.

[Southwell, Robert]. *A Short Rule of Good Life.* S. Omers: J. Heigham, 1622.

S[outhwell], R[obert]. *The Triumphs over Death.* London: V[alentine] S[ims] for John Busbie, 1595.

Stapleton, Thomas. *The Life and Illustrious Martyrdom of Sir Thomas More, Formerly Lord Chancellor of England. Part III of "Tres Thomae," printed at Douai, 1588.* Translated by Philip E. Hallett. London, 1928.

Sulpicii Severi Libri qui Supersunt. Edited by Karl Halm. (Corpus Ecclesiasticorum Latinorum, Vol. I.) Vindobonae, 1866.

Surius, Laurentius. *De Probatis Sanctorum Historiis. . . . Tom I.* Coloniæ Agrippinæ: apud Gervinum Calenium et hæredes Quentelios, 1570.

Tertullianus, Quintus Sept. Flor. *The Writings of . . . Tertullianus.* Translated by R. S. Thelwall and Dr. Holmes. Vol. I. (Ante-Nicene Christian Library.) 3 vols. Edinburgh, 1869–70.

Van Ortroy, Fr[anciscus], ed. *A Treatis Contayninge the Lyfe and Maner of Death of that Most Holy Prelat and Constant Martyr of Christ John Fysher Byshop of Rochester and Cardinale of the Holy Church of Rome,* in *Vie du Bienheureux Martyr Jean Fisher Cardinal, Évêque de Rochester* (†*1535*): *Texte Anglais et Traduction Latine du XVIᵉ siècle.* Extrait des *Analecta Bollandiana,* X (1891), et XII (1893). Bruxelles, 1893.

Vives, Juan Luis. *On Education.* (*De Tradendis Disciplinis.*) Translated by Foster Watson. Cambridge, 1943.

Whitaker, William. *Ad Rationes Decem E. Campiani, . . . Responsio.* London: T. Vautrollier for T. Chard, 1581.

———. *An Answere to the Ten Reasons of Edmund Campian the Jesuit.* Translated by Richard Stocke. London: Felix Kyngston for Cuthbert Burby and Edmund Weaver, 1606.

———. *Edmundi Campianae Jesuitae Rationes Decem . . . Guilielmi Whitakeri . . . Responsio.* Antverpiae: Aegidius Radaeus, 1582.

———. *Responsionis ad Decem illas Rationes quibus fretus E. Campianus Defensio.* London: T. Vautrollier for T. Chard, 1581.

———. *Responsionis ad Decem Rationes quibus fretus E. Campianus Defensio.* London: H. Midleton for T. Chard, 1583.

White, Tristram. *The Martyrdome of Saint George of Cappadocia.* London: T. [Snodham] for William Barley, 1614.

Whittingham, William. "The Life and Death of Master William Whittingham, Dean of Durham," edited by M. A. Everett Green, in William Whittingham, *A Briefe Discourse of the Troubles at Frankfort, 1554–1558 A.D.* Edited by Edward Arber. London, 1907.

Wilkinson, William. *A Confutation of Certaine Articles delivered unto the Familye of Love.* London: John Daye, 1579.

W[ilson], J[ohn]. *The English Martyrologe.* St. Omer, 1608.

Worthington, Thomas. *Relation of Sixtene Martyrs Glorified in England in Twelve Monethes.* Doway: the Widow of James Boscard, 1601.

Secondary (Selected)

Aigrain, René. *L'Hagiographie: ses sources, ses méthodes, son histoire.* Paris, 1953.

Albright, Evelyn May. *Dramatic Publication in England, 1580–1640.* New York and London, 1927.

Allard, Paul. *Dix Leçons sur le Martyre.* Paris, 1907.

Allison, A. F., and D. M. Rogers. *A Catalogue of Catholic Books in English Printed Abroad or Secretly in England, 1558–1640,* in *Biographical Studies,* Vol. III, No. 3. Bognor Regis, 1956.

———. Review of A. C. Southern, *Elizabethan Recusant Prose: 1559–1582,* in *The Library,* 5th Ser., VI (1951), 48–57.

Auclair, Marcelle. *Saint Teresa of Avila*. Translated by Kathleen Pond. New York, 1953.

Aurner, Nellie Slayton. *Caxton, Mirrour of Fifteenth-Century Letters*. Iowa City, 1926.

Bartoli, Daniel. *Histoire de Saint Ignace de Loyola et de la Compagnie de Jesus*. 2 vols. Paris, 1844.

Bennet, Josephine Waters. "Genre, Milieu, and the 'Epic-Romance,'" in *English Institute Essays, 1951*, edited by Alan S. Downer. New York, 1952.

Bett, Henry. *Nicholas of Cusa*. London, 1932.

Bouyer, Louis. *Erasmus and the Humanist Experiment*. London, 1959.

Butler, Pierce. *Legenda Aurea — Légende Dorée — Golden Legend: A Study of Caxton's Golden Legend with Special Reference to its Relations to the Earlier English Prose Translation*. Baltimore, Md., 1899.

Butterworth, Charles C. *The English Primers (1529-1545)*. Philadelphia, 1953.

———. *The Literary Lineage of the King James Bible, 1340-1611*. Philadelphia, 1941.

Chambers, R. W. "Life and Works of Nicholas Harpsfield," in Nicholas Harpsfield, *The Life and Death of Sr Thomas Moore* . . . , edited by Elsie Vaughan Hitchcock. Early English Text Society, O.S., No. CLXXXVI. London, 1932.

———. Introduction, "The Continuity of English Prose from Alfred to More and his School," in Nicholas Harpsfield, *The Life and Death of Sr Thomas Moore* . . . , edited by Elsie Vaughan Hitchcock. Early English Text Society, O.S., No. CLXXXVI. London, 1932.

———. *Thomas More*. London, 1949.

Collins, Joseph B. Introduction to *The Roman Martyrology*. Westminster, Md., 1946.

Daniel-Rops, H[enri]. *The Church of Apostles and Martyrs*. Translated by Audrey Butler. London and New York, 1960.

Delehaye, Hippolyte. *Les Origines du Culte des Martyrs*. Bruxelles, 1912.

———. *Les Passions des Martyrs et les Genres Littéraires*. Bruxelles, 1921.

———. *The Legends of the Saints, an Introduction to Hagiography*. Translated by V. M. Crawford. London, 1907.

———. *L'Oeuvre des Bollandistes, 1615-1915*. Bruxelles, 1920.

Devlin, Christopher. *The Life of Robert Southwell, Poet and Martyr*. London, New York, Toronto, 1956.

———. "The Patriotism of Robert Southwell," *The Month*, N.S. Vol X (1953), No. 5, pp. 345-54.

De Vocht, Henry. *Acta Thomae Mori: History of the Reports of His Trial and Death with an Unedited Contemporary Narrative*. Louvain, 1947.

———. *The Earliest English Translations of Erasmus' Colloquia, 1536-1566*. Louvain and London, 1928.

Dickens, A. G. "Aspects of Intellectual Transition among the Parish Clergy of the Reformation Period: A Regional Example," *Archiv f. Reformationsgeschichte*, XLIII (1952), 51-69.

Douillet, Jacques. *What is a Saint?* Translated by Donald Attwater. *Twentieth Century Encyclopedia of Catholicism*, Vol. XLVI. New York, 1958.

Dudden, F. Homes. *The Life and Times of St. Ambrose.* 2 vols. Oxford, 1935.

Duff, E. Gordon. *Fifteenth-Century English Books.* Oxford: The Bibliographical Society, 1917.

Ellis, F. S. Introduction to *The Golden Legend; or, Lives of the Saints, as Englished by William Caxton.* 7 vols. London, 1900.

Festugière, A. J. *La Sainteté.* Paris, 1942.

Gee, Henry. *The Elizabethan Prayer-Book and Ornaments.* London, 1902.

Gerould, Gordon Hall. *Saints' Legends.* Boston and New York, 1916.

Günter, Heinrich. *Die Christliche Legende des Abendlandes.* Heidelberg, 1910.

Haile, Martin. *An Elizabethan Cardinal, William Allen.* London, 1914.

Haller, William. "John Foxe and the Puritan Revolution," in Richard Foster Jones et al., *The Seventeenth Century: Studies in the History of English Thought and Literature from Bacon to Pope.* Stanford, 1951.

Hawkes, Arthur J. "The Birchley Hall Secret Press," *The Library,* 4th Ser., VII (1926–27), 137–83.

Herrtage, Sidney J. H., ed. *The Early English Versions of the Gesta Romanorum.* Early English Text Society, E.S., No. XXXIII. London, 1879; reprinted 1932.

Hicks, L. *Letters and Memorials of Father Robert Parsons, S.J.* Vol. I. Catholic Record Society, Vol. XXXIX. London, 1942.

Hogrefe, Pearl. *The Sir Thomas More Circle.* Urbana, Ill., 1959.

Hügel, Baron Friedrich von. *The Mystical Element of Religion as Studied in Saint Catherine of Genoa and Her Friends.* 2 vols. London, 1909.

Hughes, Philip. *A History of the Church.* 3 vols. New York, 1949.

——. *The Reformation in England.* 3 vols. London, 1950–54.

——. *Rome and the Counter-Reformation in England.* London, 1944.

Hummel, Edelhard L. *The Concept of Martyrdom according to St. Cyprian of Carthage.* Washington, D.C., 1946.

Janelle, Pierre. *The Catholic Reformation.* Milwaukee, 1951.

——. *Robert Southwell the Writer.* Clermont-Ferrand, 1935.

Jeremy, Sister Mary. "Caxton's *Golden Legend* and Varagine's *Legenda Aurea,*" *Speculum,* XXI (1946), 212–21.

——. "The English Prose Translation of *Legenda Aurea,*" *Modern Language Notes,* LIX (1944), 181–83.

Jessopp, Augustus. *One Generation of a Norfolk House: A Contribution to Elizabethan History.* London, 1879.

Jones, Charles W. *Saints' Lives and Chronicles in Early England.* Ithaca, N.Y., 1947.

Jungmann, Josef A. *The Early Liturgy: To the Time of Gregory the Great.* Translated by Francis A. Brunner. Notre Dame, Ind., 1959.

Kapp, Rudolf, *Heilige und Heiligenlegenden: Studien zum 16. und 17. Jahrhundert.* Vol. I. Halle Saale, 1934.

Kennedy, Charles W. *Early English Christian Poetry.* New York, 1952.

Kennedy, V. L. *The Saints of the Canon of the Mass.* Città del Vaticano, 1938.

Kennedy, W. M. *Archbishop Parker.* London, 1908.

Kidd, B. J. *The Counter-Reformation, 1550–1600.* London: Society for Promoting Christian Knowledge, 1933.

Klein, Edward J. Introduction to *The Imitation of Christ*, translated by Richard Whitford. New York and London, 1941.

Knappen, M. M. *Tudor Puritanism: A Chapter in the History of Idealism.* Chicago, 1939.

Loomis, C. Grant. *White Magic, an Introduction to the Folklore of Christian Legend.* Cambridge, Mass., 1948.

MacCulloch, J. A. *Medieval Faith and Fable.* London, 1932.

McDonald, James H. *The Poems and Prose Writings of Robert Southwell, S.J.: A Bibliographical Study.* Oxford: for the Roxburghe Club, 1937.

McGuire, Martin R. P. "The Christian Funeral Oration," Introduction to *Funeral Orations by Saint Gregory Nazianzen and Saint Ambrose.* New York, 1953.

Mackie, J. D. *The Earlier Tudors, 1485–1558.* Oxford, 1952.

Maclure, Millar. *The Paul's Cross Sermons, 1534–1642.* (University of Toronto Department of English Studies and Texts, No. VI.) Toronto, 1958.

Mâle, Émile. *L'Art Religieux du XIIIe Siècle en France.* Paris, 1898.

Martz, Louis L. *The Poetry of Meditation.* New Haven and London, 1954.

Mathew, David. *Catholicism in England, 1535–1935.* London and New York, 1936.

————. *The Celtic Peoples and Renaissance Europe.* London and New York, 1933.

————, and Gervase Mathew. *The Reformation and the Contemplative Life.* London, 1934.

Mecklin, John M. *The Passing of the Saint.* Chicago, [1941].

Mozley, J. F. *John Foxe and His Book.* London: Society for Promoting Christian Knowledge, [1940].

Nock, A. D. *Conversion: The Old and the New in Religion from Alexander the Great to Augustine of Hippo.* Oxford, 1933.

Oliver, Leslie M. "The Seventh Edition of John Foxe's *Acts and Monuments*," *Papers of the Bibliographical Society of America*, XXXVII (1943), 243–60.

Owen, E. C. E. General Introduction to *Some Authentic Acts of the Early Martyrs.* London: Society for Promoting Christian Knowledge, 1933.

Pamp, Frederic E., Jr. "Walton's Redaction of Hooker," *Church History*, XVII (1948), 95–116.

Pearson, A. F. Scott. *Church and State.* Cambridge, 1928.

Perry, Edith Weir. *Under Four Tudors, being the story of Matthew Parker sometime Archbishop of Canterbury.* London, 1940.

Pijper, F. *Martelaarsboeken.* s-Gravenhage, 1924.

Plomer, Henry R. *William Caxton (1424–1491).* London, 1925.

Pollen, John Hungerford, ed. *Unpublished Documents relating to the English Martyrs, Vol. I, 1594–1603.* Catholic Record Society, Vol. V. London, 1908.

Poncelet, Albert. "Le Légendier de Pierre Calo," *Analecta Bollandiana*, XXIX (1910), 5–116.

Read, Conyers. *Mr. Secretary Cecil and Queen Elizabeth*. New York, 1955.

Reynolds, E. E. *Saint John Fisher*. London, 1955.

Robertson, Jean. Introduction to *Poems by Nicholas Breton*. Liverpool, 1952.

Rupp, Gordon. *Six Makers of English Religion, 1500–1700*. London, 1957.

Saintyves, P. [E. Nourry]. *En Marge de la Légende Dorée: songes, miracles et survivances*. Paris, 1930.

Seybolt, Robert Francis. "The 'Legenda Aurea,' Bible, and 'Historia Scholastica,'" *Speculum*, XXI (1946), 339–42.

Sherman, James Edward. *The Nature of Martyrdom*. Paterson, N.J., 1942.

Simpson, Richard. *Edmund Campion: a Biography*. London, 1896.

Southern, A. C. *Elizabethan Recusant Prose, 1559–1582*. London and Glasgow, [1950].

Stauffer, Donald A. *English Biography before 1700*. Cambridge, Mass., 1930.

Sylvester, R. S., and D. P. Harding, eds. *Two Early Tudor Lives: Cavendish's Wolsey and Roper's More*. New Haven and London, 1962.

Thompson, E. Margaret. *The Carthusian Order in England*. London: Society for Promoting Christian Knowledge, 1930.

Turner, Celeste. *Anthony Mundy, an Elizabethan Man of Letters*. (University of California Publications in English, Vol. II.) Berkeley, 1928.

Veech, Thomas McNevin. *Dr. Nicholas Sanders and the English Reformation, 1530–1581*. Louvain, 1935.

Wakeman, Henry Offley, rev. S. L. Ollard. *An Introduction to the History of the Church of England*. London, 1927.

Waugh, Evelyn. *Edmund Campion*. London, 1947.

Weisinger, Herbert. "The Renaissance Theory of the Reaction against the Middle Ages as a Cause of the Renaissance," *Speculum*, XX (1945), 461–67.

White, Helen C. *English Devotional Literature (Prose) 1600–1640*. Madison, Wis., 1931.

————. *The Tudor Books of Private Devotion*. Madison, Wis., 1951.

Willey, Basil. *The Seventeenth Century Background*. London, 1934.

Winship, George Parker. *William Caxton and His Work*. Berkeley: The Book Arts Club, 1937.

Workman, Herbert B. *John Wyclif: A Study of the English Medieval Church*, Vol. II. 2 vols. Oxford, 1926.

Wyzewa, Teodor de. *La Légende Dorée*. Paris, 1925.

Young, Karl. *The Drama of the Medieval Church*, Vol. II. 2 vols. Oxford, 1933.

Zuidweg, Jacobus Jan. *De Werkwijze van Jacobus de Voragine in de Legenda Aurea*. Oud-Beijerland, 1941.

INDEX

Abdon, Saint, 48
Achilleus, Saint, 44–45
Acta, acts of martyrs, 14, 115, 116
Acta Sanctorum, 321
Actes and Monuments. See Foxe, John
Act of 1585 against Jesuits and seminary priests, 242
Act of Persuasions, 242
Act of Succession, 96
Act of Supremacy of 1534, 78–79
Act of Supremacy of 1559, 198
Acton, Lord, 99, 124
Acts of the Apostles, 10, 274
Acts of Uniformity, 124, 198
Adamnan, Saint, 21
Adon (Ado), Archbishop of Vienne, 23, 130
Adrian, Saint, 62–63
Adventure, in saint's legend, 21
Agatha, Saint, 38–39, 41, 42, 55, 59
Agazzari, Alfonso, Jesuit rector of English College at Rome, 205, 230, 259
Agnes, Saint, 55–56, 60
Aleph, Judge, 248
Alexander III, Pope, 69
Alexander VI, Pope, 299–300
Alexius, Saint, 284–85
Alfield, Thomas, 224, 227, 228, 230; present at Campion's execution, 217–18; executed in 1585, 218
— *A True Reporte of the Death and Martyrdome of M. Campion Jesuite and Preiste, and M. Sherwin, and M. Bryan Preistes, at Tiborne the First of December 1581,* ed. Stephen Vallenger, 217; report of priest witness, 217; printed on secret press, 217–18; defense against treason charge, 218; on excellence of Campion, 218–19, on Campion's demeanor at execution, 219–20; on compassion in crowd, 220–21; marvel in death of Briant, 221; defense of comrades'

honor, 221; appeal for Queen's compassion, 221; Vallenger punished for authorship, 222
Allen, Rose, 183
Allen, William, 202, 203, 207, 236, 237, 255, 257; *Apologia pro Seminariis Anglorum,* 235; *Vitas Duodecim Præclarissimorum Martyrum,* 235; *An Apologie and True Declaration of the Institution and Endevours of the Two English Colleges,* 243; "An Admonition to the Afflicted Catholikes," 243
— *A Briefe Historie of the Glorious Martyrdom of Twelve Reverend Priests Father Edmund Campion and His Companions,* 228–31; purpose classic martyrologist's, 229–30; as expansion of Alfield's account, 230; includes Campion and others, 230–31; on asceticism, 237; on marvels, 238
— *A True Sincere and Modest Defence, of English Catholiques that Suffer for Their Faith both at Home and Abrode,* 218, 232, 235; answer to Cecil, 231; rebuttal of Protestant charge of Catholic treason, 231, 232
Alphege, Saint, 50, 53
Ambrose, patron of Origen, 9
Ambrose of Milan, Saint, 16, 54, 62, 139; favorite authority of *Golden Legend,* 61
Amos, 191
Anabaptists, 142, 197–98, 247, 300, 302; as martyrs, attitude of Catholics and Protestants toward, 144, 198, 247, 300, 302
Ancrene Riwle, 280
Andrew, Saint, the Apostle, 285
Anemyr, King, 59
Angel, 50
Anglican archbishop's life, 313–14; Puritan view of, 309–13, 315–16
Animals and saints, 19, 56
Anniversary, saint's, 14

An Answeare for the Time, unto that Foule and Wicked Defence of the Censure that was given upon M. Charkes Booke, and Meredith Hanmers, anonymous answer to Parsons, 212; on racking of martyrs, 222
Anthony of Italy, Saint, 285
Antiochus, King of Syria, 298
Antony the Abbot, Saint, 19, 21, 49; life by Athanasius, 21, 278
Apocalypse, 247. *See also* Revelation
Apocrypha, 60
Apologia Martyrum, 235
Apostles, 12, 37, 243, 293; simplicity and wisdom, 47–48, 174; fishermen, 191
Apostolic age, 171
Apparitions, 55
Appellant controversy, 257
Aquaviva, Claudio, Father General of Jesuits, 244
Archbishop of Trèves, 232, 233
Arden, Edward, 227
Arden, Mary, 227
Arian martyrs, 198
Aristotle, 139
Art, 262; and politics, 270
Arthur, Thomas, 150–51
"Articles devised by the Kynges Highnes Majestie, to stablyshe Christen Quietnes and Unitie amonge us," 79–80
Arts, visual, use for religion idolatrous, 180–81
Arundel, Countess of, 243
Arundel, Dorothy, 267
Arundel, Philip, Earl of, 243
Asa, King: Queen Elizabeth reminded of, by Geneva Bible-makers, 92
Asceticism, 128, 147–48; not emphasized in English Mission, 237
Ascetics, 18–19; feats of, 19; glorification of life of, 21
Askew, Anne, 49, 55
Aston, John, 137
Athanasius, Saint, life of Saint Antony, 21, 278
Athlete of religion, designation for martyrs, 12–13, 223
Attack on saint's legend. *See* Legend, saint's
Attila, 57
Augustine of Canterbury, Saint, 49; and restoration of dead lord, 58
Augustine of Hippo, Saint, 16, 19, 36, 48, 61, 260, 311, 312; scepticism about some relics, 77
Aurelius, Marcus, Roman emperor, 170
Authority, reverence for, 61

Ba., Ro., 98; *The Lyfe of Syr Thomas More,* 129–31; writes in English, 129; and literature of tradition, 129–30; and criticism of legends, 130; and enthusiasm of hagiographer, 130; occasionally dramatic, 130–31; place among More biographers, 131
Babington plot, 242
Baily, Thomas, 107, 111
Bainam, James, 164
Baker, Augustine, 275–76
Ball, John, 183
Ban against unlicensed printing of Bible in English, 67
Barbara, Saint, 42
Barker, Christopher, licensed to print Geneva Bible in English, 92
Barlaam, Saint, 59–60
Barlaam and Josaphat, Christianized legend of the Buddha, 21
Barley, William, 288
Barlow, William, Bishop of St. David's, 85
Barnes, Doctor, 151, 177
Baronius, Caesar, 24
Baroque, 241, 280–81; complexity of effect in *Legenda Aurea,* 63–64; and Foxe, 161, 162; development in seventeenth century, 162; and saints' lives, 277
Basil, Saint, 43, 57, 60
Basilides, Saint, 13
Bayfield, Richard, 151, 160
Beaufort, Lady Margaret, 108
Beaumont, Sir John, 291
Bede, the Venerable, 23, 130, 278; *Ecclesiastical History,* 23
Benedict, Saint, 20, 49, 57, 115
Benedictine order, 24, 276
Bennett, Josephine Waters, 288
Bernard of Clairvaux, Saint, 39, 48, 49, 244, 249, 260; *Versus Sancti Bernardi,* 70–71
Beuno, Saint, 42–43
Beza, Theodore: life of, by Laing, 223
— *A Discourse . . . Conteyning in Briefe the Historie of the Life and Death of Maister John Calvin,* trans. I. S., preface to Calvin's *Commentaries upon the Book of Josua,* 301; pattern of Puritan saint's life, 301; battle note in, 301–2; as classic hagiographic account, 302–3, 305
Bible, 7, 95, 150, 244, 245, 273, 275; Biblical lives added to *Legenda Aurea,* 33–34; romantic handling of Scripture, 60, 279; displaced by saints' legends in Church service, 87–88; lack of agreement on meaning of, 145; and Southwell's *Marie Magdalens Funeral Teares,* 263; examples of virtue and grace, 271, 279, 290, 294; Biblical hero, 289–92, 295; New Testament saint, wariness of, 292
— in English: prohibition of circulation, 33–34; ban against unlicensed printing of, 67; first printing of Tyndale's version, 67; translations, 145–46, 187; to be kept in churches, 168; Marian ban of texts on

church walls, 187–88. *See also* Geneva Bible

Bilney, Thomas, 147–48, 149, 150–51, 187

Bishops: Anglican, and Puritans, 143; discrimination from priests, second stage of Church, 154; Foxe's attitude toward, 154–55; opposition of, to Gospelers, 155; Bishops' Bible, 167–68; ancient lives of, as martyrology, 309; bishop's life, 309–13; Marian, 314; history of bishops of England, 316–21

Bishops' Book, The. *See The Institution of a Christen Man*

Blackwell, George, Archpriest, 257

Blaise, Saint, 57

Blandina, Saint, 12

Blind bell-ringer of Westminster, 58

Blood of Hailes, 85

"Bloody Question," the, 252, 255

Bock, Henry, 233

Bodley, Thomas, 310

Bokenham, Osbern, Augustinian, trans. *Legenda Aurea*, 32

Boleyn, Anne, 115, 116, 121, 125, 128, 131, 146–47, 175–76, 314

Bollandists, 95, 321

Bolton, John, 158

Bonaventura, Saint, life of Saint Francis of Assisi, 21

Bongeor, Agnes, 158–59

Boniface I, Pope, 173

Bonner, Edmund, Bishop of London, 187–88

Book of Common Prayer of Edward VI, first: imposed by Parliament, 87; preoccupation with corruption, 87–88; to be based on Scripture, 88; omission of certain ceremonies because of abuses, 89

Book of Common Prayer of Edward VI, second, 306; omission of ceremonies, 89; basis of Elizabethan Prayer Book of 1559, 89; any other service forbidden, 198

Book of Martyrs, The. See Foxe, John

Books: lack of, in Middle Ages, 22–23; Recusant attempts to print, 200; importation forbidden under penalty, 200–201; smuggling of, 201, 278

Borgia, Francis, Saint, 262

Bradford, John, 149, 155, 162–63; traditional conversion story, 150

Bradshaw, Henry, 282

Brendan, Saint, 21, 55, 56–57

Breton, Nicholas, *Auspicante Jehova. Maries Exercise*, 271–72; influence and echoes of Southwell, 271–72; *Marie Magdalens Love*, 271, 292; *A Solemne Passion of the Soules Love*, 271; warmth of feeling serving hortatory purpose, 271

Briant, Alexander, 217, 219, 221, 228; letter from Tower describing tortures, 224

Brice, Thomas, *A Compendious Register in Metre, conteining the names, and pacient suffryngs of the membres of Jesus Christ*: rhymed accounts of Protestant martyrs in calendar, 134–35; deplored killing of Reforming preachers, 134; helped create audience for Foxe, 135

Bridget of Sweden, Saint, 86 *n78*

Bridgewater, John, 233–36. *See also Concertatio Ecclesiæ*

Bristowe, Richard, 216

Broxup, William, *Saint Peters Path to the Joyes of Heaven*, 274

Bryan. *See* Briant, Alexander

Bucer, Martin, 137, 150

Buchanan, George, 310

Bullinger, Heinrich, trans. Thomas Twine, *Tragedies of Tyrantes*, 296; history of persecutions, 297–98; current persecutions, 298; persecutions as punishment of human frailty, 298; punishment of persecutors, 298

Bull of Excommunication of Queen Elizabeth, 202–3, 206, 216; and Recusants, 255

Butterworth, Charles C., 33

Butts, Sir William, 176

C., I. or J., *Saint Marie Magdalens Conversion*, 279

Caesarius of Heisterbach, 26

Calendar, 16, 23, 24, 72, 140; entries reduced in Joye's *Hortulus Animae*, 87; and first Prayer Book of Edward VI, 88; Foxe's reformed, 136–38, 140

Calvin, John, 307; *A Very Profitable Treatise . . . Declarynge what great Profit might come to al Christendome, yf there were a a Regester made of al Sainctes Bodies and other Reliques*, 77–78

Calvinism in Geneva Bible, 92

Campion, Edmund, 142, 196, 203, 204, 206–23, 224, 232–33, 234, 236, 237, 238, 240, 240–42, 248, 253, 255, 256, 281; stellar role in English Mission, 206; qualities of martyr in, 206; resembled courtier, 206; origins and education, 206–7; fled England, 207; joined Jesuits, 207; patriotism and cosmopolitanism, 207; open letter of, stating purpose, 207; betrayed by George Eliot, 212; tortured, 214; reports of his breaking, 214; condemned and executed, 214; hostile accounts of execution printed, 214–17; execution important occasion, 216; Alfield's account of execution, 217–21; Allen's account of, 230–31; printing of letters of, 232–33; pride of followers in, 238–39; and "Bloody Question," 255; compared with Southwell, 275–76. *See also* Alfield, Thomas; Allen, William

— *Rationes Decem*, 234; secretly printed and

distributed in St. Mary's, Oxford, 209; reply by Whitaker, 209; printed with Whitaker's *Responsio* at Antwerp, 210

Canonization: difficulties of popular canonization, 69; efforts to control, 69

Canossa, 174

Carthage, persecution at, 6, 11

Carthusian order: martyrs under Henry, 97, 110, 128, 152; and resistance to Henry, 102; community enthusiasm, 105–6; dangers of withdrawal from world, 203–4. *See also* Chauncy, Dom Maurice; Houghton, John

Carver, Dirick, 149

Castiglione, *The Courtier*, 117

Catherine of Alexandria, Saint: famous for wisdom and beauty, 46–47; Caxton's enthusiasm for mystical marriage of, 50

Catherine of Genoa, Saint, 14

Catherine of Siena, Saint, 22

Catholic criticism of saints' legends, 130

Catholic martyrs' lives of seventeenth century, 126

Catholic political intrigues, 203

Catholic princes, 203

Catholic Recusants. *See* Recusants, Catholic

Catholic religious system: priest essential in, 201

Cause makes martyrs, principle of, 20, 69, 140, 239, 246–47

Cavendish, George, life of Wolsey, 114

Caxton, William, 36, 41, 132; middle-class origins, 31; success in foreign trade, 31; in service of Court of Burgundy, 31–32; translations from the French, 32; learned art of printing in Germany, 32; printed translation of Troy book at Bruges, 32; established in Westminster under royal patronage, 32; various works printed by, 32; translation of *Vitas Patrum*, 32; translation from various languages, 32

— *The Golden Legend*, 31, 71, 321; sources used for translation, 32–33; and basic pattern of original, 33–36, 37–38; addition of Bible stories, 33, 289; popular character of, 34, 52–54, 64, 65–66; style, 34, 62–63, 64; tone of, 35, 36–37, 56, 64–65; qualities of saints, 36, 37–41, 42, 47–52; recapitulation of history of Church and saint's cult, 37; four classes of saints, 37–38; wide social range represented, 38; psychology of martyr, 41–42; prominence of women in, 43–47; good works indispensable, 48–49, 52–54; romantic elements, use of, 50, 59–60; marvels associated with saints, 54–56; critical spirit, 60–61; last printing of, coincided with first printing of Bible in English, 67. *See also* Jacobus de Voragine

Cecil, William (Baron Burghley), 198; *The Execution of Justice in England*, 231; official policy toward Recusants, 254

Cecilia, Saint, 43

"Certain Injunctions," published by royal authority in 1539, 175

Challoner, Richard, 109

Chambers, R. W., 124

Chambers, Robert: *Palestina*, 279–81, 289

Charity, works of, 50–51

Charke, William: *An Answere to a Seditious Pamphlet lately cast abroade by a Jesuite*, 207; comparison of Sanders' expedition to Ireland and Campion's mission, 207; on Campion's defense of Catholic faith, 207–8; known as extreme Puritan, 208

Charles V, Emperor, 129

Charles the Bald, 23

Chaucer, 72, 73

Chauncy, Dom Maurice: attitude toward submission to Henry, 103; left England, 103; account of Houghton, 103–5. *See also* Houghton, John

— *Passio XVIII. Carthusianorum in regno Angliæ*: published 1550, 101; not translated until 1890, 101; as work of contemplative, 101; as official report, 101–2; scriptural language of, 101–2; involvement of author with subject, 102; as transition from *Golden Legend* to later martyr's life, 106–7

Childeric, King, 39–40

Christ, early life of, 279–80

Christina, Saint, 42

Christmas, Thomas, 166

Christopher, Saint, 40, 52–53

Chrysostom, Saint, 62, 139

Church and State, 22, 143–44, 171; use of secular authority by Church unpopular, 143; princes and Reformation, 146–47; foundation of prince's power in Saint Paul, 174; refusal of obedience to heretical prince, 183–84; persecution of Church under Roman emperors, 297

Church of England, 198, 277, 309, 311; in 1563, 179–80; and Catholics and Puritans, 183–84; attendance at services enforced by law, 254; hagiographic revival, 277, 281–301

Church Triumphant, 36

Civil War, 184

Clare, Saint, 55

Clarke, Samuel, collections of lives of Puritan ministers, 301

Clement, John, 127

Clement, Margaret, 127

Clement, Mother Margaret, 105

Clients of saints: as problem, 51–52

Cobham, Eleanor, 138

Cochlaeus, John, 129
Codex Velseri, 24
Colchester, 151, 159, 160–61, 163, 191
Colet, John, 127
Colley, Dorothy, 129
Colte, Gratian, 75–76
Columba of Iona, Saint, 20, 21
Commons, House of: hostile reaction to Henry's innovations, 152–53, 177
Communion of the saints, 17, 30
Companies of London, 168
Concertatio Ecclesiæ Catholicæ in Anglia, adversus Calvinopapistas et Puritanos: as record of controversy, 232; addressed to Catholic world, 232; success on Continent, 236
— first version of: published 1583, 232; edited by John Fen and John Gibbon, 232; as record of martyrs, 232–33; on 1580 mission of Parsons and Campion, 232–33; contents of, 233
— second version of: published 1588, 233; edited by John Bridgewater, 233; tone of, 234; as record of martyrs, 234–35; contents of, 234–36
Confessors, 18, 37–38
Conformity, 241
Constantine, Roman emperor, 138, 170; peace of the Church, 13
Contemplation, 49–50, 259, 271–72, 275–76, 292–93; and Briant, 224
Contemplative life, 21–22, 127
Controversy between Anglicans and Catholics, 190, 236; in martyr story, 196; and authorities, 238
Cooper, Elizabeth, 157
Corruption, Foxe's interest in growth of, 170–71
Cosmas, Saint, 58
Cottam, Thomas, 228, 230, 237
Council, Queen's, 208, 215, 232–33
Councils, 172
Counselors of kings: problem of, 176–78; bad counselor as explanation of king's failing, 178–79
Countess of Northumberland, 234
Courtier martyr, 163
Court of Elizabeth, 168, 206, 295, 301, 305, 306
Court of James VI, 290
Coverdale, Miles, 145–46, 150, 182–83
Cowper, Thomas, 213
Cranmer, Thomas, Archbishop of Canterbury, 86, 115, 134, 140, 154, 161, 176, 178, 181, 188–89, 312
Crespin, Jean, Protestant martyrologist: *Le Livre Des Martyrs*, 299
— *État de l'Église des le temp dès apôtres jusqu'a 1560*: trans. Simon Patrick as *The*

Estate of the Church, 298–99; publication of, 299; continuation of, 299; as Protestant history of world, 299; slight narrative element, 299–300; accounts of Turkish events, 300–301; mentions ambassadors from Moscow at Elizabeth's Court, 301
Crispinus. *See* Crespin, Jean
Croesslius, Joannes, 264
Crofts, Richard, 106–7
Cromwell, Oliver, 71
Cromwell, Thomas, 115, 132, 153, 176–77, 304; *Injunctions gyven by Thauctoritie of the Kynges Highnes to the Clergie of this his Realme*, 80; and popular propaganda, 80–82, 84–85; *Injunctions for the Clerge*, 83–84
Cuthbert of Lindisfarne, Saint, 20, 56
Cynewulf: *Andreas*, 21; *Elene*, 21
Cyprian, Saint, Bishop of Carthage, 14, 120, 139, 243, 244; *The Lapsed*, 9; on retribution, 9–10, 246; martyred, 10

Dagobert, King, 38
Dalaber, Anthony, style of, contrasted with Foxe, 156–57
Damian, Saint, 58
Daniel, prophecies of, 298
Dare, Christopher, 149
Dauncy, Elizabeth, 128
David, King, 295
David, Saint, patron of Wales, 285
Day, William, Dean of Windsor and later Bishop of Worcester, 223
Decius, Roman emperor, 9
Dedication of Temple or Church, 36
Defense of faith against heresy, 49
Delehaye, Hippolyte, Bollandist, 14
Demons, tales of, 20
Denis, Saint, patron of France, 43, 56, 285
Denny, Sir Anthony, 176
Deportation of Catholic priests, 226, 227
De Roma at Avignon 166
Desert: Fathers of, 19; saints of, 237
Development of religious rite, Foxe on, 182–83
Devil, 50, 60, 244, 300
De Vocht, Henry, 80–81, 82, 98, 117
Devotion, including prayer and meditation, professionally practical view, 49
Diary of the Tower, 214, 234, 236; printed by Wolfgang Eder, 225; work of priest prisoner, 225; prisons of Recusants, 225; tortures, 225–26; resembles monastery calendar, 226; author presumably deported in 1585, 226, 227; tone of entries, 226–27; records arrival of Campion, 227; reports fate of Arden family, 227; reports episode of John Nichols, 227–28; rejoicing in prisoners who withstood torture, 228

Dinocrates, 11
Diocletian, Roman emperor, 13, 298
Discipline, 302–3, 307
Disputations: Campion's in Tower, 222–23, 224; and sermons in Tower, 228; sought by both sides, 238
Divorce case, Henry's, 100, 121, 146, 175–76, 229
Dominic, Saint, 37, 49
Dominican order, 24, 25, 278
Domitian, Roman emperor, 298
Douai, 126; seminary at, 202; priests sent to England in 1574, 202; martyr roster opened in 1577, 202; 100 priests in England by 1580, 203
Dramatic element: in *Golden Legend*, 50; in More, 122; in Foxe, 160–61, 194
Drayton, Michael, *Moyses in a Map of his Miracles*, 291–92
Dreams, 11, 55; prophetic, 56, 165
Du Bartas, G. Saluste, 290–91
Duchess of Richmond, 133
Dunstan, Saint, 50, 54, 55
Dury, John, Scottish Jesuit: answer to Whitaker's *Responsio*, 210; Whitaker's rebuttal of, 210
Dwabene, Arthur, Merchant Adventurer, 282
Dyson collection of proclamations, 200–201, 249–50

Earthly Paradise, 55
Edict against Strangers, 304
Edmund, Saint, 51, 55
Edmund Rich, Archbishop of Canterbury, Saint, 115, 319
Education, importance of, to revolution, 186–87
Edward, King, martyr, Saint, 53, 59
Edward IV, King, 31
Edward VI, King, 86, 100, 137, 146, 147, 150, 155, 172, 178, 185, 191, 307, 314
Edward the Confessor, King, Saint, 38, 49, 53–54, 55, 58
Egles, George, "Trudgeoner," 191
Eleazar, 9
Elene, 21
Eleutherius, Saint, 56
Eliot, George, 227; *A Very True Report of the Apprehension and Taking of that Arche Papist Edmond Campion the Pope his Right Hand*, 212; commissioned for apprehension of priests, 212–13; discovered Campion, 213–14
Elizabeth, Countess of Lincoln, 295
Elizabeth, Queen, 90–92, 100, 134–35, 141, 147, 165, 172, 178–79, 185, 196, 198, 199, 205, 281, 307, 312, 314, 316, 320
Elizabeth, sister of John Fisher, 109
Elizabethan age, 240, 254
Elizabethan Settlement of Religion, 229, 242;

unity of religious faith and national feeling, 141; hope opposition would die out, 141–42; and Christian tradition, 172; designed to be comprehensive, 196; ready to be conciliatory, 197; and admirers of Geneva, 197; and Anabaptists, 197–98; enforcement of conformity to, 198; and exile of Catholic leaders, 200; nominal conformity to, 200; defense of, against Rome, 255–57
Elizabeth of Hungary, Saint, 55, 95
Eloy, Saint, 38, 52
Emperors, Roman, 41; and structure of Eusebius' history, 170
Encomium, classical, influence on saint's legend, 20–21
England and Germany, relations between, 232
English Books, 200; position of Henry VIII on, 132; popularized religious controversy, 190
English College in Rome, 241
English Mission, 203, 204, 205, 236, 237, 240, 242, 255, 275–76; and impact on Elizabethan age, 203. *See also* Campion, Edmund; Parsons, Robert; Southwell, Robert
— of 1580, 196, 224, 232–33; as dramatic episode, 203; and Bull of Excommunication of Queen Elizabeth, 206; Munday's charges of conspiracy against, 215–16
English Mission martyrology: heroes chiefly priests, 236–37; virginity and asceticism not emphasized, 237; and marvels, 238; stress on learning, controversy, and preaching, 238; pride in disputation successes, 238–39; tone of, 239; and salvation of England, 239
Episcopacy, 154, 171. *See also* Bishops
Epistle of Comfort to persecuted: classic type from antiquity, 8–9; More's, 108, 121–22, 125; Fisher's, 109; Catholic and Protestant, 242–43; Southwell's, 243–49
Equivocation, 312
Erasmus, Desiderius, 71, 73, 108, 120, 127, 129, 137, 180, 260, 304; *Colloquies* censured by Sorbonne, 76–77; *Colloquies* condemned by Council of Trent, 77; accounts of More's death, 98; Paris News Letter, 98, 124; *Expositio Fidelis de Morte D. Thomae Mori et quorundam aliorum insigniorum vivorum in Anglia*, 98, 117; letter of July 23, 1519, to Ulrich von Hutten, 116–17
— *The Pilgrimage of Pure Devotion*: published as *A Dialoge or Communication of Two Persons*, 73; attack on absurdities of pilgrimage cult, 73–74; possibly used by Cromwell, 80–82
Esdras, 295
Established Church. *See* Church of England
Esther, 295

Ethelbert, King of Kent, Saint, 49, 64
Eugenia, Saint, 46
Europe, medieval, poverty of, 22–23
Eusebius Pamphili, Bishop of Caesarea, 130,
138, 170, 171, 274
— *Historia Ecclesiastica*, 12–13, 243; trans.
Meredith Hanmer, 169–70, 281–82, 295–
96
Eustace, Saint, 59, 61
Evagrius, 295, 296
Exmew, William, 99

Fagius, Paul, confessor, 135
Fathers of Church, 33, 93, 244, 245
Feast of Corpus Christi, 36
Feasts of liturgical year, 26
Featley, Daniel, 310–13
Felician, Saint, 42
Felicitas, Saint, 6, 246
Felix of Nola, Saint, life of, by Bede, 278
Fen, John, Chaplain to Saint Ursula's convent
of Austin canonesses in Louvain, 232;
worked in collaboration with Jesuit John
Gibbon, 232. *See also Concertatio Ecclesiæ*
Ferrar, Robert, Bishop of St. David's, 159,
166
Filby, William, 214, 230
First Book of Homilies, 86
Fish, Simon, *Supplication of the Beggars*, 78,
179
Fisher, John, Bishop of Rochester, Saint, 85,
96, 97, 99, 100, 101, 107–16, 152, 319;
compared with More, 108, 110, 111–12,
113; as reformer, 108; interest in education, 108; as model bishop, 108; success
in career, 108, 110; sense of failure, 108–9;
*A Spirituall Consolation . . . to hys sister
Elizabeth*, 109, 242; "The wayes to perfect Religion," 109; attitude toward martyrdom, 110–11; claims of Henry on, 112–
13; devotion to poor, 113; devotion to
learning, 113–14; asceticism, 114
—, biography of (*A Treatis Contayninge the
Lyfe and Maner of Death of that Most
holy Prelat and Constant Martyr of Christ
John Fysher*): printed 1655, as work of Dr.
Thomas Baily, 107; preliminary drafts
survive, 107; problem of authorship, 107–
8; blamed Wolsey for insinuation of scruple about Henry's marriage, 113; stressed
asceticism, 114; pains to establish facts,
114; hagiographic pattern, 114; resembles
early *Acta* of martyrs, 114–16; tone of,
115; and marvels, 115–16
Flavia, Saint, 44–45
Florus, Canon of Lyons, 23
Folkes, Elizabeth, 160–61
Forgeries, hagiographic, 14
Forrest, Friar, 152
Fortunatus, 278

Four Ages of the Church, 26, 170–71
Foxe, John, 82, 85, 89, 96, 98, 108, 115,
198, 236, 253, 295, 296, 298, 299, 310,
317; began book on Protestant martyrs under Henry, 132; middle-class origins, 132;
educated at Oxford, 132; growth of Protestant convictions of, 132–33; became tutor
in Lutheran household, 133; began to publish in Reforming cause, 133; fled to Continent, 133; published *Commentarii Rerum
in Ecclesia Gestarum, maximarumque per
totam Europum persecutionem*, 133; gathered materials on Marian persecution,
133; published *Rerum in Ecclesia Gestarum, quae postremis et periculosis his
temporibus evenerunt . . . Pars Prima*,
133–34; returned to England, 135; *Book
of Martyrs* and English Puritanism, 154,
190–91; narrative art of, 160–62, 190, 193–
94; apologetics of, as representative of
contemporary English Church, 179–80
— *Actes and Monuments* as martyrology, 167,
169, 172, 196, 204, 232, 238; title page
sets tone, 135–36; *Eucharisticon* in, on vindication of martyrs, 136; and calendar,
136–38; name of Eusebius invoked in address to Queen, 138, 169; on cruelty of
Papists, 138, 155–56, 158, 160; on honoring martyrs, 138–40, 155; on love of
praising famous men, 139; on value of contemplating fate of tragic heroes, 139; on
zeal of ancient Christians for martyrs,
139; Foxe's attitude toward, 140; differences in tone from *Golden Legend*, 141;
as rationalization of victory, 141; position
on problem of supporters of old order,
141–42; attitude toward Anabaptists, 142,
144–45; on punishment for treason, 142,
152; on heresy, 142–43, 144, 145; on persecution on false grounds, 143; on bishops,
143, 154–55; on Henry's divorce, 146;
princes as religious heroes, 146–47, 174–
78; ministers as religious heroes, 147–49;
variety of martyrs, 149–50; foreshadowing of seventeenth-century sectarianism,
149–50; as testimony of dissemination of
Protestant ideas, 150–52; attitude toward
adversaries of martyrs, 152–53; and triumph of the martyr, 155, 156–57, 158–59,
162–63, 164–66, 167; style, 156–57, 159,
160, 161–62, 163, 188, 189, 193–94; as
record of simple souls caught in pressures
of times, 157; emphasis on records of examinations, 157–58; emphasis on records
of disputations, 157–58; dramatic quality
in, 160–61, 163, 193–94; and exploitation
of sensuous detail, 161–62; and portents
and miracles of Providence, 164–67; as
substitute for *Golden Legend*, 167; record

of publication indication of success, 167;
prescribed for various places, 167–68; in
parish churches, 168
— *Actes and Monuments* as ecclesiastical history: modeled on Eusebius' outline of *Historia Ecclesiastica*, 169–70; other influences
on organization, 170; interest in growth of
corruption, 170–71; and lineage of religious settlement, 172; as religious history
of England, 173–76, 194–95; on Henry
VIII, 176–79; central theme of, rebellion
against Rome, 179; as encyclopedia of Reformation in England, 179–80, 192; and
iconoclasm, 180–83; as reflection of Foxe's
confidence in his position, 184; Foxe as
propagandist in, 184–86, 187, 188, 195;
on conscience of dissenters, 186; on education, 186–87; on benefits of printing,
187, 190; on English books, 187–88; use
of emotional appeal in, 188; techniques of
denigration and caricature in, 188–90; appeal of, to unlearned public, 190, 191;
intellectual tone of, 192–93
Foxe, Simeon, 142
Franciscan order, 24, 25
Francis of Assisi, Saint, 21, 51, 55, 188
Frankfurt, 307, 308, 312
Friars, 188
Frideswide, Saint, 320
Frith, John, 149, 151, 181
Froben[ius], Johannes, 98

Galerius, Roman emperor, 13
Gallicanism, 258
Gardiner, Germain, 155
Gardiner, Stephen, Bishop of Winchester, 145,
154, 157–58, 177–78; as Foxe's favorite
villain, 152–54
Gardiner, William, 155, 182, 183
Garnet, Henry, Superior of Jesuits, 257, 276
Gaul, persecution in, 12
Geneva, 197, 251, 302–3, 307, 308
Geneva Bible, 91, 307; commended for au-
thenticity and availability to unlearned, 91;
issue of idolatry stressed, 91–92; Calvin-
istic bias of, 92; plainness of style, 92
Genevieve, Saint, 39–40, 56, 58
Geninges, Edmund, 237
Genoa, 25
Gentlemen martyrs, 149
George, Dutchman, 144, 147
George, Saint, patron saint of England, 137;
patriotism and piety of, 285–88
Germanus, Saint, 50
Gervasius, Saint, 16
Gesta Romanorum, 288
Gibbon, John, Jesuit, 232. *See Concertatio
Ecclesiæ*
Gilbart, Thomas, ballad on execution of John
Lewes, 198

Godwin, Francis, Subdean of Exeter, afterward Bishop of Llandaff and of Hereford,
316–21
— *A Catalogue of the Bishops of England*:
popular history, 316; author's delight in
history, 317; purpose of, to redress balance
in current controversies, 317; treatment of
prelates of past, 317–18; portrait of
Thomas à Becket, 318–19; penance of the
King, 319; Edmund Rich victim of Pope's
tyranny, 319; length of account of Fisher,
319; account of Parker, 319–20; critical
sense of author, 320; success of, 320–21;
and career of author, 321
Golden Legend, Caxton's, 47, 68, 95, 106,
110, 115, 116, 123, 125, 135, 136, 140–41,
149, 158, 159, 163, 164, 167, 190, 286,
291–92, 311. *See also* Caxton, William;
Jacobus de Voragine
Gospelers, 155, 176–77, 178
Gospel story, 263
Green, Bartlet: as case of university conver-
sion, 150
Greenham, Richard, Puritan minister, 305–6
Gregory I, the Great, Saint, Pope, 38, 69, 93,
311
Gregory VII, Saint, Pope. *See* Hildebrand
Gregory XIII, Pope, 206
Gregory of Nazianzus, Bishop, Saint, 139
Gregory of Tours, 278
Grey, Lady Jane, 149
Grindal, Edmund, Archbishop of Canterbury,
133; and Geneva Bible, 92
Grosart, Alexander B., 263
Guide to the devout life, Catholic, 294
Gunpowder Plot, 276

Hagiography: saint's and martyr's lives in
England as episode in larger story, 321;
examples of human devotion, 321
—, classic: genres, 8–14; stages of evolution,
14; expansion of martyrology, 18–23; varieties of martyrology, 23–24; collections of
saints' lives for preachers and lay readers,
24–30. *See also* Legend, saint's and martyr's
—, emergent Protestant types: development
on classic pattern, 301; Beza's life of Calvin, 301–3; oration of Wygandus Orthlius
on Hyperius, 303–5; life of Puritan minister (Holland's life of Greenham), 305–6;
saint's life (life of Whittingham), 306–9;
life of bishop (Humphrey's life of Jewel,
trans. Featley), 310–13; emphasis on particular principle, 313; archiepiscopal life
(Josselin's life of Parker), 313–16; history
of bishops of England by Godwin, 316–21
—, sixteenth-century: Catholic revival, 277;
Whitford's translation of Martyrology of
Salisbury Use, 277–78; work of Lippomanus, 278; work of Surius, 278; work of

Villegas, 278; work of Ribadaneyra, 278; work of Southwell, 279; work of Chambers, 279–81; Protestant revival of, 281–82; popular romantic versions, 282–88; straight treatment of, 288; and *Gesta Romanorum*, 288–89; Old Testament saints, 289–92; New Testament saints, 292–95; Primitive Church saints, 295–96; Protestant history of Christianity, 296–301; scientific, 321

Hales, Master, 183

Hall (Halle), Edward, official view of Catholic resistance to Henry, 96, 99–100

Hall, Hugh, 227

Hall, Richard, 107, 108

Haller, William, 192, 195

Hallett, Philip E., translation of Stapleton, 126, 131

Hamilton, Patrick, 149

Hanmer, Meredith, 289, 305, 309; trans. Eusebius' *Historia Ecclesiastica*, as *The Auncient Ecclesiasticall Histories of the First Six Hundred Years after Christ*, 169, 281–82, 295; *The Great Bragge and Challenge of M. Champion a Jesuite*, 208; on popular taste for romance, 281; devotional character of reading saint's life, 295; on miracles, 295–96; on duration of first age of Church, 296

Harding, Thomas, 236, 311

Harpsfield, Nicholas, Archdeacon of Canterbury, 89–90, 98–99, 123–24, 125, 126, 127

— *The Life and Death of Sr Thomas Moore, knight*: compared with Roper's life, 124; first modern complete biography in English, 124; aspects of More stressed, 124; on Henrician revolt, 124–25; on intercession of More and fellow martyrs as explanation of Marian restoration of religion, 125; sense of form in, 125; and prophetic element, 125; style of, 126

Harris, Dorothy, 127

Harris, John, 127

Hatotus, Edmundus, 232

Haunce, Everard, 214–15

Hawkes, Thomas, 163

Heath, Nicholas, Archbishop of York and Chancellor of England, 236

Helena, Saint, 21

Helenopolis, 19

Hemerford, Thomas, 255–56

Henrician martyrs, Catholic, 184–239, 278; accounts of, not possible in England, 100

Henry II of England, King, 318–19

Henry VII of England, King, 108, 112

Henry VIII of England, King, 96, 97, 100, 108, 111, 112–13, 115, 116, 120, 121, 127, 128, 129, 130, 131, 145–46, 150, 151, 152–53, 154–55, 172, 175, 199, 242, 278, 314; campaign against monasteries, 78;

Act of Supremacy, 78–79; as Supreme Head of Church of England, 79, 82–86; effort to secure religious peace, 79–80; on honoring of saints, 79–80; progress in Protestant direction, 80–86; *Institution of a Christian Man*, 85, 86; on use of images, 85; lack of resistance to, 96–97; aware of dangers of martyrology, 97–98; Foxe on, 146, 176–78, 187

Henry IV of Germany, Emperor, as model of virtue, 174–75

Heresy, 132, 142–43, 156; charges of, resented by Protestant apologists, 172

Herman Contractus, 24

Herod, 297, 298

Heroic tale, 21

Heywood, John, 127

Hide, Thomas, *A Consolatorie Epistle to the Afflicted Catholikes*: cited example of apostles and Polycarp, 242–43

Hilary of Poitiers, Saint, life by Fortunatus, 278

Hildebrand, Pope (George VII, Saint): Foxe's opinion of, 174–75

Hilsey, John, Bishop of Rochester, 85

Historical criticism: Foxe's principle of, 170–71

Historical martyrology, new hagiographic type, 23

Historical studies, 315, 317

History: Foxe's view of, as defense against Catholics, 190; used for controversy, 296

Holland, Henry, life of Richard Greenham, preface to *The Works of Richard Greenham*, 282; stress on cure of souls, 305–6

Holy Innocents, 54, 297

Homily, medieval, 294

Honoring of martyrs and saints: middle ground, 310

Hooker, Richard, 184

Hooper, John, Bishop of Gloucester and Worcester, 145, 158, 161–62

Hore of 1527. *See* Regnault, François

Horror, 159–60, 161–62

Houghton, John, Carthusian prior: attitude toward martyrdom, 102; concern for house, 102–3; unworldliness of, 103; personality of, 103–4, 105; as administrator, 103–4; importance of Divine Office, 104–5

Hours, 36, 70–71, 86

House of Convocation of Canterbury, 167–68

Howlet, I., pseudonym of Robert Parsons, 205

Hudson, Thomas, trans. Du Bartas *The Historie of Judith in Forme of a Poeme*, for popular audience, sober and godly, 290–91

Hügel, Baron Friedrich von, study of Saint Catherine of Genoa and her friends, 14

Hughes, Philip, 97, 104, 204

Humanists, 77, 116–17, 124, 132; impatient

of absurdities of saints' cult, 73; view of awakening from Middle Ages, 189

Humble martyrs, 158–59; take on power of the Lord, 191

Humphrey, Laurence, *J. Juelli Episcopi Sarisburiensis Vita*: popular influence limited by use of Latin, 310; formal plan indebted to classic saint's life, 310; trans. Daniel Featley, *The Life of the Worthie Prelate and Faithfull Servant of God John Jewel*, 310; etymological analysis of names, 311; education and career, 311–12; classic Anglican picture of good bishop, 312; almost monastic household, 312–13; remarkable memory and gift of prophecy, 313; nearly died preaching, 313

Hunter, William, 159

Hus, John, 137

Hyperius, Andreas [Gerardus], 304–5. *See also* Orthlius, Wygandus

Hypocrisy: attack on, 80; of old order, 82; charge against Catholic bishops, 145

Iconoclasm, 76–77, 80, 84–85, 180–83; warning against private action on, 81–82; and avoidance of idolatry, 84; problem with regard to secular monuments, 90–91

Idolatry, 79, 82, 187, 222, 292; as major charge against saints' cult, 77; elements of, magic, 78; in use of images, 84; abolishing of, essential to peace of kingdoms, 92; arraigned in second homily of *The Seconde Tome of Homelyes*, 92; caused by pilgrimages, shrines, and images, 180; and obedience to magistrates, 183–84; elimination to be left to magistrates, 290

Ignatius of Antioch, Saint, 41, 55; epistle to Romans, 8

Ignatius of Loyola, Saint, 203, 261–62

— *Spiritual Exercises*, 266; way of making techniques of meditation available to layman, 204; and problems of meditation for sixteenth century, 259–60; technique of meditation, 261; basic scheme clear, 261–62; affords basic orientation and confidence, 262; method of transformation, 262

Images, 180, 296; of saints, destruction of, 68; Caxton on importance of, for popular religious instruction, 68–69; proper use of, 79, 82–83; and charge of idolatory, 81–82; Reforming appeal for poor against images, 83; propaganda against veneration of, 85; restoration of, under Mary, 89–90; inquiry in Visitation Articles of first year of Elizabeth, 90; in Foxe's index, 179

Incarnation, 4

India, 21

Inner life, 260

Innovation: charges of, resented by Protestant apologists, 140, 174; Protestant-Catholic controversy over, 172

Institution of a Christen Man, The, 82–83, 85

Interrogatories of martyrs, 13, 14

Iona, 21

Ireland, 216; expedition under papal banner, 229

Irenaeus, Saint, 295–96

Isaiah, 249

Israel, kings of, 298

Jacobus de Voragine, Archbishop of Genoa, 25–27, 31, 32–33, 34, 35, 170; man of learning and practical experience, 25

— *Legenda Aurea*, 71, 73, 238, 281, 288, 321; directed to lay audience, 25–26; problem of sources, 26, 71; popularity of, 26; later expansion, 26; abbreviation of, in Mirk's *Festial*, 26–27; as aid to preachers, 27–28; narrative qualities, 62; sense of comedy, 62; awareness of human frailty, 62–63; favorite heroes of, 236. *See also* Caxton, William

James VI, King, 290, 320–21

James, Saint, Numidian martyr, 11, 56

James of Compostella, Saint, 74, 285

Janelle, Pierre, 202, 264, 338 *n12*

Jarrow, 23

Jean de Mailly, *Abbrevatio in Gestis et Miraculis Sanctorum*, 24

Jean de Vignay, Hospitaler, French translation of *Legenda Aurea*, 32

Jenkins, David, 213

Jeremy, Sister Mary, 35, 64

Jerome, Saint, 23, 130, 139, 274, 278

Jerusalem, 39; heavenly, 279

Jesuits, 224, 237, 240, 257, 258–59, 262, 275–76, 278; Haunce's execution, printing of hostile account of, 214–15; Briant believed vow to join them brought grace, 224–25; techniques of meditation, 225; newsletters, 253. *See also* Society of Jesus

Jetter, John, 228

Jewel, John, Bishop of Salisbury, life of, by Laurence Humphrey, 309–13. *See also* Humphrey, Laurence

Joan of Kent, 144, 147

Job, 295, 298

John, Archbishop of Trèves, 232

John, King: oppressions caused by treasons of bishops and barons, 175; poisoned by monk, 175

John XV, Pope, first recorded example of formal approval of a canonization, 69

John Damascene, Saint, *Barlaam and Josaphat*, 21

John of Salisbury, life of Saint Thomas à Becket, 22, 300

Johnson, Richard, *The Most Famous History of the Seaven Champions of Christendome*, 285–87

John the Almoner, Saint, 52

John the Baptist, Saint, 115

John the Evangelist, Saint, 60, 274, 279
Josaphat, Saint, Christianized Buddha, 55
Josephus, 33
Joshua, 295
Josiah, 84
Josias, example commended to Queen Elizabeth by makers of Geneva Bible, 92
Josselin, John, *Historiola Collegii Corporis Christi*, 313
— "Matthaeus," life of Archbishop Matthew Parker, 313; trans. in *The Life off the 70. Archbishopp of Canterbury Presentlye Sittinge*, 313; classic account of subject, 314; perfect pattern of archbishop, 314–15; interest in history, 315; translation published from hostile motives, 315–16; translation gives Puritan view of see of Canterbury, 316
Jovius, Paul, 129
Joye, George: *Hortulus Animae*, reduction of calendar entries, 87; *A Present Consolation for the Sufferers of Persecucion for Ryghtwyseness*, 242
Judah, Kings of, 298
Judas, 55, 60
Judith, 290–91
Julian, Saint, 39, 42
Juliana, Saint, 40
Julian the Apostate, 61, 296
Justice, saints' concern for, 51–52
Justification, 157

Katherine, Countess Dowager of Huntington, 305
Keltridge, John: complaint of Campion's and Howlet's challenges, 209
Kempis, Thomas à, *Imitation of Christ*, 260, 264
Kenelm, Saint, 56
King of Spain, 204, 252
Kings, 112–13, 190; goodness of, benefit to realm, 49; Scripture-devoted king to be trusted, 176; raised by God against popes, 298. *See also* Church and State; Supremacy, Royal
Knowles, Sir Francis, 220
Knowles, William, Lord, 210
Knox, John, 307
Koprîs, 19

Labor, respect for, 51
Laing, James, summary of Catholic Campion literature, 223
Lambert, John, 150–51, 153, 154, 155, 157–58, 176–77
Lamentation literature, 262–75, 292–93; pious tearfulness, 262; reversal of earlier feeling against emotional embellishment of Scripture, 275; appeal of Southwell's work across religious barriers, 275
Lanfranc, Archbishop of Canterbury, 53–54

Lark, John, 155
Latimer, Hugh, Bishop of Worcester, 137, 150, 159–60
Laurence of Rome, Saint, 36, 43, 61
Lausiac History. See Palladius
Laxity, 9–10
Lay artisan preachers among martyrs, 191
Leake, Thomas, 258
Learning and sanctity, 47–48; *Golden Legend* does justice to both simple and learned, 47–48
Legend, saint's and martyr's: definition of "martyr" as witness, 4–5; problems of writing, 4, 13–14, 17; problem of truth, 5; self-criticism, 5; and the great persecutions, 5–6; edifying use of, 27–29, 68; as entertainment, 27–29; role in medieval art and life, 29–30
—, attack on: central to religious revolution, 67–69; and problems of saints' cult, 69–72; medieval recognition of absurdities, 72–73; humanist reaction, 73–77; and charge of idolatry, 77–78, 90–92, 92–94; Henry VIII's caution about, 85–86; Edwardian strategies of attack and omission, 86–89; and Marian restoration, 89–90; Catholic criticism, 94–95
— cult of the martyr: commemorative rites at tomb, 14; miracles of intercession, 15; pride of group, 15–16; *legenda*, to be read, 16–17
— expansion of martyrology: of local calendar, 18; of categories, 18–20; responsiveness to climate of opinion, 20–22; expansion of complexities, 22–23
— martyrological genres: address of consolation and encouragement, 8; exhortation to martyrdom, 8–9; rebuke of the lapsed, 9–10; letters reporting martyrdoms, 10; early accounts of martyrdoms, 10–11; account of historian Eusebius, 12–13; transformation by popular imagination, 13–14; stages of hagiographic evolution, 14
—, varieties of: historical martyrology, 23–24; monastic calendars, 24; legendaries or passionaries, 24; collections of saints' lives for preacher and laymen, 24–28
Legendary, as hagiographic type, 24
Leicester, Earl of, 206, 306
Leo I, Pope, Saint, 57
Leofric, Earl, 55
Letter from Smyrna to Philomelium about Polycarp, 10
Letter from the brethren at Lyons and Vienne, 12
Lewes, John, 198
Lewis, Joyce, 151
Lippomanus, Aloysius, Bishop of Verona, *Historiae de Vitis Sanctorum*, 130; lack of order in, 278

Litel Treatise ageynste the Mutterynge of Some Papistis in Corners, A, 84–85
Liturgy, advantage of familiarity in, 17–18
Local pride, monastic, 20
Lollards, 133, 200
London prisons of Recusants, 225
Loyalty to Queen against Pope, Munday's account of Campion's answer, 216
Ludham, John, Vicar of Weathersfield, 304
Lupus or Leu, Saint, Archbishop of Sens, 45
Luther, Martin, 133, 137
Lutherans, 128, 132; attack upon cult of saints, 74; Paris edicts of 1542 against, 300
Luxury, 262
Lyons, 12
Lyric element in saint's life, 280–81

Macarius the Alexandrian, Saint, 19
Maccabees, Seven, 9; mother of, 246
Machiavelli, Niccolò, 174
Mackie, J. D., 97
Magic, confused with idolatry, 78
Magus, Simon, 57–58
Malory, Sir Thomas, and Arthurian legend, 21
Marbecke, John, *The Lyves of Holy Sainctes, Prophetes, Patriarches, and Others, Contayned in Holye Scripture*, 289–90
Marburg, 304
Marcellinus, Pope, Saint, 39
Margaret, Countess of Cumberland, 305
Margaret, Duchess of Burgundy, 31
Marian and Elizabethan persecutions, compared by Whitaker, 210
Marian priests, 201, 202
Marianus, Saint, 11
Marie Magdalens Lamentations for the Losse of Her Master Jesus: indebted to Southwell, 272–73
Markham, Gervase, *The Teares of the Beloved*, 274
Marsh, George, 155
Martin of Tours, Saint, 17, 20, 56, 57, 62
Martyr: as witness, 4, 167; revelation to brethren, 6; Christ in, 6; passion, 6–7; power of example, 9–10; divine grace in, 12–13; constancy greatest marvel of, 13; contribution to spiritual treasury of Church, 16, 37–38, 41; triumph, 41, 155–56, 162–63, 164–65, 172–73
—, cult of: commemorative rites at burial place, 14; invoking of intercession of patron, 15–16; pride of group in, 15–16; essentials of, 16; revelation of unknown burial place, 16, 53; in seventeenth century, 162
Martyr, Peter, 137, 150, 311, 312
Martyrdom: pagan, 6; supreme glorification of God, 9; readiest way to God, 10; problem of heretical martyr, 20; standards, 61; not expected by men in settled society,

97; magnetism of, 151–52, 221–22, 233, 275
Martyrology: beginning of literary records, 10; accounts of passions, 10, 16; official reports, 13; acts of martyrs, 15–16; difficulties of record-keeping, 16; common stock of, 17; Roman, 18, 24; expansion of area and categories, 18–24; historical, 23–24; Catholic under Henry, difficulties of, 98; development of Recusant, 228–29; types and patterns, 236; ascribed to Jerome, 274; of Salisbury Use, 277–78; value of, 295, 297. *See also* Hagiography; Legend, saint's and martyr's
Martyrs, sixteenth-century: stories of, and foundations of *Golden Legend*, 95; compared to ancient, 151–52, 155; at Colchester, 159, 163; at Stratford-the-Bowe, 159; at Coxehall in Essex, 163; at Ipswich, 163; of Bohemian and other churches, 172; Catholic under Elizabeth, fragmentary record of, 196. *See also* Campion, Edmund; Carthusian order; English Mission; Fisher, John; Foxe, John; More, Sir Thomas; Southwell, Robert
Marvels, 13–14, 115–16, 238; Palladius, 19; Adamnan's life of Saint Columba, 21; medieval sense of, 30; prenatal wonders signaling saint, 54; jewels, 55; lights, 55–56; animal wonders, 56; at execution of Briant, 221; at execution of Campion, 248. *See also* Miracles
Mary, Queen of England, 89, 98, 134, 135, 142, 146, 147, 151, 165, 181, 229, 243, 299, 307, 309, 312, 314; commissioners punished for cruelty, 160; bloody time of, 172; stubbornness, 178; misled by Pole and bishops, 178; changes in religion, disaster, 185
Mary, Queen of Scots, 200, 234, 242
Mary, Virgin, 37, 74, 86, 279–80; Marian prayers omitted in Joye's *Hortulus Animae*, 87; Marian elements eliminated from hours in First Prayer Book of Edward VI, 88; Marian poems, 270; cautious revival of attention around turn of century, 293–94; Protestant concern about overemphasis, 294
Mary Magdalene, Saint, 46, 49–50, 60, 86, 137, 262–68, 271–72, 272–73, 274, 279, 293
Mary of Egypt, Saint, 19, 38, 39, 46, 56
Mass, 36, 151, 190; idolatry, 166, 182–84; King John's attitude, 175; Foxe's caricature of, 189; cornerstone of old religious order, 201; attack on, 300
Matilda, Countess, 174
Matthew, Saint, 43
Maxentius, Roman emperor, 46–47
Maximin Thrax, Roman emperor, persecution of, 9, 61, 63

Mayne, Cuthbert, 202, 230, 232, 238
Meditation, 259–62, 262–67, 275; way of acquiring wisdom, 48; problems of communication, 260; adaptation to sixteenth-century conditions, 260–61; Ignatian technique, 261–62; *Meditations of St. Bridget*, 275
Melanchthon, Philipp, 137
Melania the Younger, Saint, 19
Mellitus, Bishop of London, afterward Archbishop of Canterbury, Saint, 64
Menedmus, 74–76
Merchant Adventurers at Antwerp, 150
Merchants, 111
Mercurian, Everard, General of the Society of Jesus, 232
Middle Ages: credulity and curiosity in, 22; Foxe's history of decay, 171
Middle class: culture of, 68–69; and attitudes toward saints' legends, 72; spiritual challenge of, 260–61; appeal to, 282
Middlemore, Humphrey, 99
Milan, 16
Miracles, 120; functional, 13; healing, 15, 62; of martyrs near or after death, 43; restoration of dead, 51–52, 57–58; revelation of spiritual reality, 53–55; manifestation of grace, 56–57; and preservation of saint, 57, 115; homeliness of, 57–58, 74; Reformers' contempt for, 164; treatment by Foxe, 164–67
Mirk, John, prior of Lilleshall in Shropshire, *The Festial* or *Festyvall*, 26–27, 288; printed by Caxton, 27
Missionary work, 20, 48–49; for conversion of ruler, 49
Mohammed, 297, 298
Mombritius, 130
Monasteries, 127, 180: dissolution of abbeys, 68; charges of slothfulness against, 75; and pilgrimages to shrines, 78; abolition of, one of Henry's means of withdrawing Church in England from Rome, 78, 241; suspicion of corruption in, 237; asceticism, 237
Monastic development of meditation, 260–61
Monastic wealth, actual disposition of, 78, 83–84
More, Henry, historian of English Province of Jesuits, 243
More, Sir Thomas, Saint, 41, 77, 96, 97, 99, 101, 108, 152, 180, 260, 322; *A Dialoge of Comfort*, 108, 112, 121–22, 125, 242; *Utopia*, 111; publication of lives of, 98–99; legend recapitulates development of martyrological tradition, 116; genius and personality, 116; portrait by Erasmus, 116–17; human excellence stressed, 218–19. *See also* Ba., Ro.; Harpsfield, Nicholas; Roper, William; Stapleton, Thomas
Morontas, Saint, 128

Morton, John, Cardinal, Archbishop of Canterbury, 122
Moses, 33, 57, 291–92, 295; persecutions of, 297
Mountjoy, Charles, Lord, 258
Mountjoy, William, Lord, 304
Mozley, J. F., 142
Munday, Anthony: purpose in going to Rome, 214–15; *A Discoverie of Edmund Campion and his Confederates, their Most Horrible and Traiterous Practises, against her Majesties Most Royall Person, and the Realme*, 215–16; troubled over effect of Campion's personality, 216–17; credibility attacked, 221; *An Answeare for the Time*, 223
Music, rejection of, 148, 308
Mustapha, strangled by Sultan Solyman, 301
Mystic, 241
Mysticism. *See* Contemplation

Natalie, wife of Saint Adrian, 63
Nazianzen. *See* Gregory of Nazianzus
Nereus, Saint, 44–45
Nero, Roman emperor: persecution of, 16, 298
Newdigate (Carthusian), 99
"New Learning," attitude toward Middle Ages, 73, 74
Nicholas, Saint, 36–37, 51–52
Nicholas of Cusa, Cardinal, 73
Nichols, John, 227–28, 233, 235
Nicomedia, 40
Nominal conformity, 200
Nonconformity, not furthered by tradition of social human being, 199
Norfolk, Duke of, 111, 120
Notary, Julian, 34
Notker of Saint Gall, 23
Nowell, Alexander, Dean of St. Paul's, 223, 310; *A True Report of the Disputation or rather Private Conference had in the Tower of London, with Ed. Campion Jesuite* (with William Day), 222–23
Numidian martyrs, 11

Obedience of a Christian Man, The, 157, 187
Ogygius, 74–76
Oliver, Leslie M., 168
Origen, *Exhortation to Martydom*, 8–9, 220
— (attributed) homily on Mary Magdalene, 263–64; Italian version, 263; Latin versions, 263–67, 272; English translation, 263–64
Ormes, Cicelie, 159
Orthlius, Wygandus, oration on Hyperius, 304–5
Our Ladie hath a New Sonne, 279

Palladius, Bishop of Helenopolis, 19, 130; "The Book of the Triumphs of the Holy Fathers" added to the *Paradise*, 19

Pancras, Saint, 52

Panegyric, Protestant, 14, 304

Papacy, 171; as usurpation with regard to other sees, 173; supremacy not known in Primitive Church, 173–74; threat to royal authority, 173–74

Papists, 158; cruelty of, 138, 160; consciousness of error, Foxe's attitude toward, 186

Par, Lord, 134

Paradinus, William, 129

Parker, Matthew, Archbishop of Canterbury, 92, 296, 310, 313–16, 319–20; *De Antiquitate Britannicæ Ecclesiæ et Privilegiis Ecclesiæ Cantuariensis*, 313; emphasis on continuity of Church of England, 313; career of, 314. *See also* Josselin, John

Parker, Mrs., wife of Archbishop Parker, 314

Parliament, 185–86, 198

Parsons, Robert, 196, 203, 204, 229, 231, 232–33, 236, 255, 257; head of English Mission, 204, 205, 206; writer and controversialist, 205; underground press of, 205, 209

— *A Brief Censure uppon Two Bookes written in Answere to M. Edmonde Campions Offer of Disputation*: defense of Campion, 211; challenged charge of treason, 212

— *A Brief Discours contayning certayne Reasons why Catholiques refuse to goe to Church*: dedicated to Queen Elizabeth under pseudonym I. Howlet, 205; impact of persecution for refusal of church attendance, 205; considered conformity damnable, 205; attitude toward ruler, 205; as indication of intention at this time to keep English Misson clear of politics, 205–6

— *A Defence of the Censure, gyven upon Two Bookes of William Charke and Meredith Hanmer Mynysters, whiche they wrote against M. Edmond Campian preest*: published 1582, 212; reply to Charke, 212

— *Elizabethæ Angliæ Reginæ Hæresin Calviniam Propugnantis, Sævissimum in Catholicos sui regni Edictum*: published under pseudonym Andreas Philopatrus, 250; reply to charges of treason of anti-Jesuit Proclamation of October 18, 1591, 250, 252

— *First Booke of the Christian Exercise Appertaining to Resolution* (1582), 205; known as *The Book of Resolution*, 205; Anglican adaptation of, 205, 259; expanded into *The Christian Directory*, 294

— *De Persecutione Anglicana libellus*, 224, 234, 235; trans. from French version into English as *An Epistle of the Persecution of Catholickes in England*, 224; protest against persecution, 224; added Briant's letter, 224

Partridge, John, *The Worthie Hystorie of the Most Noble and Valiaunt Knight Plasidas*, 282–84

Passion, Christ's, 265

Passionaries, hagiographic type useful for monastic reading, 24

Pathology, physical, in Foxe, 162

Patrick, Saint, patron saint of Ireland, 20, 36, 285

Patrick, Simon, trans. Jean Crespin's *État de l'Église* as *The Estate of the Church*, 298–301

Paul, Saint, 3, 39, 70, 123; Thirteenth Epistle to Romans, 173–74; classic text for martyr, 220

Paula, Saint, 19; life by Jerome, 278

Paulinus, Saint, 16, 19

Paul's Cross, 85

Paul the Hermit, Saint, 19

Peckham, John, Archbishop of Canterbury, 83

Pecock, Reginald, Bishop of Chichester: attitude towards absurdities of saints' cult, 72–73, 138

Pedagogical element, 280

Pelagia, Saint, 39, 46, 55

Pelagius II, Pope, 300

Penal Statutes of 1571: Parliament's reply to Bull of Excommunication, 202; designation of Traitors in, 202–3

Perpetua, Saint, 10–11

Persecutions of antiquity, 5–15, 18; Saracens, 93, 297; Turkish, 93, 297–98

Petarpemôtîs, 19

Peter, Saint, 37, 41, 52, 57–58, 63, 74–75, 120, 171, 293; and hallowing of Westminister, 64–65; as penitent, 267–69, 273, 274

Peters (Collington or Colleton, John), 213

Petronilla, Saint, 41

Pettie, George, *A Petite Pallace of Pettie His Pleasure*: retelling of Alexius story, 284–85

Pharaoh, 298

Phillips (Philips), Walter, last Prior and first Dean of Rochester, 100

Philomelium in Phrygia, 10

Philopatrus, Andreas, pseudonym of Robert Parsons, 250

Philpot, John, 137

Pico della Mirandola, 137

Pilgrimage of Grace, 81

Pilgrimages, 180; Erasmus' attack on, 73–77; injunctions against, 83–84

Pilgrims, rascally, 74

Pilgrim's Progress (John Bunyan's), 168

Pius V, Pope, Saint, 202

Plain style, 194

Plato: complaints in *Republic* on scandalous picture of gods, 71; *Phaedo*, 117

Pole, Reginald, Cardinal, 125, 129, 178; considered by Foxe archenemy to God, 152

Political and religious interests confused, 202–3

Pollen, J. H., 230

Polycarp, Bishop of Smyrna, Saint, 10, 11, 12, 162; *Passio Polycarpi*, 10; on swearing to Caesar, 243

Polychronius, Bishop of Jerusalem, 171

Pontus, The, persecution in, 13

Pope, 145–46, 249; renunciation of authority of, 68, 84–85, 146, 175, 175–76, 177; usurpation of authority by, 82, 86; resistance to rejection of, 84–85; archvillain to Foxe, 154, 155, 173–75; in Foxe's index, 179; and cardinals, 190; enemy of Queen, 199; conspiring against England, 249–50

Pope Joan, 193

Popular passion for affairs of state, 190

Portents of greatness, 128; as evidence of Heaven's concern, 165

Potamioena, Saint, 13, 19

Potten's wife, 163

Poverty: spirit of, 21; voluntary, 51; evangelical, 108

Praemunire, 203

Prayer Book. *See* Book of Common Prayer

Prayer Book battles at Frankfurt, 307–8

Prayer Book battles at Strasbourg, 306

Preaching: medieval, 27–28; increased importance for Catholics, 238; Puritan emphasis on, 303, 304, 308; importance to Jewel, 313. *See also* Hyperius

Precocity of saints, 54–55

Press, secret, 205, 209, 217, 243

Priesthood of Antichrist, 157

Priests, Catholic: necessity of, 201; impossible to function publicly, 201; depletion of ranks, 201; seminaries on Continent as source of, 201–2; tradition of praying for Queen at execution, 258

Primer or Book of Hours, 70–71; in English, omitting litany, 87; Reforming primers and books of devotion, 260–61

Primitive Church, 93, 139–40, 171, 179; Bishop of Rome obedient to emperor, 174

Primus, Saint, 42

Printing, invention of, 187; furthered circulation of English books, 260

Prisons of sixteenth century, 158

Privy Council, 213–14

Proclamation against Jesuits and seminary priests, 235

Proclamation of March 1, 1568: prototype of proclamations against unlicensed books, 200–201

Proclamation of November 22, 1538, banishing Anabaptists, 197–98

Proclamation of October 18, 1591, *A Declaration of Great Troubles pretended against the Realme by a number of Seminarie Priests and Jesuits, sent, and very secretly dispersed in the same*, 249–50

Proclamation of offenses of Campion and his companions, 215

Propaganda, 194, 195; of pulpits, 85; Foxe's mastery of, 184–90; for Elizabethan Settlement, 198–99; reinforced by folk piety, 199; Munday as master of, 216

Prophecy, 120–21, 122, 125, 313; foretelling child's greatness, 54–55; in Chauncy, 106

Prosperity, problem of, 262

Protasius, Saint, 16

Protestant history of Christianity: Foxe, 170–79, 296; Bullinger, 296–98; Crespin, 298–301

Protestant history of Popes, 170–79, 298

Protoctetus, 9

Prudentius, 139

Psychology: medieval, 260; sixteenth and seventeenth century, 261; seventeenth-century emphasis on systematic organization, 261; Jesuit attitude toward passions, 262; growing interest in, 275

Puritans, 71–72, 143; of seventeenth century, foreshadowing of, 177–78; "tender conscience" in Foxe, 180–81; conflict with Established Church, 184; leaders of seventeenth-century appreciated Foxe, 191; and Elizabethan Settlement, 197; martyrs of later period, 197; movement within Church of England, 301; saints' life, pattern in Beza's life of Calvin, 301; movement for Reformed Church, 306; of sixteenth century, 308; tone of lives of ministers, 309

"Quietness," problem of, 79

Quintianus, Provost, 42

Quiricus, Saint, 54–55

Rack, 225, 228, 230–31; unusual in Marian persecution, 158

Raimondo of Capua, life of Saint Catherine of Siena, 22

Rainolds, John, President of Corpus Christi College, Oxford, and Dean of Lincoln, 310

Rastell, William, 117, 127; nephew of Sir Thomas More, 98; English account of More's trial trans. in *Ordo Condemnationis Thomae Mori*, 98, 117; source of account in *Acta Thomae Mori*, 110

Rebellion in the North, 216

Recusants, Catholic, 112, 124, 183, 198, 204, 214, 228, 230, 235, 254–55, 277; reactions of crowds at executions of, 151–52; resistance of underground, 196, 241; life of, described, 212–13; prisons in which confined, 225; social classes, 234; priests as heroes of martyrology, 236–37; periods of history marked by executions of Campion and Southwell, 240; problem of loyalty, 242, 252, 255; plight as described by Southwell, 252–56; situation at end of sixteenth century, summed up in Southwell's career, 275; foreshadowing of seventeenth-century predicament, 275–76; translations of continental hagiography, 278–79

Reed, A. W., 122

Reformation, Catholic, 109, 240, 262–63; failure of, 108–10

Reformation, Protestant: zeal of Cranmer, 86; and attack on saints' cult under Henry VIII, 96; and ministers, 147–49; popular nature of, in Marian times, 150; Reforming books, 151; Foxe's attitude toward, 172, 189; in England, Foxe's encyclopedia of, 178–79; history of, in Foxe, 192–93

Regnault, François, published *Hore Beatissime Virginis Marie ad Legitimum Sarisburiensis Ecclesie Ritum*, 70, 86

Regulus, Bishop of Arles, Saint, 56

Relics, 14, 74–75, 139; veneration of, 21; problems of, 69–70; effort to regulate, 69–70; duplication, 77; as source of idolatry, 77; existence of, proof of corruption, 77–78; necessity of abolishing, 78, 82; and Protestant martyr, 164

Renaissance, 262; interest in study, 282; magnificence of, 286–87

Reprobus. *See* Christopher, Saint

Retribution, 9–10, 13, 115, 121; false swearers, 52; lack of, in saints' legends, 71–72; in Chauncy, 107; judgment of God on persecutors, 248; examples of, 298

Revelation xi:12, 170

Revet, George, 166

Ribadaneyra, Pedro de, *Flos Sanctorum*, 278

Richard III, King, 35

Richardson, William, 220, 230

Ridley, Nicholas, Bishop of Rochester, 85, 137, 150, 164

Rishton, Edward, 229; continuation of Sanders' *De Schismate Anglicano*, 234

Rivius, John, 129

Robert of Molesme, 24

Robinson, Richard: modernization of *Gesta Romanorum*, 288–89; *The Vineyarde of Vertue*, 294–95

Rock, Saint, 38

Rogers, John, 133, 150, 163

Romance, religious, 29; historical, in legends, 14; imaginative, in legends, 14; difficulty discriminating from legend, 21; in legend and heroic tales, 40; in *Golden Legend*, 50, 59–60; and Greek romance, 279; in Catholic saint's legend, 279–80; in Anglican saint's legend, 281–89

Romances, secular, 95; Italian, 281–82

Roman Empire, 5, 37

Rome, see of, 202–3. *See also* Papacy

Romuald of Camaldoli, Saint, 24

Rood of Dovercourt, 181

Rood of Grace from Boxley, 85

Roper, Margaret, 108, 110, 117, 120, 122, 124, 125, 127, 128

Roper, Thomas, of Kent, 213

Roper, William, 98, 110, 112, 125, 126, 127, 128

— *The Mirrour of Vertue in Worldly Greatnes, or the Life of Syr Thomas More Knight*: as personal memoir, 117–19, 121–22; hagiographic elements in, 117, 119, 120–21, 123; to preserve memory, 118; sense of drama in, 122–23; basis of later lives, 123

Rosweyde, Heribert, 95; *Vitae Patrum*, 321

Rudolf of Swabia, 174

Rupp, Gordon, 179 *n44*

Rusticus, Saint, 56

Sackville family, 247

Sacrament of the Altar, the, 144, 145–46, 153, 157–58, 176–78; theory of, 36; position of Henry VIII on, 132; Foxe's attitude on, 155, 176, 181–82; people conservative on, 177; disputes about, main causes of Marian martyrdoms, 181; disputes about, frequent among women, 181

"Saint Peters Complaynt," 272, 273

Saint Peters Ten Teares, 273

Saint's legend. *See* Legend, saint's and martyr's

Salisbury Mass book, 182–83

Sampson, Elizabeth, 181

Sander (Sanders), Nicholas, 207, 216, 225, 231, 236, 255; *De Visibili Monarchia*, 228–29, 234, 235; and exiles at Louvain, 229; expedition to Ireland, 229; *De Origine ac Progressu Schismatis Anglicani*, 229; treatment of religious issues in writings of, 229, 234, 235

Sandys, Edwin, Bishop of London, afterward Archbishop of York, 307–8, 310

Saracens, 93; and persecutions of Christian religion, 297

Satwell (Ford, Thomas), 213

Sauer, Lawrence (Surius), Carthusian, *De Probatis Sanctorum Historiis*, 130, 278

Saunders, Laurence, 151, 159, 162, 188

Savonarola, Hieronimus, 137

Scavenger's daughter, 226, 228

Scholastica, Saint, 38

Scripture. *See* Bible

Seconde Tome of Homelyes, The, second homily of: condemnation of images, 93; idolatry cause of schism between East and West, 93; confutation of arguments for images, 93–94; complaint of spending money on images instead of needy, 94

Secularization of culture, 262

Seminaries on Continent, 202, 203, 228; defended by Southwell, 251–52

Sennen, Saint, 48

Sermon to prisoners, 228

Servetus, Michael, 302–3

Services of Church explained by Caxton, 36

Seven Sleepers of Ephesus, 59, 61

Shakespeare, treatment of history: Foxe resembles, 190
Sheriffs, brutality of, 158
Sherwin, Ralph, 217, 221, 224
Sherwood, Thomas, 230–31
Shilliton, George, Justice of the Peace, 288
Shrines, 3, 180; tomb of ancient martyr, 13, 14, 15; gifts at tomb, 15; cures and miracles at tombs of saints, 53–54; Erasmus and attack on, 74–76; wealth of, and neglect of poor, 75–76, 78, 80; destruction of, 81
Silbecke, Richard, 137
Simeon Metaphrastes, 130
Smith, Mistress, widow of Coventry, 160
Smith, Robert, 164–65
Smyrna, persecution at, 10
Sobriety of godliness, 162–63
Social disorder, attitude toward, 142
Society of Jesus: product of new age, 203; understanding of resources of time, 204; and *Spiritual Exercises*, 204; character of personnel, 204. *See also* Jesuits
Socinian martyrs, 198
Socrates, 295
Somerville, Elizabeth, 227
Somerville, John, 227
Somerville, Margaret, 227
Song of Mary the Mother of Christ, The, 293
Song of Songs, 285
Southern, A. C., 232
Southwell, Robert, 277, 292, 293; compared with Campion, 240–41; background, 241; mission to England, 242; *The Triumphs over Death*, 247, 270; betrayal of, 258; serenity of, 258; and Ignatian spiritual development, 258–59; poetry from meditation, 267–69; memory of, as martyr, 275; influence of private meditations of, 275; career as epitome of Recusant situation, 275
—, imitators of, 270, 279; Nicholas Breton, 270–72; anonymous poets, 272–73; William Broxup, 274; Gervase Markham, 274
— *Epistle of Comfort*: dedicated to Countess of Arundel, 243; printing of, 243; reminder of tradition, 243–44; motive to show affection toward God's prisoners, 244; enumerated grounds of consolation, 244–49; reprinting of, 249
— *An Humble Supplication to Her Majestie*, 249; address of loyalty to Queen, 250–51; defended colleagues from charges of anti-Jesuit proclamation, 251; on purpose of Continental seminaries, 251–52; on charge of supporting King of Spain, 252; defense of ordination oaths of chastity, 252; basic premise that Queen unaware of situation of Recusants, 252; on torture of Catholics, 252–53; on economic strictures, 254; on "Bloody Question," 256–57; printing of, in Appellant controversy, 257; position not Gallican, 258

— *Marie Magdalens Funeral Teares*, 271; significance of choice of subject, 262–63; relation to possible sources, 263–65; treatment of subject, 265–66; use of love poetry for divine love, 266; call to action, 266; example of Ignatian influence, 266; devices of contemporary rhetoric, 266–67; development of psychological possibilities and homely details, 267; reprinting of, witness to contemporary appeal, 267, 270
— *Mœoniæ, or Certaine Excellent Poems and Spirituall Hymnes*: success of, 269, 270; care in selection of material, 270
— *Saint Peters Complaynt, with Other Poems*: emotional exploration of scriptural material, 268; companion piece to Magdalene meditation, 268; expansion of figures of speech in baroque fashion, 268–69; reprinting of, 270
— *A Short Rule of Good Life*: commended by seventeenth-century editor, 258–59; on foundation of good life, 259; published under both Catholic and Protestant auspices, 259; tone of, humane, 259; technique of development Ignatian, 259
Spanish Armada, 242, 244, 252, 258
Spanish friar, 161
Spenser, *Faerie Queene*, 287–88
Spiritual predicament, sixteenth-century, 262
Stapleton, Thomas, 98
— *The Life and Illustrious Martyrdom of Sir Thomas More*: Part III of *Tres Thomae*, 126; hagiographic elements in, 126, 127, 128–29; resembles seventeenth-century Catholic martyrs' lives, 126; organization, 126, 128; source materials, 126–27; praise of genius of More, 126, 129; portrait of More in, 127–29
Star Chamber, 222
Stauffer, Donald, 28
Stephen, Saint, 10, 123
Stevens, Thomas, 137
Stock, Richard: printed English version of Campion-Whitaker controversy, 210–11
Stokesley, John, Bishop of London, 155
Stonyhurst College, 263
Story, John, 211
Strasbourg, 302, 304
Student of the Temple, friend of Whittingham, 306
Sulpicius Severus, life of Martin of Tours, 21, 130
Supernaturalism, revolt against, 180–84
Superstition, 58–59; and abuses of saints' cult, medieval criticism of, 72–73; Erasmus' attack on, 73–75; Cromwell's attack on, 80; of Popery, 86; of old order, attack on, 88, 89; inquiry on, in Visitation articles of Elizabeth, 90; crusade against, 180; Foxe equated with support of monasteries, 180
Supremacy, 152; basic issue for Foxe, 173
Supremacy, Royal: Henry VIII assumed title

"Supreme Head," 78–79, 99, 111, 122–23, 127–28, 176–78, 198; security in uniting secular and religious piety, 196–97, 243, 255

Supremacy of Papacy: More's support of, described by Hall, 99; disastrous result of claims of, 171; controversy over, as cause of sects and schisms, 171; not claimed until year 1000, 174

Surius. *See* Sauer, Lawrence

Surrey, Earl of, 133

Swinderby, priest martyr, 137

Swithin, Saint, 57

Sylvester II, Pope, 171

Symson, Cuthbert, 158, 165

Taylor, Dr. Rowland, Archdeacon of Exeter, 148–49, 151, 155, 157

Taylor, William, Wycliffite martyr, 172

Tender conscience, 95, 180, 306

Teresa of Avila, Saint, 110

Tertullian, 4, 5; *Ad Martyres*, epistle to "Blessed Martyrs Designate," 8, 244

Tewksbury, John, 151, 157

Thais, Saint, 19

Theodora, Saint, 45–46

Thomas à Becket, Archbishop of Canterbury, Saint, 22, 75–76, 83, 120, 126, 140, 175, 318–19

Thomas Aquinas, Saint, 41, 270; and learning, 48

Thomas the Apostle, Saint, 126

Three Wise Men, 295

Time, division of: according to Jacobus de Voragine, 170; according to Foxe, 170–71

Tobias, 295

Toleration, 121, 142

Topcliffe, Richard, 258

Torture, 222, 253; of ancient martyrdoms, 42–43; sharpness of, increases glory, 43; not many charges of, in Marian executions, 158; Tower instruments, 225–26; variety, 228; described by Southwell, 253, 256; Southwell's witness, 258

Tower of London: conditions in, 225; tortures, 225–26

Tradesmen martyrs, 160

Transubstantiation, rejection of, 181

Treason charge, 132; against Recusants, 112; difficult for Fisher and More, 112–13; approved by Foxe for those who refused King's supremacy, 176; suspicion of, 245–46

Treatis Contayninge the Lyfe and Maner of Death of that Most holy Prelat and Constant Martyr of Christ, John Fysher. *See* Fisher, John

Trent, Council of, 135, 202, 263

True Cross, 21, 39

Trunchfield, Michael, wife of, 163

Trussell, John, address to reader in 1594 edition of *The Triumphs over Death*, 270

Truth, problem of, 5, 95, 321

Turkish persecutions: idolatry responsible for, 93; compared to Assyrian and Babylonian captivities, 297–98

Turncoats, 235; John Nichols, 227–28, 235

Twine, Thomas, 296

Tynbygh, William, 106

Tyndale, William, 150, 151; translation of New Testament, 67, 145–46, 157, 187; and juggler at Antwerp, 164

Tyrrwhit, Sir Robert, 226

Tyrrwhit, Robert, son of Sir Robert, 226

Tyrrwhit, William, 226

Ulric, Bishop of Augsburg, Saint, 69

Uniformity: and settlement of religious problem, 255

Uniformity, Second Act of, 89

Unity of Church, 21–22, 125

Universities: at beginning of sixteenth century, 188–89; source of anxiety to authorities, 206–7

Urban VIII, Pope: defined procedure of canonization, 69

Usuard, 23–24, 26, 130

Vallenger, Stephen: editor of Alfield's *A True Reporte of the Death and Martyrdome of M. Campion*, 217–18; added "A caveat to the reader touching A,M his discovery," 221; and Walpole's verses on Campion's death, 221; punished for authorship of *A True Reporte*, 222

Valvasone, Erasmo di, *Le Lagrime della Maddallena*, 263

Van Ortroy, Fr[anciscus], 107–8, 114

Victorines, 260

Vienne, 12

Villegas, Alfonso, *Flos Sanctorum*, 278

Vincent, Saint, 41

Vincent of Beauvais, *Speculum Historiale*, 24–25, 26

Virginity, 37–38; and virtues required, 44; curious arguments in favor of, 44–45; unconventional stories of, 45–46; early Christians who killed selves for, 183; in martyrology of English Mission, 237; and Southwell's appeal to Queen Elizabeth, 252

Visions, 11, 16, 49, 55; in Chauncy, 106

Visitation articles of first year of Elizabeth, 90

Visitors to Protestant leaders in prisons, 158

Vitas Patrum, translated by Caxton, 32

Vives, Juan Luis, 73

Waldo, Peter, 173

Walpole, Henry: "The Complaynt of a Catholike for the death of M Edmund Campion," 221–22; executed in 1595, 222

Walton, Izaak, 309, 311, 317, 321

Warham, William, Archbishop of Canterbury, 127

Wattes, William, 166

Wealth of Church, 75–76, 90; problem of distribution to poor, 78

Well, healing, miracle of, 43

Whitaker, William: Latin *Responsio* to Campion in 1581, 209–10; *Defensio* of *Responsio*, 210; denied cruelty in Elizabethan persecution, 210; warned university scholars against deceits of Campion, 210–11

White, John, Bishop of Winchester, 243

White, Richard, 245

White, Tristram, *The Martyrdome of Saint George of Cappadocia*, 288

Whitford, Richard: translation of *Imitation of Christ*, 260; and meditation, 260–61; English translation of Martyrology of Salisbury Use, 277–78

Whittingham, William, Dean of Durham: biography of, by "Student of the Temple," 306; career, 306–7; at Frankfurt, 307; at Geneva, 307; defense of liberties of his church against Archbishop of York, 307–8; suspected of authorship of Puritan account of Frankfurt disputes, 308; example of sixteenth-century Puritan ready to conform on minor but not essential matters, 308; concern for duties of office, 308; death of, 308–9; and concern for perfected reformation, 309

William the Conqueror, 53–54

Wilson, John, *The English Martyrologe*, 278

Wilson, Nicholas, 96

Winchester, melancholy citizen of, 128, 131

Winifred, Saint, 39, 42–43

Wolsey, Thomas, Cardinal, 97, 108, 114, 119, 193; pride and ambition cause of disaster, 113; Foxe's attitude toward, 152; considered villain by Sanders, 229

Women: noble young woman, as type in *Golden Legend*, 38–39, 149, 236; sharptongued, 41–42, 149, 183; part played by, in ancient times, 43–44; stories of, in *Golden Legend*, 44–46; in Foxe, 149, 151, 155, 157, 159, 160–61, 163, 181, 183; martyrs at Colchester, 160–61; Recusant, 227, 237

Worthington, Thomas, prisoner in Tower, 227

Wray, Sir William, 299

Wright, Dean (Walter Wright, Archdeacon of Oxford?), 312

Wulfstan, Saint, 53–54

Wycliffe, John, 75, 137, 165, 171–72, 181

Wynkyn de Worde, 34, 278; continued Mirk's *Festial*, 27; last printing of Caxton's *Golden Legend*, 67

Yates, Master and Mistress, 213

Young, John, Master of Pembroke Hall, 108

Zerubbabel, example commended to Queen Elizabeth, 91

Ziska, Jan, 137

Zwinglians, 76